D0996116

AS Level for OCR

Applied **ICT**

Series Editor:
K. Mary Reid

Heinemann

Inspiring generations

Heinemann Educational Publishers
Halley Court, Jordan Hill, Oxford OX2 8EJ
Part of Harcourt Education

Heinemann is a registered trademark of
Harcourt Education Limited

© Maggie Banks, Glen Milbery, Karen Scott, Sonia Stuart, 2005

First published 2005

10 09 08 07
10 9 8 7 6 5 4 3 2

British Library Cataloguing in Publication Data is available
from the British Library on request.

10-digit ISBN: 0 435449 96 6
13-digit ISBN: 978 0 435449 96 4

Edited by Sian Morris
Designed by Lorraine Inglis
Typeset by Thomson Digital, India

Original illustrations © Harcourt Education Limited, 2005

Cover design by Wooden Ark Studios

Printed in China by South China Printing Co.

Cover photo: © Zefa Images

Acknowledgements
Every effort has been made to contact copyright holders of material reproduced in this book.
Any omissions will be rectified in subsequent printings if notice is given to the publishers.

Websites
Please note that examples of websites suggested in this book were up to date at the time of writing.
It is essential for tutors to preview each site before using it to ensure that the URL is still accurate and
the content is appropriate. We suggest that tutors bookmark useful sites and consider enabling
students to access them through the school or college intranet.

Contents

Acknowledgements

The authors and publisher would like to thank all those who have granted permission to reproduce copyright material.

The author would like to thank the Royal Artillery Museum for the use of their newsletter on page 35.
Microsoft product screen shots reprinted with permission of Microsoft Corporation.
Jazzprojects.co.uk
Crown copyright material is reproduced with the permission of the Controller of HMSO
© 2005 Google
Tesco plc
Mozilla Firefox
Sun Java applet/Copyright 1994–2005 Sun Microsystems, Inc.
Symantec (UK) Ltd
Corel Corporation

The authors and publisher would like to thank the following for permission to reproduce photographs:

BBC/page 8
Alamy/pages 10, 47
Corbis/pages 54, 71, 82, 133
Hewlett Packard/pages 126 (2), 136, 137 (2)
Harcourt Education Ltd/Gareth Boden/page 128
Art Directors/Helene Rogers/page 135

Every effort has been made to contact copyright holders of material produced in this book. Any omissions will be rectified in subsequent printings if notice is given to the publishers.

Introduction

This is one in a series of four volumes that covers the OCR qualifications in Applied Information and Communication Technology for GCE.

The books are organised like this:

* AS (Single Award), which covers units 1 to 3
* AS (Double Award), which covers units 1 to 8
* AS A2 (Single Award), which covers units 9 to 14
* AS A2 (Double Award), which covers units 9 to 20

The two AS Level (Single and Double Award) qualifications are covered by one book each. The two A Level (Single and Double Award) qualifications are covered by two books each, one at AS and one at A2 level.

This book covers the eight units that are offered in the AS (Double Award):

* Unit 1: Using ICT to communicate
* Unit 2: How organisations use ICT
* Unit 3: ICT solutions for individuals and society
* Unit 4: System specification and configuration
* Unit 5: Problem solving using ICT
* Unit 6: Software development – design
* Unit 7: Communicating using computers
* Unit 8: Introduction to programming

To complete the AS (Double Award) you should study Units 1 to 4, plus two chosen from Units 5 to 8. To complete the AS (Single Award) you should study Units 1 to 3 only.

Assessment

Your achievements on this qualification will be assessed through portfolios of evidence and an examination. The examination will be assessed externally and the portfolios will be assessed internally.

Unit 2 will be assessed externally, and you will sit a 90 minute examination, set by the examination board. You will be given a case study in advance and will be expected to do research before the examination itself. You will also carry out some tasks based on the case study, which you must then take into the examination. The tasks will count towards your mark for this unit.

All the other units will be assessed internally. You will be expected to construct a portfolio for each unit. Further guidance on this is given in each unit.

Further information

You can find further information about this qualification at www.ocr.org.uk. Remember to search for GCE Applied ICT. You can download the complete specification, which gives full details of all the units, both AS and A2, and how they are assessed. This document is nearly 300 pages long.

A Tutor Resource File will provide additional material for these units.

We hope you enjoy your studies and wish you every success.

K Mary Reid
April 2005

Using ICT to communicate

Introduction

The C in ICT stands for communications. ICT has provided us with new ways to communicate information, such as email and telephone text messaging. It has also improved more traditional communication methods. For example, word processing has made it easier to produce paper-based communications, such as this book. The author can check and correct spellings and make changes without the need to rewrite or retype the text. In this unit you will learn about the different types of information, methods of communicating information and the technologies that support them.

Being able to communicate information effectively is important for both organisations and individuals. You will learn how to create effective communications that meet their purpose and the needs of their audience. You will also look at how organisations communicate and present information and understand why they use standard layouts for documents.

While you carry out your work for this unit – and all the others – you need to follow standard ways of working. This includes managing your own work, taking steps to keep information secure and working safely. What you learn in this unit will form the basis for the whole course and will provide you with skills and knowledge that will be valuable in the future, whether you continue in education or enter the world of work.

Throughout this unit and chapter, we will refer to a document, a communication, a presentation or a report. Whichever term is used, you should take it to mean any suitable way of communicating information. For example, a document does not have to be printed out on paper and a presentation does not have to be an on-screen presentation created using presentation software such as MS PowerPoint®.

This unit will be assessed on a portfolio of evidence you will provide. The Assignment Evidence at the end of this unit provides you with the ability to develop a portfolio.

By studying this unit you will:

* learn about the information age: know about the characteristics and significance of different types of information, the methods used to communicate information and the technologies that support these methods of communication. You will need to be able to describe the communication methods and technologies that support them.

* be able to identify the audience for a communication, its purpose and how it will be communicated. You will be able to match the writing style you use to the communication's audience and purpose. You will need to be able to plan and create communications that use writing styles that clearly match their audience and purpose.

* be able to check the accuracy of communications and improve their readability by using spell checkers and grammar checkers and by proof-reading both content and layout. You will need to be able to use these tools effectively so that you produce final copies that contain few obvious errors.

* be capable of using a range of features and formats to create layout styles to suit the purpose of communications and that will appeal to their audience. This will include using and combining different types of media, positioning important items correctly, creating templates, creating new information and blending it with existing information and maintaining a consistent style. You will also need to evaluate the communications you produce.

* understand why and how organisations present information, the standards and layouts for formal documents, the methods of presenting a corporate image and how templates can be used to enforce corporate standards. You will need to be able to describe and compare similar documents in terms of their writing style, presentation style and their use of common standards for layout.

* be able to follow standard ways of working including managing your work effectively, keeping information secure, and working safely.

You probably already know how to use word processing software, although you may need to learn how to use some new tools and facilities. You may also need to learn how to use other types of software such as desktop publishing, presentation, multimedia authoring and web design.

The information age

How many different types of information have you received today? Reading this book you are receiving written information. You may have received audio information from your teacher (i.e. listening in class) or from the radio. Has a friend sent you a text message – again written information? If you saw an advertisement hoarding on your way to school or college, it was probably mostly graphical information. If you have been searching the World Wide Web (WWW) you will have received web-based information. This may have included words, pictures, sound and video and so becomes multimedia information or you may have been playing a computer game or using a CD-ROM. It is almost impossible not to receive information in one form or another most of our waking lives. The volume of information we receive and the different types of information have increased considerably in the last 50 or 60 years.

Types of information

Written

Written information is text based. It uses words on a page or screen to convey meaning. The words used will be part of a language and will be understood only by people who understand that language. Also, the person who is to receive the information must know how to read it. A pre-school child, for example, is unlikely to be able to receive written information because they have not yet learnt to read. An advantage of written information is that the reader can read the information at a pace that suits them. They can also backtrack and reread passages if necessary to ensure that they have understood the information. The text of this book is written information. Other examples include a text message, an email, an article in a newspaper, a note to the milkman, a letter or a memo.

> **Think it over...**
>
> When was the last time you used written information as a means of communication?

Multimedia

> **Key terms**
>
> *Multimedia*: using more than one medium to express or communicate information.
> *Media*: (singular medium) has several different but related meanings. In multimedia it means the methods by which something is expressed, communicated, or achieved, for example text, graphics, sound or video. People also refer to the media, by which they mean newspapers, television, radio, etc. In ICT we also refer to types of data storage as media, for example floppy disks and CDs to convey information.

Multimedia information, as its name suggests, uses many different types of *media*. This may include text, graphics, sound and video. Multimedia information is designed to grab the recipient's attention and make the information more interesting or entertaining than one type of information on its own. Often, when multimedia information is presented, the recipients can *interact* with the presentation, for example to choose their own paths through it. Multimedia information is used in many different ways such as entertainment, for example computer games; training and information, for example multimedia encyclopaedias.

> **Key term**
>
> *Interact*: able to select options, for example by clicking with a mouse, to affect what happens.

> **Think it over...**
>
> Can you think of three examples of multimedia communication you've encountered recently, for example ordering online?

Graphical

Graphical information is information conveyed using pictures, graphs or charts. A picture can often convey information more directly than words and may be easier to remember. Some people remember important information by imagining a picture to represent it.

An advantage of graphical information is that it is not language dependent. You do not need to understand the language of the country you are in to know which is the men's and which the women's toilet if there is a picture of a man or a woman on the door (see Figure 1.1). Similarly, it is easier to see which product provides the highest sales if the sales of the different products available are shown in a bar chart, rather than if they are simply presented as a table of figures. Road signs are another example of graphical information. We all know that a picture of a man digging means that there are roadworks ahead.

FIGURE 1.1 *Different types of graphical information understood across cultures*

Think it over...

Video clips are also used as entertainment. Can you think of any, for example Police Camera Action?

Audio

Audio information is information that we hear. This may be spoken language, in which case, the recipient needs to understand the language being used. However, the spoken word is often able to convey more information than the written word, because how something is said is frequently as meaningful as what is said. There are other forms of audio information that are not language dependent. The sound of a door-bell tells you that there is someone at the door, your computer will beep to tell you that you have hit the wrong key, a car alarm going off indicates that someone has tried to break into a car. There are many other examples of non-verbal audio information. Music, for example can convey information that we respond to in different ways (see Figure 1.2).

Video

Video information is conveyed using moving images. The images themselves may be moving or the camera recording the images may be moving or a mixture of both. Like still images, moving images convey information more directly and are more memorable than words. However, whilst a still picture supplies us with information at an instant in time and at a particular place, video information allows us to see what is happening over a period of time and/or at different places. Moving images also attract attention. There are many different uses for video information. A football manager will often look at videos of his or her team's matches to analyse the team's performance and look for ways to improve it. Close Circuit Television (CCTV) cameras provide video information to the police which helps them to detect crime and catch the people responsible. Video information about a holiday resort will give potential visitors a better idea of what the resort is like than still photographs.

FIGURE 1.2 *We can respond to music through our emotions*

Web-based

As its name suggests, web-based information is information available on the WWW. This may be written information, graphical information, video information, audio information or, indeed, multimedia information. What distinguishes web-based information is its source, its volume and its accessibility. Providing you have a computer connected to the Internet with browser software installed, you can access web-based information on almost any topic imaginable from anywhere in the world. It is also possible to access web-based information if you have a WAP (wireless application protocol) mobile phone.

> **Key term**
>
> *Browser software*: software that allows you to access and view web pages.

There are some problems associated with this volume of information and the fact that anyone can generate web-based information. It is difficult to know whether the information is accurate or simply one person's interpretation. It is also difficult, if not impossible, to police web-based information, resulting in undesirable information such as pornography or criminal information also being easily accessible.

Methods of communicating information

With so many types of information, we have gained as many, if not more methods of communicating it.

Paper-based

Computers were supposed to reduce paper-based communication and lead to a paperless office, but this is still a distant dream. Paper-based communication is anything that is written, printed, typed or drawn on paper. Both written and graphical information can be communicated on paper. This book is one example of paper-based communication but there are many others. Newspapers, letters, reports, photographs, architects' plans, examination papers and brochures are just some examples of communications that can be paper-based. An advantage of paper-based

communication, and one reason why it is still widely used, is the fact that no equipment is needed to access the information. You can read a book in bed (Figure 1.3) or on the train without the need for a computer to display the information.

FIGURE 1.3 *Reading in bed!*

Printed photographs can be put in an album and handed around for people to look at, rather than needing access to a computer to view them. It is possible to spread out an architect's plan and see the whole of it at once, rather than having to scroll around it a section at a time on-screen. Some communications, such as contracts, must be paper-based for legal reasons. It is also true that many people prefer to read from paper than from a computer screen.

> **Think it over...**
>
> Is this likely to change as children are brought up with screen reading?

Screen-based

It is possible to communicate video, multimedia and web-based information on screen as well as written and graphical information. Screen-based communication does not apply only to a computer screen. Television is an obvious example of screen-based communication but more and more communications in our daily lives are also screen-based. Buses, trains and even doctors' surgeries use screen-based communication to convey information. This might simply be a scrolling text message, for example listing the stations a train will stop at, or it might provide more detailed information such as the times and destinations of the next three trains to arrive at a station and whether they are on time or not.

Mobile phones can be used for screen-based communication through text and picture messaging, emails and web pages. Many people use a *PDA* to replace a diary, address book and notepad amongst other things. The information contained in the PDA is communicated on screen rather than on paper.

Key term

PDA (personal digital assistant): a handheld computer that provides facilities for maintaining a diary, address book, notebook, etc.

SMS (short message service – telephone text messaging)

As already mentioned, mobile phones can be used for screen-based communication using text messaging. This is more correctly known as SMS. Messages are entered using the phone's keypad and then sent to another phone with SMS capabilities. Some home phones now offer such capabilities. The main feature of SMS communications is that there is a limit on the total number of characters that can be sent in a message – hence **short** message service. To communicate as much information as possible in the number of characters available, a texting language has developed using abbreviations and numbers to convey the message. Examples are w8 = wait, 4 = for, 2 = to, tmw = tomorrow, u = you and so on. I'm sure you know many more.

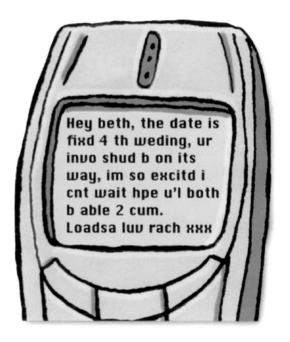

FIGURE 1.4 *How would you write this paragraph or any paragraph in this book using SMS text?*

Radio

Radio is a means of communicating audio information. Most radio is broadcast to the public on many different channels and as such it is a method of one-way communication. You can only listen to a radio broadcast. Some of these channels are local to a particular area, others are broadcast to a whole country and a few are broadcast over longer distances. There are channels that are devoted to broadcasting a particular type of music, others that are devoted to sports and others, often known as talk radio, that only broadcast the spoken word. Alongside these are channels that broadcast a range of different types of audio information. However, all radio stations will have a specific audience that they are aiming to communicate with. The advent of digital radio has provided additional channels, and radio players in web browsers enable people to listen to radio stations from the other side of the world via their computers.

Key term

Frequency: the particular waveband at which radio signals are broadcast or transmitted.

Another use of radio communication is two-way radio. This allows both parties to send and receive information. However, unlike the telephone, information can be sent in only one direction at a time. For this communication to take place, both the sending and receiving radios must be set to the same channel or *frequency*. As there is a limited band of radio frequencies, these are allocated for different uses by the government. Each broadcast radio station has its own channels, some channels are reserved for the police and other emergency services, and others for air traffic control. Citizen Band (CB) Radio is a public two-way radio service with a limited number of channels. This is frequently used by truck drivers and other motorists to communicate with each other, for example about traffic conditions. The advantage of two-way radio over mobile telephones is that the message can be received by any radio tuned to the same channel as the transmitting radio. This means that, on receipt of a 999 call, the emergency services dispatcher can broadcast the details to all vehicles, and those nearest to the scene can respond as required. Also, two-way radios often work in areas that mobile phones do not. Two-way radios may be useful for the rescue services, delivery work and security on buses.

Two-way radio is also used within a limited area, for example within a dock area for communication between staff organising the loading of vehicles onto a ferry. In these situations, there is less restriction on the frequency used because the range is too limited to cause interference with other systems.

Television

Like radio, most television is broadcast to the public and is also essentially a method of one-way communication. However, unlike radio, television communicates video as well as audio information. Like radio, there are many different channels communicating different types of information, such as sport, news, films, weather or music videos, as well as general channels that broadcast a balance of different types of information.

Digital broadcasting (see Figure 1.5) has increased the number of television channels available and has enabled viewers to interact with the programmes.

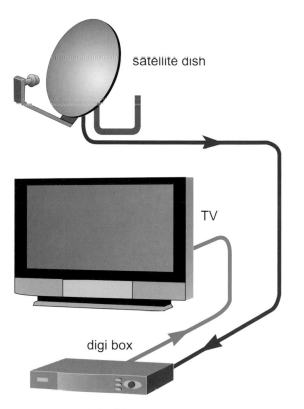

FIGURE 1.5 *Digital broadcasting*

The broadcast programmes do not use all of the available signal. There is some spare capacity that is used to transmit teletext. This consists of pages of textual information that viewers can access providing they have a television with a teletext decoder and a remote control. The viewer can access the information they require either by selecting from a series of menus or by entering the relevant page number.

Television is also used on a more local scale. This is known as close circuit television or CCTV. One of the main uses for CCTV is security. Cameras are positioned in shopping centres and other public areas as well as in and around shops, offices, banks and other buildings. The video images obtained are usually displayed on a screen that is monitored by security or other personnel. The images are also recorded so that, if anything happens, the event can be viewed again and the recordings passed to the police as evidence.

```
 P100 CEEFAX 1 100 Wed 09 Jun 10:39/37
 BBC CEEFAX
 News
 IRAQ PLAN GETS UNANIMOUS UN BACKING 104

 A-Z INDEX       199  NEWS HEADLINES    101
 BBC INFO        695  NEWS FOR REGION   160
 CHILDREN        570  NEWSROUND         571
 COOKERY         560  RADIO        BBC1 640
 COMMUNITY BBC2  650  READ HEAR    BBC2 640

 ENTERTAINMENT   500  SPORT             300
 FILMS           540  SUBTITLING        888
 FINANCE   BBC2  200  TRAVEL            430
 GAMESTATION     550  TV FEATURES       520
 HORSERACING     660  TV LINKS          615
 LOTTERY         555  TV LISTINGS       600
 MUSIC           530  WEATHER           400
 Ceefax: The world at your fingertips
 Headlines   News Indx   Sport   Main Menu
```

Telephone

Traditionally, telephone has been a method of communicating audio information, but modern telephones, both mobile and landline, enable written, graphical and even video information to be communicated. The essential feature of telephone communication is that it is two-way. You can listen to what the other person is saying and you can speak to them at the same time. The increase in the use of mobile telephones has meant that people can be contacted almost anywhere when they are away from their home or place of work. It is also possible to make conference calls so that more than two people can be involved in a telephone conversation, making it possible for meetings to take place remotely.

Email

Email is written information that is communicated electronically. This is most often via a computer network, either within an organisation or the Internet, but can also be via mobile phones. With emails, it is possible to send attachments. These may be documents, pictures, video or sound files. The recipient of the email does not have to be available to receive the communication as it can be stored in an inbox and viewed later. This makes email a particularly useful method of communication between people or organisations located in different parts of the world where different time zones make telephone communication inconvenient (see Figure 1.6). It is also possible to send the same message to any number of people at the same time. However, this has led to people receiving large numbers of unsolicited, or 'junk' emails, known as spam.

FIGURE 1.6 *The difficulty of time differences!*

WWW (World Wide Web)

The WWW allows the communication of web-based information. This can be accessed using a web browser. If you know the web address (URL) of the site you want to view, this can be entered in the browser. More usually you will want to find information on a particular topic. As the amount of information available is so vast, to find the information you will need to use a search engine. You will learn more about search engines and finding web-based information in Unit 3: ICT solutions for individuals and society.

Technologies that support communication

There are many technologies that support these forms of communications.

Personal computers

Personal computers enable a number of different methods of communicating information providing they have the necessary hardware and software. All visual information will be communicated on screen, although a graphics card or video card may be needed for high-quality graphic and video information. A printer will allow you to produce paper-based communications using different types of software including word processing, desktop publishing, graphics, spreadsheet and database. A modem, cable modem, broadband modem or router and communications software will allow you to communicate using email, and a web browser will provide access to the WWW. A sound card and loudspeakers or headphones will allow you to hear audio information, and the addition of a microphone and appropriate software will allow you to communicate by telephone through your PC. We have already said that with a radio player you can listen to radio through your computer; it is also possible to have a TV adapter so that you can watch television on your computer screen as well.

Think it over...

What technologies do you need in order to send an e-card?

Touch screens

A touch screen allows people to interact with a computer without the need for a keyboard, mouse or other input device. This interaction is much more direct – instead of having to manoeuvre the mouse and then click the button, you just have to touch the relevant point on the screen. The fact that no mouse or keyboard is required also has other advantages. Less space is needed, there is less possibility of theft or vandalism and there is greater data security – without a keyboard, only the options available on screen can be accessed.

There are several different types of touch screen. The most common is known as a resistive touch screen (see Figure 1.7). This type requires you to exert a certain amount of pressure on the screen. This is because there is a plastic membrane over the screen that is separated from a glass layer by small clear dot-like spacers. The plastic and glass layers are both *conductive* but the spacers are not. When you press the screen, contact is made between the plastic and glass layers at that point so that an electrical circuit is created and a signal is sent to the computer.

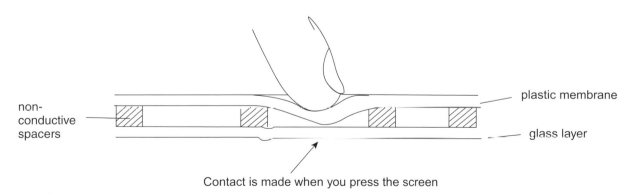

non-conductive spacers

plastic membrane

glass layer

Contact is made when you press the screen

FIGURE 1.7 *Cross-section of a touch screen*

The other types of touch screen do not require pressure to be applied. They rely on identifying the co-ordinates of the point being touched. One of these, known as a capacitive touch screen, has a thin conductive film fused onto a glass layer, with another layer of anti-scratch glass on top of it. Electrical circuits at the corners of the screen distribute a uniform low-voltage alternating current electrical field across the conductive film. When you touch the screen, the electrical field is disrupted. The change in electrical current from each corner is measured and used to calculate the x and y co-ordinates of the point you are touching. Other types of touch screen use ultrasound or infrared to find the position of your finger.

Touch screens are particularly useful in public places where other devices might be easily damaged or take up too much space. They allow the user to make choices by touching an area on the screen to access the information they need. One example of this is in the Bullring shopping centre in Birmingham where visitors can use touch screens to find the location of a particular shop or find shops of a particular type, as well as other information. Other examples include tourist information screens and car supermarkets, where customers can use touch screens to find out what cars are available matching their requirements. Touch screens are also used on small portable devices such as PDAs. Here, because of the small size, a pointer or stylus is used to select options, rather than a finger. It is also possible to 'write' on the screen to input text and numbers.

Digital broadcasting

Key terms

Bits: binary digit, i.e. 0 or 1.
Set-top box: a box about the size of a DVD player that is connected between the satellite dish, aerial or cable input and the television set.
Bandwidth: the number of bits per second that can be transmitted.

Until the mid 1990s, most radio and television broadcasting was analogue – the picture or sound was provided by a constantly changing signal and each channel could broadcast only one programme. Since then, digital broadcasting has become more and more widely available and will eventually replace analogue broadcasting. Digital television broadcasting transmits multimedia data in much the same form as data received by a computer via the Internet – streamed *bits* of data. This data can be broadcast by satellite, cable or using terrestrial broadcasting – through an aerial that was used for receiving analogue broadcasts. The signal must then be converted back to pictures and sound (decoded), either using a *set-top box* or an integrated digital television (iDTV) where the decoder is built into the television set. Digital television provides improved quality of pictures and sound. It also allows more programmes to be transmitted over the same *bandwidth* than is possible for analogue broadcasts. This enables a television station to broadcast different versions of a sporting event taken from different camera angles, for example, allowing the viewer to select the one they want to watch. This provides viewers with some limited interaction – the viewer is merely selecting one of the many signals being broadcast, rather than sending data back to the source of the broadcast. It is also possible to broadcast a film on several different channels, starting at different times so that viewers can choose when they want to watch it. Digital television also offers truly interactive services. This can include gaming, betting, shopping, banking, email and Internet access. Where digital television is provided by satellite, this is made possible by connection to a standard telephone line. With cable services there is a built-in return path that allows such two-way communication.

Digital radio provides digital-quality sound – similar to a CD or MP3 player. However, a special digital receiver is needed to listen to it. As well as the improved sound and reception quality, it is possible to broadcast text, data and even still pictures alongside the audio signal.

DVD (digital video disk)

> **Key term**
>
> *Optical storage medium*: a disk that stores data by altering the optical characteristics of the surface material, e.g. the way light is reflected off it.

A DVD is an *optical storage medium* that can hold 4.7 Gb or more of data. This means that a DVD can store two hours of full motion video, such as a full-length feature film. As on a pre-recorded CD, the data is stored as a pattern of microscopic pits on the surface of the disk, which are read by reflecting light from a laser. The presence or absence of a pit represents the 1s and 0s that make up the digital data. DVDs can store much more data than CDs because the pits are closer together and the wavelength of the laser used to read them is shorter. Double-layered DVDs are also available. These have two parallel layers of pits at different depths. The reading laser is able to focus on each of these layers. These DVDs can hold 8.5 GB or over 4 hours of video. DVDs can be read by a DVD player, usually connected to a television, or by a DVD drive on a computer. DVD writers make it possible to store data and television programmes on DVD-R or DVD-RW disks, making magnetic videotapes and video recorders obsolete. However, DVD-R and DVD-RW use different methods of recording the data onto the blank disks.

Mobile phones

Mobile phones have transformed the way we communicate with others. Some people no longer have a landline telephone and rely exclusively on a mobile phone to keep in touch with family and friends, and for business. With mobile phones, people can be contacted anywhere there is a signal, be that in town, on the beach or even the other side of the world. Mobile phones are also known as cell phones. This is because they operate in cells. When you make a call, your phone is connected to the nearest cell via an antenna. The network is then searched to find the cell where the number you are ringing is located. When the connection is made (see Figure 1.8) the signal is sent from your phone to the nearest cell, then across the network to the receiving cell and finally from this cell to the phone you are calling and vice versa.

This means that a phone has to transmit signals only to the nearest cell. As well as voice communication, as we have already discovered, mobile phones can be used to send SMS messages.

The Internet

The Internet is a world-wide network of computer networks. It was first created in 1966 by the US government's defence research agency as a means of ensuring that there was no single 'nerve centre' in their communications

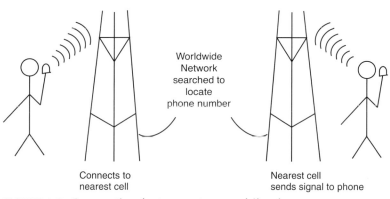

Worldwide
Network
searched to
locate
phone number

Connects to
nearest cell

Nearest cell
sends signal to phone

FIGURE 1.8 *Connection between two mobile phones*

network that could be wiped out by a nuclear attack. In the 1980s major university networks, for example JANET (the UK's Joint Academic Network) was connected to this network and since then it has continued to expand. Now, it connects all the major public, private and university networks. When you connect to the Internet, you connect to a network owned by an Internet Service Provider (ISP). This network is connected to others in a tree structure. The main 'trunk' of the tree that carries long-distance messages consists of a small number of high-speed, high-capacity networks known as Internet backbone networks. These are mainly the original military networks plus high-speed lines owned by major telephone companies.

It is easy to think that the Internet and the WWW are the same thing, but they are not. As we have discovered, the Internet has been in existence since the 1960s, the WWW since 1992. The WWW is only one of the services that the Internet provides. Other services provided include email, chat rooms and bulletin boards, all of which provide different ways of communicating information (see Figure 1.9).

WAP (wireless application protocol)
This is a way of sending information such as web pages to and from devices such as mobile phones. It provides a way of minimising the data sent because download speeds on mobile devices are slow compared with computers with normal connections to the Internet. Using WAP it is possible to access the WWW from a mobile phone but there will be less interactivity than would normally be available via a computer connected to the Internet.

Communication of information

So far you have learnt about different types of information and how they are communicated (summarised in Table 1.1). Now we will consider how to communicate different types of information effectively. When

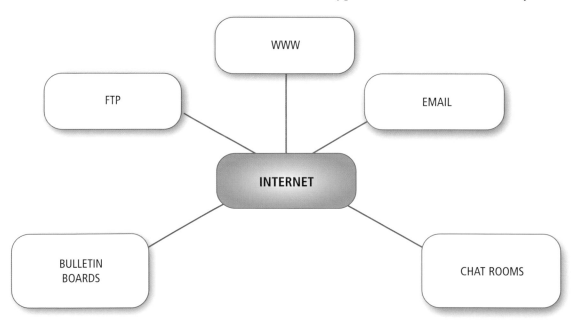

FIGURE 1.9 *Some services provided by the Internet*

TYPE OF INFORMATION	COMMUNICATION METHODS	TECHNOLOGIES
Written	Paper-based, screen-based, SMS, email, WWW	Personal computers, touch screens, mobile phones, the Internet, WAP
Multimedia	Screen-based, television, WWW	Personal computers, digital broadcasting, DVD, the Internet
Graphical	Paper-based, screen-based, WWW	Personal computers, touch screens, the Internet
Video	Screen-based, television, WWW	Personal computers, digital broadcasting, DVD, the Internet
Audio	Radio, television, telephone, WWW	Personal computers digital broadcasting, DVD, the Internet
Web-based	WWW	The Internet, WAP

TABLE 1.1 *How types of information, communication methods and technologies are linked*

you want to communicate some information, there are three questions you need to ask yourself.

1 Who is going to receive it – who will be the audience?

2 What is the communication's purpose?

3 What method will be used to communicate the information?

By answering these questions it will help you to decide on the style of language to use. If you are writing a note to a friend you will use informal language, as informal purposes demand an informal style; if you are writing a letter to apply for a job you will need to use formal language, as formal purposes demand a formal style (see Figure 1.10).

A presentation for young children will need to use short words and simple sentence constructions; a business *report* will use more complex words and sentences.

Key term

Report: a long document that presents the results of some research or the activities an organisation has undertaken during the previous year and its financial position.

Room 354, Block 6
Model Village
North Point
Hong Kong
Phone: 24862893
Mobile: 95427415
E-mail: wwm654@hkinternet.com
13 July 2005

Mr William Chan
Personnel Manager
XYZ Consulting
PO Box 583
Kwai Chung
Kowloon

Dear Mr Chan

Application for the Post of Management Trainee

I am writing to apply for the post of Management Trainee, which was advertised on the Student Affairs Office notice board of the Hong Kong Polytechnic University on 13 July 2005.

My working experience at Lucky Star Garment Manufactory Limited improved my leadership skills, communication skills and ability to work in a team environment. I have fluent spoken and written English. I also have fluent spoken and written Mandarin, and can therefore work in mainland China.

Currently I am studying a B.A. in Management at the Hong Kong Polytechnic University, graduating in 2006.

Subjects, which I am studying that are relevant to the post of Management Trainee include Operations Management, Human Resources Management, Accounting, Marketing and Strategic Management.

My final year project is entitled Knowledge Management Practices in HK. Carrying out this project has improved my communication skills, my leadership skills and my ability to lead and supervise subordinates effectively. I have also learnt how to run a project from the planning stage to its completion.

During my studies, I have held the post of Executive in the Management Society. While leading and organising Management Society activities, I have

FIGURE 1.10 *An example of a formal type of communication*

You will need to be able to use different writing styles to meet different purposes and document structures.

Attracting attention

If the purpose of a communication is to attract attention, you will need to use short punchy sentences that grab the reader's attention. An example might be 'Grand sale starts tomorrow. Don't miss the bargains.'

Think it over...

Compare two examples. What's good and bad and what improvements would you make?

Setting out facts clearly

When it is important to communicate facts clearly, you will need to use straightforward language that is easy to understand with no unnecessary descriptive words. For example, if you need to give someone directions you might write 'Leave the clockwise M25 at junction 1b (Dartford). At the top of the slip road take the third exit from the roundabout, immediately after the petrol station. Turn left at the next roundabout. The school entrance is on your right after 100 metres.'

Writing to impress

Sometimes you will need to write to impress your reader. This will give you the opportunity to use unusual words and more complex sentence structures. For example, in a job application you might write 'During the last ten years I have undertaken a plethora of responsibilities with consummate ease, enhancing my position and standing within this organisation. However, I feel I have now reached the pinnacle of the opportunities available and require new challenges.'

Summarising information

When you are summarising information, the purpose is to communicate the important points so that your audience can easily grasp them. Short bullet-pointed statements are often the best way to do this. For example, 'This unit requires you to study the following topics:

* the information age
* communication of information
* accuracy and readability
* styles of presentation
* how organisations present information
* standard ways of working.'

Creating a questionnaire

If you are creating a *questionnaire* a or if you are collecting information from individuals, you need to choose the questions you ask very carefully so that you get the response you need. Questions such as 'What do you like best about this brand of crisps?' are called open questions. If you asked 100 people, you could get 100 different responses. That would not be of much use to you if you want to do any analysis of the information you collect.

Key term

Questionnaire: a document designed to gather information and opinions from large numbers of individuals, often as part of a survey or to gain feedback on services provided.

Questions like 'Have you ever bought this brand of crisps?' are called closed questions. There are only two possible answers, yes and no. You can also ask questions that have a limited range of responses, for example 'Which of these is your favourite flavour?' with possible responses of 'cheese and onion', 'salt and vinegar', 'beef' and 'plain'. Closed and limited-response questions will help you to collect information that can be usefully analysed.

Collecting information from individuals

If you are creating a form to collect information from individuals, such as an application or booking form, you will need to ensure that it is clear what information is required. Some information may only require a simple prompt, for example 'Surname', 'Date of birth', 'Postcode', as everyone will know what is required. To obtain more complex information you may need to ask a question or write a statement to describe what is required. Some application forms have separate instructions on how to fill them in, for example an application for a passport or driving licence.

Explaining technical details

When you need to explain technical details it is important that your language is clear and accurate and that you use appropriate technical terms. For example, 'A digital television (DTV) broadcast has a 19.4 Mbit/s bandwidth. A standard DTV programme can use as few as 4.5 Mbit/s. This allows broadcasters to transmit more than one programme within a single 19.4 Mbit stream.'

Writing a reminder

A reminder is an informal document, possibly a hand-written note, a memo or an email. When you write a reminder it will be in an informal style. For example, 'Don't forget the meeting tomorrow at 2 o'clock. We're going to meet in the Sun Rise for a bite to eat, if you want to join us. We'll be there at about 1.'

Preparing a report

A report, on the other hand, is a formal document that needs a formal style. There are many different types of report but they all need to use formal language and be well structured.

Many businesses will produce an annual report for their shareholders and other interested people (see Figure 1.11). This will explain what has happened in the business in the previous year and include financial information such as the amount of money that has passed through the business and their profits for the year.

Ordering or invoicing goods

The most important consideration when creating orders and *invoices* is that they are accurate. If an incorrect address is given on an order, the goods will not get to the right place. An incorrect total on an invoice may lead to an irate customer or a loss of profit, as well as damaging the reputation of the company and losing the respect of its customers.

> ### Key term
>
> *Invoices*: A document that lists the products or services purchased from an organisation together with the cost of each, any additional costs such as carriage, the VAT due and the total amount to be paid.

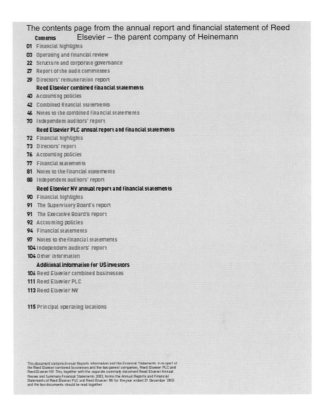

FIGURE 1.11 *The contents page from the annual report and financial statement for Reed Elsevier*

Orders and invoices may also include the terms and conditions under which the goods are supplied and payment made. The wording of these sections must be in a formal style, clear and precise, as they form part of a legal agreement between the supplier of the goods and the person buying them.

> ### Think it over...
>
> Technically explain how to open and close a file. Make sure each step is listed. Provide visual guidance.

Accuracy and readability

Some recent research has suggested that we can make sense of words, regardless of the order the letters are in, providing the first and last letters are correct.

'The rset can be a taotl mses and you can sitll raed it wouthit a porbelm.'

However, this does not make for easy reading. Imagine if you had to read a whole page like that. Inaccurate information, such as incorrect spellings, punctuation and grammar can mislead or annoy the reader. The position of a comma, for example, can totally change the meaning of a sentence. For example:

'When getting in the boat, shoes must be taken off.'
'When getting in, the boat shoes must be taken off.'

There was a court case involving a woman who lost her job because of an ill-placed comma!

Spell checkers

ICT provides us with tools to improve the accuracy of what we write. A spell checker will help you to check and correct punctuation and the spelling of words, and will also pick up repeated words, such as 'the the'. However, a spell checker only compares the words you type with an in-built dictionary. If you type 'form' when you mean 'from', or 'manger' when you mean 'manager', the spell checker will not identify these as errors. On the other hand, you may type a name, such as 'Agnew', which you know is correct, but the spell checker identifies it as an error. This is because 'Agnew' is not in the dictionary (see Figure 1.12).

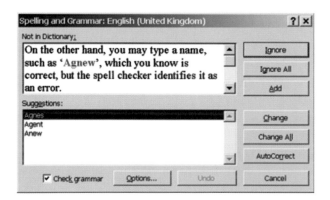

FIGURE 1.12 *Spell check*

If you use a lot of unusual words or proper names, you can create your own personal dictionary containing these words. You should not become over-reliant and expect the spell checker to spell for you. It will often provide a list of alternative spellings – you need to know which one to select. Sometimes the correct word may not be in the list or the spell checker cannot offer any

suggestions so you will need to correct the word yourself. Also, remember that the spell checker may be configured not to check certain words, such as those in capital letters, and does not tell you when you have omitted a capital letter at the start of a sentence.

> ### ✻ REMEMBER!
> Check that the spell checker is using English (UK) spellings. Quite often the spell checker is set to use US spelling, which does differ from English accepted grammar, punctuation and spelling conventions.

Grammar checker

Grammar checkers are also available to improve the accuracy of your documents. Grammar checkers compare what you type with a set of rules. You can choose which set of rules to use by selecting the style of language that you want, such as formal or technical.

A grammar checker will help you make sure that there is a capital letter to start a sentence and only one full stop at the end of it. It will also indicate if you have a single subject but a plural verb, for example 'they is', or vice versa. Also, common errors can be avoided, like writing 'you and I' when it should be 'you and me'. A useful tool of grammar checkers is to indicate where you have used the passive rather than the active voice. The passive voice is where the object of the sentence comes first, for example:

'The play was enjoyed by the audience.'

The active voice is when the subject of the sentence comes first, for example:

'The audience enjoyed the play.'

The active voice is much easier to read and has a more direct effect than the passive voice.

Grammar checkers can also provide you with readability statistics (see Figure 1.13). These will help you to meet the needs of your audience.

You need to take great care when using a grammar checker. Do not be too hasty to accept the changes suggested. Not all the changes

Theory into practice

– Selecting language style

Select *Options* in the *Tools* menu and then select the *Spelling & Grammar* tab. This dialogue box allows you to alter how the software checks spelling and grammar. In the grammar section there is a drop-down list to select the writing style. There is also a button labelled *Settings*. This takes you to another dialogue that indicates what will be checked – try changing the writing style and watch how the items selected in this list change. You can also set up your own customised writing style by selecting and deselecting these items. When you are happy, select *OK* to go back to the main dialogue box. There is a button that allows you to recheck your document. Try selecting different writing styles and options to see the effect on your documents.

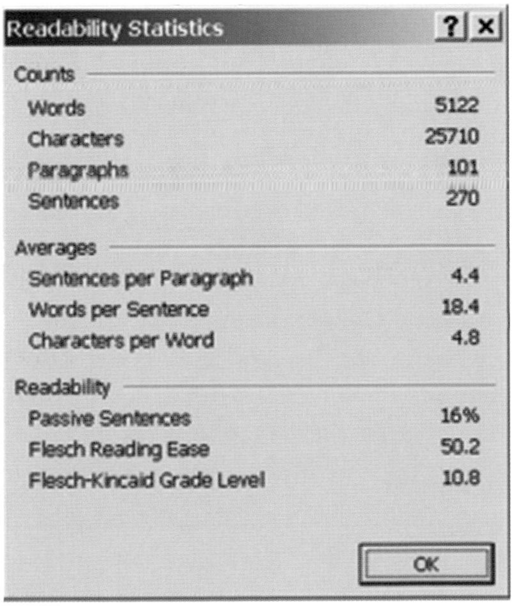

FIGURE 1.13 *Readability*

suggested improve the grammar of a sentence – some might change the meaning or make it meaningless.

Proof-reading

As you have already discovered, spelling and grammar checkers will not identify and correct all the errors you might make. It is very important that you proof-read your work. This means that you should read it through carefully to check for errors that the spelling and grammar checkers have not picked up. You should also check that what you have written makes sense, meets your purpose, and that the layout is correct. It is good practice to proof-read and correct errors on screen before you print the document. However, layout errors may not be evident until you print the work out. It is also often easier to spot errors on paper than on screen, so always give the printed copy a final check.

✱ REMEMBER!

The language used to convey information depends on:

- ✱ the audience
- ✱ the purpose
- ✱ the method of communication.

The accuracy of the information conveyed is important.

Software provides tools such as spelling and grammar checkers but these are no substitute for careful proof-reading.

Styles of presentation

How you present information is as important to your audience as the style of language you use and the accuracy of the content. Different font styles and sizes may help to differentiate between headings and the main body of a communication, or pick out a particular passage in the text, but use too many and the effect becomes confusing and annoying. Inconsistent headings and layout are common mistakes. When you are preparing a communication you need to think carefully about how you will present it to achieve the right impact and appeal to your audience.

In the following sections you will learn about the features that affect presentation style and how to use or modify them to suit your purpose.

1 What style of language should you use in a poster or flyer when you are trying to attract attention?

2 Why are open questions of limited use when you are designing a questionnaire?

3 If you have to write a report, how would the language you use differ from that you might use to write a reminder to a friend?

4 What is the most important thing you should consider when creating orders or invoices?

5 If you type manger instead of manager the spell checker does not find the error but if you type a name like Asif it is shown as an error, even though it is spelt correctly. Why is this?

6 Give three types of error that a grammar checker would find.

7 What is the difference between the active and the passive voice? Which should you try to use as much as possible and why?

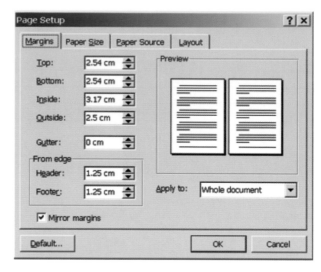

FIGURE 1.14 *Margins*

Margins are often blank, but books sometimes have wide side margins to contain marginal comments, and the top and bottom margins of many documents contain headers and footers.

Headers and footers

A header is text that lies within the top margin and that appears on every page within a section of the document. Typical header text might be the document's title or the name of the author. Long documents like a book may have the chapter title in the header for that chapter.

A footer is like a header but it lies within the bottom margin. Typical footer text might be the page number, the date it was created or amended, the version number or the filename of the document. You can have different headers and footers on odd and even pages and on the first page.

Page orientation

Page orientation arises because most documents are printed on paper that is rectangular. Portrait orientation is when the text is printed parallel to the narrow edge of the paper. Landscape orientation is when the text is printed parallel to the long edge of the paper (see Figures 15A and B). You need to consider carefully which orientation you should use for each communication you create. Business letters are always printed portrait, as are most books, brochures and newsletters. However, within these, a table, picture or chart that is wider than it is high may be printed landscape.

Page layout

Page layout features usually relate to how information is presented on the printed page. These features can be set up or modified in word processing or desktop publishing software to achieve the required layout.

Margins

Margins are the spaces between the edge of the text and the edge of the page. You can set the width of the top, bottom, left and right margins (see Figure 1.14). If you are creating a letter, the left and right margins would usually be the same but you might need to increase the size of the top margin if the letter is to be printed on headed notepaper. Reducing the size of margins is a useful trick if you are trying to fit a table, for example, on one page. If you are producing a longer document that is going to be printed on both sides of the paper and then hole-punched or bound, you would need a wider margin on the inside edge of each page. This would be the left margin on odd pages and the right one on even pages. You can set the software to 'mirror' the margins to achieve this effect.

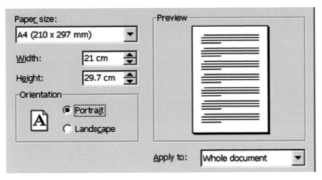 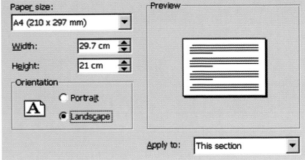

FIGURE 1.15A–B *Orientation can be portrait (1.15A) or landscape (1.15B) and applied to the whole document or part of it*

More informal documents, such as advertisements or an invitation, may be printed landscape but, in general, portrait is the more commonly used orientation.

Paper size

There are many different sizes of paper. In the USA, letter (8.5" wide by 11" high), legal (8.5" by 14") and executive (7.25" by 10.5") are used but in the UK the most commonly used paper size in business is A4. A4 paper is 21 cm wide and 29.7 cm high – 8.27" by 11.69". A4 is one of a series of paper sizes, all of which are exactly half the size of the previous one in the series. So, A4 is half the size of A3, which itself is half the size of A2, and if you fold a piece of A4 paper in half you get A5 (see Figure 1.16).

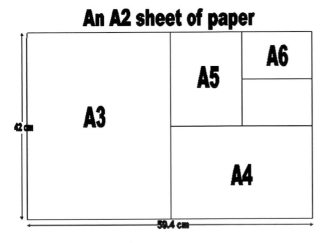

FIGURE 1.16 *Paper sizes*

This means you can create an A5 booklet by printing the pages landscape on A4 paper and folding them in half.

Pagination

Pagination is how text is distributed between the pages of a multi-page document. Software will automatically move text onto a new page when the previous one is full, but you can force text onto a new page before then by inserting a manual page break. You can also adjust where automatic page breaks occur to prevent *widows* and *orphans*. Remember this applies only to a paragraph, so you may need to manually insert a page break to keep a heading with the paragraph it relates to.

Key terms

Widow: where the first line of a paragraph is left on its own at the bottom of a page.
Orphan: where the last line of a paragraph ends up on its own at the top of a new page.

Gutters

The blank extra margin on the inside edge of pages that will be bound is called a gutter. This will be within the binding when the pages are bound.

Textual styles

Fonts

As you learnt at the beginning of this section, the use of too many different font styles and sizes can be confusing and annoying but careful selection and use of these can enhance your presentation style. There are many different font styles available in many different sizes. The font style and size you use for your communication will depend on its purpose and audience. A fancy font (see Figure 1.17) may be suitable for an invitation to a wedding but not for a business letter.

Wedding Invitation

FIGURE 1.17 *A fancy font suitable for a wedding invitation*

Many business documents will use a font style like the one used for this book – Times New Roman. This is known as a serif font. Others will use a sans serif font style such as Arial.

> ✱ **REMEMBER!**
>
> Arial, Verdana and Helvetica are conventionally used for web pages.

If you look at letters such as the i, r and l carefully, you will see how these two families of fonts differ. The letters in the serif font have short strokes – called serifs – that are missing from sans serif fonts – sans means without in French. It is considered easier to read serif fonts because the serifs draw your eye along to the next letter.

The font size you use is also important. This too will depend on the purpose of your communication and your audience. If you are creating an on-screen presentation to show to an audience, you will probably need to use a font size of at least 20 point. A book for young children may use a 14 pt font size, but for most business letters, reports and other formal documents, you should use a font size between 10 and 12 pt. Font sizes smaller than 10 pt can be difficult to read. Information that must be included in a communication for legal reasons is often printed in a small font size so that the reader's attention is not drawn to it. Such information is often known as 'the small print'.

Headings and title styles

Headings and titles give a communication structure and help the reader to know what each section is about. There may be main headings and different levels of sub-headings to break the text up further, as shown in this book. If each different level of title or heading has its own style, it will help the reader to recognise which level a heading belongs to. It is important that you use title and heading styles consistently. Software will help you to do this by allowing you to set named styles. For example, you could create a style called Main Heading that is Times New Roman 18 pt, bold. Every time you need a main heading, you would only need to select this style.

> **Theory into practice**
>
> – setting heading styles
>
> Select *Style* from the *Format* menu. Next select the *New* button. Type in a name for your style and then click on the *Format* button. You will be given different formatting options such as *Font* and *Paragraph*. Change the formatting to what you want for this style then click on *OK* to return to the previous dialogue box. When you have made all the changes, click *Apply* on the main *Style* dialogue.

Bold, italic and underline

Bold, *italic* and <u>underline</u> are all ways of drawing attention to particular words or sections of text. They are effective only if you use them sparingly. Underline is now commonly used to indicate a *hyperlink*. It is not normally used for headings except in hand-written documents. Emboldening the most important word in a phrase or sentence will make it stand out and grab the reader's attention. Italics are also commonly used for emphasis but, if a whole document is in italics, it just becomes more difficult to read. Titles and heading styles often use bold to make them stand out.

> **Key term**
>
> *Hyperlink*: an area of an on-screen document or presentation that takes the user to another part of the presentation or to a different location, such as another file or a web page, when it is clicked on.

Superscript and subscript

Usually, letters appear on an imaginary line, with only the 'tails' of letters like g or p below it. Sometimes you may need letters to appear above the line, for examplest 1st. The 'st' is in superscript – MS Word will do this automatically but you can switch this feature off. Similarly, if you want to type the chemical formula for water, H_2O, the 2 needs to be below the line,- or in subscript. This is achieved by highlighting the 2 and then checking subscript in the Format Font dialogue (see Figure 1.18).

Text orientation

Most text you type will appear horizontally on the page, like this does. However, if the text is in a frame, it is possible to change the orientation of some of the text on the page so that it appears vertically on the page.

FIGURE 1.18 *Subscript*

Text animation (on-screen)

If you are producing an on-screen communication, you can also animate the text (see Figure 1.19). This can either be how it arrives on the screen, such as letter by letter or word by word, or how it appears, such as a flashing background or moving border. Both text orientation and text animation should be

used only for effect and sparingly so that the reader does not become confused or distracted.

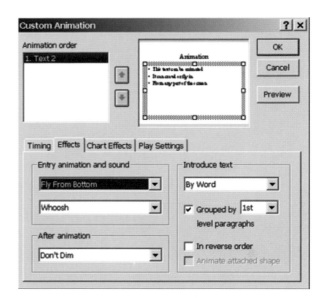

FIGURE 1.19 *Animating text in a slide presentation*

Theory into practice

– animating text in a slide presentation

Set up your presentation and enter the text onto your slides. Select the text you want to animate and then select *Custom Animation* from the *Slide Show* menu. Select the *Effects* tab. You can then choose from the drop-down lists the effects (including sounds) that you want to apply.

Paragraph formats

There are a number of options available that allow you to control how the text within a communication is set out in paragraphs.

✱ REMEMBER!

As far as word processing software is concerned, you start a new paragraph every time you hit the **Enter** key.

Tabs and indents

A tab allows you to move the typing cursor to a certain distance along the line. You can set tabs at different positions on the line and every time you press the **Tab** key, the cursor will move to the next position. Tabs are usually used with individual items in a list to ensure that each starts at the same distance from the margin. The standard tab setting starts the word at the tab position – it is left aligned. It is also possible to set tabs that are centre aligned, right aligned, or decimal aligned. The last of these is used for columns of figures so that the decimal points are all under one another.

$$23.4$$
$$361.35$$
$$\underline{3.671}$$

Total   388.421

Another feature of tabs are the leaders. These give a line of dots, dashes or a solid line leading to the tab position. For example:

Item 1 . . . . .Page 24
Item 2 . . . . .Page 139

This is an example of a right aligned tab with leader dots.

Theory into practice

– setting tabs

Select *Tabs* from the *Format* menu. Type in a tab position and select the tab alignment and any leader by clicking the radio buttons. Don't forget to click on the *Set* button to set each tab, which will be used within the document from then on. To clear a tab, select it in the list and then click the *Clear* button. Experiment with different combinations of tab positions, alignments and leaders.

An indent is usually used with paragraphs of continuous text. If you set an indent, you can make every line in a paragraph start and finish a set distance in from the margins. This is often used when a quotation is included in a document to differentiate it from the rest of the text. This paragraph has left and right indents of 1 cm.

A first line indent is when only the first line starts at the set distance from the left margin. First line indents used to be used to indicate a new paragraph but a blank line is usually used for this purpose now. This paragraph has a 1 cm first line indent.

With a hanging indent, the first line starts at the left margin and the rest of the paragraph is indented. This is mostly used with bullets or numbering. This paragraph has a 1 cm hanging indent.

Paragraph numbering

The paragraphs within a document can be numbered. In a long document such as a report, multi-level numbering may be used. The main sections in the document may be numbered 1, 2, 3, etc., sub-sections may be numbered 1.1, 1.2, 1.3, etc. and these sections may also have sub-sections numbered 1.1.1, 1.1.2, 1.1.3, and so on (see Figure 1.20).

1 Customers
1.1 Shops
1.1.1 High Street
The number of customers buying from our high street shops this Christmas has shown a marked decline over previous years.
1.1.2 Shopping Malls
Although the reduction in customer numbers has not been as great as for our high street outlets, there has still been some reduction from last year.
1.2 Remote
1.2.1 Mail Order
Customer numbers from our mail order catalogue has seen some reduction this year.
1.2.2 The Internet
This is the main growth area. Customer numbers have more than doubled since last Christmas.
2 Suppliers
2.1 UK-based
2.2 Overseas

FIGURE 1.20 *Multi-level numbering*

Such numbering makes it possible for a reader to refer accurately to a particular part of the report. Numbering is also used to indicate points or actions that are in a specific order, for example in recipes and instructions.

Widows and orphans

As you learned on page 19, widows and orphans are where the first or last line of a paragraph is on a different page from the rest of the paragraph. The automatic page breaks can be set to avoid widows and orphans.

Theory into practice

– preventing widows and orphans

Select *Paragraph* in the *Format* menu and then the *Line and Page Breaks* tab. Checking the *Widows/Orphans control* box will ensure that these are avoided.

Alignment

A paragraph that has a straight left edge and a jagged right edge is left aligned. If the left edge is jagged and the right edge is straight, the paragraph is right aligned. Centre alignment is where each line starts and ends the same distance from its centre. If a paragraph is justified, both left and right edges are straight. The spaces between words are extended as necessary (see Figure 1.21 for examples of alignment).

A paragraph that has a straight left edge and a jagged right edge is *left aligned*.

If the left edge is jagged and the right edge is straight, the paragraph is *right aligned*.

Centre alignment is where each line starts and ends the same distance from its centre.

If a paragraph is *justified*, both left and right edges are straight. The spaces between words are extended as necessary.

FIGURE 1.21 *Alignment*

Left alignment is commonly used for many types of document. Right alignment may be used to align an address on the right margin of a letter, for example. Centre alignment may be used for headings or for communications such as greetings cards, menus, posters or flyers with limited text.

Newspapers and newsletters use justified paragraphs. Justified paragraphs are also used in business letters that use a style called 'fully blocked'.

Spacing before/after

Adding space before or after a paragraph is useful when you want some space but not a whole line between a heading and the following paragraph or before a bullet list. You can specify the point size of the space you want to leave. Adding spacing before and after items in a table provides some white space between the text and the borders of the cells. These options can be found in the **Format Paragraph** dialogue box.

Use of tables

Tables help to organise information on the page or screen. You can use a table rather than tabs to align columns of short items. If you do not add borders to the table, the effect will be exactly the same. However, with a table, each item can extend onto more than one line. Table 1.2 shows the flight details for a trip to Australia. A 3 pt space has been added before and after each paragraph to move the text away from the borders making it easier to read. The cells in the first and fifth rows have been merged to allow each heading to appear on one line and to differentiate them from the details.

Bullet points

Bullet points are similar to numbered paragraphs but are used to identify a list of points that are in no particular order.

Line spacing

It is possible to adjust the space between the lines within a paragraph. Line spacing within a paragraph is most commonly single, 1.5 or double, relating to the font size being used. However, you can set the line spacing to be at least a set point size or exactly a set point size, or larger multiples of the font size such as 2.5 or 3 times. Many documents use single line spacing, but adding extra space between the lines may make the text easier to read. Double line spacing is often used for the draft copy of a document as it allows space to annotate the text with suggested changes and comments.

| FLIGHT DETAILS – OUTBOUND | | | | | |
AIRLINE	FLIGHT NO.	DEPARTURE AIRPORT AND TERMINAL	DESTINATION	DEPARTING	ARRIVING
Malaysia Airlines	0003	London Heathrow Terminal 3	Kuala Lumpur	28/03/05 1200	29/03/05 0730
Malaysia Airlines	0129	Kuala Lumpur	Melbourne Victoria	29/03/05 0950	29/03/05 2030
FLIGHT DETAILS – INBOUND					
AIRLINE	FLIGHT NO.	DEPARTURE AIRPORT AND TERMINAL	DESTINATION	DEPARTING	ARRIVING
Malaysia Airlines	0148	Melbourne Victoria Terminal 1	Kuala Lumpur	28/04/05 1540	28/04/05 2030
Malaysia Airlines	0002	Kuala Lumpur	London Heathrow	29/04/05 2340	29/04/05 0550

TABLE 1.2

Hyphenation

Hyphenation allows a long word that will not fit on the current line to be split and a hyphen inserted. You can switch hyphenation off so that words are not split in this way.

Special features

There are a number of special features you need to be able to use to develop special presentation styles.

Borders

You can use borders around paragraphs as well as in tables. A border around a paragraph will make it stand out from the rest of the text and draw the reader's attention to it.

Shading

Shading behind the text can also draw attention to it. However, you need to be careful that the shading is not too dark, so that the text can still be read easily.

Background and text colour

For screen-based communications, or those that will be printed in colour, you can select the colour of the background and the text colour. You need to be careful which colours you choose to use together. For example, if you use red text on a green background, it will be unreadable by anyone who is red-green colour blind. You should also limit the number of different colours you use (see Figure 1.22). A rainbow of different colours is likely to annoy the audience and distract them from the information you are trying to communicate.

FIGURE 1.22 *Too many colours have been used on this page*

A contents page

A contents page is an important feature of a multi-page document. It should list the main sections of the document with their page numbers. If you use named heading styles, you can make the word processing software create a contents page automatically (see Figure 1.23).

Theory into practice

Check the contents page of this book.

– creating a contents page

Before you can create a table of contents, you must have set up and used named heading styles in your document. Select *Index and Tables* from the *Insert* menu and select the *Table of Contents* tab.

You can select different pre-set formats for the contents table, whether to include page numbers, whether these should be right aligned and whether to include a leader or not. You can also select how many levels of heading should be listed in the table of contents. Clicking the *Options* button will enable you to select the named style you have used and the level of each. The *Modify* button will allow you to change the style of each level of heading in the table of contents.

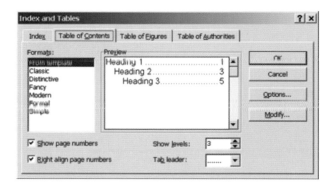

FIGURE 1.23 *Creating a table of contents*

An index

An index is also a feature of longer documents. You will find one at the end of this book. The index lists important words in alphabetical order, along with the pages each word appears on. You can mark the words you want to appear in an index, and the word processing software will create the index for you – this is also done using the **Index and Tables** dialogue box.

Try this on a document you've already created.

A bibliography

A bibliography lists all the sources of information you use when creating a communication. You will need to create a bibliography to list all the sources of information that you use when you are producing the assessment evidence for this unit. The purpose of a bibliography is to allow someone else to find the same information as you did. You must provide enough information for them to do so. For a book, you should list the name of the author(s), the title and the publisher as a minimum (see Table 1.3). A formal bibliography will also state where and when the book was published. If you use information from a web page you should list the exact URL of the page you used. If you use a magazine or other publication, you will need to list its title, publisher and the date it was issued (and/or the volume number and issue number).

Bessant, A	Learning to Use Your Computer	Heinemann	Dec 2002	ISBN 0435455478
de Watteville, A & Gilbert L	AVCE ICT Student Book 2nd Edition	Heinemann	Oct 2000	ISBN 0435453076
http://www.io.com/~hcexres/tcm1603/acchtml/genlett.html				
http://esl.about.com/cs/onthejobenglish/a/a_basbletter.htm				
http://www.textmatters.com/tm/guides/dbd.html				

TABLE 1.3 *Part of a bibliography*

An appendix

Information that you want to refer to but that you do not want to include in the main body of the document should be put in an *appendix* at the end of the document. You should clearly number each appendix, e.g. Appendix 1, Appendix 2, and refer to them in the main document, for example 'see the sales figures in Appendix 1'. If no reference is made to an appendix, it should not be included.

Text/picture boxes

Text and picture boxes allow you to position a picture or some text where you want it to appear on the page or screen. You can then choose how you want the rest of the text to wrap around it. Desktop publishing software uses text and picture boxes (or frames – see Figure 1.24) to hold and position all text and pictures.

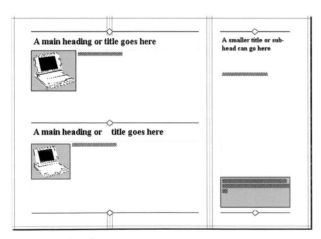

FIGURE 1.24 *Frames*

Types of media

Much of what we have looked at so far relates to presenting textual information. We have already said that graphical information is more direct and memorable than written information. So, many types of presentation can be improved by incorporating various types of media such as different types of graphics, charts, video clips and sound.

Graphs or charts

If you have to communicate numerical information, a graph or chart may make it easier for your audience to understand than a table or list of figures. For example, a line graph is often used to show the variation in temperature in a holiday resort for different months of the year. You could use a pie chart to show the proportion of boys and girls studying ICT in your school or college, or a bar chart to show the number of boys and girls taking each subject. Do be careful, however, that you choose the correct type of graph for the data you need to display.

Lines or borders

Lines and borders are effective ways to visually break a page or screen up into separate areas. You can use a horizontal line below the title on each slide of a slide presentation, or above the footer on a printed document. You can place a vertical line between the columns of a two or three-column newsletter to help guide the reader's eye down each column or put a border around an article to draw attention to it (see Figure 1.25).

FIGURE 1.25 *Vertical lines between columns*

Video clips

On-screen communications such as multimedia presentations and web pages allow you to include video clips and sound to liven up the presentation and attract the audience's attention. For example, if you are producing a multimedia presentation about your local area for the tourist office, including a video clip will give people a better idea of what the area is like than still photos alone.

Pictures

There are a number of different types of graphic images that you can include to improve presentation style. These include:

* pictures created using painting packages (*bitmap* images)

* line drawings created using *vector graphic* packages

* photographs taken with a digital camera can be imported directly into your presentation

* photographs taken with a digital camera that can be imported directly into your presentation

* extensive libraries of clipart images can illustrate the information you are trying to convey

* scanned images such as printed photographs can be imported.

One point to bear in mind, however, is that whichever images you use they must be appropriate to the purpose of the communication and the needs of your audience.

Sound

Sound can make a presentation more accessible as well as attracting attention. Spoken instructions can be recorded and added to the presentation or the text of the presentation can be read aloud and recorded. Both of these additions would help a young child or a person who is visually impaired to access the presentation. Other types of sound such as music or sound effects can also be used effectively.

Positioning important items

Addressee details, dates, logos, signatures and headings should follow standard layouts (see Figure 1.26).

FIGURE 1.26 *A business letter*

There are standard conventions for the layout of some documents such as business letters. A reference and the date are positioned above the main body of the letter, as are the name and address of the person being written to – the addressee. One reason for this is to allow the use of 'window' envelopes. Conventionally used in business, these are envelopes that have a see-through window that allows the name and address to be seen and which does away with the need to write or print the address on the envelope. Business letters often include a heading to indicate what the letter is about. This is positioned at the beginning of the letter below the salutation (the Dear …). Space needs to be left for a signature at the end of the letter. This will come after the complimentary close (Yours faithfully or Yours sincerely). The person's name and their position are usually printed below their signature. Many organisations will also have their own rules for positioning items such as the company logo as part of their house style. We will look at house style in more detail in the section about how organisations present information.

Knowledge check

1 Which page orientation is used for most business documents? Give three examples when it would be appropriate not to use it.

2 What is a widow and what is an orphan in a multi-page document?

3 What should you consider when choosing font styles and sizes for a communication? What font style and size would be appropriate for a business letter?

4 What is the difference between a tab and an indent? Give an example when each might be used.

5 What should you consider when choosing background and font colours for a presentation?

6 Give two examples of when a graph or chart might improve a presentation.

✳ REMEMBER!

There are many different features that affect the style of a presentation. The features you use will depend on the purpose of your communication, what you want to achieve with it and what will appeal to your audience. These features apply to:

✳ page layouts – margins, headers and footers, page orientation, paper size, pagination and gutters

✳ textual style – fonts, headings and title styles, bold, italic and underline, superscript and subscript, text orientation and text animation

✳ paragraph formats – tabs and indents, paragraph numbering, widows and orphans, justification, spacing before/after, use of tables, bullet points, line spacing and hyphenation

✳ special features – use of borders, use of shading, background colour, text colour, a contents page, an index, a bibliography, an appendix and text/picture boxes

✳ types of media – graphs or charts, lines or borders, video clips, pictures, drawings, digital photographs, clip art, scanned images and sound

✳ position of important items – references, signatures, dates, logos, addressee names and headings.

Creating communications

So far you have learnt about the different writing and presentation techniques that you can use to create different types of communications. You will need to learn to judge when to use different techniques to match the purpose and audience for each communication.

How to create templates to standardise styles of presentation

Templates will help you to create a standardised presentation style. A template allows you to set

Theory into practice

– creating and using a template

Open a new document, set the page layout and any textual styles. Type in any standard text that will appear on every document and import any graphics such as a logo. Instead of just clicking the *Save* button, select *Save As* from the file menu. Type in a name for the template and then select *Document Template (*.dot)* from the *Save As Type* drop-down list. Click the *Save* button. To use the template, select *New* from the *File* menu, then select your template and click *OK*.

things like the style and size of fonts and the position of items so that these are the same every time you use the template.

When to use existing information

There is a saying 'Why re-invent the wheel?' Sometimes, the information you want to communicate already exists. It may be better to use the existing information than to try to recreate it.

How to select and adapt existing information to the needs of your communication

There may be different sources of the information you want to convey in different forms. You will need to be able to select the existing information that most closely matches the purpose of your communication and the needs of your audience.

You may not be able to find information that exactly matches your requirements. If that is so, you will need to adapt the information you find. This may involve simplifying the language used in a text article, cropping a photograph or adding an arrow to a map to indicate a location, for example. If you use or adapt existing information, it is important that you identify and credit its source.

When to create original information

Sometimes you will need to create your own original information. If you are producing a *curriculum vitae (cv)* and letter to apply for a job, the information you include in it will be original information about you.

Key term

Curriculum vitae: called a resume in the US, this is a document that includes your personal details and your education and employment history.

When to blend existing and original information

Often you will need to blend your own original information with existing information. For example, you may carry out a survey to find out how your fellow students spend their leisure time and present your results alongside national statistics obtained from existing sources.

How to maintain a consistent style throughout a communication

When you are creating a long document or presentation, it is important that it has a consistent style throughout. The use of named heading styles, templates and master page layouts will help you to achieve this. A master page layout allows you to set the layout that all the pages in a document or presentation will follow. This will include things like the background and text colours, the size of margins, the position of page numbers, the font style and size for titles and body text and the style of bullets. Slide presentations can be formatted in a similar way (see Figure 1.27).

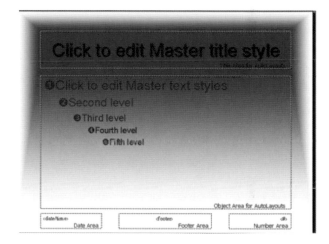

FIGURE 1.27 *Master slide*

How to combine text, sound, graphics, video and number information harmoniously

In a previous section we discussed the use of different types of media to improve presentation style. Often you will need to combine different types of information and media in a communication. It is very easy to combine different types of information badly. Too many graphics or video clips will compete with each other for the viewer's attention, reducing their effectiveness. When you are combining text and graphics you need to consider the position of each carefully, so that there is an overall balance to the document, and so that pictures are as near as possible to the passage of text they illustrate. Whichever types of information you are combining, you should try to achieve a harmonious balance, so that each type of information is communicated effectively without undermining others.

How to evaluate the communications you produce

You will need to produce many different communications to refine your skills in presenting information and to evaluate each communication you produce so that future ones will be more effective. You will need to ask yourself and others a number of questions such as:

* is the style of language suitable for the purpose?

* is the style of language suitable for the intended audience?

* does the presentation style match the purpose of the communication?

* does the presentation style appeal to the intended audience?

* will the audience understand what I am trying to say?

* does the communication have the impact I wanted to achieve?

* how could I improve the communication to make it more effective?

Think it over...

In a group, discuss and evaluate some of the communications you have created. Use the questions just listed as the basis for your discussion.

How organisations present information

Every organisation is made up of a group of people who work together to make something or provide a service. You will learn more about what organisations are and how they operate in Unit 2: How organisations use ICT. In this chapter we will look specifically at why and how organisations present information, both within the organisation and outside it.

Why, and how, organisations present information both within, and outside, the organisation

All organisations need to communicate information. Internal communications may include memos and emails sent by managers to their staff, or from one member of staff to another. Large organisations may create multimedia presentations for training staff or informing them of developments within the organisation. The larger the organisation, the more internal communication will be needed to keep it running smoothly. Organisations also need to communicate with outsiders, including other organisations. External communications will be with customers, suppliers, official bodies such as the Inland Revenue and with the general public. Communication with customers may include letters, invoices, brochures and, increasingly, emails and websites. Organisations will send orders to suppliers and will have to send financial information to the Inland Revenue. There are many different ways that organisations communicate with the general public, including advertisements, posters and flyers. Some may even display visual presentations in public places to inform people about the organisation and its products or services.

Organisations present information externally through branding and advertising. This helps customer loyalty, gives quicker identification and reinforces the link between validity and reliability, therefore giving an impression of trust. The presentation of internal information gives branding for employees, consistency of standards, and saves time and money.

Typical uses of illustrations, technical drawings, pictures and artwork

Letters, invoices and similar documents will not include graphical information other than the company logo and possibly logos of other organisations, such as trade bodies, that they belong to. Other types of communication from organisations will include graphical information in different forms. A builder developing a new block of flats may produce publicity material that includes artists' impressions to illustrate what the finished block will look like (see Figure 1.28).

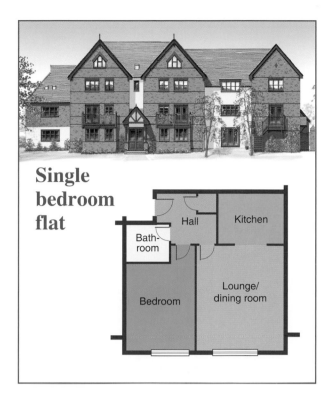

Single bedroom flat

Hall

Kitchen

Bathroom

Bedroom

Lounge/dining room

FIGURE 1.28 *An artist's impression*

The material may also include technical drawings such as the floor plans of different flats. All of this graphical information will enable the builder to sell the flats before they have even been built. A company that makes and sells self-assembly furniture will provide instructions, including technical drawings, for assembling it. A school prospectus is likely to include photographs of staff, pupils and different features of the school. Most advertisements, publicity flyers, newsletters and similar documents, as well as visual and multimedia presentations will include pictures and artwork of one kind or another.

Commonly accepted standards for the layout of formal documents

There are commonly accepted standards for the layout of formal documents and certain items of information that must appear on them. We discussed the positioning of information on business letters in a previous section. Most business letters use a style called open punctuation. This means that the only punctuation used is in the body of the letter so that it makes sense: there are no commas after

each line of the address, for example. It is also usual for all the items in a letter to start at the left margin with paragraph breaks being shown by a blank line. Some letters are fully blocked, which means that the text of the letter is fully justified (see page 27). Where the organisation sending the letter is a company, the company's full name, registration number and the address of the registered office must appear on the letter (see Figure 1.29). The address may be different from that from which the letter is being sent and is often included in a smaller font size as a footer.

Harcourt Education Limited
Registered Office: Halley Court, Jordan Hill, Oxford OX2 8EJ

Registered in England: Number 3099304

FIGURE 1.29 *Section of Heinemann notepaper showing registered office details*

Essential information that appears on formal documents

Other documents also have information that must be included for legal or other reasons. An invoice (see Figure 1.30) will include an invoice number for easy reference. It must show the address of the company sending the invoice so that the customer knows where to send payment. As with a letter, the company's registration details must also appear. The invoice will also include the terms under which payment must be made, for example within 30 days. If the company is VAT registered, their VAT registration number and the amount of VAT charged must appear on the invoice. The invoice will also include the customer's address and the delivery address if it is different.

A fax header sheet should indicate the number of pages being sent and the telephone number of the sender. The receiver then knows when all the pages have arrived and can contact the sender if there is a problem.

Walter's Widgets,
Unit 24,
Sprocket Industrial Estate,
Anyhampton,
Somewhereshire
SM1 2AB

INVOICE

Invoice No. INV1234567
Invoice Date: 1/8/05

Customer:
The Widget Shop,
123 Rubble Road,
Anyhampton,
Somewhereshire
SM1 2CD

Item	Quantity	Price per unit	Total
Round Widget	10	£3.50	£35.00
Square Widget	10	£4.50	£45.00
Curved Widget	20	£2.50	£50.00
		Sub Total	£130.00
		VAT @ 17.5%	£22.75
		GRAND TOTAL	**£152.75**

Payment Terms: 30 days

VAT No. 1234567890

FIGURE 1.30 *A sample invoice*

FIGURE 1.31 *Logos*

Methods of presenting a corporate image

Most organisations want to present a corporate image when they communicate externally. Indeed, some organisations spend very large sums of money designing and implementing a corporate image so that all their communications are instantly recognisable.

Part of an organisation's corporate image may be a logo (see Figure 1.31), but there will also be presentation rules, or house style, that all communications must follow. These rules may include the style, colour and size of fonts used for different documents, the size of margins, when and how the company logo is used, where it should be positioned, and so on. Some large organisations may provide their staff with a booklet or other document containing detailed instructions on how to create different communications in the house style.

How templates might be used to enforce corporate standards

Another way of ensuring that all communications conform to the organisation's house style is to provide staff with templates that they must use. These templates can be set up with the correct page layout and font styles so that staff simply need to click on them and enter the information.

Types of documents

Earlier in this chapter we looked at different writing and presentation styles. In this section we are going to consider these in relation to different types of communications used by organisations.

Publicity flyers

Publicity flyers (see Figure 1.32) may be handed out to people, posted through letterboxes or left in places such as reception areas or stations for people

FIGURE 1.32 *A flyer*

to pick up. They are usually printed on a single sheet of paper (usually A4 or A5) either on one or both sides, and, if A4, may be folded in half or into three. Publicity flyers need to grab people's attention. Presentation techniques such as large font sizes, colour and images will be used to do so. The writing style will often be informal, with short, easy-to-read statements rather than long sentences.

Questionnaires

Organisations use questionnaires for a variety of reasons. A common reason is to get feedback from customers on the quality of the goods or services the organisation provides. Organisations that provide a guarantee for the goods they sell often ask customers to register the product and complete a 'lifestyle' questionnaire (see Figure 1.33).

This allows the organisation to build a profile of the type of customers who buy its products. Whatever the purpose of the questionnaire, it is important that it is easy to understand and easy to complete. Instructions and questions must be clear and easy to understand. Closed or limited response questions will probably be used with tick boxes for responses. A common method to obtain an opinion is to ask the respondent to indicate a number on a given scale or select a descriptor. For example, How would you rate the quality of our service? 1 Excellent, 2 Good, 3 Average, 4 Poor, 5 Unacceptable. Where this technique is used, the numbers and descriptors need to be used consistently. It is common to find a

A. YOUR NAME & ADDRESS

GUIDANCE NOTES
1. Please answer questions on behalf of yourself, your partner or your household as appropriate. Of course, you can always discuss your answers with other members of your family.
2. Please feel free to ignore particular questions if you wish. Your remaining answers are still of value.
3. Please write in CAPITAL letters – tick boxes like this. ✔
4. If you make a mistake, simply cross it out and continue.
5. Some of the questions will relate to you or your partner. Please ask your partner before providing information on their behalf.

Your name: Mr ☐   Mrs ☐   Miss ☐   Ms ☐
Initials
Surname
Address

Town
County
Postcode
Telephone number:
Your mobile number:
e-mail address: @
Are you?
Married **01** ☐   Single **02** ☐   Divorced/Separated **03** ☐   Widowed **04** ☐   Living Together **05** ☐
If applicable, please write in the date you were married:
Your partner's name: Mr ☐   Mrs ☐   Miss ☐   Ms ☐
Initials
Surname
Your partner's mobile number:
Your partner's e-mail address: @
What are the dates of birth of: You   Your Partner

GENERAL INTERESTS

1. Please tick the leisure interests and activities which you and your partner enjoy regularly: *(Please tick all that apply)*

	You	Ptnr		You	Ptnr
Art	01 ☐	18 ☐	Football Pools	35 ☐	52 ☐
Arts & Crafts	02 ☐	19 ☐	Foreign Travel	36 ☐	53 ☐
Antiques	03 ☐	20 ☐	Gardening	37 ☐	54 ☐
Astrology/Horoscopes	04 ☐	21 ☐	Health Foods	38 ☐	55 ☐
Betting	05 ☐	22 ☐	Home Baking	39 ☐	56 ☐
Book Reading	06 ☐	23 ☐	Live Sports Events	40 ☐	57 ☐
Bingo	07 ☐	24 ☐	Motoring	41 ☐	58 ☐
Catalogue Shopping	08 ☐	25 ☐	Motorsports	42 ☐	59 ☐
Cigarette Smoking	09 ☐	26 ☐	National Lottery	43 ☐	60 ☐
Cinema	10 ☐	27 ☐	National Trust	44 ☐	61 ☐
Collectibles	11 ☐	28 ☐	Nightclubs	45 ☐	62 ☐
Computer Games	12 ☐	29 ☐	Personal Finance	46 ☐	63 ☐
Cookery	13 ☐	30 ☐	Science/Technology	47 ☐	64 ☐
Current Affairs	14 ☐	31 ☐	Slimming	48 ☐	65 ☐
D I Y	15 ☐	32 ☐	Theatre	49 ☐	66 ☐
Eating Out	16 ☐	33 ☐	Visiting Pubs	50 ☐	67 ☐
Fashion	17 ☐	34 ☐	Wildlife	51 ☐	68 ☐

2. Have you taken (in the last 3 years), or are you considering taking, any of the following types of holiday? *(Please tick all that apply)*

	Taken	May Take		Taken	May Take
Apartment/Self Catering	01 ☐	07 ☐	Motoring	13 ☐	19 ☐
Citybreak	02 ☐	08 ☐	Package Holiday	14 ☐	20 ☐
Coach Holiday	03 ☐	09 ☐	Skiing	15 ☐	21 ☐
Cruise	04 ☐	10 ☐	UK Short Break	16 ☐	22 ☐
Hotel UK	05 ☐	11 ☐	Walking/Trekking	17 ☐	23 ☐
Long Haul	06 ☐	12 ☐	Winter Sun	18 ☐	24 ☐

3. On average, how many weeks a year do you spend abroad?
One-two **01** ☐   Three-four **02** ☐   Five or more **03** ☐

FIGURE 1.33 *A lifestyle questionnaire*

number of such questions in a table format. Often, an even number of options is provided to prevent people simply choosing the middle one. Depending on the purpose of the questionnaire, there may also be lines for the respondent to write comments.

Business letters

We have already discussed many of the presentation styles and common standards used for business letters. The writing style used will depend on the reason the letter is being sent. Many organisations send out letters to existing and potential customers using mailing lists. These letters try to persuade people to buy the product or service the organisation offers. Such letters will often be written in a more informal style and using persuasive language. On the other hand, a letter to a customer in response to a complaint is likely to be written in a more formal style of language.

Newsletters

Newsletters may be internal to an organisation to keep its employees informed about what is happening in the organisation, for example the vocational department internal newsletter may make the organisation aware of the newly formed team; or it may be an external document for customers or the general public. There are few common standards for such documents, although most will use a fairly informal writing style. Most newsletters will have a title, even if it is just the name of the organisation such as 'Banks and Co Staff Newsletter'. A date or some indication of when it was issued, such as 'Spring 2005', is vital. Many newsletters will use columns and most will include at least some pictures. The size of the newsletter and the presentation techniques used will depend on a number of factors such as the size of the organisation and how often it is published. A large organisation that produces a quarterly newsletter for its staff may produce a high-quality, colour document of several pages, which includes a number of photographs and other graphics (see Figure 1.34). A small charity that produces a monthly newsletter for subscribers may produce a single-page black and white newsletter with few pictures so as to keep production costs to a minimum.

Visual presentations

Organisations use visual (or slide) presentations for two main purposes. One of these purposes is to accompany a talk to an audience; the other is as an unattended, automatic 'rolling' presentation in a reception area, airport or other public place. In either case, the amount of text on each slide should be kept to a minimum, using large font sizes that are easy to read from a distance. The text is often displayed as bullet points. Presentation techniques should be used consistently and colours chosen carefully. Most slide presentations include graphic images, including charts or graphs. The golden rule is only one graphic image per slide.

Brochures

Brochures come in all shapes and sizes and for a variety of purposes. Many brochures will advertise the goods or services that an organisation sells. It is, therefore, vital that the name of the organisation and its contact details are clearly displayed. Such brochures will almost always include photographs and other images. The text may be fairly informal and descriptive, trying to show the products or services in the best light. However, many brochures will include terms and conditions that will be written in a formal style to meet legal requirements.

Itineraries

An itinerary provides details of a trip that is going to happen. Travel agents and tour operators will provide itineraries for their customers; other organisations may provide itineraries for staff going on business trips. An itinerary will include

FIREPOWER

THE ROYAL ARTILLERY MUSEUM

CELEBRATIONS AS DAME VERA LYNN OPENS PHASE TWO OF FIREPOWER – by Brigadier Ken Timbers

CONTENTS

Opening the two new galleries in Building 41 at the end of March was, for me, an occasion of mixed feelings. On the one hand, it was wonderful to have the opportunity at last to show off the big guns of the post-WW2 era, together with some of the splendid trophies from the Rotunda. On the other, it was a moment to reflect on the fact that we still have much of the RA Historical Trust's collection to bring into play, and little prospect of being able to show it until the funding situation improves.

The opening ceremony, performed so gracefully by Dame Vera Lynn, was very well attended by a large gathering of supporters of the Museum, including Mrs April Clavell and Major Tony Howitt, two of our major benefactors. Included among the guests were representatives of the firms which had done the work of developing the galleries. It is impossible in the space available here to name all those who had a hand in the project, but I would like to pick out the Project Manager, Peter Thompson of Slough Estates, the architects, Austin:Smith Lord and, in particular, their design team headed by Bob Aitken, and the main building contractors, Hillmans. The supporting team from the Museum, too, deserves a mention: Les Smith, Matthew Buck, Paul Evans and Marc Sherriff all played a significant part in bringing the project to a successful conclusion.

The Cold War gallery was produced on a shoestring. The grant from the European Regional Development Fund had to be directed primarily towards the preparation of the building, so there was little left with which to develop the gallery itself. With this in mind, it is amazing what can be done by a designer with flair, using modern museum techniques. The use of high screens to break up the space into manageable proportions, with huge poster images to provide contemporary images, proved to be a major contribution to the success of the gallery. Innovative lighting stands, display boards and audio handsets have added another interesting dimension, so that the collection of objects on display is given the best possible interpretation.

Dame Vera officially opens the Cold War Gallery

Smiles all round as Mitchell Mannion (aged 10) from Mulgrave Primary School, Woolwich presents Dame Vera with a beautiful basket of flowers.

There remains much to be done. One of the aspects which we would have liked to highlight—a large 'sand table' map display of an armoured division deployed in Germany during the Cold War—had to be shelved for lack of funds, but the concept has been fully developed and will be brought forward as soon as funding permits. Another feature to come in due course is the grouping of ammunition displays with the equipment exhibited: it was delayed at this point simply to ensure that the objects could be enclosed to protect them from careless handling—we can't afford to be sued by a visitor who topples a 155mm shell onto his foot!

Mrs Clavell unveiling the sign with the assistance of Regimental Colonel Simon Hutchinson

Naming of James Clavell Square

On the same day as the opening of the Cold War Gallery Dame Vera joined visitors to welcome Mrs April Clavell to officially open 'James Clavell Square'. This is the area immediately outside the Clavell Library and Archives.

The Regimental Colonel, Simon Hutchinson, warmly introduced Mrs Clavell as one of Firepower's loyal supporters. Mrs Clavell sponsored The Library and Archives in memory of her late husband, the author James Clavell and Colonel Hutchinson gave the audience gathered an insight into the author's works such as 'King Rat' and 'Shogun'.

Mrs Clavell said she was extremely proud to have his name associated with Firepower and the Royal Arsenal.

FIGURE 1.34 *A newsletter*

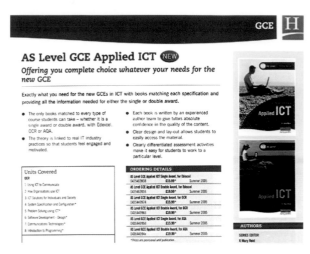

FIGURE 1.35 *Extract from Heinemann catalogue*

details of the date, time, departure and arrival point for each journey, along with dates and the location of any accommodation booked. These will usually be in the order they are to happen. For clarity, the information is often shown in a table (see Figure 1.36). It is vital that the information on an itinerary is accurate. If not, people may miss trains or flights, or go to the wrong hotel.

Forms to collect information from people

Questionnaires are one way that organisations collect information from people, but they are not the only way. You have probably filled in application forms for all sorts of reasons, for example to apply for your college or a job, to get a passport or a driving licence or to become a member of a club.

The layout of such forms is very important. It must be clear where the person filling it in should write their information and there must be enough space for them to do so. Boxes and tables are often used for this. There are many poorly designed forms that do not provide sufficient space for responses. The language used needs to be clear so that the reader knows what information they must provide. Passport application forms, for example, come with a separate instruction booklet to help you complete them correctly. Many government agencies use forms to collect information from people. For example, each year many people have to complete a Tax Return for the Inland Revenue, and once every ten years every household in the country must complete a census form.

Think it over...

Why do government agencies often ask you to write in ink and capital letters?

Business reports

Business reports are usually fairly long formal documents. They may be written to summarise some research findings or they may be a report on the year's activities for shareholders and others. Reports will probably start with an introduction or an abstract. An abstract is a summary of what is included in the report so that people can get an overview without having to read the whole report. The report will be divided up into sections with headings and often numbered paragraphs. It will end with a conclusion or some closing remarks. Most reports will include a list of contents and an alphabetical index. There may also be a number of appendices. Reports may include photographs, other pictures and graphs or charts, as well as tables of figures. Some end-of-year reports issued by large organisations are very glossy high-quality documents.

Technical specifications

Manufacturing organisations produce technical specifications (see Figure 1.38) to give precise technical information about their products. They will use clear technical language and numerical information. This may be presented in tables for ease of reading. Technical drawings may also be included.

Web pages

Most organisations have their own website, as many people will search the WWW for what they require (see Figure 1.39). It is very important that the web pages are well designed, easy to navigate and provide the information people need.

Itinerary for forthcoming visits to Regional Offices

The following meetings have been organised for the week beginning 22/06/05.

Day	Regional Office	Start time
Monday	Midlands Region, Birmingham	10.30
Tuesday	North Region, Leeds	10.00
Wednesday	Scotland and Islands Region, Edinburgh	11.00
Thursday	North and Borders Region, Newcastle	10.00
Friday	Central Region, Manchester	11.00

Travel and overnight accommodation details are shown below. You may use taxis to travel from the train station to the regional office and from the regional office to your hotel – don't forget to get receipts. Location maps are attached.

Date	Depart	Arrive	Hotel
22/06/05	London Marylebone Time: 0715	Birmingham Snow Hill Time: 0943	Holiday Inn, Great Barr
23/06/05	Birmingham New Street Time: 0703	Leeds Central Time: 0905	Holiday Inn, City Centre
24/06/05	Leeds Central Time: 0710	Edinburgh Waverley Time: 1018	Holiday Inn, City Centre
25/06/05	Edinburgh Waverley Time: 0807	Newcastle Central Time: 0939	Holiday Inn, Washington Tyne & Wear
26/06/05	Newcastle Central Time: 0726	Manchester Picadilly Time: 1026	Crowne Plaza, Manchester Airport
20/00/05	Manchester Picadilly Time: 1820	London Euston Time: 2110	

FIGURE 1.36 *An itinerary*

Poorly designed web pages will reflect badly on the organisation. If people can't move around the site easily and find what they are looking for, they will become frustrated and look elsewhere. Also, whilst high levels of graphics and other multimedia features may seem appealing, not everyone has fast access to the Internet.

Multimedia presentations

Organisations may use multimedia presentations internally for training staff or for annual reports on how well the company has done and to outline future strategy. Multimedia presentations are also used externally for promoting products and services, for example at trade fairs. High-quality multimedia presentations are expensive

> ✱ **REMEMBER!**
>
> ✱ Organisations communicate internally with members of their staff and externally with customers, suppliers, the general public and other organisations.
>
> ✱ Many organisations adopt a house style for all external communications, to present a corporate image.
>
> ✱ As you have learnt throughout this chapter, the writing and presentation styles used in business communications are dependent on the purpose, audience and communication method and must be appropriate to these.
>
> ✱ There are common standards for the layout of many business documents.

Product type	:	Digital camera (for shooting and displaying)
Recording system		
Still picture	:	Digital recording, JPEG (in accordance with Design rule for Camera File system (DCF)), Exif 2.2, Digital Print Order Format (DPOF), PRINT Image Matching II
Movie	:	QuickTime Motion JPEG support
Memory	:	xD-Picture Card (16 – 256MB)

No. of storable pictures (when a 16 MB Card is used) :

Resolution	Record mode/ No. of storable pictures			
		Model A	Model B	
2272 × 1704	SHQ	5	—	—
	HQ	16		
2048 × 1536	SQ1	20	SHQ	6
			HQ	20
1600 × 1200	SQ2	24	SQ1	24
1280 × 960		38		38
1024 × 768		58	SQ2	58
640 × 480		99		99

Record mode	Resolution (Frames/sec)	Memory capacity in sec. per movie
HQ	320 × 240 (15 frames/sec)	16
SQ	160 × 120 (15 frames/sec)	70

No. of effective pixels

MODEL A	: 3,200,000 pixels
MODEL B	: 4,000,000 pixels

FIGURE 1.38 *Part of the technical specification for a digital camera*

to produce but relatively cheap to copy and distribute. For this reason, it is likely to be only large organisations who communicate in this way.

Standard ways of working

While you are carrying out your work for the GCE in Applied ICT, you will need to follow standard ways of working. Organisations in which you will work also have similar rules and guidelines to ensure the security of their data, safety of staff and the effectiveness of the workforce.

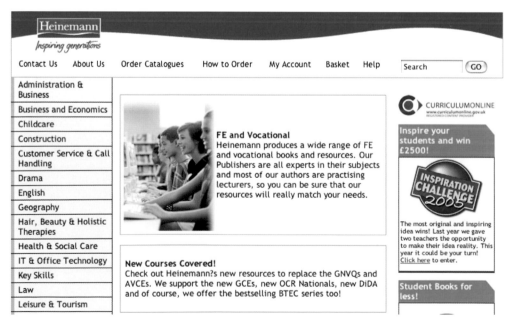

FIGURE 1.39 *Home page of Heinemann website*

Why these are important to ICT

Information that is held on computer systems can be easily lost or misused. Much of the information stored will be confidential, either personal information about individuals or information about the organisation that other people could use against it. Without standard ways of working, unauthorised persons may gain access to this confidential information. It is very easy to copy data that is held in computer files. Without standard ways of working, people could copy others' original work and present it as their own. Data files held on computer systems can be easily lost or corrupted, for example by viruses or hardware failure. If a computer system is physically damaged, it may not be possible to recover the data held on it. Also, the use of computers makes it very easy to present information in a professional way. Information that is presented professionally is likely to be believed, even if it is not accurate.

Managing your work

While you are working towards this qualification, you will have a number of assignments to complete and limited time to complete them in. When you are given an assignment, you will also be told when you must hand it in. You will need to look carefully at what you are being asked to do, decide how long each task will take you and then plan when and how you will complete each task so that you can produce everything by the deadline. If you do not plan your work you will be rushing to complete it and will produce work of poor quality. *The ability to plan work to meet deadlines is an important skill that you will find useful in the future.*

This unit is about presenting information. One aspect of managing your work is to make correct use of facilities such as spaces, tabs and indents to lay out your work consistently. This will also make editing easier.

How often have you wanted to reopen a file and not been able to remember where you stored it (see Figure 1.40) or what you called it?

An important aspect of managing your work is to use filenames that are sensible and that remind

FIGURE 1.40 *'I know I saved that file somewhere!'*

you of what the file contains. Most modern software allows you to use long filenames, making it easy to give files meaningful names. How you organise your file storage and where you store files is equally important. If you set up folders with meaningful names and make sure that you always store files in the appropriate folder, you will always be able to find the file you are looking for.

Computers and other ICT equipment do not always work as they should. It can be very frustrating and prevent you getting on with your work if problems occur. Many problems happen more than once and can be solved relatively easily providing you can remember what to do. Keeping a log of any problems that occur and how you solved them will ensure that you can solve similar problems in the future (see Table 1.4).

Keeping information secure

Information needs to be protected from, for example, theft, loss, viruses and fire. Physical security such as locks on doors and bars on windows is one way to protect information from theft. However, it is not always necessary to be in

DATE	PROBLEM	SOLUTION

TABLE 1.4 *Problem log*

the same room or even the same building as the computer storing the information to steal it. For this reason, so called logical security is also needed. This includes the use of passwords and access rights, so that only authorised people can access the information. To maintain security it is important that passwords are kept secret. You should also choose passwords that are not easy to guess – a random selection of letters and numbers is best. You should change passwords regularly and always if you think someone else knows it.

One reason for keeping information secure from theft and unauthorised access is confidentiality. Confidential information is information that individuals or organisations do not want others to know. Medical, criminal and financial records should all be kept confidential. As well as keeping such information secure, the people who work with confidential information must not pass it on to others.

Viruses are computer programs that replicate themselves and spread from computer to computer, either via removable storage media such as floppy disks, or via networks, especially the Internet.

Think it over...

How many viruses have you encountered or know of? Research the WWW for information.

Although not all viruses are malicious, most are, causing the files on infected computers to become corrupted, or allowing the writer of the virus to access the files on the infected system. The main protection against viruses is to install and use virus checking software. However, as new viruses are being developed all the time, this will be effective only if the software is regularly

updated. Restricting the use of the Internet and of removable storage media can also provide some protection against viruses.

The main way of protecting information stored on a computer system from loss is to keep a backup. This is a second copy of the information that can be used if the original is lost. To be of value, backups need to be taken frequently and dated so that you know when each was saved. Backups also need to be stored in a different location from the original information. To protect against fire, the backup should be kept in a fireproof safe, or preferably in a different building. If the original information is lost, the most recent backup can be used to restore the information. However, it will not be possible to restore any information that has been created since the backup was taken.

Theory into practice

Find out what your college/organisation does about backups.

Another way of protecting information from loss is to save your work regularly using different filenames. This is particularly important before you make significant changes. If, by making the changes, you lose the information, you can always go back to the previous version.

One of the reasons why standard ways of working are important is to stop people copying original work and presenting it as their own. Computer programs, words, pictures, graphic images and music that have been created by other people are protected by copyright. The person who created or owns the material has the copyright to it. The Copyright, Designs and Patents Act (1980) determines how others can use the material. You will learn more about this Act in Unit 2: How organisations use ICT. In general, you must not use the work of others without their permission (see Figure 1.41 for a sample letter requesting permission). Where you do use the work of others, you must acknowledge the source, either with a suitable reference, or by including it in your bibliography.

Heinemann

Halley Court
Jordan Hill
Oxford OX2 8EJ

Tel: +44 (0)1865 311366
Fax: +44 (0)1865 314140
Web: www.heinemann.co.uk

Dear XX,

I am writing to request permission to use XXX in our forthcoming educational publication, *XXX*.

The details of the forthcoming publication are as follows:

Title:	*XXX*
Author:	XX
Extent:	XX
Price:	XX
Pub. date:	XX

The rights we are seeking are world rights in all languages for reproduction in all forms and media, including electronic media, in this and any future revisions and editions of the book published by [imprint] and under licence from [imprint], and for publication in promotional material for the book. Should you not control these rights in their entirety, would you kindly let me know to whom I must write.

The deadline for this project is XX and I would be grateful if you could let me know at your earliest convenience whether you can grant us permission to use this material and, if so, what fee and form of acknowledgement you might require.

For your convenience a release form is provided below and a copy of this letter is enclosed for your files.

Yours sincerely,

XX

Permission is hereby granted to reproduce the material requested above on the terms set out in this letter for a fee of _____.

Acknowledgement: _____

Signed: _____ Date: _____

FIGURE 1.41 *A sample letter for permission*

Working safely

Although the ICT working environment is fairly safe, there are some health and safety issues that you need to be aware of. Health issues tend to relate to bad posture, physical stress and eyestrain, while safety issues relate to hazards resulting from equipment or workplace layout.

An important part of reducing problems caused by poor posture and physical stress is comfortable seating. Chairs should be adjustable

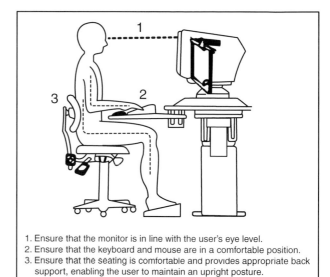

1. Ensure that the monitor is in line with the user's eye level.
2. Ensure that the keyboard and mouse are in a comfortable position.
3. Ensure that the seating is comfortable and provides appropriate back support, enabling the user to maintain an upright posture.

FIGURE 1.42 *Safe-sitting position*

and provide good support for your back. A comfortable chair alone will not prevent these problems. You must make sure that the desk, VDU and keyboard are positioned correctly and your chair is correctly adjusted. Ideally, your eyes should be level with or slightly above the top of the monitor, your wrists should be straight with your forearms parallel with the floor and your feet should be flat on the floor with your thighs also parallel to it (see Figure 1.42).

However comfortable and well positioned your workstation is, you should try to take brief rest periods at regular intervals. In particular, you should avoid long periods of continuous VDU work. Try to organise your work so that periods spent at the computer are broken up with other activities. When you take a break from work, get up and walk around, rather than play a computer game. As well as taking breaks, to help prevent eyestrain, you should exercise the muscles in your eyes by focusing on near and distant objects every so often. It is, therefore, important that the computer's surroundings provide the opportunity for you to do this.

The two main safety issues in an ICT environment are tripping and electrical hazards. Tripping hazards can be prevented by careful layout of cables and equipment. Cables should not cross walkways and should be enclosed in trunking. To prevent electrical hazards, sufficient electrical sockets should be available to prevent overloading, and all electrical cables should be properly insulated.

Knowledge check

1 Give five reasons why standard ways of working are important.

2 How can you ensure that, in the future, you will be able to find files that you save?

3 What types of information are confidential and why should confidentiality be protected?

4 How can you ensure that information is not lost if a fire destroys your computer?

5 What health and safety hazards are associated with the ICT working environment and how can they be avoided?

Assessment evidence

A new independent travel agent is opening in a town near where you live. They will specialise in organising activity holidays in the UK and overseas. They have asked you to help them create the communications they need to advertise and run the business.

Task 1

Collect two types of documents from each of three organisations. Ideally, these documents should be from three different travel agents. It should be relatively easy to collect brochures, and most travel agents will also have a website. Most brochures will also include a booking form. You may be able to get hold of letters from the travel agents or travel itineraries, but remember you must collect the same two types of document from all three travel agents.

Study the documents carefully and write a report describing and comparing them. You will need to answer some or all of these questions when you are writing your report.

✱ What is the specific purpose of each document?

✱ What layout has been used for each document?

✱ What are the good points, if any, of each document's presentation?

✱ What are the bad points, if any, of each document's presentation?

✱ What comparisons can be made between the presentation styles of similar documents?

✱ What are the good points, if any, of each document's writing style?

✱ What are the bad points, if any, of each document's writing style?

✱ What comparisons can be made between the writing styles of similar documents?

✱ Has a house style been used for the two documents from the same organisation?

✱ How is this house style demonstrated?

✱ How well does each document meet its purpose?

✱ Are there any improvements that could be made to each document? What are they?

As a minimum you must describe the layout and/or the purpose of each document and identify some good and bad points about the writing and/or presentation styles of similar documents. To reach the second mark band, you must describe both the layout and purpose of each document and identify good and bad points about both the writing and presentation styles of similar items. You must also make some comment on their suitability for purpose, their use of house style and/or how they could be improved. Your report must contain few spelling, punctuation and grammar errors. To reach the highest mark band, your descriptions of the layout and purpose of the documents must be detailed and you must accurately identify good and bad points about writing and presentation styles of similar items. You must comment on the suitability for purpose, use of house style and how the documents could be improved. Your report must be consistently well structured and contain few, if any, errors in spelling, punctuation and grammar. If you provide detailed answers to all of the questions and take care over your use of English when writing your report, you should be able to reach this mark band.

Tasks 2–7

When you are carrying out the remaining tasks you should:

* plan the content and layout of each communication – if you produce little evidence of planning, you will reach only the lowest mark band; outline plans will gain the second mark band and detailed plans will enable you to reach the highest mark band

* include a list of any information sources you use – a simple list of sources is the minimum requirement; to reach the second mark band this will need to be organised in an appropriate way, and for the highest mark band you must produce a detailed bibliography

* create new information and locate, use and adapt existing information – as a minimum you should create new information that is clear, easy to understand and that uses a suitable style; to reach the second mark band you should locate, use and adapt existing information and combine it with information

you have created; to reach the highest mark band you must locate, adapt and combine information to create coherent easy-to-read communications of near-professional standard

* use common standards for layout where appropriate, for example use the standard layout for a business letter – you must do this to reach even the lowest mark band

* use different text styles, page layout and paragraph formatting to suit the purpose of a communication and improve its impact – to reach mark band one, these must suit the purpose of each communication; to achieve higher mark bands, they must also improve the impact of each communication

* combine different types of data – text, graphics (photographs, clipart, line drawings, graphs, charts), tables, borders, shading, sound, video clips – to suit the purpose of a communication and improve its impact – as a minimum you must combine two of these to suit the purpose of the communication; to reach the higher mark bands you will need to combine a range of types of data to also improve the impact of each communication

* use software to automate aspects of your communications, such as creating templates for standard layouts – this will contribute to the highest mark band

* include labelled and annotated draft copies of each communication to show how you developed them – if your annotations show how you placed information in appropriate positions and ensured correct and meaningful content, this will contribute to mark band two; for the highest mark band your annotations need to show how you achieved a consistent style and made good use of standard formats to organise a variety of different types of information in a coherent and easy-to-read way

* spell check and proof-read the content and layout and correct any errors found – at the lowest level you will show you can check the accuracy of the layout and content of your work and proof-read it, so few obvious errors remain; for higher mark bands your

annotations will demonstrate how you checked your work carefully

* include a labelled final version of each communication
* evaluate each communication – as a minimum you must comment on how effective each communication is and suggest improvements; to reach the second band you also need to identify good and not so good features of each communication; to reach the highest mark band you must have identified strengths and weaknesses in your initial drafts and show how you refined them to meet the purpose more closely
* evaluate your performance in completing each task – as a minimum you must comment on how you went about carrying out the tasks; to reach the second mark band you will need to analyse how you carried out the tasks so that you could do it better next time; to reach the highest mark band you must also suggest how you might approach a similar task in the future.

To evaluate each communication you need to consider:

* what worked well – what is good about it
* what did not work – what is not so good
* how well it meets its purpose
* what you could improve if you created it again
* how you refined your drafts to meet the purpose more closely.

To evaluate your own performance you need to consider:

* what went well
* what went badly
* what you would do differently if you had to carry out a similar task in the future.

Task 2

The director of the travel agent wants to know about how information is communicated. Produce a presentation for the director of the travel agent on how information is communicated and the technologies that support

these communication methods. You may use presentation software to create an on-screen slide presentation with presenter notes to add detail or you may present the information in some other way.

As a minimum, you must briefly describe some of the methods used to communicate information and the technologies that support them. You will find information to help you earlier in this chapter but you must make sure that the information you include in your presentation is in your own words. To reach the second mark band, you must describe most of the methods used to communicate information and the technologies that support them. Your descriptions need to include some detail. To reach the highest mark band you need to provide detailed descriptions. At this level, you will need to supplement the information provided in this chapter with some research of your own.

Task 3

Create a letterhead for the tourist office and use it to produce a standard letter to a potential holidaymaker, outlining the type of holidays available, to be included with a copy of the brochure. Remember to use the standard layout for a business letter. You may also want to create a template so that similar letters can be more easily produced in future.

Task 4

Create a promotional flyer for an activity holiday in the UK – the location and activity is up to you. This is an opportunity to include suitable images as well as text.

Task 5

Create a website for the travel agent or a multimedia presentation that can be displayed in the travel agent's office. This is another opportunity to incorporate different types of data but if you are creating a website, do consider download times for those using dial-up services.

Task 6

Create some sample pages for a brochure detailing the holidays available. If you did not create a website in Task 5, these could be pages for an on-line brochure.

Task 7

Create a booking form to collect holidaymakers' details and the details of the holiday they want to book. Think carefully about the information you need to collect and the space needed for the information. The booking form can be paper-based or on-line.

Signposting for portfolio evidence

Currently, all of your evidence must be produced on paper. If you have created screen-based communications, you will need to provide screen prints or printouts to evidence your work. You will need to annotate these to indicate any features, such as sound, video or animation that are not obvious from the printouts. You should get your teacher to witness these features and initial or sign the printouts to confirm that the features work. For example, printing out a slide presentation as an audience handout with three slides to a page will provide space for you to add any necessary annotations.

You need to organise your work carefully. Make sure each piece of work is clearly labelled to show what it is and that your name is on each page. In particular, make sure that the draft and final copies of each communication are clearly labelled as such.

For Task 1, make sure you include copies of the documents you have compared. Your assessor and the moderator will not know whether you have described them accurately or not if you do not include them. For Tasks 2 to 7, put the work for each task in a logical order. A sensible order would be: plan, draft 1, draft 2 etc., final copy, evaluation. When you have put all your work in a sensible order, number all the pages and create a contents page to show where each piece of work is located.

How organisations use ICT

Introduction

In this unit you will study organisations in detail. You will learn about how organisations are structured and how they use and exchange information. You will then consider how well ICT helps organisations and how it supports the different activities they undertake. Developments in ICT are offering organisations new opportunities in the ways they work and the way goods are produced. You will learn about some of these new opportunities. You will also learn about *legislation* relating to the use of ICT and the effect it has on organisations.

Key term

Legislation: laws or Acts of Parliament that must be obeyed.

How you will be assessed

This unit is assessed by an external assessment, the mark for which will be for the whole unit. You will need to be able to apply what you learn in this unit to an organisation described in a case study. You will have to carry out tasks related to this organisation and answer questions about it, as well as more general questions, in the examination.

What you need to learn

By studying this unit you will:

✱ know about the different types of organisation

* learn about the different *job functions* that appear within organisations. You will need to be able to describe these functions and the tasks that make up each particular one

* be able to interpret diagrams that show organisations' structures

* understand how organisations use information, including how it is collected, communicated and processed

* be able to describe the key systems used by large organisations

* be able to draw diagrams to describe the movement of information in organisations

* be able to describe the ICT systems used by organisations to support their operations, how the ICT systems support these operations and how they interact

* understand the impact that technological developments have had on *working practices*, including changes in working styles and employment opportunities and the possible effects on *employees*. You will need to be able to evaluate these effects on a particular organisation

* recognise how the introduction of *robotics* and other linked ICT systems have affected methods of production. You will need to be able to evaluate how a particular organisation has been affected

* understand the purpose of legislation related to using ICT, how organisations are affected by it and what, if anything, they must do to comply with the legislation.

Key terms

Job functions: staff who are responsible for carrying out specific tasks within an organisation, such as sales or finance.
Working practices: the way that work is organised and carried out.
Employees: the people who work for and are employed by an organisation.
Robotics: computer-controlled devices that are able to carry out tasks that would have previously been done by people.

Types of organisation

Organisations are made up of groups of people who use their own skills and other resources to make a product or provide a service. There are many different types of organisations of many different sizes. At the top of the range are the large multinational commercial companies, many of which are household names all over the world. Examples include oil companies such as Shell and BP; Coca Cola; sportswear companies such as Nike; electrical goods companies such as Sony; software companies such as Microsoft and many, many others.

Banks are organisations that provide financial services, and shops provide retail services. These range from large chains, such as Marks and Spencer or B&Q to small, privately owned corner shops. Other organisations provide utilities such as water, electricity and gas, or transport, including

CASE STUDY 1: FRANCEFILEZ

Introduction

Francefilez is a UK-based company that produces brochures advertising holiday homes in France and Spain. They produce a total of eight brochures, six for France and two for Spain, and each brochure is printed twice a year. All the brochures are distributed to newsagents and travel agencies throughout the UK. The company was founded in 1998 to produce a single brochure for holiday homes in France. This grew to the current six brochures by 2001, and the two Spanish brochures were launched in 2002.

The brochures are funded primarily by the advertisements placed by the owners of the holiday homes, but a number of airline and cross-channel travel companies have recently started to advertise in the brochures as well.

The company employs a total of 90 staff in two offices in Shropshire. The Head Office houses the finance and administration, sales and marketing, ICT services and human resources (HR) departments. The second office accommodates only the design and production department.

CASE STUDY 2: SOURCE COMPUTERS UK

Introduction

Source Computers UK is a wholesaler of computer components and software based in Essex. They supply computer equipment to a large number of local companies, computer shops and system builders in the area. They also sell to individuals who visit their premises. As well as selling computer components, Source Computers UK also use the components to build complete computer systems. They build and sell a small selection of standard systems, but will also build bespoke systems to meet customers' specific requirements.

Source Computers UK is a small business with fewer than 20 staff, based in a small unit in a business park. They keep the majority of components on site, but the main stock of more bulky components, such as monitors and computer cases, is kept in a secure lock-up some two miles away. The managing director, Mick, established the company in 2003, but all of the staff had previously worked together in other computer companies.

buses, trains and planes. All of these organisations aim to make a profit for their owners or shareholders.

Most hospitals, schools and colleges are examples of public-service organisations. Public-service organisations are funded by central or local government, through taxes, to provide health, education or other services to the public.

Before you learn about how ICT can help and support organisations, you will need to know how they are structured, their information needs, and describe the movement of information internally and externally within them.

In this unit we will consider two organisations: Francefilez and Source Computers UK. In the assessment for this unit, you will be provided with a similar case study about an organisation and be required to carry out tasks and answer questions based on that case study. However, you will also need to gain experience of real organisations either by visiting them, through work experience or a part-time job, or by people from the organisations coming to talk to you. You will gain more from your contacts with real organisations by having studied this unit, as it will help you to know what to look for and what questions to ask.

Functions within organisations

Within most organisations, there will be staff who are responsible for carrying out particular tasks. These tasks and responsibilities are known as job functions. In small organisations, one person may be responsible for more than one job function. Large organisations will have a *department* for each function. We will consider how organisations are structured later in this unit. In the following sections we will look at the different job functions that appear in many organisations, the tasks that make up those job functions and the other functions, organisations and people they communicate with.

Accounts or finance

The accounts or finance job function in an organisation carries out all tasks relating to the money that comes into the organisation and the money that it pays out. This will include recording payments received for goods or services provided by the organisation and banking any payments made using cash or cheques. This function will arrange payment to suppliers for stock, raw materials or services, including water, gas, electricity and telephone, and rent or mortgage repayments for premises, as well as payments for loans. Many of these payments will be made by *BACS* transfer. Another important role of this job function is to arrange payment of staff wages. This too will probably done through BACS. Careful records must be kept of all financial transactions. The Inland Revenue will require accurate accounts so that the correct amount of tax can be collected, both from the organisation and from employees. Customs and Excise will require details of all transactions involving VAT (Value Added Tax). This will involve deducting the amount of VAT paid by the organisation to suppliers from the amount of VAT received by the organisation from customers, to find the amount of VAT the organisation must pay to Customs and Excise. Shareholders will also want accurate financial records as will the bank if the organisation needs to borrow money. As well

CASE STUDY 2: SOURCE COMPUTERS UK

Finance function

A finance administrator, Jane, and her assistant Mary, control the finance function in Source Computers. Between them they manage all aspects of purchasing, sales order processing and invoicing. All of these functions are computerised using an integrated finance package.

The purchasing manager, Dick, is primarily responsible for making regular purchases. Often he will do this by making telephone calls to the company's suppliers. He will then email the finance function details of the supplies purchased. The sales function can also make purchases, as often they have to ensure the availability of components for urgent orders. Sales also email details of the purchases to the finance function, with a copy sent to Dick. Jane or Mary then raises a confirmation purchase order (see Figure 2.1) that is sometimes posted but often emailed to the supplier. When an invoice is received from the supplier, it is Jane's responsibility to ensure that the supplier is paid.

The sales staff also email details of all customer orders to the finance function. Jane or Mary raises invoices for these orders and email or post them to the customers. They keep track of the payments received and send reminders if payments are overdue.

Mary is responsible for staff wages, which are paid monthly. Every month she sends a fax to the bureau company that runs their payroll. This fax either confirms that the information used to calculate the wages is unchanged, or it details any changes to the information, such as any paid overtime that staff have worked. Staff wages are paid directly into each individual member of staff's bank account by BACS transfer.

Source Computers UK

78 Main Road

Billericay

Essex

SO11 2QQ

Purchase Order

PO No:	226/3/117
Date:	20/03/06
Delivery Date:	20/03/06

Supplier
Screens UK
Radley House
Lower Marsh Street
Reading
RG1 3AZ

Qty	Item	Description	Discount %	Unit Price	Total
20	06392/15B	15 inch TFT Monitor Black	10	82.50	1500.00
15	06392/15s	15 inch TFT Monitor Silver		82.50	1237.50

Subtotal	2737.50
VAT	479.06
Bal Due	3216.56

FIGURE 2.1 *Example of a confirmation purchase order*

as communicating with these external organisations, this function will communicate information internally with most other functions, including sales, marketing and human resources.

Key term

BACS: Banks Automated Clearing System – a system that transfers money electronically from one bank account to another.

Purchasing

As we have already said, part of the role of the accounts or finance function is to pay for goods and services from suppliers. This is sometimes handled by a purchasing function that is purely responsible for the ordering of and payment for these goods and services. The purchasing function will raise *purchase orders* and receive and arrange payment of suppliers' invoices. Most other functions will communicate with purchasing when they need supplies of one kind or another.

Sales order processing

Another section within the accounts or finance section is sales order processing. This is responsible for the administration of the organisation's financial dealing with customers. As part of this, it will organise contracts for services, receive sales orders, create and send invoices and receive and process customers' payments. There are close links between this function and the sales function.

Sales

The sales function, as its name suggests, is responsible for selling an organisation's products or services to its customers. The tasks that are carried out by this job function will vary widely, depending on the nature of the organisation. In a shop, sales staff will help customers to find the products they require, take the customers' payments and wrap the purchases. They will also be responsible for ensuring there are goods on display and possibly taking orders for out-of-stock items. In a newspaper publishing organisation, the sales function will be responsible for selling advertising space in the newspapers. This is likely to involve *telesales*. Staff will take the customers' details and the details of the advertisements. These will be input into a computer system. The staff will then either take and check credit card details in payment or add the cost to an account so that the customer can be invoiced. A salesperson in a kitchen design company, for example, may visit each customer's home to discuss his or her requirements and to measure and design the kitchen. He or she will then produce a *quotation* for the customer. If the customer decides to accept the quotation, the salesperson will create an order for the parts and labour needed to complete the kitchen and will take a deposit from the customer. The sales function will communicate closely with marketing and accounts but will also communicate with other functions such as production and distribution.

Distribution

The distribution function is most likely to be found in organisations that make or sell goods, rather than those that provide a service. It is also

CASE STUDY 1: FRANCEFILEZ

Sales function

The sales function in Francefilez is part of the Sales and Marketing department. There are two sales managers in the department, one for France and one for Spain, both of whom report to the sales and marketing director. The sales function is organised into four teams, each with responsibility for selling advertising space in two brochures. Each team has a sales team leader. The sales teams vary in size, the largest having eight members and the smallest five members. Each sales assistant has responsibility for maintaining contact with a number of established customers, but they must also try to sell to a target number of new customers. Staff are paid a commission on sales. The main contact with customers is via the telephone, although FAX and email are increasingly used for confirmations, etc.

The sales teams have the support of an on-line database, which contains details of all existing customers, their sales history, any relevant notes and an interactive reminder system. The database also holds lists of potential customers. At the beginning of each day, sales staff log on to the system, check their own reminders and then start telephoning customers. All of them have been trained by the company in telesales techniques, and they normally follow a 'script' in their conversations. When a customer confirms that they want to place an advertisement, the sales assistant logs on to the sales order processing system to input the customer and advertisement details, method of payment, etc. As soon as this is completed the order is automatically directed to the administration department for further processing. The sales assistant will only need to be re-involved if any queries have to be taken up with the customer by telephone.

The sales team leaders are responsible only for the day-to-day management of their team members, helping with any queries that they might have and assisting with more difficult customer problems. The two sales managers, in addition to the day-to-day management of their sales teams, are also responsible for selling advertising space to selected airline and cross-channel operators. Because the revenue from such advertising has become increasingly important, most of the contact with these companies is conducted face to face.

sometimes called logistics. This function is responsible for moving goods from the factory, farm or other source to warehouses and then on to shops or directly to customers. This may involve sending goods by mail or using couriers. In this case, the distribution function will need to ensure that packages are correctly addressed and then either contact the postal or courier service to arrange a collection, or apply the correct postage and take them to the post office. Where goods are moved in bulk, such as from the factory to warehouses, they may be sent by rail or air freight or using road hauliers. The distribution function will be responsible for booking these services. Some organisations will have their own fleet of vans or trucks to deliver goods. For example, large supermarket chains have fleets of lorries to distribute goods from central warehouses to their stores.

Think it over...

It is likely that some of your group have part-time jobs in shops, supermarkets or elsewhere. Discuss the tasks that they and their work colleagues carry out as part of the sales function. Are there common tasks that are carried out in different types of shops? Are there any tasks that are unique to one organisation?

Knowledge check

The sales function in Francefilez uses telesales to sell space in their brochures. What does this involve?

What are the responsibilities of the sales team leaders and sales managers in Francefilez?

CASE STUDY 2: SOURCE COMPUTERS UK

Distribution

Source Computers deliver about 60 per cent of their orders using a national courier service, who collect from their premises at 5.30pm Monday to Friday. The purchasing manager, Dick, is responsible for ensuring that all orders are picked, packed and ready for collection at this time. Only orders received before 4.00pm are guaranteed for despatch the same day.

The sales order processing system automatically produces despatch notes for orders that require delivery. Two copies are sent for printing at Dick's workstation. He passes one copy to either of his two staff, who collects the components from around the building and packages them for delivery, marking off each item on the despatch note. He or she keeps a stock of the courier's *waybills*, which are filled out by hand with the customer's details.

When the waybill has been completed the despatch note and waybill are returned to Dick. Dick checks that all items have been picked and that the customer details on the waybill are correct. He then enters the waybill number into the order on the computer system, and also into a proforma email to be sent to the customer. The customer or Source Computers can use this number to track the progress of the delivery using the courier's website.

They also have fleets of vans to deliver on-line customers' shopping to their homes. However the goods are distributed, it is the responsibility of the distribution function to ensure that the right goods get to the right place at the right time. The distribution function will mainly need to communicate with the production and sales functions.

Key term

Waybill: A multi-part form that is attached to a package for courier delivery. It includes details of who is sending and who is receiving the package and a unique number (often with a barcode) that allows the package to be tracked.

Knowledge check

Who is responsible for distribution in Source Computers UK?

What tasks contribute to the distribution function?

Marketing

The marketing function is often linked with the sales function. It is the responsibility of this function to plan for future sales and to monitor the organisation's relationship with customers and potential customers. One major task for this function will be to advertise the organisation's products or services. This may involve designing advertisements and buying advertising space, designing flyers and arranging for them to be distributed, or arranging for the organisation to have a stand at appropriate trade fairs and ensuring there are people to man it. Increasingly, this task will involve web-based advertising and ensuring that details on the organisation's website are regularly updated. Another task of this function might be to gather customer opinion by arranging for some market research to be carried out. It will be the marketing function that receives and processes the lifestyle questionnaires that we mentioned in the previous unit. In some organisations, this function will be responsible for *direct marketing*, either by themselves or by commissioning a direct marketing agency. As indicated earlier, there will be close links between the marketing and sales functions. The marketing function will also communicate with other functions such as design and production. If the marketing function is going to launch an advertising campaign for a particular product, they need to know that sufficient will be produced to meet the hoped-for additional demand.

Research and development

The research and development function is most likely to exist in organisations that manufacture products but may also exist in some organisations that provide a service. This function carries out research into new techniques, technologies and materials to see if they can be applied to the products or services supplied by the organisation. The development function, as its name suggests, then develops new products or services. This may involve creating a prototype of the new product or service that can be tested to see if there is a market for it. This prototype may never actually be put into production, but aspects of it may be applied to improving the organisation's existing products or designing new ones. For example, car manufacturers often feature concept cars at international motor shows.

These cars feature all the latest developments and are a glimpse into the future. Some features will appear in the car manufacturer's new models, but the concept car in its entirety will never actually be manufactured commercially. The research and development (R and D) function needs to work closely with marketing so that it does not waste time and money on projects that will not match the long-term needs of the organisation's customers. It also needs to communicate with the design and production functions.

Human resources

The human resources (HR) function is responsible for dealing with the organisation's employees. When more staff are needed, the HR function will organise the placing of advertisements and/or notifying the local employment agencies. They will be responsible for sending out application forms and receiving the completed application forms, cvs and application letters. These will be

HR function

The HR function in Francefilez is made up of an HR manager, Nadeem, along with three HR administrators who report to her. This function is responsible for all aspects of the recruitment, training and welfare of staff.

Sales training is one of the major responsibilities of the HR function. They maintain a staff development plan and keep training records for all staff, including sales staff. An independent consultant who has developed a number of courses especially for Francefilez carries out sales training. The HR department uses the staff development plan and training records to identify when a particular sales course is required. They are then responsible for contacting the consultant, scheduling the courses, and ensuring that all appropriate sales staff attend. After the course, it is the HR function's responsibility to update the training records.

Because sales staff are paid on commission, the HR function also has a major responsibility for payroll. When a brochure advertisement has been paid for, the HR function calculates the commission due and adds it to the monthly pay record for the sales assistant concerned. The HR function is responsible for ensuring that all information for the company's monthly payroll, including contributions to the company pension scheme, is kept up to date.

The HR function is also responsible for maintaining the information on the personnel database. They handle requests for staff leave and arrange temporary staff to cover for staff absence or at particularly busy times.

---

checked and collated by the HR function who will then liaise with senior staff to shortlist the applicants that will be called for interview. This function will organise the interview process and send letters to successful applicants, inviting them for interview. They may also send letters to unsuccessful applicants. A representative of the HR function will be part of the interview panel. When the successful applicant(s) has been selected, this function will produce and send a letter offering the applicant the job. They will also check the applicant's references and prepare and send out a contract.

Other tasks carried out by the HR function will include:

* handling requests for leave
* dealing with disciplinary matters
* arranging cover when staff are on leave or off sick
* keeping record of hours worked and calculating wages due
* organising staff pension contributions

* sending out redundancy notices when staff numbers need to be reduced
* dealing with trade unions and staff organisations
* arranging and keeping records of staff training.

The HR function will need to be in regular contact with all other functions within the organisation as they all include staff who are the responsibility of the HR function. It will also need to communicate with external organisations such as employment agencies and the Inland Revenue.

Knowledge check

Sales staff training is an important responsibility of the HR function at Francefilez. Describe four essential tasks that make up the training aspect of the HR function.

Identify one other important responsibility of the HR function at Francefilez. Describe the tasks involved.

Design

The design function takes over where the research and development function finishes. The design function takes the ideas and prototypes developed by R and D and turns them into designs for the products or services that will actually be supplied to customers. The design function may also design products from scratch, based on perceived customer needs as identified by market research. The design function will need to communicate extensively with R and D, production and marketing.

Production (or service provision)

The production function occurs only in organisations that manufacture products. It is the production function that actually takes the raw materials, parts and facilities and uses them to make the products. In a clothing manufacturing company, the people who perform this function will be cutters who cut the cloth, machinists who sew the garments together and finishers who press the finished garment and ensure it is ready for sale. In many manufacturing organisations there will be a production line where members of the production function each carry out a particular task as the product moves along the line. However, in many industries machines are taking over the tasks, and the

responsibility of the production function is more involved with overseeing and maintaining the machines and checking the quality of the products. The production function will need to communicate with all other functions within the organisation.

In service organisations, this function is called service provision. As its name suggests, the responsibility of this function is to provide the service to the customer. The tasks of this function will differ widely depending on the service provided. In an airline, the pilot and flight crew will fly the plane to get passengers to their destination while the cabin crew will look after the passengers by serving them food and drinks and looking after their safety during the flight. In a leisure centre, the receptionist will check members in and hand out towels, instructors will provide classes or individual instruction, and lifeguards will look after the safety of swimmers (see Figure 2.2) and help anyone in difficulty.

There will also be cleaners who keep the facilities clean and maintenance staff who keep the equipment in working order.

ICT services

The ICT services function is responsible for the provision of all computer facilities within the organisation. This will include obtaining, installing and maintaining hardware, managing the local area and possibly wide area network services (LANs and WANs), obtaining, installing and maintaining software and providing hardware and software support to ICT users within the organisation. They will also be

FIGURE 2.2 *Safety of swimmers*

CASE STUDY 1: FRANCEFILEZ

ICT services function

The ICT services function in Francefilez is made up of an ICT manager, Li, and an ICT executive, Mark. Occasionally they contract in extra ICT staff to cover abnormal workloads.

Li and Mark are responsible for maintaining all of the hardware and software of the two local area networks (LANs), one in each of the company's two offices. The network in Head Office is based on PC workstations, with two servers, and the other

network is made up of Apple Mac computers. Li and Mark are also responsible for ensuring that WAN communications are maintained between the two sites using a 2GB broadband link.

All of the software used in the two offices is based on standard operating systems and application packages. ICT services are responsible for specifying any changes to these systems that the company may require from time to time.

---

responsible for internal and external data communications such as maintaining the organisation's intranet and website. Small organisations will probably not have anyone fulfilling an ICT services function but will have a contract with an external ICT services provider to fulfil this role when required. This function too will communicate with all other functions within the organisation, providing they use ICT.

Knowledge check

Describe the tasks carried out by the ICT services function in Francefilez.

Administration

The administration function is usually responsible for the day-to-day running of an

---

CASE STUDY 1: FRANCEFILEZ

Administration

The main responsibility of the administration function in Francefilez is the processing of customer advertisements after they have been sold. There is an administration manager and three assistants who deal with this.

When a confirmed order for an advertisement is passed by sales to administration the customer's preferred means of communication and method of payment are included. Communications may be by FAX, email and sometimes post; the method of payment is credit card or cheque. The administration assistant uses the preferred communication method to request from the customer the information required to complete

the advertisement. This will include a description of the property for rent, sometimes including photographs, availability dates, and prices. The request will include the dates by which this information and payment for the advertisement must be received.

When the advertisement information is received from the customer, an administration assistant checks it for completeness and sends a copy to the design and production department. When payment is received, administration confirms with the design and production department that the advertisement is to be included in the brochure. They also confirm to the HR department that payment has been received so that sales commission can be calculated.

organisation. This may include things like looking after the buildings and facilities, general maintenance and cleaning, fleet management and utilities. However, administration is often used to describe other functions that do not naturally fit into any of the functions we have considered up to this point. Also, in smaller organisations, other functions such as ICT services or HR may form part of the administration function. This function will need to exchange information with all other functions in varying amounts depending on its precise role within the organisation.

The structure of organisations

As was stated at the beginning of this section, in large organisations the job functions that we have been considering are organised into departments each with a department manager. There may then be higher levels of managers responsible for several departments, and so on.

Such a structure is hierarchical – it is like an upside-down tree (see Figure 2.3). There are many levels of management between the managing director at the top of the structure and the people working in each department at its base, with little direct contact between them. Very hierarchically structured organisations are expensive to run – successive levels of managers will expect to be paid higher salaries than those they manage – and can result in poor worker morale because they are too remote from the decision-making process. There is now a tendency to reduce the management levels resulting in a flatter organisational structure. The extent to which this can be achieved in very large organisations is limited, however, as one person can effectively manage only a finite number of people. Also, in organisations with departments based on job functions, information will need to be passed extensively from one department to another, as we have seen in the previous sections, and no one department manager will have an overview of the task or project. There is, therefore, a need for someone to co-ordinate the work of the various departments involved.

Some organisations arrange their workforce into project teams rather than functional departments. Within the project team will be representatives of the job function required to work on the project. There will, therefore, be less need to pass information to other teams, and the team manager will have an overview of the project.

FIGURE 2.3 *Hierarchical organisational structure*

Even in small organisations there will be an organisation structure (see Figure 2.4), although this is likely to be much flatter. The only exceptions to this are the smallest organisations where all the work is carried out by the owner(s) and no staff are employed.

Information and its use

All organisations need information to operate, but some exist solely to gather and disseminate information.

Knowledge check

What term would be used to describe the organisational structure of Source Computers UK?

Who has overall responsibility for the company?

Which staff report directly to this person?

What information do organisations need?

Different organisations need different information, for example:

* a retail shop needs to know about the availability of stock and prices as well as other information

* a manufacturing organisation needs information about the availability and cost of raw materials or parts, the customers for its products and the method of distribution

* a tour operator needs information about the availability and cost of hotel rooms, flights and other transport from its suppliers, and information about booking requirements from its customers.

CASE STUDY 2: SOURCE COMPUTERS UK

Structure

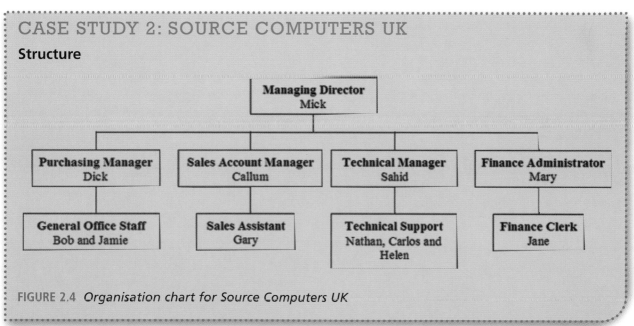

FIGURE 2.4 *Organisation chart for Source Computers UK*

CASE STUDY 2: SOURCE COMPUTERS UK

Information requirements and collection

Source Computers require the following information to complete a customer order:

* customer name and account details

* delivery address or to be collected

* date required

* details and quantities of goods

* method of payment.

This information is usually collected over the telephone, but some orders are collected by email.

Organisations such as news agencies, newspapers and radio and television news channels, along with many others, such as market research and direct marketing agencies, exist only to collect and disseminate information. News organisations, for example, collect the information from many different sources, collate and combine the information to make it more accessible and understandable and then publish the information as text and pictures on paper, as audio reports on radio, as audio and video reports on television or as multimedia information on the WWW.

How is the information collected?

The information needed by organisations will be collected in many different ways depending on the organisation and the information. Market and opinion research agencies will collect information about people's buying habits or preferences by face-to-face and telephone interviews and by sending out questionnaires. Web-based retail organisations will collect information about customers and their requirements by getting customers to complete an on-line order form. More traditional retail organisations will collect the same information over the telephone, face to face or on paper order forms.

How is information communicated?

When we were looking at job functions, we found that the different job functions within an organisation communicate with each other. All organisations will also communicate with people and other organisations externally: customers or clients, suppliers, the Inland Revenue and other official bodies. We will discuss in more detail what information is exchanged between the different job functions within an organisation and with outsiders in the following sections.

Types of information

Customers and clients

Customers and clients will place orders for goods or services. The orders will include details of the goods or services required and customer details to enable delivery and payment (see Figure 2.5).

Some organisations will require customers to make full payment when they place the order, other organisations will require payment of a deposit and will then send an invoice to the customer detailing the total cost, amount due and the terms under which this must be paid. Many business customers may set up accounts. In this case, no payment will be required with the order: the full cost will be added to the account and an invoice sent to the customer. Customers may also be sent monthly statements to show details of purchases, payments made and any outstanding amount owed. Contracts may also be exchanged between organisations

CASE STUDY 2: SOURCE COMPUTERS UK

Customers

Most of the customers of Source Computers are locally based computer system builders and small computer retailers. All of these customers have an account with the company, which they can pay by cash or credit card, but more usually by cheque on a *30-day credit* basis.

Account customers generally place orders over the telephone with one of the sales staff. The customer tells the sales staff whether they require the order delivered or whether they will collect it. When an order is confirmed for release an invoice is automatically produced for electronic transmission via email. A printed copy is given to customers who collect their orders but a copy is still automatically sent to the customer by email.

Source Computers also sell to customers who do not have an account with them. These customers can either visit the showroom or place their order by telephone. Non-account customers can pay for the goods by credit card over the telephone or by cash, credit card or cheque in the showroom. However, they will not be able to collect the goods or have them despatched until payment has been cleared.

RKingB

ORDER

Customer Name and Address	For Office Use
Mr KZ Manlay	Order: 2 office chairs
33 Woodman Road	Order No:
Gravesend	Date Received:
DA11 7QQ	

Telephone	FAX	Email
01474 998647		Kzmanlay @btconnect.com

FIGURE 2.5 *Sample order form*

and their clients. A contract sets out the precise details of the goods or services being supplied and the terms and conditions under which they will be supplied. This will be signed by both a representative of the organisation and the client and will form a *legally binding agreement* between them. Banks and other financial institutions that provide loan services will supply a contract for the provision of the loan. This will set out how much money they will lend, the interest they will charge, repayments the client must make – how much and how often – and what will happen if the client fails to meet the terms and conditions of the agreement. This type of contract also includes items that are required by law, such as a statement explaining that, even if they sign the contract, the client has 14 days to change his or her mind.

Wholesalers and retailers

Wholesalers are intermediary organisations. They buy goods from producers and manufacturers and

sell them on to other organisations. They do not usually sell directly to the public. Retailers for the most part buy goods from wholesalers, rather than directly from producers and manufacturers, and sell them to the general public. The types of information that will be exchanged between wholesalers and retailers will be similar to that exchanged between an organisation and its customers. In effect, the retailers are the wholesalers' customers. Retailers will pass orders for the goods that they require to the wholesalers – these are usually called purchase orders to distinguish them from customer orders. The wholesalers will send invoices requesting payment to the retailers, who will then send the required payments.

Distributors

Distributors are organisations that move goods from place to place. Distributors will need information about what goods are to be transported, where they are coming from and going to, when they must be collected and how quickly they need to reach their destination. The organisation wanting goods distributed will need to know about the cost of the service, how the distributor will ensure that the goods will reach their destination in good condition and on time and what will happen if they do not. This will probably be set out in a contract between the two organisations. Organisations will provide distributors with delivery notes that detail the goods being delivered and the delivery address. Distributors will provide the organisation with delivery confirmations, usually signed by the person receiving the goods, to confirm that they have been delivered as agreed.

Suppliers (of services or goods)

Wholesalers and distributors are two types of supplier. Wholesalers supply goods to retailers; distributors supply transportation services to manufacturers, wholesalers and retailers. There are many other types of suppliers to all different types of organisations. The information exchanged will depend to some extent on the type of organisation and the type of supplier but will often involve purchase orders being sent to the supplier. The supplier will send invoices to the organisation who will then make payment.

Knowledge check

In a previous section of Case Study 2, another supplier was mentioned. Who is this supplier? Who in the company does the supplier deal with, what information do they exchange and in what form?

Manufacturers

Manufacturers are organisations that make products. They will need information about raw materials and parts from their suppliers and will send purchase orders to order what they need. Manufacturers will also receive orders from wholesalers and others wanting their products and will send invoices to request payment. Manufacturers will also need specifications for the products they produce, for new products and for any changes to the specifications. These may be supplied internally from the organisation's own design department or from

Theory into practice

– suppliers

Try to find out about some of the suppliers to your school or college and the information that is exchanged.

CASE STUDY 2: SOURCE COMPUTERS UK

Suppliers

Most of the suppliers to Source Computers are companies who they deal with on a regular basis and with whom they have a credit account. These suppliers are usually the UK offices of computer component manufacturers or bulk importers of components such as RAM and CPUs. When purchasing from importers, Source Computers will usually talk to several before confirming an order, to ensure that they get the best available price, as this is subject to considerable fluctuation. Occasionally, when products are in short supply and their normal suppliers cannot provide what they need, they will order from computer wholesalers to fill the shortfall.

In all cases, when the purchasing manager confirms an order from a supplier, a purchase order is raised by the finance function and sent to that supplier. The supplier will send an invoice when the order is despatched which must be paid within the terms of the credit agreement.

external sources. The information will depend on the product being made but may include precise details about the colour, size, shape and materials to be used. The specifications will also probably include technical drawings.

Managers and employees

All organisations will hold information about their managers and employees. This will include their name, address, education and qualifications, employment history, position, salary, contracted hours, pension rights, etc. The information that is exchanged between managers and employees will differ depending on the organisation and the job function involved. In most cases, however, managers will give instructions to employees about the work they are required to do and employees will report back to managers the outcomes of those tasks.

Briefs

Specifications may be provided in a design brief. A brief is a summary of the specification of a product or service – the term is also used in different contexts by different organisations.

Services

Those looking to buy services will want to know the price and what the service includes for that price. For example, if you are buying an insurance policy, you would want to know exactly what is covered and what is not as well as the cost of the *premium.* If you want to buy airline tickets to Australia, you would want to know the price of each class of ticket, departure and arrival times, where the plane stops en route and for how long, whether you can break your journey there without paying extra and, most importantly, whether there are seats available at a particular price on the flight you want to take.

General information about services will be provided in brochures and on websites. However, clients may need to provide their own information or discuss their precise requirements with the service provider to obtain more specific information.

> ### Key term
>
> *Premium*: the amount of money you pay to an insurance company to provide insurance cover. Premiums are calculated based on the statistical evidence of the likelihood of you making a claim. This is why young people have to pay much higher car insurance premiums than their parents. Statistics show that young people are more likely to be involved in motoring accidents and make insurance claims.

Goods

Customers and clients will need information about the goods that they are hoping to buy. Customers looking to buy goods will want to know the price, availability and the features offered. For example, if you are going to buy a laptop computer, you would want information about its size and weight, screen size, processing power, memory and storage capacity, the software, installed, etc., see Table 2.1. You would also want to know how much each model costs and whether there are any in stock.

This information will be provided in catalogues either on paper, or increasingly on websites. Retailers will also require similar information about goods from wholesalers. However, they may be less interested in the

LAPTOP	CPU	SCREEN	MEMORY	HDD	DIMENSIONS	WEIGHT	SOFTWARE	PRICE
Toshiba	1.6GHz	15" standard	512MB	60GB	365×275×38	3.1kg	XP Home	£1000
Apple	1.5GHz	15" wide	512MB	80GB	348×280×24	2.6kg	MAC OS	£1600
Sony	1.7GHz	17" wide	512MB	80GB	405×280×45	3.9kg	XP Home	£1500
HP	3.4GHz	17" wide	1024MB	100GB	398×288×42	4.2kg	XP Home	£1400

TABLE 2.1 *Information about laptop computers*

INFORMATION	FROM	TO
Orders or purchase orders	Customers and clients	Retailers or service providers
Invoices	Retailers	Wholesalers, distributors and other suppliers
	Wholesalers	Manufacturers, distributors and other suppliers
	Manufacturers and service providers	Distributors and other suppliers
	Retailers or service providers	Customers and clients
	Wholesalers, distributors and other suppliers	Retailers
	Manufacturers, distributors and other suppliers	Wholesalers
	Distributors and other suppliers	Manufacturers and service providers
Delivery notes	Retailers, wholesalers or manufacturers	Distributors
Delivery confirmations	Distributors	Retailers, wholesalers or manufacturers
Product specifications and design briefs	Internal design function or external organisation	Manufacturing function
Work instructions	Managers	Employees
Work reports	Employees	Managers
Goods information (catalogues/websites)	Retailers	Customers
	Wholesalers	Retailers
Service information (brochures/websites)	Service providers	Clients (brochures/websites)

TABLE 2.2 *Senders and receivers of information*

precise specification of the goods and more interested in the quantity available and the likely profit margin.

Key information and supporting ICT systems

There are a number of key information systems that are used by many organisations. Increasingly, organisations will use ICT systems to support these key systems. In this section, we will look at these key information systems and the ICT systems that support them.

Personnel

Personnel systems are maintained by the HR function in an organisation. Information is collected from the employee when he or she first joins the company, usually from the application form. This information will include the employees full name, address, date of birth, gender, marital status, education and qualifications, employment history, etc. A unique employee number will be allocated. All this information will be stored along with the date the employee joined the organisation, his or her current position, salary grade, contracted hours, holiday entitlement and other job-related information. This information will need to be updated whenever there is a change in employees' details, for example if they move house, marry or get a promotion. It is vital that the information stored is accurate. Inaccurate information may result in an employee being paid the wrong salary or not receiving the number of days' holiday they should. Inaccurate information may even lead to an employee losing his or her job in error. When an organisation needs to shed employees, this is often done on a last in, first out basis – the employees who have joined the organisation most recently are the first ones to be made redundant. If the employee's joining date has been entered incorrectly, he or she may be wrongly issued with a redundancy notice. It is also likely that information about the number of days of sick leave taken will be stored. If an employee applies for a new job or promotion, a reference will be required that will include such details taken from the personnel system. An error may result in the employee not getting the new job or promotion.

This information is also confidential so its security is important. Only the employees themselves and authorised members of the HR department and management should have access to the information held. Personnel records will also be subject to the requirements of the Data Protection Act that you will learn more about later in this unit.

In nearly all organisations, the personnel records will be held in a database on a computer system. The data will be entered from the original application forms and other documents via the keyboard. In small organisations this might be a simple *flat-file database;* in larger organisations the data is likely to be stored in several linked tables, i.e. a relational database (see Figure 2.6). For example, all employees on a certain salary grade are likely to be entitled to the same number of days' leave, contracted hours and overtime rates, etc. Rather than

EMPLOYEES

Employee_No

Surname

Forenames

Date_of_Birth

Gender

Home_Address_1

Home_Address_2

Home_Address_3

PostCode

Home_Telephone

Department

Salary_Grade

Job_Title

Location

Extension

SALARY_GRADE

Grade

Hourly_Rate

Contracted_Hours

Overtime_Rate

Leave_Days

FIGURE 2.6 *Relational database tables*

repeating this information for each employee, if the salary grade is recorded in the employee's record, the other details can be stored in a separate related table with a record for each salary grade.

It is also likely that the personnel database will be linked to the training records and payroll systems that we shall consider shortly.

> **Key term**
>
> *Flat-file database*: a database consisting of a single table of data.

Records can be sorted on different criteria, such as alphabetically by surname, length of service, salary grade or by the number of days' sick leave in the previous year. The records can be searched to find employee records that match a particular criterion, such as those who have been with the organisation for more than ten years. It is also easy to locate an individual employee's record to update it or to use it to produce a reference. Updating is also more straightforward as the old information can simply be replaced with the new.

Training

Ensuring that employees have the skills they need and updating those skills is important to most organisations. This will involve the HR function in organising training for employees and in keeping training records. These will be a natural extension of personnel records. The information stored will include details of courses attended and skill levels reached. Large organisations may also develop training plans for their staff as part of a *staff development plan.* In some industries, there is a requirement for certain staff to update their skills at regular intervals. In these cases, training records are particularly important. Training records may also include details of the particular skills of each employee. This enables the organisation to easily identify employees with the skills needed for a particular project or in an emergency, for example to identify employees with first aid skills, if there is an accident. Depending on the size of the organisation and the extent of the training records, these may simply be additional fields in employee records, or one or more linked tables in a relational personnel database.

Key term

Staff development plan: a document that identifies the existing knowledge and skills of employees and how these can be extended and updated to improve performance. It will allocate resources to ensure that any training provided is relevant to the needs of the organisation and the employees.

Payroll

Payroll systems link the HR function to the accounts or finance function. These systems will have links with the personnel system. Each employee's rate of pay, either salary or hourly rate, and their current *tax code* will be linked to their employee number. All but the smallest organisations will use computerised payroll systems, although some may use an external bureau instead. As payroll calculations are carried out on a weekly, or more usually, a monthly basis, they are often *batch processed*. For hourly paid workers, the hours worked will be entered. This may be done manually or calculated from an electronic clocking-in system that records when each employee starts and finishes work. This too will be linked to the employee number. The calculation carried out will be to multiply the hours worked by the hourly rate. The income tax due will be calculated and deducted from the total, as well as National Insurance and other deductions such as pension contributions. Most systems will then print out a pay advice slip (see Figure 2.7). This will include the employee number, name and address, details of pay and deductions, as well as other information such as National Insurance number, tax code and the payment date. Often, the name and address will be printed in a text box so that the pay advice slip can be put in a window envelope and sent to the employee.

Key terms

Tax code: a code issued by the Inland Revenue and based on each individual's personal circumstances that is used to calculate how much income tax should be deducted from their wages or salary.
Batch processed: processing where all the data is collected or input and then all the records are processed in a single operation. As little or no human intervention is needed, such processing is often carried out overnight when processing power is not required for other operations.

There will be both external and internal links to the payroll system. Externally, there will be links with the Inland Revenue that will require details of wages paid and tax deducted. In most organisations, there will also be links with BACS to pay employees' wages directly into their bank accounts. Internally, accounts managers will need to know the amount paid in wages so that this can be included in the profit and loss statements in the organisation's accounts. Profit and loss statements list all the monies taken in by the organisation (income) and all the monies paid out (expenditure). The expenditure is subtracted from the income to show the profit or loss that the organisation has made.

PAY ADVICE PAY PERIOD 05 2003/4 PAYMENT DATE 15/08/03
BEXLEY COUNCIL   120/LB18

CONSULTANT REL   EST7   1B

PAY AND ALLOWANCES			INDICATORS (SEE NOTES BELOW)			
DESCRIPTION	HOURS / UNITS	AMOUNT	-	T	N	P
HOURS PAY @ 1.0	14.00	369.89	*	*	*	*

DEDUCTIONS	(STATUTORY & VOLUNTARY)			
DESCRIPTION		AMOUNT +	BALANCE	I/R +
TAX (CODE BR PD 05)		81.40	526.02	I
NATIONAL INSURANCE (CAT A)			137.63	I
PENSION				

TOTAL	Box 1	GROSS TAXABLE	369.89
	Box 2	NON TAXABLE	

NET PAY (Box 1+2-3) **AMOUNT DUE** 288.49

C/FWD DEDUCTIONS GREATER THAN PAY, BALANCE TO BE DEDUCTED FROM NEXT PAYMENT

Pay point HOME   **MOP** DIRECT CREDIT
Bank/Building Society account details

TOTAL	Box 3	81.40

DEDUCTION NOTES
I INCREASING BALANCE
R REDUCING BALANCE
+ REFUND

TOTAL EARNINGS THIS FINANCIAL YEAR   2391.06
TOTAL TAXABLE PAY THIS FINANCIAL YEAR   2391.06

INDICATOR NOTES
- NEGATIVE PAYMENT, AMOUNT TAKEN BACK
T SUBJECT TO TAX
N SUBJECT TO NATIONAL INSURANCE
P SUBJECT TO PENSION

BEXLEY COUNCIL

FIGURE 2.7 *Sample pay advice slip*

There are likely to be many changes made to payroll records. These will include staff leaving whose records need to be deleted, new staff being employed so that new records must be added, changes to personal details, changes in pay rates, etc. Like the personnel records, it is vital that payroll records are accurate and up to date. Inaccurate payroll information may result in employees being paid the wrong amount, either too much or too little, or possibly not being paid at all. It is particularly important that tax codes are correct. If the tax code is wrong and too little tax is deducted, the employee is still liable for the unpaid tax. When the error is discovered the employee may have a large bill to pay that he or she cannot afford. Payroll information is also very confidential and must be kept secure, with only authorised members of staff having access to the information.

Design and development

Design and development systems will vary depending on the organisation's specific products or services. In the past, designs would have been drawn on paper by skilled draughtspeople and developed by building and testing physical models. Most organisations designing products now use computer aided design (CAD) systems to design products and 2-D or 3-D modelling tools to test the designs. The CAD systems may even be linked to computer aided manufacturing (CAM) systems to automatically manufacture the product. Records will need to be kept of any new products designed and any changes made to existing products. These records will need to include precise details of sizes, materials, components, etc., so that technical specifications can be produced. Such records may be kept in a database with links to files containing production drawings created using a CAD system.

Purchasing

All organisations need to purchase goods or services. These can be anything from light bulbs to computers, paper clips to conveyor belts, paper to sheet steel, printing Christmas cards to supplying power. The purchasing system will create purchase orders for the goods or services required. One copy of a purchase order will be sent to the supplier and one will be kept by the purchasing function. When the goods or services and the supplier's invoice are received, they can be checked against the purchase order. Purchase orders may be produced on carbonised paper so that the top copy is posted to the supplier and the second copy kept in a file. However, purchase orders may be created and stored on a computer system and sent electronically to the supplier, either by email or by *electronic data interchange (EDI)*.

The purchasing system will provide input to the *purchase ledger* in the accounts system. As well as accounts, purchasing will have links with the stock control and manufacturing functions of organisations that supply or make goods. The goods or raw materials purchased will be added to the quantity in stock and the stock control or manufacturing systems will determine when more goods or raw materials need to be purchased as stocks are used up. However, all functions within an organisation will need supplies of one sort or another, so there will be links between the purchasing system and most functions within the organisation. Purchasing will also be responsible for generating contracts for the supply of services.

Key terms

Electronic data interchange (EDI): the exchange of standardised document forms between computer systems for business use. EDI is most often used between different companies and uses certain standards so that the different systems can communicate.
Purchase ledger: the section of the accounts system that keeps records of all the purchases made by the organisation and the money paid out for these purchases. The term 'ledger' is a reference to when accounts used to be kept in large books called ledgers.
Sales ledger: the section of the accounts system that keeps records of the sales made by the organisation and the money paid in for the goods or services sold.

Sales

The sales system is responsible for keeping records of orders and contracts placed by customers. The inputs to the system will be the customer's details and the details of the goods or services required (see Figure 2.8). These details

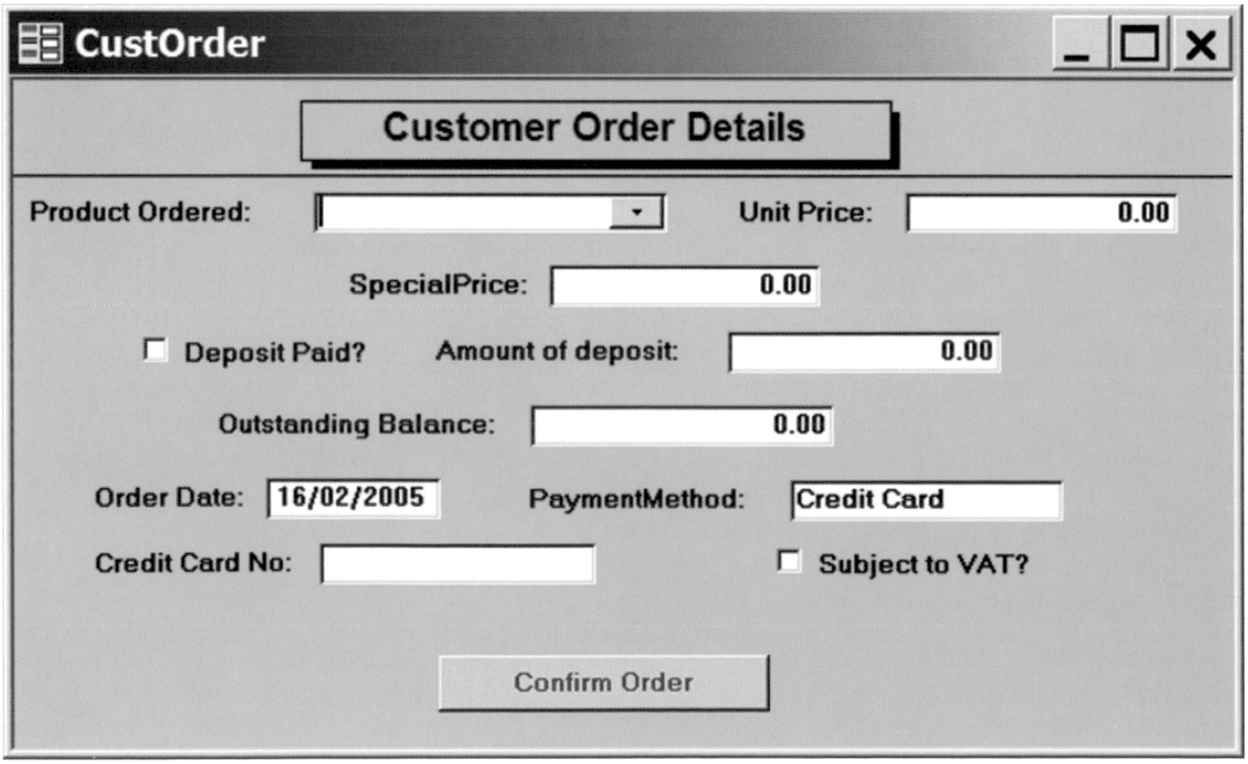

CustOrder

Customer Order Details

Product Ordered:	Unit Price: 0.00

SpecialPrice: 0.00

☐ Deposit Paid? Amount of deposit: 0.00

Outstanding Balance: 0.00

Order Date: 16/02/2005 PaymentMethod: Credit Card

Credit Card No: ☐ Subject to VAT?

Confirm Order

FIGURE 2.8 *Sales order input screen*

will be used to generate internal requests for the supply of the goods or services required. In the case of goods, this may take the form of a picking list, which is sent to the warehouse so that the required items can be picked from the shelves and packed ready for delivery. Delivery notes may also be created and passed to the despatch or delivery department. The sales system will also create an invoice that will be sent to the customer. Most organisations will use ICT for sales order processing. Inputs may be taken from a paper order form and manually entered, they may be entered by a telesales assistant, or by the customer using an on-line order form. The processing carried out to produce the invoice will include looking up the unit price for each item and multiplying it by the number required, adding the totals for all the different items, adding any carriage costs, calculating and subtracting any discounts and calculating and adding VAT. The order processing system will often have direct links with the stock control system so that the items sold can be deducted and sales staff – or the customer in the case of

on-line ordering – can have up-to-date information on the availability of goods. The sales system will also provide the input to the sales ledger in the accounts system.

Research

The research function will need to keep detailed records of any new products that are being trialled or investigated. This will include details of the product and of the research being carried out on it. These records will be used to produce reports on the research that will allow directors to make decisions. Analysis of market research findings using spreadsheet models may enable the research function to forecast future trends, such as how long an existing product will remain saleable, or possible new areas that the organisation might venture into.

Accounts and finance

We have already discovered that other systems such as payroll, purchasing and sales will have inputs into the accounts and finance system. The purpose of this system is to keep track of the money paid out by the organisation and the money paid in or owed to it. The sales and

CASE STUDY 2: SOURCE COMPUTERS UK

Finance system

The finance function of Source Computers uses an integrated software package specifically designed for computer companies. Purchase orders are raised automatically by the system on entry of the product details. The system also keeps a record of all purchase orders raised. The system produces daily reports of supplier invoices due for payment and, depending on the supplier, cheques are produced or money is transferred electronically.

Details of all orders are input directly into the sales order processing module. This includes most of the information listed in the 'Information requirements and collection' case study section. However, the only details about goods that need to be entered are the product code and quantity. All other information such as the product description and unit price is stored on the system and retrieved by the product code. Unit price is multiplied by

quantity to give a product total. The product totals are added to give a sub-total before the VAT due is calculated and added. All these details are included on an invoice.

When an order is ready for despatch or collection, sales telephone finance to release the order and proceed to issue the invoice. This is done only after the system has checked the customer's account to ensure that payments are up to date. Invoices are printed locally, but the system also automatically sends a copy of the invoice by email to the customer. The invoice total is added to the customer's account.

The finance system automatically calculates and produces the VAT returns for Source Computers. The finance function then raises a cheque to pay the VAT owed. The system also produces information at the end of the company's financial year. This information is sent by the finance function to their accountants who produce the company reports.

purchase ledgers we discussed in previous sections, along with payroll and other financial information, will be used to prepare a general ledger that summarises the organisation's accounts. Most organisations will use ICT systems to keep their accounts. In a small business, this may be a simple spreadsheet or one of the several off-the-shelf accounting packages that are readily available. Large organisations will have *bespoke software* to keep their accounts. The software will be used to prepare a balance sheet and an income statement. A balance sheet is a financial statement that lists the *assets*, debts and owners' investment at a particular date. An income statement lists the money taken in (revenue), the money paid out (expenditure) and the net income (revenue minus expenditure) during a particular period. These financial statements are important to the organisation, as they provide the basis of financial planning so that the organisation remains profitable in the long term. They are also required by the Inland Revenue and by shareholders. To remain profitable in the short term, organisations need to control their cash flow. Cash flow is a measure of the money coming into and going out of the organisation, usually on a monthly basis. The accounts and finance system will keep track of cash receipts and payments so that future cash flow can be forecast (see Figure 2.9).

Stock control or inventory systems

Whilst accounting systems keep track of the money coming into and going out of an organisation, it is the job of the stock control system to similarly keep track of goods by recording the number, cost and place of stocked items. All goods will be identified by a unique serial number. Part of a typical stock record is shown in Table 2.3.

The stock records will need to be updated when goods are sold, by subtracting the number sold. When new stock arrives, the stock records will also need to be updated by adding the number received. As there is a continual need to update the records, most organisations use ICT systems to store them. In small organisations, the updating may still be done manually by typing in the product number to locate the record and then adding or subtracting the quantity.

Microsoft Excel - cash2006.xls

	A	B	C	D	E	F	G	H	I	J	K	L	M	N
1						Cashflow Forecast 2006								
2														
3		Jan-06	Feb-06	Mar-06	Apr-06	May-06	Jun-06	Jul-06	Aug-06	Sep-06	Oct-06	Nov-06	Dec-06	
4	Income													
5														
6	Product Sales UK	117.20	117.79	121.32	124.96	128.71	132.57	136.55	140.64	144.86	149.21	153.68	158.29	
7	Product Sales Europe	52.30	52.46	52.61	52.77	52.93	53.09	53.25	53.41	53.57	53.73	53.89	54.05	
8	Services UK	9.38	9.42	9.71	10.00	10.30	10.61	10.92	11.25	11.59	11.94	12.29	12.66	
9	Services Europe	4.71	4.72	4.74	4.75	4.76	4.78	4.79	4.81	4.82	4.84	4.85	4.86	
10	Consultancy	24.20	24.32	24.44	24.56	24.69	24.81	24.94	25.06	25.19	25.31	25.44	25.56	
11														
12	Total Income	207.78	208.71	212.82	217.04	221.39	225.85	230.45	235.17	240.03	245.02	250.16	255.44	
13														
14	Expenditure													
15														
16	Product Costs	53.47	53.70	54.81	55.96	57.14	58.35	59.60	60.89	62.21	63.57	64.97	66.41	
17	Services Costs	5.87	5.89	6.01	6.14	6.26	6.39	6.53	6.66	6.81	6.95	7.10	7.25	
18	Salaries	95.20	95.20	95.20	95.20	95.20	99.96	104.96	104.96	104.96	104.96	104.96	104.96	
19	Premises	11.75	11.75	11.75	11.75	11.75	11.75	11.75	11.75	11.75	11.75	11.75	11.75	
20	Other	10.39	10.44	10.64	10.85	11.07	11.29	11.52	11.76	12.00	12.25	12.51	12.77	
21														
22	Total Expenditure	176.68	176.98	178.41	179.90	181.42	187.74	194.36	196.02	197.73	199.48	201.29	203.14	
23														
24	Cashflow													
25														
26	Monthly	31.10	31.73	34.41	37.14	39.97	38.11	36.09	39.15	42.30	45.54	48.87	52.30	
27	Cumulative		62.83	97.24	134.38	174.35	212.46	248.55	287.70	330.00	375.54	424.41	476.71	
28														
29														

FIGURE 2.9 *Spreadsheet cash flow forecast*

PRODUCT NUMBER	DESCRIPTION	COST PRICE (£)	LOCATION	QUANTITY
123456	Parcel tape × 6	0.95	H7	125

TABLE 2.3

In larger organisations, stock control is becoming more and more automated. Product codes are stored in barcodes attached to the item or container (see Figure 2.10). These will be scanned by barcode readers attached to the stock control system when goods are received and sold. This will automatically alter the quantity in stock.

In shops, barcode readers attached to the electronic point of sale (EPOS) terminals are used to scan the barcodes. The product number is then used to find the item description and price for the customer receipt as well as deducting the item from the quantity in stock. Each stock record will include a re-order level. When the quantity in stock falls below this level, a warning can be given so that the item can be re-ordered. Alternatively, this re-ordering process may also be automated. Rather than giving a warning, the system can simply add the item to an order that is automatically sent to the supplier.

We have already suggested that the stock control system may be linked to the sales system. This may be taken one stage further and linked to robotic systems in the warehouse. Each product code is linked to a location within the warehouse. When goods arrive, the product codes are used to identify where each should be stored and the robots are programmed to deliver the goods to the right places. When goods are purchased, rather than providing warehouse staff with picking lists, the product numbers are used to program the robots to select the goods required.

Email

The use of email is becoming more and more widespread as a means of communication within organisations and with outsiders such as customers and suppliers. Internal email obviously requires that the organisation has a computer network, and external email requires connection to the Internet. Where, in the past, managers would have sent memos to staff to inform them of a meeting, for example, they are now much more likely to send emails. There are several advantages to this. The manager can send an email requesting a meeting and asking when staff are available. This needs to be typed in only once, as it can be sent to any number of people simultaneously. Staff can reply with their availability and the meeting details

FIGURE 2.10 *A barcode*

confirmed, all in a relatively short time. Unlike telephone calls, the member of staff does not need to be at his or her desk when the email is sent: it will be stored in the inbox until he or she is able to pick it up. This is particularly useful for international communications when different time zones make scheduling business telephone calls very difficult – 9 am to 5 pm in the UK is 8 pm to 4 am on the east coast of Australia during our winter.

There are, however, disadvantages to using email. One disadvantage is the sheer ease of sending messages. It is not unusual, for example, for someone to send an email to the person sitting at the next desk, rather than just turning round to speak to them. Also, care is needed to ensure information is sent only to the people who need it. Irrelevant information simply adds to the volume of emails people receive. Dealing with this volume of emails can be very time-consuming, reducing the time staff have for their work. The other issue is to ensure that information is not sent to people who should not know it. It is very easy to reply to all the people in a list, rather than just to the person who sent the email. If the email is requesting personal information, for example, your reply might inadvertently provide others with information they should not have access to.

Internet and intranet

Internal networks provide organisations with the possibility of setting up an intranet. An intranet is a network that provides similar services within the organisation to those provided by the Internet outside it, but it is not necessarily connected to the Internet. It allows the distribution of information within the organisation that can be viewed using standard web browser software. The intranet can provide an electronic notice board to keep staff informed but can also provide access to documents, reports and a wide range of other information. Intranets can usually be accessed only by staff within the organisation. However, some organisations give limited access to their intranets to other organisations and the general public. This is known as an extranet.

The Internet provides new opportunities for organisations to communicate externally. Many organisations have a presence on the WWW, in the shape of a website that the general public can visit to find out about the organisation and what it has to offer. An increasing number of organisations have gone beyond this and offer the opportunity for e-commerce. E-commerce is the buying and selling of goods and services on-line. There are some organisations that operate only in this way. A common form of e-commerce is where the organisation sells its goods or services to the general public. The customer selects what he or she wants from an on-line catalogue before proceeding to the checkout page (see Figure 2.11). This shows the items selected, prices, total and any carriage charge. If the customer is happy he or she proceeds to the payment section. This will be held on a secure server and the details entered

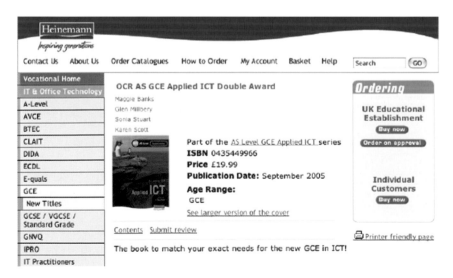

FIGURE 2.11 *On-line shopping site*

CASE STUDY 2: SOURCE COMPUTERS UK

Internet and email

Source Computers currently do not have a website, but one is under development. In fact, their current integrated package is web-based and the website will be integrated into that system. This will allow them to sell their products on-line. A draft of their proposed homepage is shown in Figure 2.12.

As you will have discovered from reading previous sections of this case study, Source Computers make extensive use of email to communicate with customers and between the various functions in the company. They also use Internet banking to pay suppliers and staff.

FIGURE 2.12 *Draft homepage for Source Computers UK's website*

Knowledge check

Discuss the improvements that a website and e-commerce will bring to Source Computers UK's operations and any problems that might arise.

will be *encrypted*. The customer enters his or her address and credit or debit card details to pay for the goods. These details are checked and, if all is well, an order confirmation is shown, which the customer can print out. Often an email is also sent to the customer confirming their order. Goods are then despatched by post or courier.

Another Internet service that is of benefit to organisations is on-line banking. This allows even small organisations to pay suppliers on-line and to move money between accounts.

Key terms

Encrypted: a security method that involves scrambling the information transmitted so that it cannot be read if it is intercepted. An encryption key is needed to unscramble the data so that it is meaningful.

Using diagrams to describe the movement of information

You will need to draw diagrams to describe the movement of information in organisations. A diagram is a helpful tool to make sense of how information moves into and out of an organisation and between individuals or departments within it. This means discovering who needs or uses what information and then showing the links There are many different types of information, most of which we have discussed over the previous pages. These need to be clearly identified in the diagrams, for example:

* customer order
* purchase orders to suppliers
* design and production drawings
* wages and tax-paid details
* records of staff training
* names and addresses of employees
* stock details
* invoices paid
* monthly income

* monthly outgoing
* web publicity pages
* monthly profit or loss.

Your diagrams also need to show the ways that the information is communicated:

* one of the most straightforward ways of communicating information is face to face. This is when the source of the information meets the receiver and either tells or hands the information to the recipient
* information that is on paper can be posted. This can be internal post from one department to another or external post from the organisation to a customer or supplier
* through EDI and e-commerce
* through internal or LAN email or external or Internet email
* the telephone is still a common method of communicating verbal information; this too can be internal or external
* through facsimile (fax)
* some organisations will share information in centralised database systems that different departments can access
* mobile devices, such as mobile phones and two-way radios can also be used to communicate information over long or short distances.

You need to be able to discover which methods are effective and efficient for various organisations, and which methods are particularly effective for various types of information.

It is important that you can interpret a written description of the movement of information during a process, or the movement of information in a process you have observed, and convert this into a diagram. The first step is to identify:

* who sends each type of information
* who receives each type of information
* what is the information
* what communication method is used.

Movement of information

On a blank piece of A4 paper, write the names of the senders and receivers of information in boxes around the page. It is likely that senders will also be receivers of information and that some may send or receive more than one type of information. Each name in its box should appear only once on the page. Next, draw an arrow from the sender to the receiver to represent each type of information. Re-organise the boxes if necessary so that the arrows do not cross. Finally, label each arrow with the type of information and the method used to communicate it. Remember it is only information we are interested in, not goods. The following generic example will help you. The senders and receivers of information are shown in **bold,** the type of information is in *italics* and the communication methods are underlined. The same convention is used in Figure 2.13 to show how they link.

A **customer** posts an *order* to the **sales department**. In the **sales department**, the *order details* are entered into a centralised database, which is accessed by the **warehouse** to make up the order. A *delivery note* is attached to the goods and handed to the **despatch department** for delivery. On delivery, the member of the **despatch department** hands the goods and *delivery note* to the **customer**. The **sales department** creates an *invoice* that is posted to the **customer**. The **accounts department** accesses a *copy of the invoice* from the centralised database. The **customer** posts *payment* to the **accounts department**.

> **Knowledge check**
>
> Draw an information diagram for the process of placing an advertisement in a brochure described in the Francefilez case study.

ICT systems

In the sections on the common key systems found in organisations, we also discussed the ICT systems that are used. Nowadays, it is almost impossible to consider the two in isolation. Even

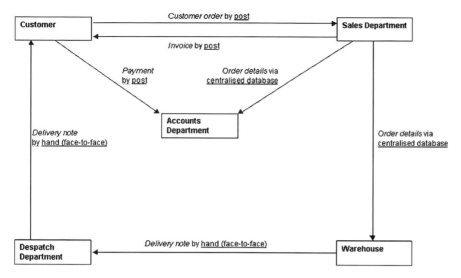

FIGURE 2.13 *Example of a flow diagram*

Information flow

The information flow when Source Computers order goods from a supplier is relatively simple. The purchasing manager, Dick, telephones a supplier to place an order. He checks that the supplier has sufficient stock and at what price the product is available. He then verbally confirms the order. Dick then emails the finance function with the name of the supplier, and details of the items ordered and an expected despatch date. The finance function sends a confirmation purchase order to the supplier by email. The supplier creates a waybill, which is collected with the goods by the courier. When the courier delivers the goods to Source Computers he or she hands a copy of the waybill to Dick. When the supplier has despatched the goods, an email is sent to finance confirming the date and method of despatch, and attaching a copy of their invoice (see Figure 2.14).

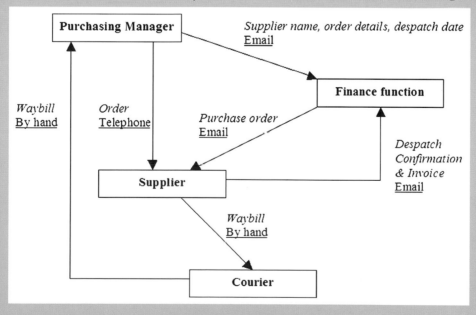

FIGURE 2.14 *The purchasing process in Source Computers UK*

small organisations rely on ICT for some or all of their key systems and would find it difficult to function efficiently without ICT. When you are considering the ICT systems used by organisations, you will need to identify the hardware and software used, data that is input, processing that takes place and outputs obtained.

You will also need to consider how well the ICT system meets the organisation's needs and suggest possible improvements that could be made. For example, an organisation may use separate and different computer systems in different areas, for example Macintosh computers for design and standard PCs for administration. This may result in duplication of data and the need to manually re-enter data.

Networking these systems would improve the information flow within the organisation. However, the fact that the two systems are different may cause problems and someone will need to manage the network that is created.

The impact of ICT on working practices

We said at the start of the last section that most organisations now rely on ICT for some or all of their key systems. This increased use of ICT and the technological developments that have taken place have led to changes in the way people work and the types of jobs that are available.

More and more people are able to work from home, more and more people need ICT skills in their work, and new jobs are increasingly available in the ICT field, such as web designers, ICT trainers and ICT support staff.

Location and pattern of work

As was just indicated, more and more people are able to work from home (see Figure 2.15).

This is due to easy access to a high-speed Internet connection and the availability of cheap high-powered computers and peripherals. Anyone who spends most of his or her working day sitting in front of a computer entering or accessing data on a computer network could, in theory, carry out the same function sitting in their home in front of a computer that is connected to their company's network via the Internet. There are considerable advantages to employers of their employees working at home. Firstly, smaller premises are needed, as there will be fewer staff actually in the office. This has led to a phenomenon known a 'hot desking'. This means that, rather than each member of staff having their own desk and computer, there are a more limited number of desks and computers in the office. Staff who are actually in the office can use any desk and computer that is available. Smaller premises in turn leads to lower lighting and heating bills. This will be balanced to some extent by paying for employees' Internet access, telephone and other expenses.

As well as working from home, people can now work on the move (see Figure 2.16). Laptops enable people to carry their computer with them and work wherever they happen to be. The development of wireless networks has provided wireless Internet access points in motorway service stations, hotels and other

FIGURE 2.15 *Working from home*

FIGURE 2.16 *Working on the move*

locations. These allow people to access the Internet on their laptops while they are away from their home or office. This means they can pick up and send emails and possibly access their company's network while travelling. Mobile telephones allow people to be contacted while they are travelling, both by voice and by text message. WAP-enabled mobile phones also provide email and WWW access.

The ability to work from home or on the move allows individuals greater flexibility in the way they work. There is no longer a need to work from 9 to 5. Work can, for example, be fitted around the family.

Another impact on working practices has come about due to the increased use of robots and automation. This has enabled organisations to operate 24 hours a day. In the past, the cost of employing staff to keep a production line operating round the clock may not have been economically viable. With automation, only a relatively small number of staff are needed to oversee and maintain the systems. Although the initial cost of introducing automation is high, reduced staffing levels and wage bills make 24-hour operation a more viable proposition.

Work skills

ICT has had a huge impact on the work skills needed in the twenty-first century. There are few jobs that do not require the use of ICT in one form or another. In the past, the jobs that required keyboard skills were limited to secretaries, typists, journalists and a few others. Now, a huge range of jobs requires the use of a computer keyboard. If you visit a car dealer's premises, the counter staff in the parts department will use a computer to look up the part required; the mechanics in the workshop will use computers to carry out diagnostic checks on cars they are servicing; the salespeople will use a computer to find out the price and availability of a particular car model, and so on. Where in the past, managers and other senior staff would have dictated letters to a secretary for typing, now they are more likely to send their own emails and type their own letters on a word

processor, only passing them to the secretary to check and put into house style. Apart from using ICT in their teaching, teachers now use computers to create worksheets and other resources and to write reports. All of these people will need keyboard skills.

The increase in the use of ICT has also led to an increase in the need for technical skills. People are needed to build computers and other ICT equipment and to repair them when they go wrong. Going back to the car mechanics mentioned in the previous section, many new cars have computerised engine management systems requiring the mechanics to have greater technical skills than in the past.

Linked with the technical skills required to build ICT systems are the skills of analysis and design. An analyst must be able to study an existing system to identify the inputs, outputs and processing that takes place and whether it can be computerised or upgraded. The analyst must then specify the input, output and processing requirements of the new system or upgrade. The designer then takes over to design the new system or upgrade to meet these requirements. Design skills are needed to design hardware and different types of software, such as applications software, web pages, multimedia applications and games.

Retraining

In the last section we have discussed the effect that ICT has had on the work skills that people need. Some jobs have disappeared or are much reduced due to greater automation and the introduction of robotics, while other jobs requiring these new work skills have opened up. The answer is to retrain the workforce so that they acquire the necessary work skills and can take on the new jobs available to them. For example, some car production workers may be retrained to program and maintain the robots that have taken over their jobs, while others may be retrained to repair and maintain other computer systems. This need for acquiring new skills has resulted in a whole new ICT training industry, which in itself offers new job opportunities for people who have learnt these skills.

Effects on employees and employers

These changes that ICT has made to working practices have negative as well as positive effects on employees and employers.

Social aspects

When people work from home social aspects of their lives are affected. Employees are no longer directly supervised. This means that there is no one on hand to give praise for a job well done, or to push to ensure a job is completed on time. For some, this may result in a lack of motivation and boredom, causing the quality of the employee's work to suffer. Others may be more motivated by 'being their own boss' and not having someone 'looking over their shoulder', causing the quality and quantity of their work to increase. Another possibly negative factor of working at home is the fact that there are no colleagues around to share experiences and discuss ideas. This may result in problems taking longer to solve when employees cannot brainstorm with others, and in employees feeling isolated. On the positive side, working at home gives employees greater opportunities for interaction with their family and neighbours than if they had to travel to work.

Other social aspects of the changed working practices as a result of ICT are the risk of job loss and reduced security of work. We have already discussed the changes in work skills required. This may lead to people losing their jobs if they do not possess the necessary skills. The increased introduction of ICT and automated systems has meant that fewer staff are needed, again resulting in the possibility of job losses. The nature of employment contracts between employers and employees has also changed. Rather than employing staff on *permanent contracts*, many ICT-related organisations employ staff on *short-term fixed contracts*. This allows employers to alter the number of staff as the needs of the organisation change without having to make redundancy payments. However, staff on short-term contracts will lose any sense of security of work, which makes it difficult for them to make long-term plans. Both the threat of job loss and the lack of security caused by short-term contracts are likely to cause stress for the employees

affected. When employers are considering making changes, such as the introduction of automation, they will need to ensure that employees are kept informed and that steps are taken to reduce job losses and provide training opportunities. Failure to handle such issues sensitively is likely to lead to a poor relationship with employees, union involvement and possible industrial action, such as strikes. This may cause stress for the employer as well as the employees.

> ### Key terms
>
> *Permanent contracts*: employment contracts that have no end date. If the employer wants to reduce the number of staff, employees will have to be made redundant and paid redundancy money.
> *Short-term fixed contracts*: employment contracts that last for a specified time, for example one year.

The balance of responsibilities

Changes in working patterns also change the balance of who is responsible for jobs being done. Employers may suffer stress because they will need to change the way in which staff are supervised and may feel that they have less control over their workforce. Rather than having managers who directly supervise employees, they may have to use tactics such as a performance-related pay scheme or fixed-price contracts to provide financial incentives to ensure employees get the work done. Performance-related pay schemes pay employees for what they actually achieve, while fixed-price contracts provide a pre-agreed payment for completing a job, regardless of how long it takes. Employees have greater responsibility to ensure they carry out the work and meet deadlines without direct supervision and may suffer stress as a result. Linked to this change of responsibility for getting the work done, who takes the blame when things go wrong? If confidential data is lost because computer equipment is stolen from the employee's home, is it the responsibility of the employee for failing to take proper care, or the employer for not ensuring adequate security was put in place? This too may cause the employee to suffer stress.

The amount and timing of leisure time

A largely positive effect of changing working patterns due to ICT is that, in theory, more work can be done in less time so that people have more leisure time. However, the ability for people to access their work at home sometimes means that people actually spend more time working than they might otherwise do. Rather than leave work behind when they leave the office, some people will access their files and continue working when they get home. This is linked to an expectation that employees will be more productive because of ICT, so more is expected of them. Where employees work most of the time at home, the increased flexibility means that they can take their leisure time when it suits them. Some people might stop work mid-afternoon when their children come home from school so that they can spend time with them and then start working again later in the evening when they have gone to bed. Others might take a long break in the morning or the middle of the day, or work through the weekend and take days off during the week so that they can take advantage of cheaper mid-week rates for leisure activities. Even those who actually go to work can often now work flexitime. This means that they have some choice over when they start and finish work each day, providing they work the number of hours they are contracted to over a week or month; and by starting earlier and finishing later some days, they can bank time to take a day, or part of a day off.

The fast-changing pace of ICT developments

We are all aware of the pace at which technology changes in everyday life. Not so long ago, CDs replaced tape and vinyl records as a medium for distributing and listening to music. As the author is writing this, downloading music files over the Internet and listening to them on MP3 players such as the iPod is fast taking over from CDs, and by the time you read this there may well be some new technology for distributing and listening to music. This same pace of change occurs in the workplace. New versions of operating systems and applications software appear about once a year, each with slightly different user interaction and features which employees must learn how to use. Hardware too is constantly being updated, meaning that technicians and support staff need to learn about the latest components. When we were discussing the changes in work skills, computerised engine management systems in cars were discussed. Every new model of car is likely to have a slightly different and 'improved' system from previous ones, meaning that mechanics have to keep up to date with these developments if they are to service and repair the cars effectively. Wherever ICT is used, systems are likely to be upgraded and changed over time and the more 'leading edge' the systems are, the more frequently these changes will occur. Employees will not only need to learn how to use the systems but will also need to constantly update their skills as the system is updated. It is also then very easy to become de-skilled. If, for whatever reason, an employee does not use a system for a period of time, he or she may forget how to use it and his or her skills may be out of date when they have to use it again. All of these effects of the pace of change of ICT systems may cause stress for employees. The more frequent the changes are, the more stressful it is likely to be for the employees involved.

Theory into practice

– effects of ICT on working lives

In a group, draw up a set of questions to use to interview adults about the effects that ICT has had on their working lives. Use the questions to interview your parents, grandparents and other adults. Share the results of your interviews in your group and discuss the impacts that ICT has had on the working lives of the people you interviewed. Make sure you take notes of your discussions. Individually, use your notes to describe the impact of ICT on working practices in your area.

The impact of ICT on methods of production

In the previous sections on the impact of ICT on working practices, automation and robotics has been mentioned on several occasions. In this section we will consider automation and robotics in a little more detail and discuss the impact of ICT on methods of production. The use of robots and other linked ICT systems has improved production in two main areas: process control and production control.

Production control

Production control involves the systematic planning, co-ordinating and directing of manufacturing activities to ensure that goods are made on time, of adequate quality and at reasonable cost. There are a number of ways that ICT can help in this process. One example of this is just-in-time manufacturing. Using ICT for order processing, stock control and automatic ordering means that raw materials or parts are only delivered exactly when they are needed in the production process. There are advantages to this system. The manufacturing company does not need large amounts of warehouse space to store materials as they can be taken straight from the delivery lorries to the production line. Also, money is not tied up in stock. Raw materials or parts are ordered only when required and they are used immediately to produce the product that is sold, resulting in a minimum delay in regaining the money spent. A disadvantage is the reliance on suppliers and transport systems. If a supplier fails to deliver the parts on time or there are traffic delays, the production process will be delayed until the parts arrive. Just-in-time manufacturing is used extensively in the car industry where the use of robots, rather than people, to carry out many of the processes has meant that the pace of production is more predictable.

Another example of how ICT is used for production control is in the newspaper printing industry (see Figure 2.17). A print management computer controls the whole process. Automated Guided Vehicles (AGVs) are used to transport rolls of newsprint from the lorries that deliver them to long- and short-term storage areas and on to the printing presses. They use sensors to follow a line on the floor according to a program downloaded from the print management computer. The program is downloaded when the AGV is in a docking area where its onboard batteries are also recharged. For safety, the AGVs also have sensors that detect when something or someone is in their way so that they can stop and avoid a collision. As well as controlling the AGVs, the print management computer also controls the production of printing plates, flow of ink to the presses and the cutting, folding and packing of the newspapers. The system even prints and attaches labels for the newsagents who will receive each pack of newspapers. When one press runs out of paper, the process is automatically transferred to another so there is no break in the flow of newspapers coming off the presses. There is some element of process control in the control of ink flow. If you look at a newspaper that is printed in colour, you will see that there are circles of four colours printed somewhere on the page (usually on the fold of a tabloid paper). Sensors check the intensity of these coloured dots and feed the data back to the print management computer so that the flow of each colour of ink can be adjusted if necessary.

Production control techniques have similar advantages to process control. Even if the feedback element of process control is not present, the quality of the final product is still likely to be better than if human workers produced it. This is due to the fact that a robot, once programmed, will carry out a task in exactly the same way every time, resulting in a more consistent output. Human workers, on the other hand, may get tired or distracted and produce output of a more variable quality.

Process control

An example of process control is paper production. In simple terms, paper is made by mixing wood pulp, or shredded recycled paper, with water. The resulting mixture is spread on a mesh so that excess water drains away. In an industrial system, the paper is passed through a series of rollers to remove the remaining water and produce paper of the correct thickness. The introduction of ICT has meant that sensors can be

FIGURE 2.17 *Newspaper printing*

used to test the thickness, water content and strength of the paper produced. The sensors feed back these values to the computer control system where they are compared with stored ideal values. If the two sets of values do not match, the system output automatically adjusts the pulp mixture and/or the rollers to alter the paper quality. Because the computer can monitor and reset each machine hundreds of times each minute, paper quality can be maintained at levels that are very close to the ideal.

Automated systems for process control have a number of advantages. Such processes can produce goods faster than a manual production line and, most importantly, the quality of the final product is higher, as it is being continually monitored and adjusted. This in turn means that there is less waste, reducing the cost of production. Automated production also requires fewer employees, reducing the wage bill, and can continue 24 hours a day without getting tired or needing breaks as human workers would. Processes such as sheet glass or steel production can be very dangerous as they involve handling materials at very high temperatures. The introduction of automated systems means that remaining workers no longer need to handle these dangerous materials, resulting in a safer working environment.

The impact on society

We have discussed the impact of ICT on working practices in some depth in a previous section. As further advances are made in technology, these impacts are likely to become more pronounced. The increased safety of workers due to automated systems was mentioned in the last section. However, the increasing use of ICT brings with it a range of health and safety issues. These include the risk of eye-strain from looking at a computer monitor for long periods of time, backache from poorly designed and adjusted workstations, and repetitive strain injury (RSI) from constantly repeating the same actions. Legislation designed to protect employees from these risks will be discussed in the next section.

Another impact on society of changes in production methods is the level of employment. There was much doom and gloom when automated systems were first introduced, as many expected that far fewer workers would be needed and that there would be high levels of unemployment. Indeed, when automated processes were introduced into the newspaper printing industry, there were large job losses. Now, however, despite more and more use of ICT the unemployment levels are the lowest they have been for many years. Automation may have reduced the number of jobs in some industries, but many new industries have sprung up; for example, people are needed to program and maintain systems. ICT training is another area of growth as is web design, and there are many others. There is, however, a change in the balance of the types of jobs available. It is often the unskilled, manual jobs that have disappeared due to ICT and automation. The new jobs that have replaced them tend to require higher skill levels. People therefore need training in order to take on these new jobs and it is harder for those without training or qualifications to gain employment.

Theory into practice

– automated systems and robotics

Use your school or college library, the Internet and CD-ROMs to find out about other examples of automated systems and robotics being used in process and production control – you may be able to find out at first hand by visiting a local manufacturing company. Select one example of process control and one example of production control and write an essay describing the process and how it has been improved by automation. You should include how ICT has aided the:

* speed of the process
* cost of the process
* safety of the workers involved
* quality of the final product.

Legislation

You will have discovered throughout this unit how ICT is used to store, process and communicate information. This ever-increasing use of ICT has led to the need for new laws. Some of these laws are designed to protect individuals, others to protect organisations and their information. You will need to learn the reasons for the various pieces of legislation, how it affects organisations, and what they must do to act in accordance with it. This legislation needs to be updated to match changes in the use of ICT. The following sections describe the laws as they apply at the time of writing this book. You will need to check whether there have been any updates to these laws by the time you are reading it. If there are, you will need to learn about these updates and take them into account when you are answering questions about legislation in the examination for this unit.

Data Protection Act (1998)

Information has always been kept about individuals by different organisations. In the past, this was kept on paper, in large numbers of filing cabinets, in the premises of the organisation that collected it. To find the record of an individual would involve someone physically searching through the files. It was feasible to search only using the record number or name that had been used to order the records in the filing cabinet. If another organisation wanted the information, if it even knew it existed, the record would have to be copied and sent in the post. If someone wanted to find out or steal personal information, they would need to physically break into the building where it was kept. The use of ICT to store personal information has changed all of this.

Now, huge numbers of records on individuals can be kept on computer. These records can be easily and quickly searched on any criterion, for example to find all the individuals who earn over £50,000. More worryingly for some people, the records can easily be transferred from one organisation to another electronically. Indeed, some organisations exist simply to buy and sell lists of individuals fulfilling certain criteria to

marketing organisations. The other cause for concern is the fact that, without good security, personal details on computer systems can be accessed and stolen without the thief having to go anywhere near the place where they are stored.

All of these issues led to the introduction of the Data Protection Act, which was updated in 1998 to cover all personal data, including paper records and not just data stored electronically. Since the introduction of the Freedom of Information Act in January 2005, the Information Commissioner maintains a register of organisations who store and process *personal data*. Organisations that need to store and process personal data must notify the commissioner that they want to be included in the register. The organisation must provide:

✳ the name and address of the person(s) within the organisation identified as the *data controller*

✳ a description of the data to be processed

✳ a description of the purpose of processing the data

✳ details of anyone that the data may be disclosed to

✳ details of any countries outside the European Union (EU) that the data may be transferred to

✳ The organisation must also describe the security measures they will take to protect the data.

> ### Key terms
>
> *Personal data*: data that relates to a living individual who can be identified from the data on its own or from the data along with other information held.
> *Data controller*: the person(s) who determines how and for what purpose personal data will be used.
> *Data subjects*: the individuals whose information is stored and processed.

The Act contains a number of principles that organisations must follow when storing and processing data and the rights that *data subjects* have. In the Act these are described in detailed legal terms but in essence the eight principles are:

1 data must be collected and processed fairly and lawfully

2 data may be collected and used only for one or more specified and lawful purpose

3 data must be adequate, relevant and not excessive for the purpose

4 data must be accurate and up to date

5 data must not be kept longer than necessary

6 data must be processed in accordance with the rights of the data subjects

7 data must be kept secure against unauthorised or unlawful processing and accidental loss, damage or destruction

8 data must not be transferred to countries outside the EU unless the country provides adequate levels of protection in relation to the processing of personal data.

The rights that individuals have under the Act include:

* the right of access to personal data – the individual must apply to the data controller in writing and will, in most cases, have to pay a fee

* the right to prevent processing that is likely to cause damage or distress

* the right to prevent processing for the purposes of direct marketing – when data is collected by organisations, there is a box to tick either for you to agree that the data can be used for marketing purposes or for you to indicate that it cannot

* the right to have inaccurate data corrected, blocked, erased or destroyed.

Individuals also have rights in relation to decisions that are made automatically; for example, when scores are given for particular criteria and the decision is based on the individual's overall score. If such a decision would significantly affect the individual, for example their work performance or creditworthiness, the individual must be told that the decision was made automatically. The individual can then ask for the decision to be reconsidered.

There are some areas that are exempt from some or all of these principles and rights. This includes areas such as national security, crime and taxation. Some data is termed sensitive personal data in the Act. This is often called confidential information. It includes data about a person's racial or ethnic origin, political opinions, religious beliefs, physical or mental health or any offences the person has committed. There are additional requirements in the Act about processing this type of data.

The Data Protection Act clearly affects all organisations in many ways. All organisations will hold data about their employees; many will hold data about customers or other individuals. The organisation will need to ensure that they register the data with the Data Protection Commissioner and that they take the necessary steps to comply with the requirements of the Act.

Think it over...

In a group, develop a list of all the different organisations that may hold personal data about you and your family. Try to find examples of data collection forms. Look at the 'small print' and discuss how this relates to the Data Protection Act (1998).

Knowledge check

Francefilez collects and processes personal data about the customers who advertise properties for rent. Describe what the company must do to comply with the requirements of the Data Protection Act (1998).

Copyright, Designs and Patents Act (1980)

In the 'Standard ways of working' section of Unit 1, we discussed the need to stop people copying original work and presenting it as their own. At that point, we mentioned the Copyright, Designs and Patents Act (1980). This Act essentially gives the creator of a piece of work ownership of it. For example, the copyright to this unit is owned by the author because it was written by her. If you look in the front of the book you will see the symbol © with the author's name after it. As well as written work like books, the Act applies to many different types of work, including computer programs, drama, music, art, sound recording, films, and radio and television broadcasts. Even the way the pages of this book are arranged and the different font styles are covered by this Act.

The Act makes the copyright owner the only person who can, for example, copy or adapt the work or issue copies to the public. Other people can do these things only with the permission of the copyright owner. For example, where I have used work that other people have created, such as the *Firepower* newsletter in Unit 1, I have had to obtain permission to use it and, in some cases, Heinemann will have had to pay the owner of the copyright to use the work.

There is a widely held assumption that information and, in particular, graphics that are downloaded from the WWW are copyright free. This is not the case – you should assume that anything that has been created has copyright unless there is a specific statement to the contrary. However, the Copyright, Designs and Patents Act (1980) is very complex and does allow some copyrighted material to be used for educational purposes. On this basis, you are unlikely to be breaking the law if you use a downloaded image in one of your assignments.

One type of work that is covered by this Act is a computer program. When you buy a computer program you are simply buying a licence to use it. The person who wrote the program owns the copyright to it (or most probably the company that he or she works for). The licence defines how the program can be used; for example, it will determine whether the program can be used on one computer or on a network and how many people can use it at any one time. A network licence for 30 users will allow the program to be installed on the network server, but only 30 people will be able to use it simultaneously. If you buy a computer program, it is most likely to be licensed for a single user. On this basis, if you make a copy and give it to someone else, you are breaking the law.

The Copyright Designs and Patents Act will affect organisations both as users of copyrighted material and as creators of material for which they own the copyright. The organisation will need to check the copyright status of any existing information they want to use, and apply and possibly pay for permission to use it. On the other hand, they will own the copyright of anything they create and will be able to charge others for using it. The other effect will relate to the use of computer software: the organisation will need to ensure that they purchase the appropriate licences and check that no more than the specified number of people are using it at any one time.

> **Knowledge check**
>
> Describe how the Copyright, Designs and Patents Act (1980) affects Francefilez.

Computer Misuse Act (1990)

The Copyright, Designs and Patents Act is a fairly old Act that has been updated to take into account the changes in technology that have taken place. The Computer Misuse Act (1990), on the other hand, is an Act that has been formulated to overcome problems that have occurred specifically as a result of the increased use of ICT. When we were considering the Data Protection Act, we said that people could access and steal personal information remotely. The same obviously applies to any other data that is stored on computer. The term 'hacking' is used to describe the unauthorised access to computer files, usually for malicious purposes, and the people who do this are known as hackers. Before the Computer Misuse Act became law in 1990, if hackers were caught, it was very difficult for them to be prosecuted under the existing laws.

The other problem that has become prevalent due to the widespread use of ICT is the spread of *computer viruses*. Again, it was difficult to prosecute the people responsible under the existing legislation.

The Computer Misuse Act (1990) makes it illegal to:

* gain unauthorised access to computer material

* gain unauthorised access to computer material with the intent to commit further offences

* carry out unauthorised modification of computer material.

The first two parts of the Act relate to hacking, while the third allows people who initiate viruses to be prosecuted. This part of the Act makes it an offence to intend to modify the content of any computer so that it impairs the operation of the computer, prevents access to programs or data, or impairs the operation of the programs or the reliability of the data – i.e. all the things that viruses can do. Also, the intent does not have to be directed at a specific computer, program or data: again, a feature of viruses. Finally, the hacker or person introducing the virus does not have to be in this country when he or she commits the offence, provided he or she has gained (or attempted to gain) unauthorised access to a computer in this country or the unauthorised modification of computer material took place in this country.

This Act is mainly designed to protect the data and computer systems within organisations, as they are most affected by hacking and viruses, both financially and in terms of the confidence of customers, other organisations and the general public.

Health and Safety at Work Act (1974)

Although the most recent version of the Health and Safety at Work Act became law in 1974, there have since been a number of regulations on health and safety that are also legal requirements. The 1974 Act sets out the duties that employers in organisations have towards their employees and members of the public relating to issues of health and safety, and the duties that employees have to themselves and each other. However, these duties require employers to do what is reasonably practical to ensure the health and safety of their workforce. In other words, the risk needs to be balanced against the time, cost and trouble of taking measures to avoid these risks and whether the measures are technically possible.

The Management of Health and Safety at Work Regulations (1999) made the requirements more explicit. The steps that employers must take include:

* carrying out an assessment of the health and safety risks

* making arrangements to implement any health and safety measures found necessary by the risk assessment

* keeping a record of any significant findings of the risk assessment and the arrangements implemented as a result (if there are 5 or more employees)

* drawing up a health and safety policy and bringing it to the attention of the employees (if there are more than 5)

* appointing competent people to help implement health and safety arrangements

* setting up emergency procedures

* providing clear information and training to employees

* co-operating with other employers who share the same workplace.

Employees also have legal duties. These include:

* taking reasonable care of their own health and safety and that of others

* co-operating with the employer on health and safety

* using work items provided, including personal protective equipment, correctly and in accordance with any training or instructions

* not interfering or misusing anything provided for their health, safety or welfare.

There are also specific health and safety regulations about working with visual display units (VDUs). These are based on and relate very closely to the EU health and safety directives that will be covered in the next section.

EU health and safety directives

In the early 1990s the EU issued a directive relating to the use of VDUs and related computer equipment. This directive gave rise to the Health and Safety (Display Screen Equipment) Regulations (1992). These regulations set out what an employer in an organisation must do to minimise the risk to employees who use computers as a significant part of their normal work. This includes employees who work at home and use a computer for a significant part of their work. This will increasingly become an issue for organisations as more employees work at home, as was suggested in the section on changes in working practices.

There are a number of things that the employer must do to comply with these regulations.

1 Analyse workstations to assess and reduce risk. This includes looking at the equipment, furniture and the working environment, as well as the job being done and any special needs of the individual member of staff.

2 Ensure workstations meet minimum requirements. This includes the provision of adjustable chairs and suitable lighting as well as tilt and swivel monitors, and sufficient workspace. These minimum requirements are detailed in the regulations.

3 Plan the employees' work so that there are breaks and changes in activity. The regulations do not specify how long or how often these should occur but do explain that, for example, short frequent breaks are better than less frequent, longer ones.

4 On request, arrange eye tests and provide spectacles if special ones are needed. Employees covered by the regulations can ask their employer to arrange and pay for an eye test. This can be repeated at regular intervals as recommended by the optician. However, the employer has to pay for spectacles only if special ones are needed.

5 Provide health and safety training and information. Employers must ensure that employees can use their workstation safely, for example by providing training in the best use of the equipment to avoid health problems. They must also give information to employees about health and safety using VDUs, including the steps they have taken to comply with the regulations.

Both the Health and Safety at Work Act and the regulations based on the EU directive clearly have a huge impact on all organisations. Even those with fewer than five employees that are exempt from some of the requirements are affected, as there are still many steps that the organisation must take to comply with the Act and regulations.

Knowledge check

From what you have read in the case study material about Source Computers UK, identify possible health and safety risks to the company's employees and explain what the employers would need to do to comply with the Health and Safety at Work Act (1974) and subsequent regulations.

Sales staff in Francefilez spend much of the day using a computer workstation. Describe how the Health and Safety (Display Screen Equipment) Regulations (1992) will affect the management and sales staff of Francefilez.

Electronic Communications Act (2000)

This Act, as its name suggests, deals with the electronic communication of information. The aim of the Act is to facilitate electronic communication and electronic data storage. One way that it does this is to set up a register of approved providers of encryption services. Encryption services involve the encoding of data so that it is unintelligible except to the people who are supposed to read it and who have the key to decode it. The second way that the Act facilitates electronic communication is by making electronic signatures legally binding.

The Electronic Communications Act (2000) will be of particular benefit to organisations that sell goods or services using e-commerce. It means that the organisation can be confident about the encryption services used to keep customers' personal and financial data secure. It also means that they can obtain electronic signatures from customers on contracts, rather than having to send hard copies of contracts for signature.

Knowledge check

Source Computers UK is planning to use e-commerce to sell computer components. Explain how the Electronic Communications Act (2000) will affect this venture.

UNIT 3

ICT solutions for individuals and society

Introduction

The access to information that has been created by the World Wide Web (WWW) has had a huge effect on society and how individuals live their lives. However, because of the huge volume of information available, finding the information you need is not always straightforward. In this unit you will learn how to search the WWW efficiently to find the information you need. You will also need to find out about the information disseminated by *public service websites*, the increased use of web-based communication by organisations and the effect this may have on people who do not have access to ICT. This unit will help you to find information from databases, use spreadsheets to analyse numerical information and to present the results of investigations and analysis effectively. You will also prepare a report on the sources and methods used to find information.

> **Key term**
>
> *Public service websites*: websites of organisations such as government departments, that provide services to the public.

How you will be assessed

This unit will be assessed on a portfolio of evidence which you will provide. The Assignment Evidence at the end of this unit gives you the ability to develop a portfolio.

By studying this unit you will be able to:

* select *search engines* and use them efficiently to find the information required

* understand the impact of the availability of electronic information on individuals and society

* access information from large websites

* use databases to find required information

* use spreadsheet software to analyse numerical data and present results

* combine different types of data to present the results of an investigation

* evaluate the methods you use to find information and present the results.

Key term

Search engines: computer programs that search a database to find the information required, either within a website or on the WWW.

Public-service websites

Public-service organisations, as the name suggests, are organisations that provide services to the general public, most of which have a presence on the WWW. These include:

* government, both local and national

* information services, e.g. libraries, museums, directory enquiries

* emergency services, e.g. RNLI

* the National Health Service

* education

* transport

* broadcasting.

Later we will discuss some of the information available from these large sites. You will need to access and explore the sites yourself to fully

appreciate the information they contain and the facilities they offer. You will also need to download the required information.

Navigating large websites

Many of the public-service websites are very large. Luckily, most provide a range of tools to help visitors find the information they need. It would after all be rather pointless to have a website if people cannot easily find what they are looking for. These tools include navigational bars, textual hotspots, directories and internal search engines.

Navigation bars

A navigation bar usually appears across the top of the web page. It provides links to the main areas of the site and is always visible whichever page you are viewing. For example, the BBC website has a navigation bar that includes tabs for Home, TV, Radio, Talk, Where I Live and A to Z Index. If you want to find out what is on television tonight, for example, a good place to start would be to click on the TV tab to go to the main TV page. Because the navigation bar is always visible, it is always possible to get back to the homepage or any of the other main pages.

Textual hotspots

Textual hotspots are words within a web page that, when clicked on, take you to another part of the site, or even to an external site. As you move the mouse around the web pages, the mouse pointer will change to a hand to indicate a textual hotspot. The text itself will appear underlined as the mouse is hovered over it. The text will indicate what the linked page will contain. For example, clicking on 'find a local school' on the Directgov website will take you to a page that explains how you can go about finding a local school by entering a postcode, with a further textual hotspot linking to the external site that allows you to do this.

Directories

Many large websites provide alphabetical lists of the topics covered by the website. The Directgov website has an A to Z of central government,

FIGURE 3.1 *Navigation bar on the Directgov website*

as well as an A to Z of local councils (see Figures 3.1–3.2).

Rather than having all the entries in one long list, there is a list of letters of the alphabet. By clicking on the first letter of the department you are looking for, you are taken to a page listing just departments starting with that letter. Clicking on E will list Education and Skills and the Environment Agency amongst others. The alphabetical index on the BBC's website lists a mixture of topics and programme titles. Some of the lists for individual letters may still be quite

long and you will need to scroll down to find what you want. On very large websites there may be a second level of index. In this case, if you click on M, say, in the main index, you will be presented with a second list that includes the second letter, i.e. Ma to Mz.

Internal search engines

Most websites of any size will include a search engine that enables you to find what you are looking for. This may be just a simple search, where you type in a keyword and click on the

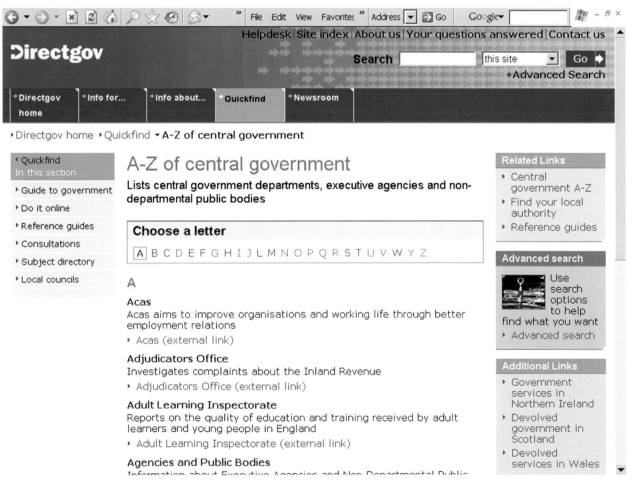

FIGURE 3.2 *A to Z of central government from the Directgov website*

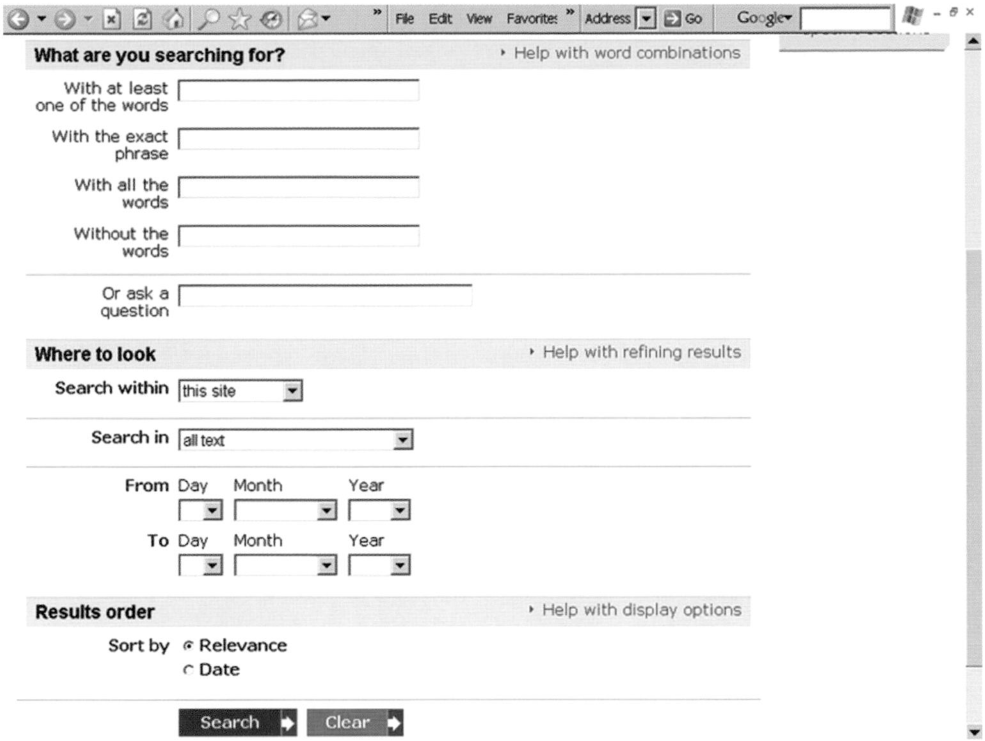

FIGURE 3.3 *Advanced search options on the Directgov website*

search button, or an advanced search facility may be provided. The Directgov site provides such an advanced search facility (see Figure 3.3).

It is possible to search for pages that include at least one word from a list, an exact phrase, all the words in a list or do not include a word. You can also choose where you want to search and to search for pages published between specified dates. Where you want to find specific information, using the search engine will probably be the most efficient method.

Downloading the information you require

When you have found the information you require you need to download it onto your computer so that you can access it without being connected to the Internet. One way to do this is to add the page to your favourites list, and select the option to 'Make available offline' (see Figure 3.4).

FIGURE 3.4 *Add to Favourites dialog*

This will allow you to view the whole web page in your web browser as if you were still connected to the Internet. However, you will not be able to move to other pages by clicking on the links. Individual elements of web pages can be saved, copied or printed. Right-clicking on a picture will bring up a list of options that include save as, print and copy. These will allow you to save the picture in your user area, print it out or paste it into a document. If you highlight a section of text and right-click on it, the options will include print and copy, allowing you to print out the text or copy it into a document.

National and local government

A huge range of information is available from government websites. At the time of writing, Direct.gov.uk is a means of accessing any other government website, both national and local (see Figure 3.5). You can find information about local schools, health, employment or motoring; you can search for jobs, find a course or even take a mock theory driving test. A facility offered by the site is to locate and complete government forms on-line. This would allow someone to complete their tax return on-line, for example.

FIGURE 3.5 *The Directgov homepage*

There is an A to Z of central government that provides links to many further sites. Under C you will find a link to the census for 2001 and to that for 1901. Here you can find out about a wide range of population statistics either for the area in which you live, or nationally. The A to Z of local government allows easy access to the website of your local council where you can find out more about the services in your local area.

Information services

Museums' websites will provide information on opening times, current and future exhibitions and any events that they are staging. They will most likely also enable you to view some of their exhibits on-line. In some cases this may take the form of a virtual tour of the museum or video clips.

Library websites will allow visitors to search the library's catalogue to locate books. They may also provide other services such as links to virtual libraries of resources that can be accessed for research or even libraries of electronic images that can be downloaded. The British Library website has a section of virtual books. These are interactive images of some of the many old and precious books that they hold. The software allows you to turn the pages of the book and there is both a text and audio commentary on what you are looking at.

There are many different directory enquiries services available on the WWW. Some of these enable you to find the telephone numbers of individuals or businesses by entering their name and address, or postcode. Others allow you to find contact details of businesses, either by entering the name of the business or by searching for the category of business and the area. Such websites also offer additional services, for example providing maps and directions to show you how to get to the business or even a car park finder so that you know where best to park your car when visiting the business.

Theory into practice

– museums

Access the websites of some museums to find out what services they offer. The British Museum (www.thebritishmuseum.ac.uk), the Natural History Museum (www.nhm.ac.uk) and the Science Museum (www.sciencemuseum.org.uk) are all worth looking at and you will find many more – try typing the word museum into a search engine. Find out the web address of your local library or follow the links to it from your local council's website. What information and facilities does it provide? Finally, visit some directory enquiries websites to see what they have to offer.

Emergency services

The emergency services such as the fire brigade, police and the RNLI (Royal National Lifeboat Institution) provide information to the public about the work that they do and the services they offer. This may include news of recent events or, in the case of the RNLI the ability to see which of their lifeboats has been launched within the last 24 hours. Such sites will also offer information and advice on safety issues, for example how to prevent fires, or the importance of installing a smoke alarm. They will also have a section for those people who want to join the service, explaining what the work involves, what qualities are needed and how to apply.

Theory into practice

– emergency services

Access the RNLI website (www.rnli.org.uk) and a fire service or other emergency service website. Find out the type of information and facilities they provide.

The National Health Service

The National Health Service (NHS) website has a section called NHS Direct. This site offers a wide range of information on medical and health issues. It includes a health encyclopaedia, a self-help guide and a frequently asked questions section. You can also send an enquiry if you cannot find the answer to your problem on the site. The self-help guide takes you through a series of questions about the symptoms you have and will then offer advice about the best way to treat the condition. The encyclopaedia enables you to search for information on different medical conditions alphabetically or by subject, while the frequently asked questions section allows you find the answer to questions on a variety of health-related topics. However, NHS Direct is just part of the wider NHS site which offers information on all aspects of the service. Here you can find details of doctors in your area or which dentists are currently registering NHS patients, for example.

Theory into practice

– the NHS

Investigate the NHS and the NHS Direct websites to find out what information they provide.

Education

There are many organisations that come under the title of education and that provide information on websites. If you look under E on the Directgov website you will find links to many educational organisations such as the Department for Education and Skills (DfES), the Qualifications and Curriculum Authority (QCA) and the Office for Standards in Education (OFSTED). All of these organisations offer information for governors, teachers, parents, students and other people on a whole range of educational issues. The DfES website (see Figure 3.6) has links to a database of the educational establishments in England and Wales that can be searched on a variety of criteria.

As well as these large organisations, other educational organisations also provide information on their websites. These will include awarding bodies, like OCR, who provide details of all the qualifications they offer, local education authorities (LEAs) who provide details of their services, and individual schools and colleges who use a website to advertise their facilities and the courses they offer.

Theory into practice

– education

Access the websites of some educational organisations, including your school's or college's website if they have one. Compare the information each provides and consider the different audiences that the information is aimed at.

Transport

Organisations that provide information on transport include National Rail. The National Rail Enquiries site offers information about the whole rail network in the UK. If you need to make a journey, you can enter where you are travelling to and from, and the date and time you want to

FIGURE 3.6 *Establishment finder on the DfES website*

travel. The site will then provide you with details of the trains that are available and any changes you may need to make. You can also find out if there are any disruptions to train services, such as engineering works, and even access live information about departure times from a particular station that can be updated every two minutes! The individual train operators also operate their own websites. Information about flight arrivals and departures, and airport facilities such as car parking can be found on the British Airport Authority (BAA) website and other airport websites, along with a wide range of other information. Information about bus and coach travel can be found on websites run by coach companies such as National Express Coaches. If you are travelling to London, the Transport for London website (www.tfl.gov.uk) provides a journey planner that includes bus, tube and train information.

For those travelling by car, there are several organisations that provide information on the UK's road network. For example, the Highways Agency site (see Figure 3.7) has an interactive map that shows where there are any problems such as roadworks or accidents on roads in England – there is a similar site for the Welsh Highways Agency.

The motoring organisations such as the AA and the RAC also provide information on road traffic conditions as well as a host of other services such as route planning.

Theory into practice

– transport

Access some websites of transport-related organisations. How would they help if you were planning a journey? Which types of organisation would benefit most from the Highways Agency website? How might organisations use other transport-related websites?

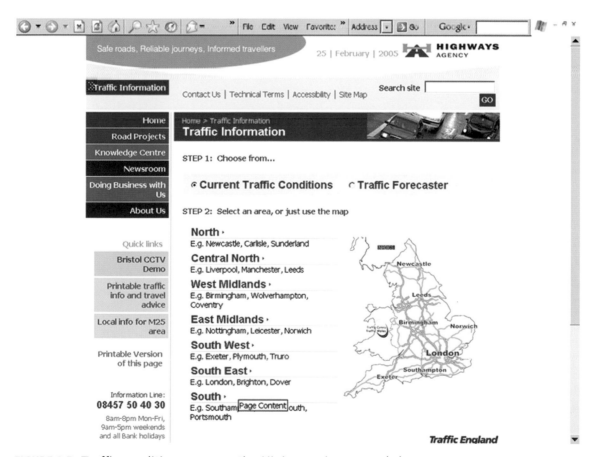

FIGURE 3.7 *Traffic conditions map on the Highways Agency website*

Broadcasting

The BBC, ITV, Channel 4, Sky and many other broadcasting organisations have their own websites. As well as providing information about forthcoming television or radio programmes, most offer a huge amount of information on a wide range of topics. For example, when you were taking your GCSEs you may have used the Bitesize revision guides section of the BBC website to help you. These sites also contain up-to-the-minute news from around the world, the latest weather forecast for your location, the latest sports news and information on a whole range of topics. On the BBC site you can also listen to live radio or to a previous radio programme you missed or want to hear again.

Theory into practice

– broadcasting

Access the websites of different broadcasting companies and investigate the information and facilities each offers. Are there information and facilities that they all provide? What is different about them?

Impact of the availability of information

Anyone who has access to the WWW can access information on almost any topic imaginable; they can also, for example, bank, shop and apply for jobs on-line.

News

In the past, if you wanted to find out about the news, you would read a newspaper, listen to the radio or watch the television news broadcasts. With newspapers, there is an inevitable delay between the story being written and the paper arriving on the counter in the newsagents or through your letterbox. Television and radio news will be up to date but, if you miss something or do not understand, there is no way of going back

to hear or see it again. Also, the finite time available for the broadcast is likely to mean that only the most important news is covered. By accessing news on-line, it is as up to date as broadcast news but without the time restrictions of a programme slot and with the possibility of revisiting the information as many times as necessary. Also, whereas newspapers and broadcast news may concentrate on stories that particularly relate to people in this country or cover them from this country's perspective, on the WWW you can access news from all over the world and from other people's perspectives. This gives individuals the opportunity to gain a more balanced view of what is happening in the world than they would have otherwise. This may eventually lead to a more tolerant society, but this seems a long way off.

National and local government websites

Access to national and local government websites makes it easier for people to find out about issues that affect their daily lives. As this is being written, there is a problem regarding a banned additive that has found its way into a wide range of prepared foods. A visit to the Food Standards Agency website has quickly provided a list of all the foods that have been affected and which should not be eaten. Parents choosing which primary or secondary school their child will attend can access information on performance tables, read OfSTED reports and find the contact details of schools in their area. This increased availability of information can lead to some schools becoming over-subscribed, while others suffer from falling pupil numbers.
It can also lead to increased pressure on schools and teachers to improve performance. In some areas, parents have been known to move house, with an associated increase in house prices, so that their children can go to a popular high-performing school.

Banking

Banking is another area that has been hugely affected by the WWW. Where in the past you would know the state of your account only when you received your monthly statement or if you went into your branch to ask, now you can gain access to your bank statement on-line at any time and from anywhere. You can also transfer money between your own accounts, transfer money to other people's accounts and pay bills. These are all tasks that in the past could be done only by going into the bank branch or writing and posting a cheque. Internet banking means that individuals are much better informed about their financial position and can manage their money much more easily.

Travel

Travel too has been affected by the availability of information on-line. In the past, information on train times, for example, was available only from often complex printed train timetables or by telephoning the rail enquiries service. Similarly, information on any disruption to services could be obtained only from notices in affected stations or from the rail enquiries telephone line, which was often busy. The National Rail Enquiries website and those of the individual train operators can provide all this information in an easy-to-access way. Instead of having to locate information in complex timetables and having to work out any connections yourself, you can simply enter the start and end points of the journey and the date and time you want to travel. The website will then provide details of suitable trains, how long it will take and where you need to change trains. Some sites then allow you to book tickets on-line, often at reduced prices. When travelling by car, websites allow you to plan your route to avoid roadworks and you can check before leaving whether there are any accidents or traffic congestion that will affect your journey.

On-line shopping

As well as train tickets, you can buy almost anything on-line. Groceries, clothes, furniture, toys, films and much more can be bought from websites offering e-commerce. As well as this, auction sites allow individuals to sell items on the WWW. On-line shopping offers many benefits to consumers. You can shop around for the best price without wasting shoe leather or petrol visiting different stores. People who are housebound or have difficulty getting to shops can buy on-line and have their purchases delivered to their door. Companies often offer extra discount to on-line shoppers, saving them more money. Also, you are not limited to the shops available in your local area; you can buy goods from companies located anywhere in the country or even overseas.

There are, however, some limitations to shopping on-line. You will almost always have to supply a credit or debit card number to pay for your purchases, making the experience of shopping on-line out of reach to people who do not have one. Some people are also concerned about the security of their personal and credit card details being transmitted. Particularly with auction sites, you may not be sure whether what you have bought will arrive or not, or whether it will be what you expected – although most auction sites have safeguards against this. You can see only the pictures of the goods on-screen, you cannot handle them or, in the case of clothes, try them on. However, most websites will allow you to return the goods if they do not meet your requirements, often without charge. The increase in on-line shopping also affects society. The more people shop on-line, the less they visit high street shops. This may result in the closure of some high street outlets, resulting in less choice for those who do not have access to on-line shopping. This may also result in a reduction in the number of retail jobs, but the number of jobs in other areas, such as courier services will increase.

Impact on methods of communication

Increased access to the WWW has led to changes in the way that organisations communicate with their clients or customers and with society in general. The prime minister has said that all priority public services, both national and local, should be available on-line by the end of 2005. There is currently an e-government unit that is responsible for ensuring that this target is met. One of their initiatives was the Directgov website that we discussed earlier in this unit. Already it is possible to carry out a range of communications with central and local government departments on-line. Until this year (2004/5), voter registration forms had to be completed by hand and posted back to the local council. This year the process could be completed on-line by visiting the local council's website. It is also possible to apply for a passport, book a driving test, complete your tax return and pay for a TV licence on-line. You can even report a minor crime on-line. In the local elections of 2002, some councils piloted e-voting, allowing people to cast their vote on a secure website. Such pilots are likely to become more widespread in future, partly as it is felt this will encourage more younger people to cast their vote.

Key term

Utility companies: companies that provide utilities such as water, electricity, gas and telephone services.

It is not just government that is increasingly using web-based communication. Utility companies too are encouraging customers to communicate with them on-line. Gas and electricity companies offer self-read schemes, where customers take their own meter reading and send it in. Often, extra discounts are offered if the reading is input on the company's website. Such companies are also offering customers on-line billing. This means that, rather than receiving a paper bill, when the bill is due the customer is sent an email so that they can visit the company's website and view and pay their bill on-line. All of these communications initiatives save the companies money. If readings are submitted on-line, the companies do not have to pay someone to enter them, while electronic bills reduce the cost of paper to print them and postage to send them. Banks too are offering the option of not sending paper statements through the post to those who bank on-line.

Effects on people who do not have access to ICT

Figures from the Office of National Statistics show that, by the end of 2003, 49 per cent of households in the UK had home access to the Internet. However, when this is broken down by income,

only 12 per cent of those in the lowest income band have home access, while the figure is 85 per cent for the highest income band. Age too is a factor when it comes to Internet access. Although by July 2004, 60 per cent of adults said that they had used the Internet, for 16- to 24-year-olds this figure is 91 per cent, falling to 50 per cent for 55- to 64-year-olds, and below 20 per cent for those who are 65 or older. Whilst these figures have increased rapidly since 1998 (only 9 per cent of households had home Internet access at that time), the increase has been slowest for the lowest income households and the oldest individuals.

If national and local government are increasingly offering on-line services, it is the people who are most likely to need those services who do not have access to ICT and the Internet. Earlier in this section, we mentioned a problem with an illegal additive getting into a wide range of prepared foods. Although this was widely reported in the press and on television, most of these reports referred people to the Food Agency's website to find out exactly which products were affected. This clearly has implications for those people who do not have Internet access. Current affairs programmes on the television, when discussing issues that are important to the less advantaged members of society then refer viewers to a website for further information. Again, it is the people who would benefit most from this information who are least likely to have access to it.

Alongside the push to get public services on-line, there are initiatives to provide Internet access to those who do not have it at home. An initiative in England and Wales called 'The People's Network' aims to make sure that every public library in England and Wales is linked to the Internet and has enough funding for computers so that people can access the Internet in their local library. Another initiative called 'everybodyonline' aims to increase access to ICT and the Internet in disadvantaged communities across the country. However, such initiatives also need to overcome people's resistance to using the Internet. The latest available figures from the Office of National Statistics (July 2004) show that 48 per cent of people who have never used the

Internet do not want to, need to or have an interest in doing so, while a further 14 per cent felt it offered no benefits to them. Only 37 per cent cited not having an Internet connection as the reason for not using it. All of the figures quoted here are the latest available at the time of writing. By the time you read this, the situation may have changed. You can check this out for yourself by going to the Office of National Statistics' website. There is a link under S on the Directgov website.

Think it over...

When you have spent some time investigating public-service websites, discuss in a group the types of information available and how access to this information might affect individuals and society. Carry out your own survey to find out who uses/has access to the Internet and who does not. Compare your findings to the figures nationally. Discuss in your group the impact on people who do not have access to ICT of the increased use of the Internet by organisations to communicate information.

Search engines

The WWW can be a powerful tool when used for searching for information, especially when search engines are utilised correctly.

What is a search engine?

A search engine is a computer program that searches a very large database to locate the information required. We have already said that large websites, such as the Directgov website, have search engines that allow you to search the site for the information you need. There are similar search engines that allow you to search the WWW to find specific information. The databases for these search engines contain extracts from millions of web pages, along with associated keywords and the location of each page. In most cases, the data on the different web pages is collected automatically using programs that search the WWW for new sites and add them to the database. The BBC website, as well as providing a search engine to search within the site, also allows searches to be made of the WWW. In this case, there is some human intervention in determining the content of the database, both in checking that inappropriate sites are not included and in providing a list of recommended sites.

Search engines allow you to find web pages via their content. When you type what you want to find into the search engine, the database is searched to find all the pages containing the word(s) you have entered. The search engine will then display extracts from the pages found that contain these word(s), and hyperlinks to take you to the page. The pages will be listed by the number of 'hits' they have received, with the most popular first. If you enter two or more words, the search engine may return pages that contain the words separately, rather than as you typed them, pages with the words in a different order, or pages that contain only some of the words. For example, a search for plant house returned pages about houseplants, several references to House of Commons/Lords proceedings that mentioned plant, and even a page on the history of astrology where the author's surname was Plant and the text included the word house. One way to overcome this is to put speech marks round the phrase that you want to find. Searching for 'plant house' reduced the number of hits from over a million to just under 2000, all of which included the exact phrase plant house. We will consider other ways of adding precision to searches later in this section.

The range of search engines

There are a number of different web search engines, for example Google, Yahoo, Alta Vista, Ask Jeeves, to name but a few. These are all general search engines that can be used to search for any topic. Ask Jeeves is a little different from the other three, as it allows you to actually type a question such as 'how do you create a website'. This will return a list of references related to building a website. If you enter a question that asks 'what is...' a definition may also be provided, while questions that ask 'who was/is...' may provide a picture and some biographical details about the person. As well as these general search engines, there are specialist search engines, for example for scientific material, fine arts, music downloads, shopping, and many other areas. Some search engines are designed specifically for children, while others combine results from a number of different search engines. There are also search engines that relate to specific countries. Most websites return the results in a similar way, but there is at least one search engine that displays the results as a sort of mind map that allows you to narrow down the search by selecting topics.

Theory into practice

– search engines

Try typing 'search engine' into your favourite search engine to find some alternatives. Try doing the same thing with some other search engines. Do you get the same results?

Results from different search engines

The results you get from different search engines will depend on the database used. Some search engines, known as meta-search engines, do not have their own database of web pages. Instead, they transmit your search to several individual search engines and their databases. You then get back results from all the search engine databases queried. This should, in theory, give better results than searches using an individual search engine. However, meta-search engines do not always have access to the largest and most useful search engine databases, relying instead on small free search engines and directories which give fewer results. Table 3.1 shows the results obtained from different search engines when the same search was carried out. In all cases, the text entered was Pentium 4 system.

SEARCH ENGINE	NUMBER OF HITS
Google	9,180,000
Yahoo	11,700,000
MSN	2,351,796
Ask Jeeves	1,978,000
WebCrawler	76
Dogpile	84

TABLE 3.1 *Search engine results*

The most striking difference is that the first four of these have hit rates measured in millions, while the last two returned less than 100 hits each. The first four are all individual search engines with their own databases; the last two are both meta-search engines.

Which search engine is best?

Which search engine you use for which purpose is, to some extent, a matter of personal preference. However, as we have just discovered, the results from different search engines are not all the same. Some things to consider when choosing which search engine to use include the subject area you are searching for, what type of media you are searching for and where you are located in the world or which part of the world you want to find out about. If you want to find out about anything that is UK-based, you need to make sure that you use a UK-based search engine, or the UK version of an international one. If you choose google.co.uk rather than google.com, ask.co.uk rather than ask.com or uk.yahoo.com rather than just yahoo.com, you will access the UK version of each search engine and will be given the option to just search UK pages. This means, for example, that if you search for 'football' you will get results relating only to soccer, rather than to American football. The best way to find out which search engine to use is to try the same search in different search engines to find which gives the most useful results.

To add precision to a search you will need to use facilities such as logical operators and advanced search options.

Logical operators (AND, OR, NOT)

Logical operators are AND, OR and NOT. These can be used to add precision to the searches you make using search engines. The way that they work can best be described using an example. This is shown in Table 3.2. All searches were carried out using google.co.uk, searching UK-based sites only.

Using the AND operator narrows down the search. The more words you include, the narrower the search becomes. The OR operator, on the other hand, widens the search. In some search engines, such as Google, it is not necessary to actually enter the word AND between search words, as the search engine includes all the search terms entered by default. In other words, it assumes that you want all the words you type

SEARCH CRITERION	WHAT IT LOOKS FOR	NUMBER OF HITS
Museum	Any pages that contain the word museum	7,540,000
Museum AND science	Pages that contain both the words museum AND science	3,410,000
Museum AND science AND technology	Pages that contain all three search words	1,120,000
Museum AND science AND technology AND London	Pages that contain all four search words	479,000
Museum AND science AND technology AND London AND industry	Pages that contain all five search words	267,000
Museum AND science AND technology AND London AND industry AND medicine	Pages that contain all six search words	158,000
Museum AND science NOT technology	Pages that contain the words museum AND science but NOT the word technology	1,980,000
Museum OR technology	Pages that contain either the word museum OR the word technology	18,900,000

TABLE 3.2 *The effect of using logical operators*

in to appear on all the hits. In other search engines you may need to use the operator if you want only pages containing all the words you enter. The other point to note from the table is that Google uses a minus sign to represent the NOT operator. This is also the case with some other search engines.

Advanced search options

Another way of adding precision to searches is to use the advanced search options offered by the search engine. You have already seen an example of an advanced search option within the Directgov website. Web search engines offer similar advanced options.

Some of the options offered in the advanced search on google.co.uk (see Figure 3.8) are the same as using the logical operators we have just been looking at. The option 'with all the words' is the same as the AND operator. Earlier we mentioned putting speech marks around two or more words to ensure that results contained only

the exact phrase. The option 'with the exact phrase' has the same effect. The option 'with at least one of the words' is the same as using the OR operator, while 'without the words' is the same as using the NOT operator.

As well as these logical options, search engines offer further advanced options to help you make your search more precise. For example, you can request that **only** pages written in a particular language are returned, for example only those written in English. You can request that the search engine returns only results that have a particular file format, for example only those in Rich Text Format (.rtf) or Adobe Acrobat format (.pdf), or you can request that results **do not** have a particular file format. As it is very easy to find information that is out of date on the WWW, a useful option is to request that the search engine returns only results that have been updated in a specified period, for example in the past three months, six months or year. You can choose where on the web pages your search term must appear,

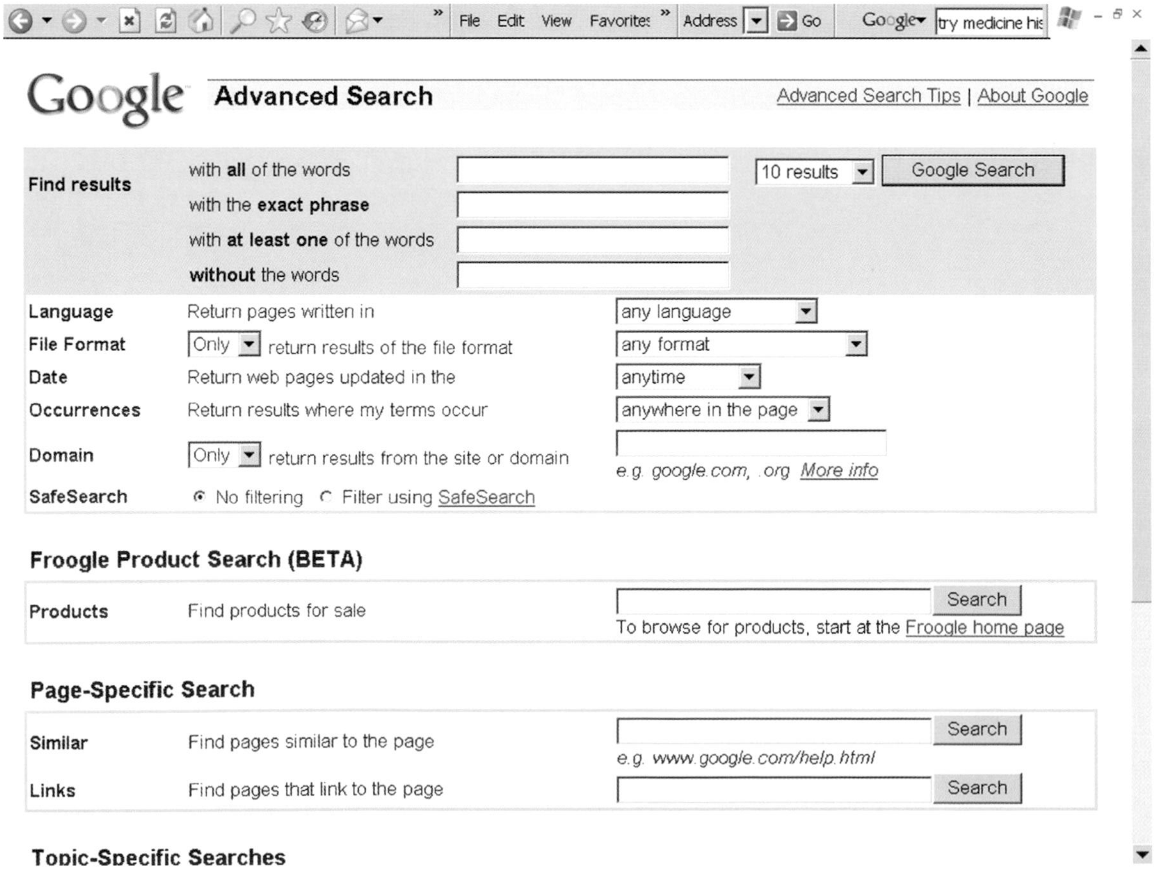

FIGURE 3.8 *Advanced search option in google.co.uk*

for example in the title, in the text or in the *URL*. You can request that only a particular site or a particular domain is searched, for example search only direct.gov.uk, or only sites that have the domain .ac.uk. You can also exclude particular sites or domains from your search. Although the advanced options described are those offered by google.co.uk, most other search engines will offer similar options, although these may appear in a different way. Advanced search options may also offer the facility to filter the search results so that inappropriate websites are not included.

Theory into practice

– logical operators

Use logical operators to carry out searches for information on the WWW. Compare the advanced search options offered by different search engines. Use the advanced search options in different search engines to search for information. Compare the results obtained using similar options in different search engines to carry out the same search.

✷ REMEMBER!

* ✷ Search engines are computer programs that allow large databases to be searched to find the information required.

* ✷ Web search engines use databases that include extracts from millions of web pages.

* ✷ There are many different search engines available, which may generate different results from the same search.

* ✷ When choosing a search engine, you should consider subject area, media and location.

* ✷ Facilities exist to add precision to searches, including logical operators (AND, OR, NOT) and advanced search options.

Databases

A database is simply a collection of data stored on a computer system in some organised way so that it is easy to retrieve information based on particular search criteria. We have already discovered that search engines use databases to locate information and that some websites include databases that can be searched, for example the educational establishment database on the DfES website. These are large on-line databases. Organisations use databases to store personnel records (see Figure 3.9), customer records, stock records, etc. The size of these databases will depend on the size of the organisation. They will most probably be stored on the server of the organisation's network. Although you do not have to know how to create a database for this unit, you may have created your own databases in the past, or your teacher may provide databases that are stored locally for you to search. These are likely to be relatively small databases. You may also find databases stored on CD-ROM.

In order to search databases effectively, you need to know something about how databases are structured. A database consists of one or

	Field Name	Data Type
🔑	EmployeeID	AutoNumber
	Surname	Text
	First Name	Text
	Addr1	Text
	Addr2	Text
	Addr3	Text
	Post-code	Text
	Tel No	Text
	Position	Text
	Contract	Text
	Plumber/ Carpenter/ Electrician	Text
	Annual Salary	Currency
	Normal hours	Number
	Hourly rate	Currency
	Overtime rate	Currency
▶	Commission Rate	Text
	Date of Birth	Date/Time
	N I Number	Text
	Tax Code	Text
	Holiday Entitlement	Number
	Pension Scheme	Yes/No

FIGURE 3.9 *Fields in a personnel database*

two. To reach mark band three you will need to explain in detail how organisations communicate with individuals and society and how this affects those who don't have (or want) access to ICT.

This task will be used to assess the quality of your written communication so you should ensure that your report is well structured and contains few, if any, errors in spelling, grammar and punctuation.

Task C

Access information from large public-service websites.

If you need some help to find the information you need, you will reach only mark band one. To reach mark band two you will need to be able to find the information without help using menus, navigation bars, alphabetical indexes and textual hyperlinks. If you can also use an internal search engine you will be able to reach mark band three.

Task D

Use databases to find information.

As a minimum you must use search criteria that involve relational operators to get information from at least one database, either local or on-line. If you can use complex search criteria that also involve logical operators, get information from both local and on-line databases and present the results, for example in a table, you will achieve mark band two. To reach the highest mark band, you must also be able to present your results as reports.

Task E

Use spreadsheet software to analyse numerical data and present results. You could, for example, find data on Internet access and individuals' use of on-line shopping on the WWW. You could also carry out a survey to find similar information for your local area and compare the results.

As a minimum, you must create a suitable spreadsheet layout and use it to carry out simple analysis of the data. You must present the output on screen or on paper and use cell formats, charts

or graphs, page or screen layout and graphic images appropriately. If you are able to carry out more complex analysis that shows you have a good understanding of spreadsheet formulae and functions and use macros to speed up data input and the production of results, you will reach mark band two. To reach mark band three, your spreadsheet must be well designed and you must test it thoroughly to make sure your results are accurate.

Task F

Combine different types of data to present the results of your investigation.

As a minimum your report must combine at least two different types of data from a small number of sources (2 or 3). You must also list the sources you use. To reach mark band two your report must combine at least three different types of data from a number of different sources (4 to 6) and you must list the sources appropriately. There should be enough detail for someone else to find the information. To reach the highest mark band, your presentation must be well thought out and coherent. You must combine a range of data from a wide range of sources (more than 6) and list your sources in a detailed bibliography.

Task G

Evaluate the methods you used to find information and present results.
You need to consider:

* what worked well – what was good about the methods you used

* what did not work – what was not so good

* how well did your methods achieve the required results?

* how did you refine your initial methods to meet the purpose more closely?

* how would you improve the methods you used if you had to do a similar task in the future?

As a minimum you must comment on how effective the methods you used were for finding the information and presenting results. If you clearly identify good and not so good features of the methods you used, you will reach mark band two. To reach the highest mark band you must show that you have identified strengths and weaknesses in the methods you used originally and how you refined these methods to meet the purpose more closely. You must also suggest how you might approach a similar task in future.

Signposting for portfolio evidence

In this assignment, the methods you use to find and analyse information are as important as the content of the presentation. As well as the presentation itself, you will need to make sure that you provide screen prints to show the search methods you have used and evidence of how you created and tested your spreadsheet. For example, you should include a formula printout. Currently, all of your evidence must be produced on paper. If you have created a screen-based presentation, you will need to provide screen prints or printouts to evidence your work. You will need to annotate these to indicate any features, such as animation or hyperlinks that are not obvious from the printouts. You should get your teacher to witness these features and initial or sign the printouts to confirm that the features work. For example, printing out a slide presentation as an audience handout with three slides to a page will provide space for you to add any necessary annotations.

You need to organise your work carefully. Make sure each piece of work is clearly labelled to show what it is and that your name is on each page. Put your work in a logical order. This might be your report on how you found the information and analysed it, followed by your presentation, with your evaluation at the end. Alternatively, you may consider the report to be most important and put that first. When you have put all your work in a sensible order, number all the pages and create a contents page to show where each piece of work is located.

Field:	EmployeeID	Surname	First Name	Position	Annual Salary	Contract
Table:	Personnel	Personnel	Personnel	Personnel	Personnel	Personnel
Sort:						
Show:	☑	☑	☑	☑	☑	☑
Criteria:				"cashier"		"full-time"
or:						

FIGURE 3.13 *A complex search to find cashiers who have a full-time contract*

EMPLOYEE ID	SURNAME	FIRST NAME	POSITION	ANNUAL	CONTRACT
9	Croker	Susan	Cashier	£14,500.00	Full-time
15	Honiker	Samuel	Cashier	£14,500.00	Full-time

TABLE 3.4

The AND operator can be used only with criteria that relate to two or more fields. The OR operator, on the other hand, can be used to select more than one item of data from the same field. In a Microsoft Access® query, entering the criteria on different rows in the query is equivalent to the OR operator. For example, to find employees with the position Sales Grade A OR Sales Grade B requires you to enter "Sales Grade A" and "Sales Grade B" on separate rows in the position column of the query. Table 3.5 shows the results of this query.

Presenting results as a report

The results of the example queries shown so far in this section have been presented as simple tables.

Using database software, it is possible to present the results in a variety of report formats. To do this, you must first create a query; you can then use the query as the information source for the report. The easiest way to create a report is to use the report wizard but you will probably need to make adjustments to the report design in design view.

The report shown in Figure 3.14 is based on the tax code query in Figure 3.10. The report uses a technique called grouping that collects together all the information about, in this case, each position.

EMPLOYEE ID	SURNAME	FIRST NAME	POSITION	ANNUAL	CONTRACT
1	McNamara	Patrick	Sales Grade A	£18,200.00	Full-time
3	Hill	Phyllis	Sales Grade B	£20,000.00	Full-time
8	Ricketts	Diane	Sales Grade A	£17,900.00	Full-time
14	Smith	Anita	Sales Grade A	£17,900.00	Full-time
18	Abdullah	Mohammed	Sales Grade A	£17,900.00	Full-time
21	Han	Yueng	Sales Grade B	£20,700.00	Full-time

TABLE 3.5

Taxcode Query

Position	EmployeeID	Surname	First Name	Annual Salary	N I Number
Cashier					
	9	Croker	Susan	£14,500.00	LD864120V
Contractor					
	17	Nicholls	Amanda		SC567420A
	11	Findlater	Martin		RA890466D
Sales Grade A					
	8	Ricketts	Diane	£17,900.00	GW121905M
Sales Grade B					
	21	Han	Yueng	£20,700.00	HA445890D
	3	Hill	Phyllis	£20,000.00	IJ289001H
Sales Grade C					
	19	Pyrda	Nana	£21,200.00	BA560963D

FIGURE 3.14 *A report based on the tax code query, grouped by position*

Theory into practice

– reports

Practise creating some queries on a local database. Use one of the queries to create a report. First select the *Reports* tab and then select *New*. Use the drop-down list to select a query to create the report from, then select *Report Wizard* and click *Next*. Add the fields that you want to appear in your report by highlighting each one and clicking the right arrow. The double arrow will add all the fields shown to the report. *Next* will move you on to the next screen. If there are records with the same data in one or more fields you can choose to group the data, as in the example. Select the field for grouping and click the right arrow to add it. You can also choose to sort the data. Work through the screens selecting options and finally click *Finish* to see the report. You may find that some field names are not completely visible or that the layout is not easy to read because of the alignment. You can change the layout by selecting *Design View*. Experiment with the layout until you achieve the effect you want. You can keep switching between *Design View* and *Layout Preview* to see the effect of each change.

✱ REMEMBER!

* ✱ A database is an organised collection of data stored in a computer system.

* ✱ Databases can be large, small, on-line or stored locally.

* ✱ Large on-line databases usually have their own search engine or search facility with easy to follow instructions.

* ✱ Databases can be searched using a single criterion, using relational operators and using logical operators.

* ✱ If a query is created, this can be used to present the results in a variety of report formats.

Use of spreadsheet facilities

A spreadsheet is a useful tool for analysing and manipulating numerical data. You will need to be able to use a spreadsheet to analyse numerical data you collect, and display the results of this analysis. In order to do that efficiently, you will need to be able to carry out a number of spreadsheet activities independently.

Different sizes of tower case and a desktop case

number of hard or optical disk drives and the drive bays to accommodate them are required. Midi, Mini and Micro tower units are more usually used for standard applications. As well as physical size, the type chosen will depend on the number of *drive bays* and *expansion slots* required. It is also possible to buy what are known as barebones main processing units for situations where space is at a premium. These are also often used as the control centre for home entertainment systems.

A desktop unit, as its name suggests, is designed to sit on the desk rather than under it. Desktop units are usually about 10 to 15 cm high by about 40 cm wide. They tend to be less flexible than tower units as they have fewer drive bays and fewer expansion slots. At one time, most personal computers used desktop units, now the vast majority use a tower unit of one size or another.

The important feature of a laptop computer is its portability. For this reason, the main processing unit in a laptop is designed to be as small and thin as possible. To achieve this, some laptops do not have built-in optical or floppy drives, relying instead on external drives that can be plugged in when needed or the use of a solid state USB flash disk to transfer data into and out of the computer.

Power supply

All static main processing units will include a power supply. The power supply is a transformer that converts mains electricity to the voltage level needed to run the electronic components in the main processing unit. The power generated by the power supply is measured in watts (W). Currently, power supplies are rated between 200W and 650W. The type of power supply needed will depend on the speed of the processor, number of expansion cards, number of drives and the amount and type of memory.

Motherboard

The motherboard is the main circuit board within the main processing unit. The processor and memory are plugged into the motherboard, which provides connections between them and to other components. Motherboards also have sockets for plugging in additional circuit boards. These too are known as expansion slots.

Processor (CPU – central processing unit)

The CPU is the main integrated circuit or chip that processes the data. The CPU includes the arithmetic and logic unit (ALU), the control unit and some memory called registers. The ALU, as its name suggests, carries out arithmetic and also compares values – the logic function. The control unit sends out signals to control different parts of the computer system. The registers store data and instructions while a program is being executed. They also store the status of the system and register the occurrence of events in the system. The CPU also contains a quartz crystal that oscillates at a known fixed rate that is used as a *clock*. The speed of the clock is measured in gigahertz (GHz) – 1 GHz is 1 thousand million cycles per second. All operations carried out by the CPU are in time with the clock pulses, so the clock speed gives an indication of the speed of the CPU. However, a 2 GHz clock speed does not mean that the CPU performs 2 thousand million instructions every second, as each instruction will require several clock pulses to complete.

A *co-processor* is a second processor that provides extra capability to the main processor, for example to provide faster or more accurate mathematical calculations. The purpose of the co-processor is to reduce the burden on the CPU by carrying out highly specific processing tasks, leaving the main processor free to continue more general tasks such as transferring data or handling multiple tasks.

Key terms

Clock: a quartz crystal that oscillates at a known fixed rate and that is used to synchronise the actions of the processor.

Co-processor: a second processor that carries out specific processing to reduce the burden on the main processor.

Peripheral controller cards: circuit boards that control external devices such as keyboards or VDUs.

Bus

A *bus* carries the electronic signals within and between components in a computer system. There are internal buses within the CPU, as well as within other components, and external buses that carry signals between components, for example, between the CPU and memory. There are three types of external bus:

* the data bus carries data between the CPU and memory and peripheral controller cards

* the address bus carries the address to which data is to be sent or from which it is to be fetched

* the control bus carries signals between the CPU and other devices to enable or disable them and to synchronise the transmission of data.

The design of the buses is known as the computer architecture and different standards have been developed.

ISA (integrated system architecture)

ISA is an older architecture that provided a 16-bit bus on IBM compatible computers. Because of its low speed and narrow data path – only the first 16 Mb of memory could be directly accessed – it has been almost entirely superseded by 32-bit and 64-bit architectures.

PCI (peripheral component interconnect)

This architecture originally provided a 32-bit bus on both IBM compatible and Apple Macintosh computers. *PCI* is not strictly a bus, but a bridge that isolates the much faster internal processor bus from the slower peripherals. This means that the CPU can run much faster than the 33 MHz of the PCI. As well as speed, a major advantage of PCI is that it supports the automatic plug and play configuration of expansion cards. Faster 64-bit PCI bus architectures have been developed and by the time you read this, PCI may well have given way to even newer and faster bus architectures.

Key terms

Bus: the channels that carry data between devices such as the processor and memory and the address the data is to be sent to or fetched from.

ISA (integrated systems architecture): an older type of bus that allowed only 16 bits (0s and 1s) to be transferred at a time.

PCI (peripheral component interconnect): originally a 32-bit bus that provided a bridge between the much faster internal processor bus and the slower peripheral devices.

AGP (accelerated graphics port): a direct high-speed bus between the system memory and a graphics card.

Expansion cards

Expansion cards are circuit boards that plug into or connect to the expansion slots on the motherboard. These include sound cards, graphics or video cards and network cards.

Sound card

A sound card typically contains a Midi synthesiser chip that can generate musical notes and sound effects under program control. It will also contain a device called an A to D converter that converts

Find data

Find allows you to locate each occurrence of a particular data item, while **Search** and **Replace** allow you to find particular data items and replace them with something else (see Figure 3.15).

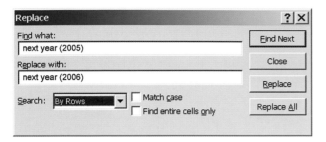

You can choose to search by row or by column and whether you want to match the case or only match the entire content of a cell. **Find Next** will move to the next occurrence of the data item, which you can then choose to replace or not. **Replace All** will change every occurrence of the data item.

Go to a specified cell

The **Go To** facility is useful if you have a large spreadsheet that is not all visible on-screen. Typing in a cell reference will take you to that cell. What's more, the **Go To** dialog keeps a record of where you started from and any cells you go to, so that you can retrace your steps.

Cut, copy, paste, move

These facilities work in a slightly different way from those in word processing software. When you select a block of cells and select **Cut** the content of the cells does not disappear, but a flashing border appears around it. When you move the cell pointer and select **Paste**, the contents of the original cells will be cleared and will appear in the new location. For the paste facility to work, you must either select exactly the same area of cells as the original, or just a single cell, which will be the top left-hand corner of the new block of cells.

Copy works in the same way, but the content of the original cells is not cleared. If you want to paste the cut or copied cells within the area of the spreadsheet that contains data, rather than **Paste** you can use **Insert Copied Cells**. This works best with a whole row or column. It is also possible to move the content of cells by selecting the cell(s) and dragging them to a new position on the spreadsheet.

Clear cell formats/contents

If you select a cell and press the delete key on the keyboard, it will clear the contents of the cell but leave any formatting intact. By selecting **Clear** in the **Edit** menu, you can choose whether you want to clear everything from the cell, the formatting, the content or just a comment that is attached to it.

Use paste special

Paste special allows you to choose what you want to paste. For example, if you are pasting values that are the results of calculations to somewhere else on the spreadsheet, or to another spreadsheet, you need to use paste special and paste the values. If you paste the formulae, the cell references may not be correct and you will get error messages or different values from what you expect.

Using cell referencing facilities appropriately

These are the facilities that allow you to perform calculations on the data in a spreadsheet so that you can obtain useful results. Cell referencing allows you to include the contents of particular cells in a formula or function. This is what allows results to be recalculated if the values in the cells are changed.

Cell referencing

Most cell referencing used in formulae is relative cell referencing. This means that if the formula is copied down a column of cells, the cell references change to match, as shown in Table 3.7.

	A	B	C
1			=A1+B1
2			=A2+B2
3			=A3+B3

TABLE 3.7

	A	B	C	D	E	F	G	H
1	Hourly rate	£8.50						
2			Hours worked					
3			Week 1	Week 2	Week 3	Week 4	Total Hours	Wages
4		Maggie	36	29	40	27	132	£1,122.00
5		Deepak	25	30	29	44	128	£1,088.00
6		Surinder	28	31	29	40	128	£1,088.00
7		Judith	15	20	17	12	64	£544.00
8		John	25	36	29	26	116	£986.00

TABLE 3.8

Absolute cell referencing is used when you want to always use the value in a particular cell in a formula. An example of this would be the hourly rate in the example shown in Table 3.8.

The wages for each member of staff are calculated by multiplying their total hours by the hourly rate. The formula in cell H4 is =G4*B1. The $ symbols show that this is an absolute cell reference. To make a cell reference absolute, you move the cell pointer onto that cell so that it appears in the formula and then press F4 on the keyboard. When the formula is copied into cells H5 to H8, the first cell reference will change but B1 will stay the same. So the formula in H8 will be =G8*B1. The advantage of this is that, if the hourly rate changes or you want to see the effect of changing it, only one value needs to be changed in the spreadsheet. Mixed referencing is when either the row or the column is absolute and the other is relative, for example B$2 or B2$.

Another way of achieving the same thing is to name the cell. Select the cell, then select **Name** in the **Insert** menu. You then select **Define**. If there is a label next to the cell to say what it contains, use this to name the cell. Otherwise, you can type a name in. The name can then be used in formulae, rather than an absolute reference. It is also possible to name a *range of cells*.

A spreadsheet workbook can consist of a number of linked worksheets. You can reference cells on different sheets in a formula. This is known as 3D referencing. This will appear as, for example, =Sheet1!B2.

All the references so far have involved columns labelled with letters A, B, C, etc. and rows labelled with numbers. There is another method of referencing where both the columns and rows are numbered. This is usually referred to as R1C1 referencing. In this case, the row number comes first, followed by the column number. The way that relative and absolute referencing appears is also different. Using the previous example, the formula for wages will appear as =R1C2*RC[-1]. R1C1 denotes an absolute reference to that cell. RC[-1] indicates that the formula should use the value in the cell in the same row, one column to the left.

Formulae
Operators are used with cell references to create formulae. When describing cell referencing we have used the arithmetic operators + (add)

mounted together in a bank. In this case they are known as *DIP (dual in-line package) switches*.

Memory

The memory in a computer is the primary data storage facility. The amount of memory the system has will determine the level of complexity of the tasks that the computer can carry out and the speed of processing. The size of computer memory and other data storage is measured in bits, bytes and multiples of these. Table 4.1 shows the relative sizes of each unit of storage.

Currently, the amount of memory in most computers is between 256 MB and 2 GB, but this is bound to increase.

Each location in the memory of a computer has a unique, numeric *address*. Each address can store a specific number of bits. The greater the number of bits stored in a single address, the more powerful the computer will be as more data can be transferred in a single operation. Earlier computers used 8-bit addressing, but now systems use 32-bit or 64-bit addressing.

There are different types of memory in a computer system. These mostly fall into two main categories, *RAM (random access memory)* and *ROM (read only memory)*.

RAM

The previous discussion about the amount of memory and the effect on the speed of processing relates to RAM. This is the memory that is used to temporarily store data and programs while they are being used. RAM can be both written to and read from but anything stored in it will be lost when the power is switched off – it is *volatile*. The effect of memory size on the speed of processing is due to the fact that the processor can access program instructions and data that is held in RAM much faster than from a disk drive. The more RAM there is available, the more program instructions and data can be stored and the less frequently data and program instructions need to be retrieved from the disk drive.

There are currently three main types of RAM used in PC systems. These are known as SDRAM, DDR and DDR2. SDRAM stands for synchronous dynamic RAM. This has largely been replaced on newer systems with DDR (double data rate). As the name implies DDR is faster than SDRAM. DDR2 is the next step up from DDR. DDR2 offers new features and functions that enable higher clock and data transfer rate operations. DDR2 transfers 64 bits of data twice every clock cycle. SDRAM is commonly available in modules from 128 MB to 1 GB. DDR is available in modules from 128 MB to 2 MB, and DDR2 in modules from 256 MB to 2 GB. The type of RAM that can be used will depend on the sockets available on the motherboard as different types of RAM have different numbers of pins. SDRAM modules have 168 pins, DDR modules have 184 pins and DDR2 modules have 240 pins.

CMOS (complementary metal oxide semiconductor) RAM is a particular type of RAM that is used to store user changeable system

Bit	A single memory unit that can store one binary digit, i.e. a single 1 or 0
Byte	Equals 8 bits
Kilobyte (KB)	1024 bytes or 2^{10} bytes $2^{10} = 2 \times 2 \times 2 \times 2 \times 2 \times 2 \times 2 \times 2 \times 2 \times 2 = 1024$
Megabyte (MB)	1024 KB
Gigabyte (GB)	1024 MB
Terabyte (TB)	1024 GB

TABLE 4.1

settings such as date and time. This uses a battery to maintain power and hence the data when the main power is switched off.

Another use for RAM is as a *buffer*. We have already mentioned several times that the CPU speed and the speed of its internal buses is much faster than the speed of peripheral devices. A buffer is simply memory within a peripheral device, such as a printer. The computer sends the data to be printed to this buffer at the speed of the data bus. The buffer holds the data and the printer accesses it at its own speed.

ROM

ROM is non-volatile memory. This means that data stored within it is not lost when the power is switched off. However, as its name suggests it can only be read from, not written to. ROM is used to contain the start-up sequence for the computer system. This includes the BIOS (basic input/output system). When the computer is switched on, the BIOS is loaded first and then loads the operating system from disk so that the system can be used.

Cache memory

Cache is very fast access memory. In modern computers, cache is actually part of the CPU, rather than a separate chip. This means that it can be accessed at the speed of the CPU's internal bus. The way that cache works is by storing the last thing that was accessed from the main memory. Then, if the same thing is requested again, it can just be loaded straight from cache much faster than if the processor had to access the main memory again. An example of caching is when you use the Internet. Your connection to the Internet is much

slower than the connection from your computer's CPU to the hard disk. The first time you open a web page it may take a while to download. As well as opening on-screen the page will be saved in a folder on your hard disk. If you go back to the page, you will notice that it loads much more quickly. This is because, providing the date is the same, the page will be loaded from your computer's hard disk rather than over the Internet.

Key terms

RAM (random access memory): volatile memory that can be written to and read from. Used for the temporary storage of data and programs.

ROM (read only memory): non-volatile memory that can only be read from. Used for storing system start-up files, including BIOS.

Address: a unique number identifying a memory location.

Buffer: memory in a peripheral device that acts as a buffer between faster bus speeds and slower peripherals.

Volatile: memory is volatile if the content is lost when power is removed.

Cache: fast access memory on the CPU that stores the most recently accessed data and instructions to speed up subsequent retrieval.

Disk drives

Computers need secondary storage in the form of disk drives so that programs and data can be stored when the computer is switched off. There are two main types of disk drive, magnetic and optical. Magnetic disks store data based on the how much of that time they spend on different activities each week; for example, using the Internet, other computer use, watching television, physical activity, etc. Record the age range, gender and occupation of each person, the hours of leisure time and the hours spent on each activity. Enter the data in a spreadsheet. Calculate the time spent on each activity as a percentage of the leisure time available. Find the maximum, minimum and average time spent on each activity for a particular age group. Do the same for a particular gender or occupation. Use cell presentation formats to make the spreadsheet easy to follow. You may need to copy data onto different worksheets to analyse the data in different ways.

Development of spreadsheets to present results of data analysis

As part of the assessment evidence for this unit you will need to use a spreadsheet to analyse numerical data and present the results. This may be data that you have collected or it may be numerical data you have found on the Internet, such as census data or other statistics. The Office of National Statistics' website, for example, provides data sets on a wide range of topic areas that can be downloaded but you may also find numerical data from many other sources.

The spreadsheet in Figure 3.16 shows how you can use the facilities available to improve the presentation of data. The original data had each year's figures beneath one another in a single column with a blank row between each year and

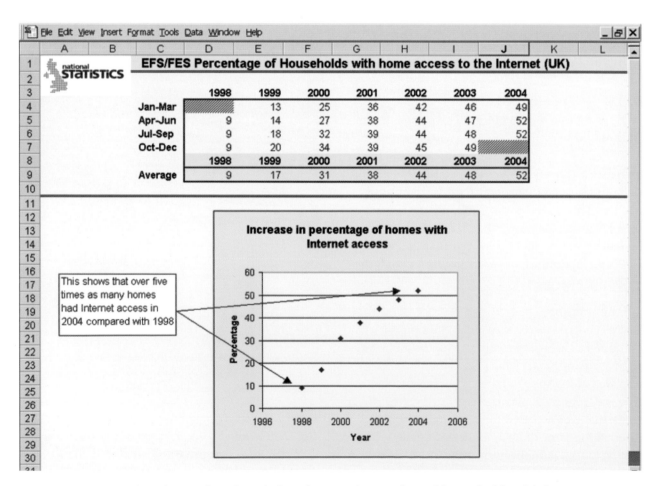

FIGURE 3.16 *Presenting the results of analysing data on the number of households with home access to the Internet (Source: Office of National Statistics)*

the next. Whilst this showed the increase quite well, it was not easy to view as the figures did not all fit on the screen and you had to scroll down to see them. It was also not clear, without looking closely, that there were only three quarters' figures for the first and last year. The data has been moved so that the years are the column headings and the quarters the row headings. The average value has been taken for each year using the AVERAGE function. As this gave decimal values for some years, INT was used as well to give whole number values, i.e. =INT(AVERAGE( )). Additional columns were added to the left so that the table is in the centre of the screen and the font size of the title has been increased and centred across the cells. Finally, the year column headings have been copied to the row above the averages, so that the two rows can be used in a chart.

To improve the appearance, two colours have been used, with borders to separate the title from the data and the data from the chart. Borders have also been added around the data and to highlight the average values. The cells for the quarters with no data have also been shaded. The years and average figures have been used to create and insert a chart – an x-y plot. This has been resized to fit the space available and so that the increase is shown clearly. The two rows of data used have been highlighted in green to link them to the chart. The Office of National Statistics' logo has been copied from the website and added in the top left-hand corner to indicate where the data was obtained, and a text box and arrows were added using the drawing toolbar.

Cell formatting

You should already be familiar with the cell formatting facilities and those for manipulating the spreadsheet from the previous section. We will now consider the other facilities used in this example in more detail.

Drawing tools and graphic images

Spreadsheet software, such as Microsoft Excel, provides the same drawing toolbar as other packages. This means that you can add shapes, lines, arrows, text boxes and WordArt to your spreadsheet. You will also be able to group drawn objects and move or copy them as one, align objects with each other or change the way objects are layered. You may have used these facilities in your work for Unit 1: Using ICT to communicate, so we will not explain again how to use them here. As with all presentation techniques, you need to take care how such objects are used – they should enhance the information in the spreadsheet, not detract from it.

As in the example, you can also add graphic images to a spreadsheet. This may be a logo, or some other images that illustrate the information being presented. Choosing **Picture** from the **Insert** menu will give you the option of using clipart or a picture from file. In either case, when you have found the image you want, it will appear on the spreadsheet and you can resize or position it as you want.

Charts and line graphs

Charts and graphs are an excellent way of showing statistical information so that it can be grasped quickly. The chart in Figure 3.16 shows very clearly how the number of households with home access to the Internet has increased. If you are going to create a chart, you need to ensure that the data is arranged appropriately. Sometimes it may be necessary to copy column or row headings and values to another part of the spreadsheet so that you can select the data you want to graph (hence the need to copy the year headings in the previous example).

Table 3.12 shows more data on Internet access from the Office of National Statistics' website. We will use this to demonstrate how to create a multiple line graph to compare the increase in home Internet access for different income bands. First you need to select the data, together with the row and column headings, that you want to graph. This will exclude the title row and the bottom row of data, but include all the rest. You then select **Chart** from the **Insert** menu (or click the chart button on the toolbar). This will open the **Chart Wizard** that will help you create the graph. Your first task is to select the type of chart. Care is needed here. The type of chart you choose must match the purpose. For example, a pie chart would show clearly the percentages for different

Theory into practice

Collect computer brochures from computer retailers – you may find you get some posted through your door – and visit computer suppliers' websites. Compare the specifications of the main processing units offered. Decide which one you would recommend to a student on a limited budget who needs a computer to produce essays and to access the Internet for research. Which would you recommend for a dedicated computer games player for whom money is no object?

Input devices

These are devices that allow data to be entered into the computer system. There are different types of input devices, each of which has a different purpose. These include the keyboard, mouse, scanner and microphone. You will need to be able to specify the most appropriate input devices to meet the needs of a user.

Keyboard

Virtually all computer systems will include a keyboard to allow the entry of textual and numeric data. There are, however, an increasing number of different types of keyboard available. Standard English keyboards have a QWERTY layout, so called because the first six letters on the top row of letter keys are Q, W, E, R, T and Y. Most have a separate block of number keys, known as a numeric keypad, cursor keys to move around the screen and function keys that can be programmed to perform particular functions.

The total number of keys on the keyboard can vary. Keyboards with 105 and 107 keys are common, but it is possible to buy keyboards for young children that have only 67 keys, while others include additional keys that allow you to open specific software packages, navigate web pages and cut, copy and paste. Most keyboards are more or less rectangular in shape, but more ergonomically designed keyboards are also available. These have a curved layout and are designed to reduce the risk of repetitive strain injury (RSI). Keyboards are available for different languages. Some, for example French, are very similar to an English keyboard but have keys for accented letters; others, such as Chinese, have a completely different set of characters.

There are also different ways of connecting the keyboard to the main processing unit. Traditionally, the keyboard was connected by a cable to a specific socket (port) known as a PS/2. This method of connection is increasingly being replaced by connection to a USB port either by a cable or wireless. In the case of a wireless keyboard, a small radio frequency receiver is connected to the USB port. The keyboard transmits radio frequency signals that are picked up by this receiver, removing the need for a physical connection between the keyboard and the computer. Usually, wireless keyboard packages also include a wireless mouse, which uses the same receiver.

Another type of keyboard is an overlay or concept keyboard. This does not have individual keys for each letter. Instead, it has a flat surface that is divided into a number of touch sensitive areas. Each area can be programmed to input a particular letter, word or phrase or perform a particular action. Concept keyboards are often used with young children or people with special needs who have difficulty using a standard keyboard. Another use of concept keyboards is in supermarkets where customers weigh their own fruit and vegetables. The customer simply presses

Wireless receiver, keyboard and mouse

a picture of the fruit or vegetable they are weighing to input the information. Concept keyboards are also used in fast food outlets and bars where there is a danger of liquids being spilled. As well as providing a wipe clean surface, data entry is also speeded up, as the operator needs only to locate and press the area corresponding to the item being sold.

There are also specialist keyboards available to help those with particular special needs use a computer. Braille keyboards are available for blind users. There are also large key keyboards for people who have difficulty reading the letters on a standard keyboard or lack the fine-motor control to press a standard sized key. Some people, such as those suffering from dyslexia, have difficulty using a standard QWERTY keyboard. Keyboards are available with keys in alphabetical order to help such people.

Mouse

A mouse or other pointing device is another essential input device on most computer systems, especially those that have a graphical user interface (GUI) – see the section on operating systems on page 140. The movement of the mouse on a surface moves the pointer on-screen and the buttons send a signal to the computer to carry out an action. Different types of mice are available. A mechanical mouse has a ball in the base that moves sensors within the casing to detect its movement. A mechanical mouse needs to be used on a mouse mat to work efficiently

and will tend to pick up dirt and dust, so the sensors need to be cleaned periodically. An optical mouse reflects infrared light off the surface it is on to detect its movement. It can be used on almost any surface without a mouse mat. Mice are available with different numbers of buttons. Two, three, four and even five button mice can be bought. A two-button mouse is adequate for most purposes – in MS Windows the left button performs an action and the right one brings up a menu. The other buttons can be programmed to perform different functions. Many mice also have a scroll wheel that allows you to scroll through a document or web page without using the on-screen scroll bars. As with keyboards, mice can be connected to a PS/2 port or, more usually, to a USB port, and can be wired or wireless.

An alternative to a mouse is a trackball. These have a ball on the top or side that is moved with the user's finger or thumb to move the pointer on-screen. As with mice, the movement can be picked up by mechanical sensors or optical ones. As trackballs do not need to be moved on a surface, they are ideal for use with laptops, some of which have a trackball built in. The other option for moving the pointer on a laptop is a touchpad. This is simply a flat touch sensitive pad with two buttons beside it that operate like mouse buttons. The user moves the pointer by simply moving their finger on the pad. Rather than use the left button to perform an action, the touchpad can be programmed so that the action can be performed by tapping it.

Scanner

A scanner is a device that converts information that is on paper into a form that can be input into a computer. It works by passing a light over the page and measuring the intensity of the reflected light. Scanners are most often used to transfer images onto a computer but, with optical character recognition (OCR) software, they can also be used to copy text into a word processing program. *Flatbed* scanners are the most common type. As the name suggests, the item to be copied is laid face down on a flat surface and the light source moves under it. This makes it possible to scan items from a book, for example. Another

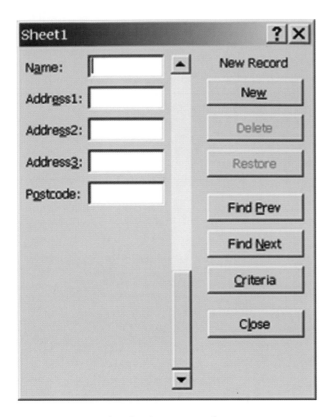

FIGURE 3.18 *A simple data entry form*

to test that the formulae you use generate the results you expect. There are several ways of doing this. You can estimate the range that results should be within and check that the actual result is within that range. For example, the average of a set of figures should be within the range of the values in the set. If the result is outside this range, there is likely to be an error in the formula. Similarly, if you estimate the result as being less than 100 and the result given is over 1000, an error in the formula is the most likely cause.

Another way of testing that the formulae in your spreadsheet do what they should is to use dummy data. In other words, use simple numbers for which you can easily work out the expected results. If the actual results are different, this will highlight any errors in the formulae. The final way of testing the formulae is to use a calculator or pencil and paper to work out what the results should be and then compare these with the actual results.

– tools and techniques

Use the tools and techniques you have learnt about in this section to further analyse the data you collected on people's leisure-time activities and present your results.

Find some numerical data on the WWW on a topic that interests you. Use a spreadsheet to analyse the data and present your results.

Presentation of the results of an investigation

In this section of the unit, you will need to use the skills described in Unit 1: Using ICT to communicate. In particular, you will need to combine different types of information into a coherent presentation. This may, for example, be a slide presentation, website or an on-screen or printed report. Whichever format you use, you need to make sure that different elements work together, rather than simply throw them together. You will need to include:

* text from existing sources as well as text you create yourself. You may need to edit or rephrase the text you use to ensure that there is a consistent writing style

* graphics, numerical spreadsheet data, graphs and charts and the results of database searches should all be incorporated so that it is clear why they are there. They should be clearly labelled, referred to in the text and positioned near the text they refer to. In some cases, it might be better to include the numerical data or database search results in a clearly labelled and referenced appendix, rather than in the body of the presentation

* if your presentation is on-screen, you will be able to incorporate hyperlinks to other information sources, either stored locally or on the WWW. Such links should be used with care. The additional information needs to be relevant to your presentation and be useful to the reader.

Accuracy and currency of information

As has been mentioned previously, anyone can create a website and display information on the WWW. Also, websites can easily become out of date – sites are rarely deleted when the person who created them loses interest and stops updating them. This means that you need to take steps to check the accuracy of any information you find and how up to date the information is.

The best way to check that information is accurate is to compare information from more than one source. If you find that two sources give different information about the same topic, you will need to look at more sources to help you determine which is accurate or to come to a consensus. The different sources may be other websites, or they may be books or other paper-based sources.

To check whether information is up to date, you need to try to find when it was last updated. Some sites, but not all, will display this information. Do not be fooled by the fact that the current date is displayed on the page. This just means that the page includes a today's date field. One way of ensuring that you download only up-to-date information is to use the 'last updated' feature in the advanced search facility of the search engine.

If you are using information from government or other large public-service websites, it is to be hoped that the information is accurate and up to date.

Acknowledging sources

When you collect and use information, it is very important that you acknowledge the sources of the information you use. You will need to list all of your sources accurately so that someone else can find the original information and check that they agree with your interpretation of it. You will also need to acknowledge the owner of the copyright of any graphics or other material you include in your presentation. An important part of presenting your results will, therefore, be a *bibliography*. You may also want to use footnotes to reference the sources of particular items.

Assessment evidence

A local retailer is considering selling goods on the Internet using e-commerce and communicating with its customers only by email. You have been asked to investigate what e-commerce might involve and the impact that relying solely on electronic communication methods might have. You need to present the results of your investigation, including the use of a spreadsheet to analyse numerical data, in an appropriate way. You also need to produce a report on the sources and methods that you used to find the information. This should include screen prints to show the methods you used. To produce the presentation and report you will need to carry out the following linked tasks.

Task A

Select and use search engines to find information on the WWW.

As a minimum you will need to identify the information you need, choose a search engine and use standard search facilities to find the information. If you use the advanced search facilities of more than one search engine and compare the results you will reach mark band two. To reach mark band three you will need to choose the most appropriate search engine and use efficient methods, including using logical operators to find the information.

Task B

Explain the impact of the availability of electronic information on individuals and society. You need to consider this in the context of the assignment as well as in general terms and use the information you collect and the results of analysing that information to aid your explanation.

As a minimum you need to make straightforward comments on how the availability of information affects people you are familiar with. If you can extend this to give a clear explanation that includes society in general and people and situations outside your normal experience you will be able to reach mark band two. To reach mark band three you will need to explain in detail how organisations communicate with individuals and society and how this affects those who don't have (or want) access to ICT.

This task will be used to assess the quality of your written communication so you should ensure that your report is well structured and contains few, if any, errors in spelling, grammar and punctuation.

Task C

Access information from large public-service websites.

If you need some help to find the information you need, you will reach only mark band one. To reach mark band two you will need to be able to find the information without help using menus, navigation bars, alphabetical indexes and textual hyperlinks. If you can also use an internal search engine you will be able to reach mark band three.

Task D

Use databases to find information.

As a minimum you must use search criteria that involve relational operators to get information from at least one database, either local or on-line. If you can use complex search criteria that also involve logical operators, get information from both local and on-line databases and present the results, for example in a table, you will achieve mark band two. To reach the highest mark band, you must also be able to present your results as reports.

Task E

Use spreadsheet software to analyse numerical data and present results. You could, for example, find data on Internet access and individuals' use of on-line shopping on the WWW. You could also carry out a survey to find similar information for your local area and compare the results.

As a minimum, you must create a suitable spreadsheet layout and use it to carry out simple analysis of the data. You must present the output on screen or on paper and use cell formats, charts

or graphs, page or screen layout and graphic images appropriately. If you are able to carry out more complex analysis that shows you have a good understanding of spreadsheet formulae and functions and use macros to speed up data input and the production of results, you will reach mark band two. To reach mark band three, your spreadsheet must be well designed and you must test it thoroughly to make sure your results are accurate.

Task F

Combine different types of data to present the results of your investigation.

As a minimum your report must combine at least two different types of data from a small number of sources (2 or 3). You must also list the sources you use. To reach mark band two your report must combine at least three different types of data from a number of different sources (4 to 6) and you must list the sources appropriately. There should be enough detail for someone else to find the information. To reach the highest mark band, your presentation must be well thought out and coherent. You must combine a range of data from a wide range of sources (more than 6) and list your sources in a detailed bibliography.

Task G

Evaluate the methods you used to find information and present results.
You need to consider:

* what worked well – what was good about the methods you used

* what did not work – what was not so good

* how well did your methods achieve the required results?

* how did you refine your initial methods to meet the purpose more closely?

* how would you improve the methods you used if you had to do a similar task in the future?

As a minimum you must comment on how effective the methods you used were for finding the information and presenting results. If you clearly identify good and not so good features of the methods you used, you will reach mark band two. To reach the highest mark band you must show that you have identified strengths and weaknesses in the methods you used originally and how you refined these methods to meet the purpose more closely. You must also suggest how you might approach a similar task in future.

Signposting for portfolio evidence

In this assignment, the methods you use to find and analyse information are as important as the content of the presentation. As well as the presentation itself, you will need to make sure that you provide screen prints to show the search methods you have used and evidence of how you created and tested your spreadsheet. For example, you should include a formula printout. Currently, all of your evidence must be produced on paper. If you have created a screen-based presentation, you will need to provide screen prints or printouts to evidence your work. You will need to annotate these to indicate any features, such as animation or hyperlinks that are not obvious from the printouts. You should get your teacher to witness these features and initial or sign the printouts to confirm that the features work. For example, printing out a slide presentation as an audience handout with three slides to a page will provide space for you to add any necessary annotations.

You need to organise your work carefully. Make sure each piece of work is clearly labelled to show what it is and that your name is on each page. Put your work in a logical order. This might be your report on how you found the information and analysed it, followed by your presentation, with your evaluation at the end. Alternatively, you may consider the report to be most important and put that first. When you have put all your work in a sensible order, number all the pages and create a contents page to show where each piece of work is located.

UNIT 4

System specification and configuration

Introduction

There are many different components that make up computer systems. These include the *hardware* components used to build the system and the *software* needed to turn, what is essentially a box of electronic circuits, into a powerful tool capable of performing many different functions. In this unit you will learn about the different types of hardware components and software so that you can select the most appropriate ones to meet a user's specific needs. You will also learn how to install software and *configure* it so that a user can make more effective use of the system.

Key terms

Hardware: the parts of a computer system that you can physically touch.

Software: the programs needed to make the hardware perform useful tasks.

Configure: make changes to the way the software looks or performs.

Specify: select and produce a detailed list of all the components and features of those components required to make up a computer system.

Learning outcomes

By studying this unit you will:

✱ understand the purpose of components in a computer system

✱ be able to identify what an individual or organisation wants to use a computer system for and how these needs might be met

✱ be able to *specify* a computer system in terms of the hardware, software and configuration required to meet the identified needs of an individual or organisation

* be able to install, configure and test software and set up suitable security procedures
* be able to configure software by installing toolbars and setting up macros and templates to meet the needs of an individual or organisation
* be able to recommend procedures to ensure the safety of computer system users and the security of the data stored on the system
* understand the basics of software development
* be able to evaluate the specification you produce and the methods you use to install, configure and test software.

An important consideration when you are specifying systems is the speed at which both hardware and software are developed. If you are reading this unit as little as a year after it was written, you may find that there are faster processors, bigger hard disks or newer versions of software than those described, while other components may have become almost obsolete. You will need to use reference materials, such as computer magazines or the websites of component suppliers and manufacturers to find out what is currently available.

What you need to learn

You need to learn about:

* hardware
* software
* basics of software development
* safety and security.

Hardware

Hardware components are the physical components that make up a computer system. You will be familiar with components, such as the keyboard, mouse, screen and printer that enable you to put data into the system and get information from it. However, there are other hardware components that are essential to the computer system, that are tucked away out of sight inside the computer's main processing unit. In this section we will consider all of these components and consider how they link together to form a working computer system. All computer systems will include input devices, a main processing unit and output devices. In this section you will learn about these different types of hardware and the technical terms that are used to describe them.

Main processing unit

The main processing unit is the box that holds all the essential electronic components that make the computer function. The components within the main processing unit will include a power supply, a *motherboard*, the *processor (CPU – central processing unit)*, memory, *expansion cards* such as sound, video/graphics or network cards, disk drives, *connectors* and *ports* to allow external devices to be connected. You will learn what each of these components does and how they are connected as you work through this unit.

Key terms

Motherboard: the main circuit board in a computer that holds the processor, memory and other components and connects them together.

Processor (CPU): the main integrated circuit (chip) that carries out the processing of data.

Expansion cards: circuit boards that plug into or connect to the motherboard to provide sound, graphics or networking capabilities, for example.

Connectors: the plugs and sockets that allow devices to be connected to a computer.

Ports: more correctly called I/O (input/output), ports are the means of connecting peripheral devices such as keyboards and printers to the computer for the input and output of data.

Case

The box or, more correctly, the case can be a *tower unit*, a *desktop unit* or the base of a laptop. A tower unit, as its name suggests, is shaped like a tower, i.e. it is taller than it is wide, and is designed to stand on the floor under a desk. Tower units come in different sizes. Full towers are the biggest and are used for servers or other applications where a

Different sizes of tower case and a desktop case

number of hard or optical disk drives and the drive bays to accommodate them are required. Midi, Mini and Micro tower units are more usually used for standard applications. As well as physical size, the type chosen will depend on the number of *drive bays* and *expansion slots* required. It is also possible to buy what are known as barebones main processing units for situations where space is at a premium. These are also often used as the control centre for home entertainment systems.

A desktop unit, as its name suggests, is designed to sit on the desk rather than under it. Desktop units are usually about 10 to 15 cm high by about 40 cm wide. They tend to be less flexible than tower units as they have fewer drive bays and fewer expansion slots. At one time, most personal computers used desktop units, now the vast majority use a tower unit of one size or another.

The important feature of a laptop computer is its portability. For this reason, the main processing unit in a laptop is designed to be as small and thin as possible. To achieve this, some laptops do not have built-in optical or floppy drives, relying instead on external drives that can be plugged in when needed or the use of a solid state USB flash disk to transfer data into and out of the computer.

Power supply

All static main processing units will include a power supply. The power supply is a transformer that converts mains electricity to the voltage level needed to run the electronic components in the main processing unit. The power generated by the power supply is measured in watts (W). Currently, power supplies are rated between 200W and 650W. The type of power supply needed will depend on the speed of the processor, number of expansion cards, number of drives and the amount and type of memory.

Motherboard

The motherboard is the main circuit board within the main processing unit. The processor and memory are plugged into the motherboard, which provides connections between them and to other components. Motherboards also have sockets for plugging in additional circuit boards. These too are known as expansion slots.

Processor (CPU – central processing unit)

The CPU is the main integrated circuit or chip that processes the data. The CPU includes the arithmetic and logic unit (ALU), the control unit and some memory called registers. The ALU, as its name suggests, carries out arithmetic and also compares values – the logic function. The control unit sends out signals to control different parts of the computer system. The registers store data and instructions while a program is being executed. They also store the status of the system and register the occurrence of events in the system. The CPU also contains a quartz crystal that oscillates at a known fixed rate that is used as a *clock*. The speed of the clock is measured in gigahertz (GHz) – 1 GHz is 1 thousand million cycles per second. All operations carried out by the CPU are in time with the clock pulses, so the clock speed gives an indication of the speed of the CPU. However, a 2 GHz clock speed does not mean that the CPU performs 2 thousand million instructions every second, as each instruction will require several clock pulses to complete.

A *co-processor* is a second processor that provides extra capability to the main processor, for example to provide faster or more accurate mathematical calculations. The purpose of the co-processor is to reduce the burden on the CPU by carrying out highly specific processing tasks, leaving the main processor free to continue more general tasks such as transferring data or handling multiple tasks.

Key terms

Clock: a quartz crystal that oscillates at a known fixed rate and that is used to synchronise the actions of the processor.

Co-processor: a second processor that carries out specific processing to reduce the burden on the main processor.

Peripheral controller cards: circuit boards that control external devices such as keyboards or VDUs.

Bus

A *bus* carries the electronic signals within and between components in a computer system. There are internal buses within the CPU, as well as within other components, and external buses that carry signals between components, for example, between the CPU and memory. There are three types of external bus.

* the data bus carries data between the CPU and memory and peripheral controller cards

* the address bus carries the address to which data is to be sent or from which it is to be fetched

* the control bus carries signals between the CPU and other devices to enable or disable them and to synchronise the transmission of data.

The design of the buses is known as the computer architecture and different standards have been developed.

ISA (integrated system architecture)

ISA is an older architecture that provided a 16-bit bus on IBM compatible computers. Because of its low speed and narrow data path – only the first 16 Mb of memory could be directly accessed – it has been almost entirely superseded by 32-bit and 64-bit architectures.

PCI (peripheral component interconnect)

This architecture originally provided a 32-bit bus on both IBM compatible and Apple Macintosh computers. *PCI* is not strictly a bus, but a bridge that isolates the much faster internal processor bus from the slower peripherals. This means that the CPU can run much faster than the 33 MHz of the PCI. As well as speed, a major advantage of PCI is that it supports the automatic plug and play configuration of expansion cards. Faster 64-bit PCI bus architectures have been developed and by the time you read this, PCI may well have given way to even newer and faster bus architectures.

Key terms

Bus: the channels that carry data between devices such as the processor and memory and the address the data is to be sent to or fetched from.

ISA (integrated systems architecture): an older type of bus that allowed only 16 bits (0s and 1s) to be transferred at a time.

PCI (peripheral component interconnect): originally a 32-bit bus that provided a bridge between the much faster internal processor bus and the slower peripheral devices.

AGP (accelerated graphics port): a direct high-speed bus between the system memory and a graphics card.

Expansion cards

Expansion cards are circuit boards that plug into or connect to the expansion slots on the motherboard. These include sound cards, graphics or video cards and network cards.

Sound card

A sound card typically contains a Midi synthesiser chip that can generate musical notes and sound effects under program control. It will also contain a device called an A to D converter that converts the analogue signals from a microphone to digital signals that can be processed and a small audio amplifier to amplify the sound output through speakers or headphones. There will also be stereo sockets to connect these external devices. Sound cards also allow music CDs to be played via the computer's CD-ROM drive and sounds to be recorded as WAV files. Many motherboards have built-in sound controllers that are capable of producing high-quality output that is suitable for most purposes. However, when the user wants to use the computer to control MIDI musical instruments and to generate music from recorded samples of actual instruments, an expensive, high-quality sound card may be needed.

Video card

A video or graphics card enables the display of graphics on a VDU. These have been developed with higher and higher capabilities to cope with the more and more complex graphic requirements of modern software. Most have a chip called a graphics accelerator that speeds up the display of graphic images. Some may include a separate graphics processor to perform the operations most heavily used in generating graphic displays to free up the CPU for other tasks – an example of a co-processor. As with sound, some motherboards have built-in graphics controllers, which are adequate for most purposes. However, where someone wants to use applications that require high-resolution, fast-changing, 3-D graphics, such as computer games, a separate graphics card will almost certainly be needed.

Network card

A network card or NIC (network interface card) enables a computer to be connected into a LAN (local area network). The LAN may provide access to a server containing applications and files to be used by the computer, or may simply provide access to a WAN (wide area network) or the Internet.

AGP (accelerated graphics port)

An *AGP* is a high-speed expansion slot that allows the processor on a graphics card to directly access the system memory, bypassing the PCI bus and the main CPU. This allows much faster access to the large amounts of graphics data required for complex 3-D images.

I/O ports

Ports are the means by which external devices are connected to the CPU. Effectively, they are the sockets on the back (and now often the front) of the computer that you can plug printers, keyboards, mice and other devices into. The ports will either connect directly onto the motherboard or onto an expansion card.

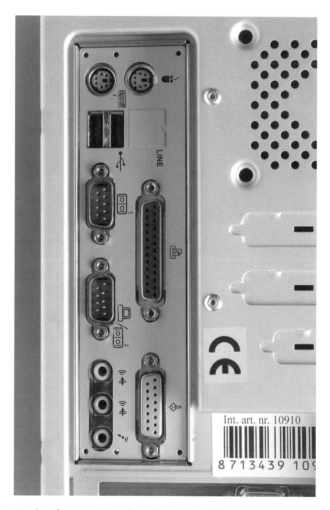

Back of computer showing the different ports

USB (universal serial bus) port

There are different types of port but the most widely used is the universal serial bus (USB) port. *USB* is a *serial* connection which can be used to connect up to 127 devices to a computer. This can be achieved by daisy-chaining – where one device is connected to another, as you would connect the daisies in a daisy-chain – or by using a USB hub. A USB hub is simply a device that is plugged into a USB port on the computer and provides a number of USB sockets that devices can be connected to. USB provides a single standard connection for a whole range of different peripheral devices and has plug and play capability. All you need to do is plug the device into a USB connector on the computer. If it is a new device the computer recognises this and asks you to insert the driver disk. If the driver software is already installed, it will simply start talking to the device. USB cables can be up to 5 metres long and can carry a power supply for devices such as digital cameras and mice.

Serial port

Another type of port is the standard *serial port*. As with USB, data is transferred in a single stream of 1s and 0s along a single wire. The serial port uses a 9-pin D-shaped connector and it is possible to use fairly long cable lengths. In the past, the serial port was used to connect communications devices such as dial-up modems that allowed access to the Internet via the standard telephone line. Now, the serial port is mainly used for connecting specialist devices, for example security cameras.

Parallel port

A *parallel port* transfers 8 bits (1s and 0s) of data at the same time along 8 separate wires. The parallel port is usually a 25-pin D connector. As any connector between a serial or parallel cable and a data bus can be referred to as a *DB series* connector, this connector can be called a DB-25. The end of the cable that connects to the device uses a *centronics* connector. This type of connector does not have pins but has a central slot with metal strips that make the contact. However, it is still referred to as a 36-pin connector. Parallel cables need to be relatively short as each of the 8 bits might travel at a slightly different speed down the individual wires, which may cause data errors over longer distances. In the past, printers were most usually connected via the parallel port, which often became known as the 'printer port'. Now, however, nearly all printers use a USB port and the parallel port is used only for specialist devices.

SCSI (small computer system interface) controller

At the time of writing, most computers have USB, serial and parallel ports as standard. Another type

of port is a *SCSI* (small computer user interface) port. SCSI ports are not usually provided but require the addition of an expansion card – a SCSI controller. SCSI is a standard parallel interface for connecting devices such as disk drives, printers and scanners to any computer irrespective of the type of CPU or operating system used. This is achieved using the SCSI controller, which uses a standard set of commands to move the data between the computer and the peripheral devices. One of the advantages of a SCSI port is the speed of data transfer, although there are a number of different standards that give different levels of performance. Like USB, SCSI devices can also be daisy-chained, but only up to 15 devices on a single controller. SCSI devices tend to be more expensive than those that use other connection methods. Also, the increased speed of newer USB ports means that these are being used more and more rather than SCSI.

Firewire

Another alternative to SCSI for fast data transfer is *firewire*. This is a fast serial port. Like USB, the cable can carry power as well as data and devices can be plugged and unplugged without turning off the computer. Firewire can transmit video or audio data in digital format at high speeds and is relatively inexpensive. Where it differs from USB is the fact that it can connect devices to each other directly as well as connecting them to a computer. This is called peer-to-peer connection. Apart from cost, an advantage of firewire over SCSI is that the cables are physically small and thin.

Connectors

There are other connectors and devices that you may come across. *RJ (registered jack)* series connectors are used to connect devices to telephone lines or to networks. These are small square plugs with a clip to keep them in place. The eight-wire RJ-45 is used to connect computers to a network, particularly an Ethernet local area network (LAN).

Some devices, such as motherboards, may need to have settings changed, for example to set the bus speed. This is achieved using small two-position switches on the circuit board called *DIL (dual in-line) switches*. These switches are often mounted together in a bank. In this case they are known as *DIP (dual in-line package) switches*.

Key terms

USB (universal serial bus): a standard serial connection for a wide range of devices.

Serial port: a port on the computer that transmits data in a single stream down a single wire. The data is transferred in a single stream of 1s and 0s.

Parallel port: a port on the computer that transmits 8 bits of data down 8 separate wires simultaneously.

DB series: a term used to describe any connector between a serial or parallel cable and a data bus.

Centronics: a type of parallel connector that usually plugs into the device, e.g. a printer.

SCSI (small computer system interface): a fast parallel connection used to connect devices such as hard disks. Devices can be daisy-chained.

Firewire: a fast serial connection often used for fast transfer of audio and video. Allows peer-to-peer connection as well as connection to a computer.

RJ (registered jack) series: a series of small square connectors used to connect devices to the telephone line or a network.

DIL (dual in-line) switches/DIP (dual in-line package) switches: small two-way switches on a circuit board used to change its settings.

Memory

The memory in a computer is the primary data storage facility. The amount of memory the system has will determine the level of complexity of the tasks that the computer can carry out and the speed of processing. The size of computer memory and other data storage is measured in bits, bytes and multiples of these. Table 4.1 shows the relative sizes of each unit of storage.

Currently, the amount of memory in most computers is between 256 MB and 2 GB, but this is bound to increase.

Each location in the memory of a computer has a unique, numeric *address*. Each address can store a specific number of bits. The greater the number of bits stored in a single address, the more powerful the computer will be as more data can be transferred in a single operation. Earlier computers used 8-bit addressing, but now systems use 32-bit or 64-bit addressing.

There are different types of memory in a computer system. These mostly fall into two main categories, *RAM (random access memory)* and *ROM (read only memory)*.

RAM

The previous discussion about the amount of memory and the effect on the speed of processing relates to RAM. This is the memory that is used to temporarily store data and programs while they are being used. RAM can be both written to and read from but anything stored in it will be lost when the power is switched off – it is *volatile*. The effect of memory size on the speed of processing is due to the fact that the processor can access program instructions and data that is held in RAM much faster than from a disk drive. The more RAM there is available, the more program instructions and data can be stored and the less frequently data and program instructions need to be retrieved from the disk drive.

There are currently three main types of RAM used in PC systems. These are known as SDRAM, DDR and DDR2. SDRAM stands for synchronous dynamic RAM. This has largely been replaced on newer systems with DDR (double data rate). As the name implies DDR is faster than SDRAM. DDR2 is the next step up from DDR. DDR2 offers new features and functions that enable higher clock and data transfer rate operations. DDR2 transfers 64 bits of data twice every clock cycle. SDRAM is commonly available in modules from 128 MB to 1 GB. DDR is available in modules from 128 MB to 2 MB, and DDR2 in modules from 256 MB to 2 GB. The type of RAM that can be used will depend on the sockets available on the motherboard as different types of RAM have different numbers of pins. SDRAM modules have 168 pins, DDR modules have 184 pins and DDR2 modules have 240 pins.

CMOS (complementary metal oxide semiconductor) RAM is a particular type of RAM that is used to store user changeable system

Bit	A single memory unit that can store one **b**inary dig**it**, i.e. a single 1 or 0
Byte	Equals 8 bits
Kilobyte (KB)	1024 bytes or 2^{10} bytes $2^{10} = 2 \times 2 \times 2 \times 2 \times 2 \times 2 \times 2 \times 2 \times 2 \times 2 = 1024$
Megabyte (MB)	1024 KB
Gigabyte (GB)	1024 MB
Terabyte (TB)	1024 GB

TABLE 4.1

settings such as date and time. This uses a battery to maintain power and hence the data when the main power is switched off.

Another use for RAM is as a *buffer*. We have already mentioned several times that the CPU speed and the speed of its internal buses is much faster than the speed of peripheral devices. A buffer is simply memory within a peripheral device, such as a printer. The computer sends the data to be printed to this buffer at the speed of the data bus. The buffer holds the data and the printer accesses it at its own speed.

ROM

ROM is non-volatile memory. This means that data stored within it is not lost when the power is switched off. However, as its name suggests it can only be read from, not written to. ROM is used to contain the start-up sequence for the computer system. This includes the BIOS (basic input/output system). When the computer is switched on, the BIOS is loaded first and then loads the operating system from disk so that the system can be used.

Cache memory

Cache is very fast access memory. In modern computers, cache is actually part of the CPU, rather than a separate chip. This means that it can be accessed at the speed of the CPU's internal bus. The way that cache works is by storing the last thing that was accessed from the main memory. Then, if the same thing is requested again, it can just be loaded straight from cache much faster than if the processor had to access the main memory again. An example of caching is when you use the Internet. Your connection to the Internet is much

slower than the connection from your computer's CPU to the hard disk. The first time you open a web page it may take a while to download. As well as opening on-screen the page will be saved in a folder on your hard disk. If you go back to the page, you will notice that it loads much more quickly. This is because, providing the date is the same, the page will be loaded from your computer's hard disk rather than over the Internet.

> ### Key terms
>
> *RAM (random access memory)*: volatile memory that can be written to and read from. Used for the temporary storage of data and programs.
>
> *ROM (read only memory)*: non-volatile memory that can only be read from. Used for storing system start-up files, including BIOS.
>
> *Address*: a unique number identifying a memory location.
>
> *Buffer*: memory in a peripheral device that acts as a buffer between faster bus speeds and slower peripherals.
>
> *Volatile*: memory is volatile if the content is lost when power is removed.
>
> *Cache*: fast access memory on the CPU that stores the most recently accessed data and instructions to speed up subsequent retrieval.

Disk drives

Computers need secondary storage in the form of disk drives so that programs and data can be stored when the computer is switched off. There are two main types of disk drive, magnetic and optical. Magnetic disks store data based on the polarity of microscopic magnetic fields or domains on the magnetic surface of the disk. Because the data is stored magnetically, it can easily be erased and rewritten. This is done using read/write heads that travel across the surface of the disk without actually touching it. An *optical disk* stores data based on the way laser light is reflected from its surface. On CD and DVD-ROMs the data bits are represented by the presence or absence of tiny pits on the surface of the disk. In this section we will look at the different types of magnetic disk drives and disks that may be required for a computer system. This is most likely to be a *hard disk* drive and possibly a *floppy disk* drive. Although there are others, such as zip drives, these have largely been replaced by re-writable optical drives.

Hard disks

An internal hard disk drive is the main secondary storage facility on a stand-alone computer system. It is where all the programs, including the operating system, and much of the data will be stored. A hard disk consists of one or more aluminium or glass platters that have a magnetic coating. The platters are mounted on a central spindle and are rotated by a motor. The three parameters that need to be considered when selecting a hard disk are its *rotation speed, access time* and *capacity*. The rotation speed is measured in revolutions per minute (rpm). Faster rotation speeds allow for faster access times. At the time of writing, a high-specification SCSI hard disk drive has a rotation speed of around 15,000 rpm. Access time is the time from the start of one disk access to the time when the next access can be started. This is measured in milliseconds (ms) and values between 5 and 15 ms are typical. The capacity is the amount of data that can be stored. Not so long ago, this was measured in MBs but at the time of writing, the smallest hard disk available is around 40 GB and 400 GB hard disks are available.

Many internal disk drives use *IDE* (integrated drive electronics) to connect to the motherboard. This is also known as ATA (advanced technology attachment). This means that the hard drive and the controller are combined. The controller is a circuit board with chips that provide guidance as to how the hard drive stores and accesses data. Most controllers also have some onboard memory that acts as a buffer to enhance the performance of the hard drive. IDE uses a parallel or ribbon cable for connection between the motherboard and the controller. Serial ATA (*SATA*) is a newer standard that uses a serial connection. As we discussed earlier, serial connection allows for longer cable lengths and thinner cables. This means there is more room for air to circulate within the case, keeping the components cool. The other alternative standard for connecting hard disks is SCSI. However, these are much more expensive and are used only when very fast access times are required or when a number of hard disks are needed, as they can be daisy-chained together.

So far we have talked about internal hard disk drives. It is also possible to have external hard drives. This means that the drive can be unplugged and locked in a safe, stored off-site or connected to another computer. The computer being used to type this unit has an external hard disk that mirrors the content of the internal one, thus providing a complete backup to the system. External hard drives can be connected via a USB, firewire or a SCSI port.

Floppy disks

A floppy disk has a flexible plastic circle covered with the magnetic material rather than a rigid platter. This is contained in a rigid plastic case for protection. The floppy disk must be placed into a floppy disk drive in the main processing unit to be read or written to. The main advantage of a floppy disk is its portability. It can be used on any computer that has a floppy disk drive. The main disadvantage of the floppy disk is its limited capacity – 1.44 MB. One way to increase the amount of data that can be stored on a floppy disk is to use *data compression* software. This works by removing unnecessary characters such as spaces to reduce the file size. However, this has a limited impact on the size of many graphics files, which are likely to exceed the capacity of a floppy disk. There are already computers that do not have a floppy disk drive. Writable CDs and solid state USB flash memory are largely replacing floppy disks.

USB flash memory

Flash memory sticks are about the size of a finger so are easily carried. They plug directly

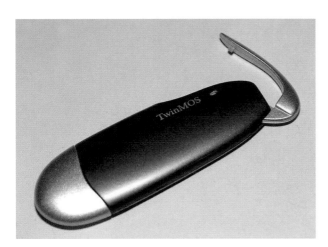

A USB memory stick

into a USB port on the computer and can be treated just like any other disk. They are currently available with capacities up to 1 GB. With both floppy disks and flash memory it is possible to *write protect* the disk. This means that it cannot be written to, preventing the deletion of important data. Flash memory also provides facilities for much more sophisticated security procedures to prevent anyone else gaining access to the data stored.

Optical disks

As we have already said, optical disks store and retrieve data by changing the optical properties of the surface of the disk using a laser. Originally, this was achieved by burning pits into the reflective surface of the disk. This required special equipment and so could only be used commercially to produce disks that could be read only by a *CD-ROM* drive. Subsequently, different methods were developed that provided disk drives capable of writing to optical disks: initially CD-R that can only be written to but not erased and then *CD-RW* that can be rewritten to many times. A standard CD has a capacity of 720 MB.

A *DVD-ROM* is another type of optical disk with a minimum capacity of 4.7 GB. As on a pre-recorded CD-ROM, the data is stored as a pattern of microscopic pits on the surface of the disk, which are read by reflecting light from a laser. DVDs can store much more data than CDs because the pits are closer together and the wavelength of the laser used to read them is shorter. Double-layered DVDs are also available. These have two parallel layers of pits at different depths. The reading laser is able to focus on each of these layers. These DVDs have a capacity of 8.5 GB. *DVD-RAM* is used to describe DVDs that can be written to, either once (DVD-R) or many times (DVD-RW). However, as with CD-R and CD-RW, DVD-R and DVD-RW use different methods of recording the data onto the blank disks.

Both CD drives and DVD drives use the same method of indicating the speed at which they read, write and rewrite. This is given as, for example, 16X. The same drive may read and write CDs at 52X but read DVDs at only 16X. Drives will usually have slower rewrite speeds than read and write speeds.

Theory into practice

Collect computer brochures from computer retailers – you may find you get some posted through your door – and visit computer suppliers' websites. Compare the specifications of the main processing units offered. Decide which one you would recommend to a student on a limited budget who needs a computer to produce essays and to access the Internet for research. Which would you recommend for a dedicated computer games player for whom money is no object?

Input devices

These are devices that allow data to be entered into the computer system. There are different types of input devices, each of which has a different purpose. These include the keyboard, mouse, scanner and microphone. You will need to be able to specify the most appropriate input devices to meet the needs of a user.

Keyboard

Virtually all computer systems will include a keyboard to allow the entry of textual and numeric data. There are, however, an increasing number of different types of keyboard available. Standard English keyboards have a QWERTY layout, so called because the first six letters on the top row of letter keys are Q, W, E, R, T and Y. Most have a separate block of number keys, known as a numeric keypad, cursor keys to move around the screen and function keys that can be programmed to perform particular functions.

The total number of keys on the keyboard can vary. Keyboards with 105 and 107 keys are common, but it is possible to buy keyboards for young children that have only 67 keys, while others include additional keys that allow you to open specific software packages, navigate web pages and cut, copy and paste. Most keyboards are more or less rectangular in shape, but more ergonomically designed keyboards are also available. These have a curved layout and are designed to reduce the risk of repetitive strain injury (RSI). Keyboards are available for different languages. Some, for example French, are very similar to an English keyboard but have keys for accented letters; others, such as Chinese, have a completely different set of characters.

There are also different ways of connecting the keyboard to the main processing unit. Traditionally, the keyboard was connected by a cable to a specific socket (port) known as a PS/2. This method of connection is increasingly being replaced by connection to a USB port either by a cable or wireless. In the case of a wireless keyboard, a small radio frequency receiver is connected to the USB port. The keyboard transmits radio frequency signals that are picked up by this receiver, removing the need for a physical connection between the keyboard and the computer. Usually, wireless keyboard packages also include a wireless mouse, which uses the same receiver.

Another type of keyboard is an overlay or concept keyboard. This does not have individual keys for each letter. Instead, it has a flat surface that is divided into a number of touch sensitive areas. Each area can be programmed to input a particular letter, word or phrase or perform a particular action. Concept keyboards are often used with young children or people with special needs who have difficulty using a standard keyboard. Another use of concept keyboards is in supermarkets where customers weigh their own fruit and vegetables. The customer simply presses

Wireless receiver, keyboard and mouse

a picture of the fruit or vegetable they are weighing to input the information. Concept keyboards are also used in fast food outlets and bars where there is a danger of liquids being spilled. As well as providing a wipe clean surface, data entry is also speeded up, as the operator needs only to locate and press the area corresponding to the item being sold.

There are also specialist keyboards available to help those with particular special needs use a computer. Braille keyboards are available for blind users. There are also large key keyboards for people who have difficulty reading the letters on a standard keyboard or lack the fine-motor control to press a standard sized key. Some people, such as those suffering from dyslexia, have difficulty using a standard QWERTY keyboard. Keyboards are available with keys in alphabetical order to help such people.

Mouse

A mouse or other pointing device is another essential input device on most computer systems, especially those that have a graphical user interface (GUI) – see the section on operating systems on page 140. The movement of the mouse on a surface moves the pointer on-screen and the buttons send a signal to the computer to carry out an action. Different types of mice are available. A mechanical mouse has a ball in the base that moves sensors within the casing to detect its movement. A mechanical mouse needs to be used on a mouse mat to work efficiently

and will tend to pick up dirt and dust, so the sensors need to be cleaned periodically. An optical mouse reflects infrared light off the surface it is on to detect its movement. It can be used on almost any surface without a mouse mat. Mice are available with different numbers of buttons. Two, three, four and even five button mice can be bought. A two-button mouse is adequate for most purposes – in MS Windows the left button performs an action and the right one brings up a menu. The other buttons can be programmed to perform different functions. Many mice also have a scroll wheel that allows you to scroll through a document or web page without using the on-screen scroll bars. As with keyboards, mice can be connected to a PS/2 port or, more usually, to a USB port, and can be wired or wireless.

An alternative to a mouse is a trackball. These have a ball on the top or side that is moved with the user's finger or thumb to move the pointer on-screen. As with mice, the movement can be picked up by mechanical sensors or optical ones. As trackballs do not need to be moved on a surface, they are ideal for use with laptops, some of which have a trackball built in. The other option for moving the pointer on a laptop is a touchpad. This is simply a flat touch sensitive pad with two buttons beside it that operate like mouse buttons. The user moves the pointer by simply moving their finger on the pad. Rather than use the left button to perform an action, the touchpad can be programmed so that the action can be performed by tapping it.

Scanner

A scanner is a device that converts information that is on paper into a form that can be input into a computer. It works by passing a light over the page and measuring the intensity of the reflected light. Scanners are most often used to transfer images onto a computer but, with optical character recognition (OCR) software, they can also be used to copy text into a word processing program. *Flatbed* scanners are the most common type. As the name suggests, the item to be copied is laid face down on a flat surface and the light source moves under it. This makes it possible to scan items from a book, for example. Another type of scanner is a page scanner. This type of scanner can copy only from a single sheet of paper. In this type of scanner, the light source is stationary and the paper moves. Both flatbed and page scanners are often combined in a single unit with a printer and sometimes a fax machine to form what is known as an all in one printer. These are useful for people who have limited space, particularly those who work from home, as they provide scanning, printing, photocopying and sometimes fax facilities in one device.

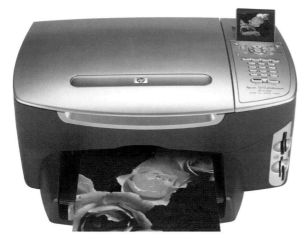

All in one printer with page scanner

Scanners are available in both A4 and A3 size – this is the size of page they can copy, although some modern scanners are physically not much larger than the paper size – and usually connect to the USB port. The most important parameter when choosing a scanner is the *resolution*. This is measured in dots per inch (dpi). The higher the resolution of the scanner, the higher the quality of the scanned image will be. Higher resolution will also enable you to enlarge an image more without it becoming *pixelated*.

Microphone
A microphone allows the input of sound into a computer. This allows the recording of sound as WAV files to include in multimedia presentations. A microphone can also be used with voice recognition software to dictate text directly into a word processing package, rather than typing it. This can be very useful for people who have difficulty using the keyboard. Another use for a microphone is for audio or, together with a

webcam, video conferencing. Microphones can be mounted on the computer monitor or made to stand on the desk. They can also be bought combined with headphones or combined with a webcam. All microphones use a jack plug to plug into the microphone socket on the sound card or onboard sound controller.

Output devices
Computers would be of little use without devices to output the results of processing. The most important output device is the VDU. Most general purpose computer systems will also need a printer for hardcopy output and multimedia computer systems will include loudspeakers to output sound.

VDU (visual display unit)
A VDU is essential for all computer systems. In the past, all desktop computers used a VDU with a cathode ray tube (CRT). Using a CRT the text and images are displayed by a stream of electrons hitting a special surface, causing individual dots to glow – as in a standard television set. CRT VDUs are physically bulky, being at least as deep as they are wide, so they take up a lot of desk space – they have a large footprint. They are also quite heavy. Laptop computers needed to use a different technology to display data on screen and thin film transistor (TFT) screens were developed. These use the properties of materials that exist in a *liquid crystal* state to display the image. There was, originally, a limit to the size of TFT screens and the possible resolution was lower than for a CRT. However, this technology has improved to allow larger screens to be produced at lower prices and with the same resolution capabilities as CRTs. Consequently, TFT VDUs are increasingly replacing CRT VDUs for use with desktop computers.

The main advantage of TFT VDUs over CRT VDUs is the very much smaller footprint, which is no more than the base the VDU stands on – 20 to 30 cm. The display size of a VDU is the corner to corner diagonal measurement (see Figure 4.1), in inches, of the actual display area. The most common sizes are 15, 17, 19 and 21 inch. The larger the screen size, the easier it is to see the detail of images. Fifteen-inch monitors are

A CRT and a TFT VDU to show relative sizes

adequate for text-based applications but larger monitors are better for highly graphical applications such as desktop publishing, photo editing or computer aided design (CAD).

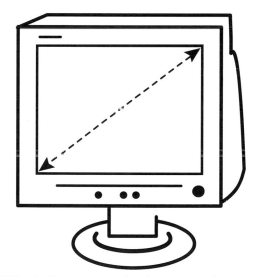

FIGURE 4.1 *How screen size is measured*

An added benefit of a TFT screen is the fact that the display area is slightly larger than a CRT screen for the same stated size. This is because the TFT is flat, while the front of the CRT is curved.

Whether the VDU uses CRT or TFT technology, the display is made up of individual dots called pixels. Each pixel can be displayed in a range of colours depending on the *colour mode* that is set. The number of bits used to hold the colour information for a single pixel determines the number of different colours that can be displayed – the colour quality.

Eight bits can display 256 different colours, 16 bits can display over 65,000 different colours, while 24 or 32 bits can display more than 16 million different colours. This is sometimes known as true colour because it is more than the 10 million different shades discernible by the human eye.

The resolution of a monitor refers to the number of pixels that can be displayed. This is given as the horizontal number × the vertical number, for example, 1024 × 768 pixels. The physical number of pixels that can be displayed will determine the maximum resolution but lower resolutions can be set.

In CRT VDUs, the beam of electrons moves along the rows of pixels line by line. As the display on a VDU is not static, this must be repeated each time the screen changes. This can lead to a slight flickering of the display. If this flickering is too noticeable it can lead to eyestrain and headaches. The features of the VDU specification that affect the amount of flicker are the *scan frequency*, the *refresh rate* and the *interlace* mode. Scan frequency is the number of lines of pixels a VDU can display in a second. This is measured in kilohertz (kHz) and is generally between 20 and 100 kHz. The higher the frequency, the less flicker there will be. The refresh rate is the maximum number of frames (whole screens) that can be displayed in a second. Again, the higher the refresh rate, the less flicker will be apparent. Interlace mode makes the display easier to look at byblending the changes between repeated image displays.

Printer

There are several different types of printer with a wide range of specifications. The most common types of printer are *laser* printers and *inkjet* printers. Laser printers fuse dry ink powder called toner onto electrically charged areas of the paper using heat. Inkjet printers spray tiny dots of ink onto the paper. Inkjet printers are almost always capable of printing in colour, while both black and white and colour laser printers are available. The relative cost to buy different types of printer is less varied than it used to be although there is a wide range of prices within each type, depending on the printer's specification. However, buying the printer is not the only cost. When selecting a printer, you should also consider the cost of replacement toner or ink cartridges and how frequently these will need replacing.

The specification of a printer will be given by the resolution, which like a scanner is measured in dots per inch (dpi), and the print speed measured in pages per minute (ppm). The higher the resolution, the higher the quality of the printed image will be. However, the print quality of inkjet printers is also dependent on the media being used as normal paper absorbs the ink dots. Special matt or glossy photographic paper is needed to obtain the best-quality image. Laser printers tend to offer greater printing speeds but lower resolution than inkjets but, because dry toner is used, better-quality is possible using standard paper. The choice of printer will depend very much on what it will be used for and how much it will be used. Most printers can print on A4 paper as a maximum, but it is possible to buy A3 or even A2 printers. At the time of writing, the latest innovation is a printer than can be connected directly to a digital camera without needing a computer. These print up to 10×20 cm photographs.

An older type of printer is a dot-matrix printer. This type of printer is known as an impact printer because it works by hammering pins against an inked ribbon to make up the characters or image. Because of this, dot-matrix printers are noisier than inkjets and lasers. They are also slower and offer much lower resolutions. The main reason that dot-matrix printers are still used is for printing on multi-part stationery, such as orders or invoices. The physical impact of the pins ensures that, when the top copy is printed, the text is transferred to the other copies. Dot-matrix printers used to be the cheapest to buy and run. As they are no longer in common use, this is no longer the case.

A completely different method of producing hardcopy output is a plotter. The most common is a flatbed plotter. The paper is placed on the bed of the plotter and the computer controls a number of pens that literally draw the image. Plotters are most often used with computer aided design (CAD) systems and can be A1 size or larger.

As was mentioned in the section on memory, a printer or plotter will contain some RAM that acts as a *buffer* between the CPU and the printer. The CPU outputs the data to the buffer and the printer can then access it at its own speed.

Most printers now are designed to connect to the USB port, although some also offer the capability of connecting to the parallel port. A few older dot-matrix printers offer connection only to the parallel or serial ports.

Speaker

Speakers are needed to output sound from a computer. Internal speakers offer only low-quality sound. For multimedia systems or

Key terms

Resolution: a measure of the number of pixels on a VDU or the dots per inch in a printed or scanned image.

Pixelated: where the individual pixels become visible and the image appears as square blocks of colour.

Liquid crystal: having some properties of solids and some properties of liquids.

Flatbed: a scanner where the image to be scanned is placed on a flat surface and the light source moves or a plotter where the paper is placed on a flat surface and the pens move to draw the image.

Inkjet: a printer that sprays dots of ink onto the paper to create the image.

Laser: a printer that uses heat to fuse dry ink powder onto electrically charged areas of the paper.

Buffer: RAM in a printer where the CPU sends the data to be printed.

Colour mode: the number of bits used to hold the colour information for each pixel and hence the number of possible colours.

Scan frequency: in a CRT monitor, the number of rows of pixels that can be displayed in a second.

Refresh rate: the number of frames that can be displayed on a CRT monitor per second.

Interlace: the blending of changes between repeated displays of images.

CASE STUDY – JOHN

John works for a construction project management company. Apart from normal office work, he uses his computer to produce architectural drawings and 3D architectural models which he sends to his clients both electronically and on paper.

His system consists of a 3 GHz CPU, 512 MB of DDR RAM, a 120 GB SATA hard disk, a 256 MB graphics card, a 21" monitor and a CD-RW. His system has a dedicated A2 printer and a broadband link to the Internet.

CASE STUDY – JAMES

James is a music student who also works part-time for a local radio station. He uses his computer mainly for his university work, but also produces compilations of music and jingles for the radio station.

His computer consists of a 2.4 GHz CPU, 256 MB of DDR RAM, an 80 GB hard drive, on-board graphics, a 15" TFT monitor, a CD-ROM and a CD-RW. The system also has on-board sound, which has 6-channel speaker output and digital input/output.

Knowledge check

Explain the technical terms used in the specifications for John's and James's computer systems. Compare the likely performance of the two systems and explain how each meets the particular needs of its user.

listening to music CDs, powered external speakers are needed. These use a stereo jack plug to connect to the audio-out socket of the sound card or onboard sound controller. Some 'multimedia' VDUs have built-in speakers but these do not tend to offer particularly good sound quality. For personal listening, headphones can be used as an alternative to loudspeakers.

Configuring and testing systems

Configuring a system means changing the settings so that the components of the system work together and the system works as the user requires. As you do not have to upgrade the physical components in a system as part of this unit, the configuration activities you need to carry out will be done using software and will be covered in more detail later in this unit. However,

whenever you change settings on a computer system you will need to carry out tests to check that the system works correctly and the changes do what you want them to.

It is good practice when you are planning to set up and configure a system to also plan the tests that you will carry out. This is best done as follows, using a table as shown in Table 4.2.

You should fill in the first two columns at the planning stage. The remaining two columns should be completed during the system configuration, as you carry out each test. Hopefully, in most cases the actual result will be what you expected and so no further action will be necessary.

Software

Software is the range of programs that turn a box of electronic components into a complex tool capable of carrying out a wide range of tasks. There are different categories of software for different purposes. These include BIOS (basic input/output system) start-up software, operating systems, GUI (graphical user interfaces) and applications software. In the following sections we will consider the purpose of each category of software and how each can be configured to meet a user's needs.

TEST TO BE CARRIED OUT	EXPECTED RESULT	ACTUAL RESULT	ACTION REQUIRED
Try to print a document.	Document will print correctly.	Document failed to print.	Check correct printer driver selected and retest.

TABLE 4.2

BIOS (basic input/output system) start-up software

When you press the power button on a computer to switch it on, it is the BIOS and start-up software that is the first to load. This software is stored in the ROM on the motherboard. As its name suggests, BIOS enables the CPU to communicate with basic input and output devices. This means it recognises input from the keyboard and allows output to the VDU. The BIOS then loads the operating system and GUI from disk.

There are a number of settings that can be configured within BIOS, but you need to be careful what you change as you could make the system unusable by making some changes. To access the start-up settings you need to press the **DEL** key when the computer is first switched on. You will need to use the keyboard to move around the screens and make the changes required. There will be instructions on-screen to tell you which keys to use. When you have finished, you will need to select the option to save changes and exit. This will take you back to the start-up screen and continue to load the operating system. The following are some of the settings you might need to change in BIOS:

* *system time and date* – this is one of the simplest changes that can be made in BIOS. This may be necessary if, for example, the computer's internal battery has run down and had to be replaced
* *start-up (boot) disk drive* – this specifies where the operating system is located. Usually, this will be set to the computer's main hard disk but sometimes it may be necessary to boot from a different disk drive, such as a floppy disk or CD. You will need to do this when you install an operating system from CD-ROM. Once the operating system is installed, you

will need to change the boot disk drive back to the hard disk. Otherwise, it should be necessary to change to a different disk drive only if a fault occurs in the hard disk, its controller or the operating system installed on it

* *defining a new disk drive* – if an additional disk drive is installed, the BIOS may need to be changed to recognise it, but most modern BIOS will automatically change to recognise a new drive
* *system password* – this will allow you to set a password that will have to be entered before the computer can be used. It will usually also need to be entered before any changes to system settings can be made, so if you apply a system password, make sure you remember what it is!

Think it over...

Access the BIOS on a stand-alone computer. Find out what settings are included and how to change them. Exit **without** saving the changes this time so that you don't change anything you didn't mean to.

Operating systems

The operating system is the software that enables the user to interact with the computer system and that allows the hardware and software to work together. There are many different types of operating system, although the choice for a particular type of hardware may be limited. Examples of operating systems include Microsoft Windows®, MS-DOS, MacOS, Linux and Unix. Some operating systems, such as MS-DOS and Unix, provide a command line interface (CLI) for the user. This means that the user has to type in commands to get the computer to do what they want. For example, in MS-DOS, if you wanted to copy a text file to a floppy disk you would have to type COPY filename.txt A:, where A: is the floppy drive. Obviously, to use a CLI you need to know the commands for different tasks, so they are not easy to use. Other operating systems, such as Windows® and MacOS offer a GUI. This type of interface allows the user to give the computer instructions by selecting icons or items from a menu by clicking with a mouse.

As mentioned previously, whichever operating system is chosen, it will need to be installed on the computer's hard disk, most usually from a CD-ROM. To install an operating system, first set the BIOS to boot from the computer's CD-ROM drive. Put the operating system CD-ROM in the drive and follow the instructions on screen, selecting options from the displayed menus as appropriate. When the operating system has been installed, change the boot disk drive back to the hard disk drive in BIOS.

GUI (graphic user interfaces)

A GUI is a user-friendly interface between the user and the computer system. A GUI uses windows, icons, menus and a pointer (WIMP) on a desktop (the main screen of a GUI from which the user can launch programs – see Figure 4.2).

Most personal computers use a GUI and the majority of these use a version of Microsoft Windows® although other interfaces are available.

Configuring the operating system and user interface

Once the operating system has been installed, it can be configured to meet the user's needs. Peripheral devices, such as printers, and extension cards, such

FIGURE 4.2 *A GUI desktop*

as sound cards or network cards, will need device drivers to operate correctly. A device driver is a program that allows the device and the operating system to communicate. The operating system may include some generic device drivers but most will need to be installed from the disk provided with the device. If you are upgrading to a newer version of the operating system, you may need to download new versions of device drivers from the Internet. Plug and play systems will search the computer's hard disk for device drivers and prompt you to insert the relevant CD-ROM if no suitable driver is found.

As well as installing device drivers, there are many other ways that the operating system and GUI can be configured. The way that the configuration is carried out will depend on the operating system and GUI installed on your computer. You will need to find out how to perform different changes to the configuration on the particular system you are setting up. The descriptions and illustrations in the following sections relate to an MS Windows XP operating system.

Time and date

The time and date can be changed either by selecting **Date and Time** from the **Control Panel** (see Figure 4.3), or by simply double clicking on the time shown on the taskbar of the desktop. The correct date can be selected on the calendar and the correct time by selecting the hours, minutes or seconds and then using the arrow buttons to increase or decrease the value.

Password properties

It is possible to set up different users each with their own user account. Each user can then be assigned a password so that others cannot access their personal user area and files (see Figure 4.4).

Notice that when the new password is typed in it does not appear on-screen. This is so that someone else cannot read it. Notice also that you need to enter the password twice. This is to ensure that it is entered the same both times and is, therefore, what was intended.

Scheduled tasks

You can tell the operating system when and how often to run particular tasks, such as performing a backup. For example, you could schedule a backup for 5.30 pm each day. To do this you need to select **Scheduled Tasks** in **Control Panel**, double click on **Add Schedule Task** and then use the wizard to set up the task you want to schedule.

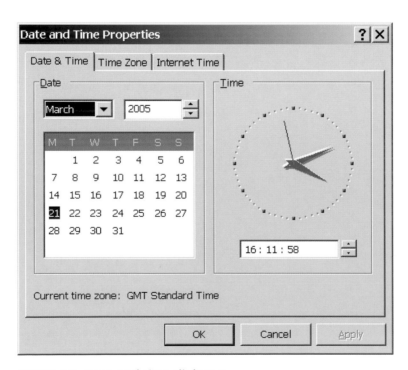

FIGURE 4.3 *Date and time dialogue*

FIGURE 4.4 *Setting a password*

Virus protection configuration

Virus protection software can be configured by selecting what is checked for viruses (see Figure 4.5), when it is checked and how often the software is updated.

To ensure that the computer system is as protected as possible, it is best to set the software to check files automatically and to update automatically as soon as new virus definitions are available. The way that the software is configured will depend on the particular virus protection software installed.

Directory (folder) structure and settings

The directory or folder structure is the way that the operating system organises files. The operating system will set up a structure for storing the files it needs and the files for any applications software installed. Setting up the folder structure to store user files so that they are easy to locate is an important part of

configuring a system. A folder structure can have a number of hierarchical levels, like a tree with its root at the top. Indeed, the main directory on a disk drive is known as the root directory. It is shown as 'drive letter':\, for example C:\ (see Figure 4.6). When setting up a new system, you need to find out from the user what the computer will be used for and what files will be stored. For example, if the computer is for both business and home use, you might start off by creating two folders called 'business files' and 'home files'. The next stage might be to create sub-folders in the business files folder for different types of files such as documents, spreadsheets, publications, etc. The documents folder could then have sub-folders for different types of document, such as letters, memos, contracts, etc. The letters folder might then have a separate sub-folder for letters to particular companies, or about particular subjects and so on. The home files folder could be organised in a similar way.

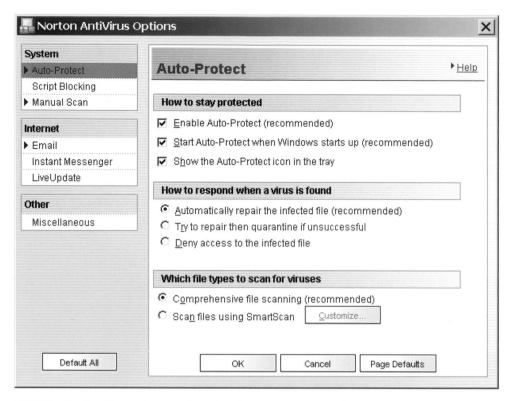

FIGURE 4.5 *Configuration options in virus protection software*

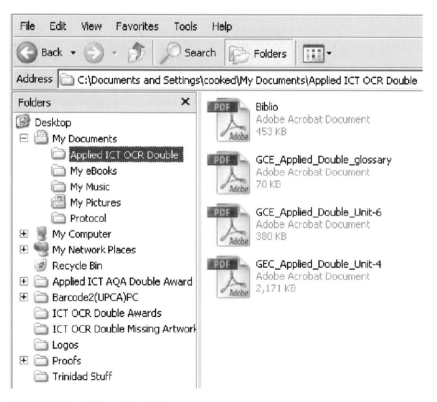

FIGURE 4.6 *Folder structure*

To start creating the folder structure, you select **My computer** from the desktop and then the drive or folder the structure will be in. **Select File, New** and **Folder** and then enter a name for the folder. To create sub-folders, select the folder and then **File, New, Folder** and enter a name for each sub-folder required.

Selecting **Folder Options** from **Control Panel** allows you to change the settings for folders, such as how they are displayed.

Multimedia configuration

How you configure the settings for multimedia will depend on the media player you have installed on the computer system. You may be able to configure video settings, sound in and sound out, language, music and other options. You will also be able to configure the sound and audio devices such as the speakers by selecting **Sound** and **Audio Devices** from **Control Panel** (see Figure 4.7).

Printer, mouse and keyboard configuration

The settings for all of these devices can be accessed by selecting the relevant icon in **Control Panel**. You can add a new printer to those available by selecting **Add Printer**. You may need to load the printer driver from disk during this process. You can also delete printers that are no longer in use.

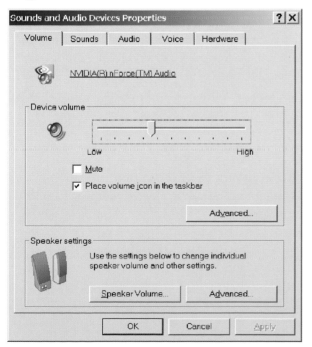

FIGURE 4.7 *Volume settings dialogue*

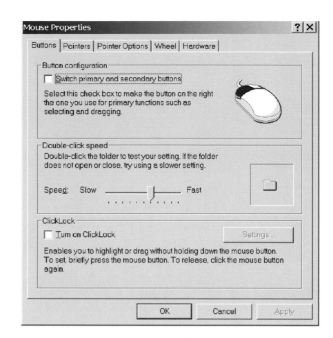

FIGURE 4.8 *Mouse settings dialogue*

The mouse can be configured in many different ways (see Figure 4.8).

If the user is left-handed, swapping the primary button from left to right is a good idea. You can change the double click speed, for example to slow it down if the user finds it difficult to select by double clicking. You can change the speed with which the pointer moves (see Figure 4.9) and you can add mouse trails to make the pointer more visible. This may be helpful to a user whose eyesight is poor. Another

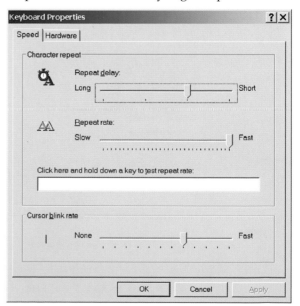

FIGURE 4.9 *Keyboard settings dialogue*

setting that can be changed is the shape of pointer that is used for different purposes – the scheme. You can select from a range of options or you can select your own pointer for each purpose. Within the available options are enlarged pointer schemes that would also be helpful to users who have difficulty seeing the standard pointers.

For young children or users who have difficulty pressing and releasing keys on the keyboard, it may help to make the keyboard repeat delay as long as possible and make the key board repeat rate as slow as possible. This will mean that, if the user continues to press a key inadvertently, he or she will not end up with a whole row of the same letter.

GUI desktop and display set-up

There is a multitude of ways that the GUI desktop and display can be configured (see Figure 4.10). You can change what appears on the taskbar at the bottom of the desktop and in the start menu that appears when you click the **Start** button. You can do this by selecting **Taskbar** and **Start Menu** from **Control Panel** or by right clicking on an empty part of the taskbar itself. In the same way, you can change display settings by selecting the **Display** icon in **Control Panel** or by right clicking on a blank area of the desktop.

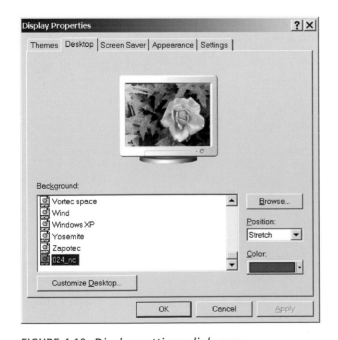

FIGURE 4.10 *Display settings dialogue*

Within the display settings dialogue you can choose a theme for the desktop or choose a background – or wallpaper – that will appear on the desktop. This can be any graphic file – the rose in the screen print is a photograph taken in my garden. You can choose a screen saver, set how long the computer should be inactive before it switches on and set a password to regain access to the work in progress. This last option is useful when a computer in a public place may be left unattended. Once the screen saver is activated, only authorised people who know the password will be able to switch off the screen saver and access the files. You can also change the appearance of the desktop by selecting the style, colour scheme and font size, as well as other options such as the size of the icons. Selecting large or extra large font and large icons may be helpful for a user with poor eyesight. Finally, you can change the display settings such as the screen resolution and the colour quality.

Application software icons

We have already said that the size of the icons on the desktop can be changed. It is also possible to change how the icons are organised on-screen, such as by name or by type. You can tidy up the desktop by deleting icons of programs that are rarely used – they will still be accessible from the start menu. To delete an icon, right click on it and select delete from the menu that appears. You can also add icons to the desktop for commonly used programs. To add an icon to the desktop, find the program in the start menu and right click on it. Select **Send to** from the menu that is displayed and then select **Desktop**.

Checking and setting system properties

Selecting the **System** icon from **Control Panel** gives you access to the system properties. This is where you can find out what processor is installed, its speed and the amount of RAM installed. Here, you can also use **Device Manager** to check what devices are installed on the computer and set up hardware profiles so that you can select from different hardware configurations when you start up the computer. Other system properties that can be changed include scheduling live updates, setting disk space for system restore and advanced settings relating to performance, user profiles and startup and recovery.

Applications software

Applications software is the software that allows you to carry out particular processing activities. By now, you will almost certainly have used a range of different applications software packages while studying other units in this course, in other subjects prior to starting the course or at home. You will need to be able to specify, install and configure applications software to meet users' particular needs.

Installing software

Once you have installed the operating system and user interface, installing most applications software is relatively straightforward. Most software will be supplied on a CD-ROM. You should put this in the CD-ROM drive. The installation software will most probably load and run automatically. If it doesn't you will need to select **Run** from the **Start** menu and then browse the CD-ROM for an appropriate file (often called startup.exe) to install the software. Depending on the software being installed, you may have to enter various items of information and select various options. You will almost always have to click to agree to the licence agreement before the software will install; you may also need to enter a product key that is included with the software documentation. Most software will tell you where the program files will be stored on the hard disk and give you the option to change this. For example, if there are two hard disk drives on the computer, you may want install all the software on one drive and use the other for data files, so you might need to change the drive letter. You may also be asked to enter details such as the user's name and company. Many software packages will give you options regarding which parts of the software you want to install. You will usually be offered a full installation, a typical installation and a custom installation. As its name suggests, the full installation will install everything, including facilities that the user may never

CASE STUDY

Mary has just bought a computer so that she can keep in touch with her daughter and grandchildren in New Zealand by email. She has asked you to configure it for her so that it is easy to use. Mary is left-handed and, as a result of suffering a stroke, she has lost some control of her finger movement. At the moment she finds it difficult to double-click the mouse and often gets unwanted repeated characters when using the keyboard. Mary says her eyesight is not what it was and that she has difficulty seeing the standard icons and reading standard size text on the desktop. Mary has heard about the problems that viruses can cause and wants to ensure that her virus protection software is set up to check all files and emails automatically; she also would like the software to be updated automatically. As well as using email and accessing the Internet, Mary will use word processing software to write letters to friends, to keep the minutes of her senior citizens' club committee meetings and to write invitations to potential speakers for club meetings. She wants no unnecessary icons on the desktop and wants a folder structure to keep her files organised.

Knowledge check

Write a specification for the configuration of Mary's computer. Configure a system to match the configuration you have specified.

need. The typical installation installs the components that most people will use. Custom installation allows you to select precisely which components of the software you want to install, so you need install only exactly what the user requires. When the installation is complete, most software will automatically place an icon on the desktop and some will add an icon to the taskbar as well. You will need to decide whether to leave them there or remove them so that the program is accessed only from the **Start** menu.

Document (word) processing

Although modern word processing packages have fairly sophisticated facilities for including graphics within documents, they still deal better with text than graphics. Consequently, you should specify this type of software when the user needs to carry out mainly text-based processing, such as producing letters, reports, essays, etc.

Desktop publishing

Desktop publishing (DTP) packages provide greater control over the positioning of text and graphics than even the most sophisticated document processing package. A master page layout can be set so that items appear in the same position on each page and text or image frames can be accurately aligned with layout guides. Often, DTP packages also offer templates and wizards for a wide range of types of document. A DTP package should be specified when the user wants to create documents that combine text and graphics such as newsletters, brochures, flyers, etc.

Multimedia reference

An example of multimedia reference software is a multimedia encyclopaedia but there are many others. Multimedia reference software will usually provide a menu system, possibly a search engine, buttons and hyperlinks to navigate through the software and locate the information required. You may need to specify a generic package, such as an encyclopaedia, if the user wants a general reference source, or a more specific package if the user has a particular interest.

Programming languages

A programming language is the applications software used to write other programs. There are many different programming languages; the one you specify will depend on the user's expertise and the type of programs he or she wants to create. To find out more about programming languages, you should read Unit 8: Introduction to Programming.

Web browsers

A web browser is the software used to view web pages. It provides facilities to move back and forward through the pages viewed, to stop a page loading or refresh a page, to add pages to a list of favourites and to access a history of the sites visited. You can also use a search engine and print web pages. If you install MS Windows® as the operating system, the web browser Internet Explorer (IE) will also be installed. However, there are other web browsers available and the user may want you to specify an alternative to IE.

Email software

In order to send and receive emails, the user will need email client software. As well as being able to compose and send emails and receive emails from others, you can reply to an email or forward it to someone else. There will also be a facility to delete emails and to print them out. The email client software specified will depend on the user's preferences.

Database (record structure)

Database software is more correctly called database management software (DBMS). A database, as you will probably have discovered in Units 2 and 3, is an organised collection of data in the form of records, where a record is all the data about one person or thing. So, for example, a personnel database will contain a record for each employee – usually identified by a unique employee number. Each record will contain all the data about one particular employee. The records in the database can be sorted and searched to find records that match particular criteria. The results of searches or queries can then be output as reports. A database may consist of a single table of records – a flat-file database – or it may consist of more than one related table – a relational database. You will need to specify database software if the user wants to store and manipulate records of data, particularly when the records will be in related tables.

Spreadsheet (numeric structure)

You will also have met spreadsheet software if you have already studied Unit 3. It is possible to use spreadsheet software to create a simple flat-file database but the strength of spreadsheet software lies in its use to manipulate numeric data and perform calculations. A spreadsheet consists of a table of cells, each of which can hold a label, data or a formula. If the formulae relate to other cells, if data in those cells is changed, the formula will be recalculated and the cell will display the new result. This allows the user to answer 'what if' questions. The data in a spreadsheet can also be displayed in charts or graphs. Most spreadsheet software provides the facility for linking a number of spreadsheets in a workbook, which can be saved as a single file. This means that a separate sheet could be used to calculate the sales figures for each quarter (three months) with the totals copied onto a fifth sheet to provide an annual summary. You should specify spreadsheet software if the user needs to manipulate or analyse numeric data and make predictions by asking 'what if' questions.

Vector graphics

Vector graphics software is often called drawing software. It stores graphic images mathematically; for example, a line could be determined by the co-ordinates of its start and end point. This makes this type of software particularly appropriate for geometrical drawings, such as floor plans or scale drawings. With vector graphics software, it is possible to manipulate individual objects within the drawing by, for example, copying, pasting or reflecting them. Because the objects that make up the drawing are stored mathematically, it is also possible to enlarge the drawing with no loss of clarity. Computer aided design (CAD) is one type of vector graphics software. You will need to specify vector graphics software when the user wants to create scalable drawings, such as kitchen or garden designs, house plans, production drawings, etc.

CASE STUDY

The Li family has just bought a computer and requires a specification for the applications software to be installed on it. All the family will use the computer. Both Mr and Mrs Li sometimes bring work home in the evenings and at weekends. Mr Li's work mostly involves writing letters and reports, while Mrs Li has to analyse the number of responses from direct marketing campaigns. Both Mr and Mrs Li belong to a local amateur dramatics group and want to use the computer to produce posters and programmes for the group's productions. These will include edited digital photographs of the actors and sets. Mr and Mrs Li have two teenage children who want to use the computer to help with their homework. They will use the Internet for research but would also like a multimedia encyclopaedia that they can search for information. All the family would like to use email to communicate with family, friends and business colleagues.

Bitmap graphics

Bitmap graphics software is often called painting software or photo-editing software. It stores images as a series of pixels. Images taken with a digital camera or input from a scanner will produce this type of image and need photo-editing software to manipulate them. Individual objects within the image cannot be manipulated; the available editing tools change the individual pixels that make up the image. For example, a brush tool changes the colour of all the pixels it 'paints', while a spray tool will change individual pixels to simulate a spray of paint. Depending on the resolution of the original image, when a bitmap graphic image is enlarged, it may become blurred and appear as a series of blocks (pixellated). This effect is less apparent when the original image has a high resolution. Bitmap graphics software should be specified when the user wants to manipulate and edit images from a scanner or digital camera, or create images using painting tools such as brushes and sprays.

Knowledge check

Produce a software specification for the Li family. If possible, install the software you specify on a computer.

Configuring applications software

As it is possible to configure the operating system and user interface, so it is possible to configure applications software to meet the needs of the user more closely. You can configure how the software appears on startup, where it looks for files, how frequently it automatically saves your work and whether it creates an automatic backup. You can also create shortcuts called macros to carry out frequently performed tasks and templates that include all the data that is the same every time, so that only the data that has changed needs to be added.

Preferences (or configuration files)

Most software will allow you to change settings using preferences or options (see Figures 4.11 and 4.12). These settings will be saved in the configuration file for the software so that they will be the same each time the software is opened. The settings that can be changed may vary from software package to software package.

A common option is the units used for measurement on the ruler and when positioning objects. This can be set to centimetres, inches, pixels, points or pica depending on the software. We will consider some of the other options that can be set in more detail later in this section.

Macros

In many applications packages it is possible to create macros to carry out frequently required tasks. For example, I frequently have to insert a tick symbol into a table in documents. To do this, I would have to select **Insert**, then **Symbol**, then select the font that includes the symbol, then select the symbol and click **Insert** and then close the dialogue. Finally, I would need to change the font size and centre the tick in the cell: a total of more than 10 mouse clicks. I have created a macro to perform this task which is activated by a tick button on the toolbar. Now when I need to insert a tick, I simply make sure the cursor is in the correct cell and click the tick button.

To record a macro, you select **Macro** from the **Tools** menu and then **Record new macro**. You will be asked to give the macro a name. You will also have the option of assigning a shortcut key and deciding where the macro is stored – this will determine where it can be used. Next you carry out the steps that you want the macro to perform and, when you have finished, you click the stop recording button. To run the macro, you can select **Tools**, **Macro**, select it from the list of macros and select Run, or you can press the key combination assigned to it. However, the easiest option is to add a button to the toolbar to run the macro. We will look at this in the next section. There are many different tasks that could be carried out using a macro depending on the needs of the user. You could create macros to insert a signature, or different standard paragraphs in a letter, or you could create a macro to select a particular print area and print out part of a spreadsheet, for example.

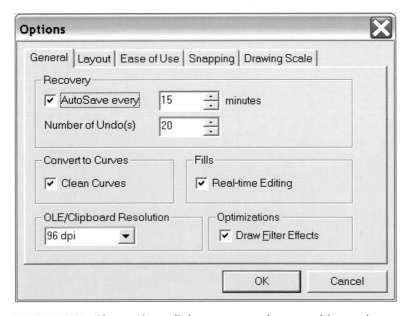

Options

| Track Changes | User Information | Compatibility | File Locations |
| View | General | Edit | Print | Save | Spelling & Grammar |

General options

☑ Background repagination
☐ Help for WordPerfect users
☐ Navigation keys for WordPerfect users
☐ Blue background, white text
☐ Provide feedback with sound
☑ Provide feedback with animation
☐ Confirm conversion at Open
☑ Update automatic links at Open
☑ Mail as attachment
☑ Recently used file list: 4   entries
☑ Macro virus protection

Measurement units: Centimeters ▼

OK   Cancel

FIGURE 4.11 *The options dialogue menu in a word processing package*

Options

| General | Layout | Ease of Use | Snapping | Drawing Scale |

Recovery
☑ AutoSave every   15   minutes
Number of Undo(s)   20

Convert to Curves
☑ Clean Curves

Fills
☑ Real-time Editing

OLE/Clipboard Resolution
96 dpi ▼

Optimizations
☑ Draw Filter Effects

OK   Cancel

FIGURES 4.12 *The options dialogues menu in a graphics package*

Toolbars and the buttons available

It is possible in most software to determine which toolbars are shown on-screen and to edit, or even create, new toolbars to meet the needs of the user. The available toolbars are usually listed in the **Toolbars** option in the **View** menu. They can also be accessed by right clicking anywhere in the toolbar area. Those that have a tick by them are displayed on-screen. It is possible to add or remove a tick by clicking on the toolbar name. Within the list there will probably be an option to customise toolbars. This provides the option to add or remove buttons, or to create a completely new toolbar. Within MS Office applications, to create a new toolbar, you select **New** and then give the toolbar a name. You can then add commands to the toolbar by dragging them onto it – you add new buttons to an existing toolbar in the same way. To remove buttons you can simply drag them off the toolbar. To add a button for a macro, select **Macros** from the list of commands and then select the macro you want to use and drag it onto the toolbar. Initially, the button will display the name of the macro, but right clicking on it will produce a menu that includes the option to change the button image. However, the options available for customising toolbars and how you add and delete buttons will depend on the software being configured.

Directory structures and defaults

We have already discussed creating directory/folder structures when configuring the operating system. It is also possible to create folder structures within applications software. The **Save** or **Save As** dialogue will include a button that allows you to create a new folder. Within applications software, it is also possible to configure the default folder for different types of files. This is where the software will load and save files if you do not specify otherwise and where it will look for clipart, templates and other resources (see Figure 4.13).

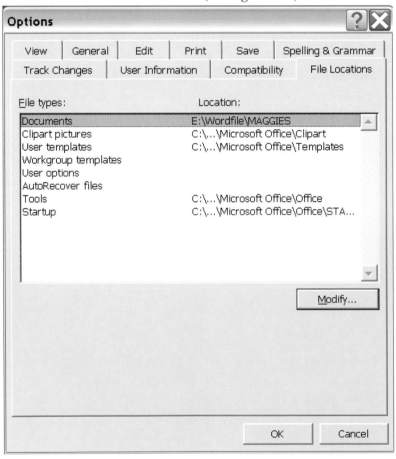

FIGURE 4.13 *File location dialogue*

Where available, the file location dialogue can be accessed by selecting **Options** from the **Tools** menu. Clicking on **Modify** will allow you to change the default folders.

Data templates

A template allows documents to be created that have a standard layout and style. Unit 1 describes how to create a template in word processing software. It is also possible to create templates in other software such as a spreadsheet template. This is created in much the same way. First you set up the spreadsheet with suitable titles, column and row headers and the formulae required. You then select **Save As** and choose **Template** as the file type. To use the template, select **New** from the **File** menu and then the template you want to use. A possible use for a spreadsheet template would be an invoice where the user only needs to enter the purchaser details, items and prices and the spreadsheet automatically calculates the total, VAT, etc.

Saving and backup security

In some software, it is possible to change the settings for how and what is saved (see Figure 4.14), whether a backup is automatically created and to protect files with a password.

Where available, these settings are changed in the **Save** dialogue, which can be accessed from **Options** in the **Tools** menu.

Menu layout and contents

In some software, it is possible to change the layout and content of menus in much the same way as toolbars (see Figure 4.15).

By dragging **New Menu** onto the menu bar, you can then drag other commands onto it. Right clicking gives you the option to change the name of the menu. While the **Customize** dialogue is open, you can also change the order of items within menus, change the order of menus on the menu bar and add items to or remove items from menus by dragging with the mouse.

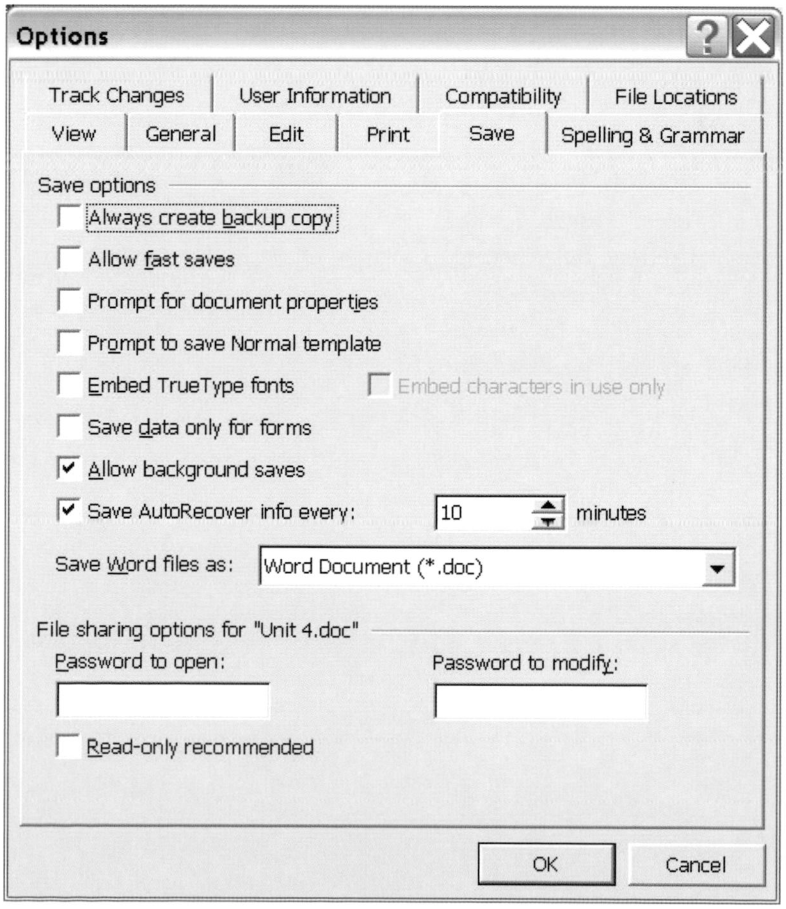

FIGURE 4.14 *Save dialogue options*

FIGURE 4.15 *Customize dialogue options*

Borders, rules and scroll bars

Depending on the software, it is possible to add or remove the rulers at the top and side of the work area. This is usually done by selecting or deselecting **Ruler** in the **View** menu. Some software also lets you remove the horizontal and/or vertical scroll bars and the status bar at the bottom of the screen. The **View** dialogue in **Options** allows you to do this.

Theory into practice

Investigate the options available for changing the configuration of different software packages and the effects that different changes to the settings have on the way the software appears and operates.

CASE STUDY

Simon is a self-employed carpenter. He has recently bought a computer to help with the administration of his business. The computer has a graphical user interface, a web browser, email client, word processing and spreadsheet software installed on it. Simon is not very computer literate and would like the software configured to make it as easy to use as possible. He finds there are too many options in the menus and toolbars, many of which he doesn't use. He would like a simpler system that includes only the facilities he uses regularly. He would also benefit from a standard layout for letters with the ability to add standard paragraphs and his signature from a toolbar or menu. A standard invoice would also be helpful to Simon, so that he just needs to enter the customer details and the details and cost of the work carried out.

Specify how the software should be configured to meet Simon's needs. If possible, carry out the configuration changes you specify.

Basics of software development

This section provides only a brief introduction to the concepts of software development. If you want to find out more, you should read Unit 6: Software Development – Design and Unit 8: Introduction to Programming.

All software, however complex, simply consists of a set of instructions that are carried out in a specific order. The following set of instructions was created when I recorded my tick macro. MS Word and other similar applications use a programming language called Visual Basic for Applications (VBA) to create macros.

```
Sub TICK()
'
' TICK Macro
' Macro recorded 19/06/04 by Maggie
'
With Selection.Font – {this section selects
the font size and indicates that it is not
bold, etc.}
.Name = "Univers"
.Size = 16
.Bold = False
.Italic = False
.Underline = wdUnderlineNone
.StrikeThrough = False
.DoubleStrikeThrough = False
.Outline = False
.Emboss = False
.Shadow = False
.Hidden = False
.SmallCaps = False
.AllCaps = False
.ColorIndex = wdAuto
.Engrave = False
```

✱ REMEMBER!

There are a number of different types of software each with a different purpose (see Table 4.3)

TYPE OF SOFTWARE	PURPOSE
BIOS startup software	The software stored in ROM that is used when the hardware first powers up. It allows input from the keyboard and output to the VDU and loads the operating system from disk.
Operating system	The operating system manages all the hardware in the computer including the main memory, disk storage and any peripheral devices. It receives and acts on commands from the user and loads other programs when requested to do so by the user.
GUI	An interface between the user and the computer that allows interaction by selecting icons or items from menus by pointing and clicking with a mouse.
Applications software	Software that allows the user to carry out particular tasks, such as word processing.

TABLE 4.3

All types of software can be configured to meet the needs of individual users. A specification should include details of the operating system and applications software required and how the different types of software should be configured to meet the user's needs. How the software is installed and configured will depend on the computer system and the type of operating system and software involved.

```
.Superscript = False
.Subscript = False
.Spacing = 0
.Scaling = 100
.Position = 0
.Kerning = 0
.Animation = wdAnimationNone
End With
Selection.ParagraphFormat.Alignment =
wdAlignParagraphCenter {This centres the tick}
Selection.InsertSymbol Font:="Wingdings",
CharacterNumber:=-3844, Unicode _
 :=True {This selects Wingdings and the tick
(character –3844)}
End Sub
```

For the macro to work, the instructions must follow the rules set out by the VBA programming language. This is known as the *syntax* of the language. If you want to write a macro from scratch or edit one you have recorded, you will need to learn and follow the correct VBA syntax. There are many different programming languages that can be used to develop software. Each programming language has its own syntax.

If the software that is being developed is to be of use, there are a number of aspects that need to be considered. Firstly, you need to consider what data will be input into the software to be processed and what output is required. This will determine the processing that must be carried out to obtain the required output from the input data. You will then need to consider how the data will be stored, for example whether it will be stored as records in a file or in some other structure. You will also need to consider how the processing of data will be controlled. This will include the way in which the user will interact with the program and also how control of processing will be passed between different sections of the program. You can find out more about how these aspects are considered in Unit 6. The other aspect that you need to consider is the instructions that are used and the way that these are organised within the program. This will determine how efficiently the program runs; large numbers of redundant instructions, for example, will slow down the running of a program. You can find out more about the way in which programs are structured in Unit 8.

Information that is to be processed needs to be organised in a suitable way. For example, if information is to be entered in a database, it will need to be organised under the same headings as the fields in the database. Any documents used to collect the information should be organised in the same way if the information is to be collected and input efficiently.

✳ REMEMBER!

* ✳ Software consists of a set of instructions in a specific sequence
* ✳ Different programming languages can be used to develop software
* ✳ Each programming language has its own set of rules called syntax
* ✳ When developing software there are a number of aspects that must be considered including:
  - input data and the output required
  - how data will be stored
  - how processing will be controlled
  - how the precision of instructions affects the efficiency of the program
* ✳ Information to be processed should be organised in a suitable way.

Theory into practice

Use Units 6 and 8 to help you understand the basics of software development.

Safety and security

Ergonomics

To ensure the user can work safely with the computer systems you specify, you will need to consider the ergonomics of the system and the workstation that it will form part of. Ergonomics is defined as the study of people's efficiency in their working environment. It is easy to consider ergonomics in relation to furniture such as desks and chairs, but it also relates to computer hardware, software and the way the workstation is set out. The Health and Safety (Display Screen Equipment) Regulations (1992) sets out minimum requirements for computer workstations including hardware, software and furniture. These requirements are based on ergonomic principles.

Hardware

As this health and safety regulation has now been in force for a number of years, virtually all hardware is produced to meet at least the minimum standard – manufacturers would not be able to sell the hardware if it did not. Nowadays, all CRT VDUs have tilt and swivel stands so that the user can adjust the screen to suit them – TFT VDUs have stands that enable them to be tilted; there is no need for swivel as it is easy to just turn the VDU on its base. The brightness and contrast of the display is easily adjustable, the level of flicker on all CRT VDUs is within acceptable limits and is not present on TFT screens. Keyboards are all separate from the screen (except for laptops, which should not be used for long periods) and all have fold down feet at the back so that they can be tilted. Both VDUs and keyboards have non-reflective surfaces to avoid glare. As we discussed earlier in this unit, some keyboards have a curved shape with two blocks of keys at an angle to each other. This is a more ergonomic design for those who can type using both hands but would be more difficult to use for those who cannot. Mice were not specifically covered by the regulations. When choosing a mouse or other pointing device, you should find one that you, or the user, finds comfortable to use. It should fit comfortably under the palm of your hand so that your fingers rest over the buttons and require the minimum of movement to click. Some people prefer to use a trackerball, with the ball either on the side so it can be moved with the thumb, or on the top.

Software

Software ergonomics is based around reducing stress caused by poorly designed software. Software should be suitable for the task so that the task can be completed without encountering any unnecessary problems or obstacles. Software should be easy to use and, where appropriate, adaptable to the level of knowledge or experience of the user. Users should be protected from the consequences of errors by the software providing warnings and enabling the recovery of 'lost' data. Feedback should be provided on the performance of the system, such as error messages, help and messages about malfunctions. This feedback should be in a suitable style and format. Information should be displayed in a format and at a pace that can be adapted to the user; in particular characters, cursor movements and position changes should be shown on screen as soon as they are input. As you have discovered from the previous sections, most software that uses a GUI meets most of these requirements, although it must be said that not all the feedback is as helpful as it could be!

Workstation layout

As the employer or the individual user, rather than the manufacturer, determines workstation layout, this is the area that is most likely to fall short of ergonomic requirements. The desk or work surface should be large enough to allow a flexible arrangement of the VDU, keyboard, documents and other related equipment. There should be sufficient space in front of the keyboard to provide support for the user's hands and arms. There should be sufficient space at the workstation for the user to find a comfortable position and to change position and vary movement while working. If a document holder is used, it should be stable and in a position that minimises uncomfortable head or eye movements. This essentially means that it should be next to and at the same height as the screen. An important consideration of workstation layout is glare. The position of the workstation needs to be considered in relation to both artificial light sources and to natural light from windows to reduce reflections and glare. Blinds or curtains may be needed to reduce the daylight from windows that falls on the workstation.

Furniture

The main ergonomic requirement of workstation furniture is that desks should have a non-reflective surface to reduce glare and that chairs are adjustable. Operator chairs must have at least five spokes in the base for stability. The seat and back must be height adjustable and the tilt of the back must also be adjustable. A footrest may be required if the user cannot place his or her feet flat on the floor. The diagram in Unit 1 (page 41) shows the correct sitting position at a computer workstation.

Management and security procedures

Unit 1 describes standard ways of working to ensure the security of data, software and equipment and to protect copyright. In this unit you have to implement or recommend procedures based on the standard ways of working described. Most of the procedures should also include an element of common sense. Possible recommendations include:

* a schedule for backing up data and software should be developed and maintained. The frequency will depend on how much the system is used but the backup should be stored in a fireproof safe or away from the computer

* confidential information should be protected by passwords so that it can be accessed only by those authorised to do so. Those who have access to the information may be asked to sign a non-disclosure agreement to agree not to share the information with anyone else

* a password policy should be implemented. This may require users to select passwords that are not dictionary words, names of family members or pets or significant dates, use passwords that contain a mixture of letters and numbers and change their password every month (or other period) or if they think someone else knows it

* virus checking of all files should be carried out automatically and virus checking software should be updated automatically on-line

* any material that is to be used should be checked for copyright before use and permission gained if the material is subject to copyright. All material used should be acknowledged

* physical security, such as locked doors, should be implemented and respected. Data and software should be protected from theft by passwords, firewalls and encryption when being transmitted

* different users on a system should be assigned only user rights and file permissions to access, or edit the information that is appropriate to them. For example, in an organisation only staff in the human resources department should have access to personnel records.

---

* REMEMBER!

When specifying systems you need to consider the ergonomics of the hardware, software workstation layout and furniture. This should, as a minimum, meet the requirements of the Health and Safety (Display Screen Equipment) Regulations (1992).

Management and security procedures should be based on standard ways of working and ensure that:

* data and software backup is maintained
* confidential information is protected
* passwords are used
* virus checking is carried out
* theft of data, software and equipment is avoided
* users are assigned appropriate user rights and file permissions.

Assessment evidence

A new independent travel agent, Activity Unlimited, is opening in a town near where you live. They will specialise in organising activity holidays in the UK and overseas. Activity Unlimited need a computer system that will be used by its staff to:

* show multimedia presentations of the types of activity holiday available to prospective holidaymakers
* keep records of holidays available that can be searched based on customer requirements
* produce large numbers of high-quality letters, holiday information sheets and other documents in colour
* send personalised letters to all customers who have taken a particular type of holiday in the past
* access competitors' websites to check what holidays they are offering
* send and receive emails.

The staff have requested that all necessary software is installed on the computer but that it is also capable of connection to the office's local area network (LAN).

Activity Unlimited would like templates for letters that include the company letterhead so that it can be printed out on plain paper. The template should insert the date and indicate where to enter the information required. They would also like a number of standard phrases that can be entered by selecting them from a menu. Other templates would also be useful. All templates should be accessible from a toolbar and standard toolbars should include only essential items.

The computer system is to be located in an area to which the public have access, so safety and security are major concerns.

Task 1

Produce a statement of Activity Unlimited's needs and how these might be met. Having done so, produce a specification for an ICT system that will meet the needs you have identified.

You need to:

* identify the tasks that Activity Unlimited want the system to perform
* identify the types of input and output
* specify the applications software required to carry out these tasks
* specify the hardware required
* specify the operating system
* specify any configuration requirements
* include designs of toolbar layouts, menus, templates and macros that provide the user with facilities to improve their efficiency and effectiveness.

You should try to demonstrate a systematic approach to specifying the system by considering what is most important and how this will affect other choices. You should make your specification as clear and detailed as possible to gain the highest marks.

Task 2

Your teacher will provide you with a computer system and software that will enable some or all of Activity Unlimited's needs to be met.

You must select, install and configure the operating system and software to meet the needs of Activity Unlimited. You must also implement suitable security procedures. Make sure your teacher or another qualified person (e.g. a computer technician) watches you carry out the installation and completes an observation record. You should also take screen prints at different stages as evidence.

You should:

* select and install the operating system
* select the most appropriate software from that provided
* select the components to install and install them
* configure the operating system, e.g. by installing drivers and setting up a printer
* configure the software to meet the requirements you identified in Task 1
* set up security procedures such as passwords

* test each stage to check that it works.

To gain the higher marks you should:

* produce a clear test procedure and carry out the tests you define

* show how you overcome problems you find using your test procedures

* set ROM-BIOS parameters

* carry out complex configuration activities such as virus protection and task scheduling.

Task 3

Install a suitable toolbar layout, menu, template and macro to meet the needs of Activity Unlimited. Make sure your teacher or another qualified person (e.g. a computer technician) watches you carry out the installation and completes an observation record. You should also take screen prints as evidence.

To gain the higher marks you should:

* test that the toolbar layout, menu, template and macro work as intended

* install the toolbar layouts, menus, templates and macros you designed in Task 1.

Task 4

Activity Unlimited is concerned about the security of their equipment and data and the safety of their staff who spend much of the day using computers.

Produce a report for the management of Activity Unlimited that provides recommendations for safety and security. Your report should consider the ergonomics of furniture, the workstation layout, hardware and software as well as management issues related to security.

You may choose the format of your report but you should try to make sure that it is well structured with headings and sub-headings to make it easy to follow. You also need to check your work carefully to eliminate spelling, punctuation and grammar errors.

Task 5

Activity Unlimited is considering having some software developed specifically for the company. They would like you to produce a simple guide to explain the basic concepts of software development in terms they will understand.

Task 6

Produce an evaluation of your specification for Activity Unlimited's computer system and of the methods you used when you were installing, configuring and testing software.

To evaluate your specification you should consider:

* what is good about it, what worked well

* what is not so good, what did not work

* how well it meets the needs of Activity Unlimited

* what could be improved if you produced it again

* how you refined your initial specification to meet the user needs more closely.

To evaluate your methods of installing, configuring and testing software you should consider:

* what went well

* what went badly

* how you refined the methods you used

* what you would do differently if you had to do a similar task in future.

 Signpost for portfolio evidence

Currently, all of your evidence must be produced on paper. You will need to provide screen prints or printouts to evidence your work and a suitable observation record signed by your teacher or other qualified person to confirm that you have carried out the installation and configuration tasks successfully.

You need to organise your work carefully. Make sure each piece of work is clearly labelled to show what it is and that your name is on each page. When you have put all your work in a sensible order, number all the pages and create a contents page to show where each piece of work is located.

UNIT 5

Problem solving using ICT

Introduction

The data and information that is used by an organisation can come from a variety of sources. Some of these will be internal to the organisation and some will be external.

In today's world, much of the information used by an organisation may come from the Internet. In order to solve the problems of an organisation through the use of ICT the source of the information used by the organisation and how it will be used within the organisation must be identified.

The assessment for this unit will require you to produce a design for a solution to a given problem.

Learning Outcomes

By studying this unit you will:

* be able to define the term 'data' clearly, identifying that data has no meaning

* be able to describe what is meant by the term 'information'

* be able to describe what is meant by the term 'knowledge'

* understand the importance of information and data within an organisation and how the use of information and data will affect the solution to a problem. You will need to describe the information that will be used by your proposed solution including the levels at which it is used

* investigate and understand the differing types of software which may be used to solve problems within an organisation. You will need to identify the different types of software that are used at different levels within an organisation

* understand how a solution to a problem may have an impact on other parts of the organisation. You will need to define the system boundaries of your proposed solution and the effect the proposed system will have on different parts of the organisation

* appreciate the need for planning, decision making and control when solving problems in organisation. You will need to discuss the aims, goals and objectives of your proposed system and the effect the proposed system will have on the end-users.

What you need to learn

You need to learn about:

* information
* software
* quality procedures
* systems
* evaluating the solution.

Information

Everyone uses information and data. From the use of data and information comes knowledge. When a problem is to be solved using ICT it is important that the difference between data, information and knowledge is understood. It is also important to know what data is being used by the organisation.

Everything is made up of *data.* Data is raw facts and figures before they have been processed. Data itself has no meaning:

* 76fg92
* sehn6i

are examples of data; there is no way of telling what they mean. They could have a meaning or they could just be a random collection of numbers and letters.

Information is the result of taking data and processing it. This means giving the data some *meaning*. Processing means to perform an action on the data, for example sorting, searching, saving or editing. Computers and people process raw data to produce meaningful information.

Data becomes information through adding specific components together (see Figure 5.1).

Data + Structure + Context + Meaning = Information

FIGURE 5.1 *Data becoming information*

Sometimes data does not need a *structure* or a *context* to become information, but when solving a problem using ICT you should be aware of the complete process.

Key terms

Data: raw facts and figures.

Meaning: putting the data into the correct structure and putting it into a context.

Structure: how the data is presented.

Context: taking the data and giving it an environment where our prior knowledge and understanding can make sense of it.

We can take raw data and put it into a structure, a context and a meaning to give information (see Figure 5.2).
Information can be described as a set of meaningful data that is useful. Information is transmitted all the time and is fundamental to every organisation and person in the world. If information was not transmitted then nothing in the world would be achieved: how

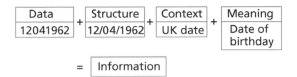

FIGURE 5.2 *Example of data becoming information*

would we know what people and systems need, and when, how and in what format it was needed?

Information can be expressed in categories of verbal or visual. Each category can then be divided into formats in which the information is transmitted. You have seen in Unit 1 how symbols can be used to convey information. For example, information can be transmitted through the use of:

* sound

* graphics

* text.

Think it over...

Complete Table 5.1 to show the advantages and disadvantages of the three methods of transmitting information.

On some occasions the information may be conveyed by more than one method. For example, the book you are reading now combines text and graphics. A fire alarm may combine sound and graphics. The important thing to remember is that the information must be conveyed in a meaningful and useful way to suit the needs of the users. Information needs to be interpreted. This

requires the appropriate representation method to be used – text, sound, graphics – and the person presenting the information must have the correct syntax and semantics. *Semantics* is the relationship between the words in the sentence. *Syntax* is the rules that should be followed. Through understanding the syntax of a sentence we can understand the semantics. For example:

> The dog chased the rabbit.
> The rabbit chased the dog.

Key terms

Semantic: the meaning of the sentence.

Syntax: the rules of the sentence.

These two sentences have the same words in them but the sentences have different meanings. To understand a sentence we must take into account the context and order of the words and not just rely on the meaning of each individual word.

The syntax of a sentence, the context, order of words and the rules of the language enable us to understand the meaning. To process a sentence we need to take into account the syntax and semantics.

The syntax of a sentence is concerned with rules. It is looking at the order of the words and being able to apply known rules to work out the meaning. For example, in the English language we know that sentences begin with a capital letter and end with a full stop. In the UK the general format of dates is dd/mm/yyyy whilst in the US the date format is mm/dd/yyyy.

METHOD	ADVANTAGES	DISADVANTAGES
Sound		
Graphics		
Text		

TABLE 5.1

Semantics is concerned with taking the different meanings of the words, applying our knowledge of syntax and being able to work out what the sentence means. Information within an organisation can be divided into specialised or general information. General information is common to any organisation and its information needs whilst specific information relates only to a particular type of organisation.

Information is crucial to any organisation – without information an organisation cannot perform its function. In an organisation information is used for many different purposes such as ordering supplies from suppliers, dealing with customer enquiries or providing information for other departments.

Different information is used at different levels within any organisation (see Figure 5.3). There are three main levels of information that can be found within any organisation. These levels are operational, tactical and strategic.

FIGURE 5.3 *Levels of information*

Operational information

Operational information lies at the bottom of the information gathering process. Typical information gathered and used at this level will be the number of units sold of an item in a shop or the overtime hours worked by hourly paid staff.

Tactical information

Tactical information is used in the day-to-day running of an organisation and the decisions that have to be made by middle management. These decisions will be based upon information that comes up through an organisation as well as information that comes into the organisation from outside sources.

Strategic information

Strategic information is used by top-level management in making decisions that will affect the whole organisation and its future. These decisions tend to be long term and involve high levels of expenditure. The decisions may include issues like investment, foreign trade and expansion of the organisation. Strategic information is very closely linked with strategic planning.

You should remember that every level within an organisation will use different categories of information. An upward flow of information takes place from the bottom (operational) level of the pyramid to the top level (strategic) level. At each level the raw data for processing is the information produced by the lower level.

Information can also be classified in relation to the time frame in which it will be used. The categories of time frames are historical, current or future. When solving problems it is important that past information is considered as well as how the information is currently used. If a problem is to be solved with long-term success then the way in which the information is to be used in the future also needs to be considered.

Quality of information

The quality of information can be affected by many factors. To provide a worthwhile solution to a problem these factors must be considered. The factors can affect the quality of the information used by an organisation. If the data entered into the system that is supposed to be solving a problem is not very good then it will not be able to be converted into worthwhile and useful information, but if correct data is put into a system then correct information will be gained. The main factors that should be considered when developing a solution are:

Accuracy

If the information is not accurate it cannot be used. *Validation* and *verification* techniques can improve accuracy but cannot guarantee it. They can be used to remove information and data that are outside the boundaries set, and any unreasonable or irrelevant data but this cannot ensure correctness. For example, if you ask the price of a car in a car showroom and you are given the wrong price then the information is worthless (see Figure 5.4).

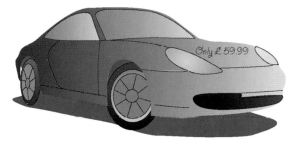

FIGURE 5.4 *A Porsche for only £59.99!*

Relevance

The information provided by the solution must be relevant to the user. If the information does not relate to the requirements of the user then the information is worthless. Irrelevant information can be a disadvantage as it increases the volume of data, and reading through it can waste time. For example, if you ask for the year a car was built and registered but you are told how many doors it has then this is irrelevant as this is not the answer to the question asked.

Age

Information, as we have already seen, can be placed within a time frame. Sometimes the time frame of information is important but information can change over time. If information is gathered from an old source it may not still be relevant or accurate. For example, if you ask the price of a new car, then to be told the price it was three years ago is of no value.

Completeness

If only part of the information is available then it is worthless. Data must have a context, structure and meaning for it to have value and be useful. For example, if you make an appointment to test drive a new car from a car showroom but you

are given only the time of the appointment but not the date then the information is worthless.

Presentation

If information is not presented in a way that the user can easily understand it or find what he or she needs then the information loses value. Presentation of information can be improved by using graphics and graphs where appropriate – remember, a picture paints a thousand words – and by being ordered into a logical format. For example, a brochure of cars contains pictures of the cars, colours and any extras that can be added. The brochure is usually ordered by model of car, i.e. a brochure about Landrovers would have all the details about each model in the range (Defender, Freelander, Discovery and Range Rover) grouped together.

Level of detail

It is possible to give too much or too little information to the user. If too much information is given then it may be difficult for the user to find the information they need; if too little is given then there may not be enough information for a decision to be made. There is a balance between too much and too little information and it can be difficult to get the balance right. For example, if all the component details about a car engine are given in the brochure (see Figure 5.5), then for most people, this is too much information. However, if the brochure just states that the car has an engine then this is, probably, too little information.

These six factors should not be viewed and considered in isolation. For example, presentation can be linked with age, and level of detail is generally linked with completeness.

There are many other characteristics of information that you will need to know about when developing a solution to a problem. Different organisations use information in different ways. When you are developing a solution to a problem you must be able to identify the characteristics of information and how these will be used in your solution. You have already seen that information is used at different levels within an organisation for different purposes and how the time frame of the information is important. There are six other

ENGINES

Item	V6 petrol	1.8 petrol	TD4 diesel
Location	Front Mounted	Front Mounted	Front Mounted
Capacity (cc)	2497	1796	1951
No of cylinders	6	4	4
Cylinder layout	"V" configured	In-line	In-line
Bore (mm)	80.0	80.0	84.0
Stroke (mm)	82.8	89.3	88.0
Compression ratio	10.5:1	10.5:1	18.1
Cylinder head material	Aluminium	Aluminium	Aluminium
Cylinder block material	Aluminium	Aluminium	Grey cast iron
Ignition	EMS 2000	MEMS 3.0	D.D.E
Fuelling	Sequential fuel injection	Multi-point fuel injection	Common-rail
Valves per cylinder	4	4	4
Valve actuation	DOHC with hydraulic tappets	DOHC with hydraulic tappets	DOHC 2 intake port design
Maximum power	177Ps (130kW) @ 6250 rpm	177Ps (86kW) @ 5550 rpm	122Ps (82kW) @ 4000 rpm
Maximum Torque	240Nm@ 4000 rpm	160Nm@ 2750 rpm	260Nm@ 1750 rpm

FIGURE 5.5 *Component list of a car*

Knowledge check

1 Describe the six factors affecting the quality of information.

2 For each factor, give an example relating to an estate agent.

characteristics of information you will need to identify when solving a problem.

Sources

There are four main sources of information. These are internal, external, primary and secondary:

* *internal* sources of information come from within an organisation. They are usually the result of processing data, and flow upwards in an organisation. In a car showroom an internal source of information might be the number of cars of a specific model that have been sold over a six-month period (see Figure 5.6). This information will be collected within the organisation

* an external source of information is outside the organisation and comes into the organisation. In a car showroom an example of external information might be the delivery date from the car manufacturer of a particular car

* *primary* sources of information are those that are generated first-hand

* *secondary* sources of information are produced from primary sources.

Primary and secondary sources of information can be either internal to an organisation or external. For example, if a car showroom belonged to a group of showrooms the accounts for the group would be a secondary source as they would be produced using the accounts from each car showroom (the primary source).

Nature

The nature of information can be sub-categorised into qualitative, quantitative, formal and informal.

* *Qualitative* information provides additional details to any existing information. For example, you might know that students have been at school for four years but the qualitative aspect will identify the subjects they have studied and if they have enjoyed the subjects. One of the best ways of finding out qualitative information is through an interview where questions can be asked to specifically gather the type of information that can be used to enhance pure statistics and facts already known.

* *Quantitative* information is based on facts and statistics. This type of information is used for

Fred's Cars
of Anytown

Sold

28/2/05
£ 9,500

2001 Blue Landrover Discovery TD5
Mileage – 21,500 miles

Last Service at 36,000 miles on 29/4/04
Next Service due 6,500 miles

Service Recommendations:
48,000 mile service including Air Conditioning Unit check

FIGURE 5.6 *Car sales receipt*

planning. Examples of quantitative information include fixed monthly expenditure, students grade at GCSEs, etc. Quantitative information is essential, as facts and statistics are easy to map and model (i.e. in graphs) unlike qualitative information, that is subjective and descriptive. When collecting information, an equal balance of quantitative and qualitative information should be gathered.

* *Formal* information is information that is usually written down or held in an electronic format. Formal information includes company records, details of qualifications – information that can be verified.

* *Informal* information is information that is known but is not written down. In an organisation an example of informal information might be that on a Monday the administration assistant goes to buy the tea and coffee supplies for the week.

Frequency

Information can be categorised as to when it is to be updated. This can be real time, scheduled or ad hoc.

* Some information needs to be kept up to date on a real-time basis. This means updating the information as soon as changes are required. An example would be if a car was sold, the buyer's name would immediately be recorded against the car. If this information was not recorded then someone else might try to buy the car.

* Information may be updated daily, weekly or monthly. An example of this might be that the hours worked by hourly paid staff will be updated on a monthly basis so that they get paid for the extra hours they have done.

* Information being updated on an ad hoc basis involves updating as and when required. This may be a customer changing his or her contact details. It is important that customer records are kept up to date but this cannot be done on a regular or scheduled basis. The customer information would be updated as customers notify the organisation of changes in their details.

Use

Information can be used for different purposes. How information is used will depend upon which level in the organisation it is being used. The main uses of information are planning, control and decisions.

* For an organisation to flourish, some planning must be done. This may be done on a long-term basis or on a day-to-day basis. Planning may be involved based on quantitative or qualitative information. Qualitative information might be gathered from users or customers in order to provide a service, whilst quantitative statistics might be used to see if the project is financially viable.

* Decisions are based upon a combination of qualitative and quantitative information. For example, the decision to employ a new member of staff would be based on the qualifications for the post they have (qualitative) and the quantitative information found out at interview based on the responses to questions.

* Information can also be used in controlling aspects of an organisation, for example using qualitative information to measure the increase in profits and to control the expansion of an organisation.

Form

The form in which information is presented is very important. Earlier in this unit we looked at the different ways in which information can be presented: sound, graphics and text. The presentation and form, formal and informal, of information is also discussed in Unit 1: Using ICT to Communicate.

Type

Information can be of different types. The three main types are disaggregated, aggregated and sampled:

* *disaggregated information* is information in its raw collected format. This could be a collection of questionnaires that has just been returned

* *aggregated information* is the information on the questionnaires collected and collated (for example, put in a table format)

* a *sample* of information is taken as part of the whole collected information. For example, if 50

questionnaires had been returned, a sample might be taken of 50 per cent (25 questionnaires) and the information would be analysed. A sample gives a 'snapshot' of the responses on the questionnaires.

Software

Each level within an organisation will use generic software and specific software related to the tasks that have to be completed (see Figure 5.7).

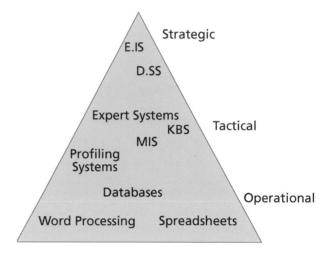

FIGURE 5.7 *Levels of information and related software*

General office software

The main type of software that will be used at operational level is general office software. A general integrated office software suite usually includes word processing, spreadsheets, graphics, presentation and database packages.

Word processing

This type of software includes word processing and desktop publishing. These are used at the operational level in the day-to-day running of an organisation. Word processing is needed to produce letters (see Figure 5.8), internal memos, email, invoices and other documents. Desktop publishing can be used to create newsletters and general information sheets for internal and external use.

Spreadsheets

Spreadsheets can be used to perform repetitive calculations and create charts and tables. Spreadsheets are commonly used to model

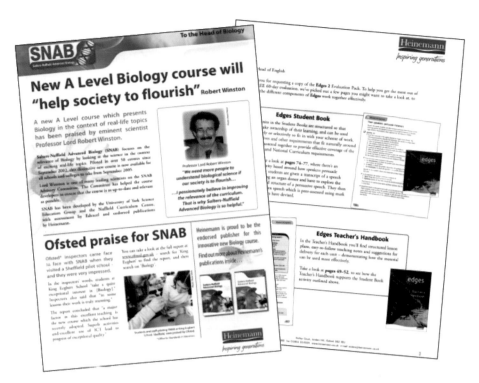

FIGURE 5.8 *A newsletter and a business letter*

numerical and financial data. Examples of their use include profit and loss accounts, monthly forecasting. The numerical information held within a spreadsheet can be shown in a graphical format. Spreadsheets provide a clear and consistent worksheet format that can assist in the understanding and interpretation of numerical data. Data can be typed in and stored as a template with the template being used to produce tables and graphs in the 'house style'. Provided that formulas have been set up on the worksheet, new data can be added and existing data updated easily, providing the user with current facts and figures. A spreadsheet that contains large amounts of data may not be easy to interpret or understand. Most spreadsheets contain an in-built chart and graph facility that will provide a visual interpretation of the data (see Figure 5.9). The 'what if' function of spreadsheet modelling also makes it useful at the tactical level.

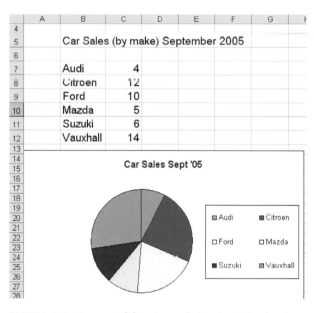

FIGURE 5.9 *A spreadsheet worksheet with charts and graphs*

Computer graphics

Computer graphics can be used within an organisation, in conjunction with other packages within the integrated general office suite, to enhance the presentation of a range of documents and to enhance a presentation itself. The use of graphics within a newsletter can be seen on this page. The graphics can be used to illustrate, entertain or enhance the reader's experience.

Presentation software

Presentation software is used for disseminating information quickly to an audience. All organisations need to ensure that information is passed around quickly and efficiently. If the information is to be sent to a small group of people, then a memo or email (produced using a word processor) may be appropriate; however, if the information needs to be disseminated to a large group at a meeting, a presentation may be used. This would be developed using presentation software. Computer generated and presented presentations have replaced the old-fashioned method of using a flip chart, white board or overhead projector and transparencies as a method of showing groups of people prepared information. This is not to say that these older methods are not still used; they are used for specific purposes usually as an addition to the computer

presentation. Presentation software enables the use of animation, sound and video files to enhance the quality of the information being presented. Presentations can be updated, edited and amended easily and quickly. This ensures that the information being presented will be up to date and that the information required to be passed around the organisation will be appropriate.

Databases

Databases carry out a range of functions to support all levels of users within an organisation. Although they are primarily used at operational level, they will be used to perform very specific queries at the tactical and strategic levels of the organisation. At the operational level databases will be used to input data, run pre-defined queries and produce reports. They will also be used, in conjunction with a word processing package, to

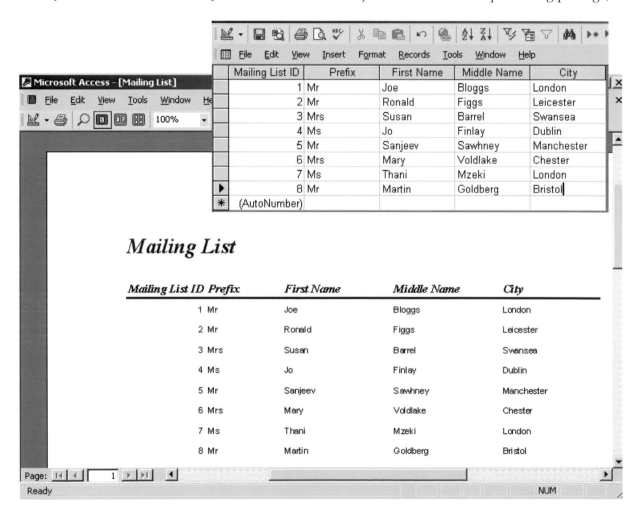

FIGURE 5.10 *A database and report*

perform a mail merge. The main function of a database is to store information in specified formats to enable easy processing and access. The data that is inputted and held in a database can be formatted into useful and meaningful information. Databases have a range of features and tools that can be used to support an organisation. These include:

* input screens including forms and tables

* output screens including reports and forms

* query and filter tools

* validation tools.

The main types of software that will be used at tactical level will be profiling systems, management information systems and knowledge based and expert systems.

Knowledge based systems (KBS)

Knowledge based systems (KBS) provide support for the users of knowledge and information within an organisation. The KBS stores human knowledge in such a way that a computer can process it. A KBS is an example of artificial intelligence (AI). The system will store facts about a specific subject area often in the form of rules that will allow questions to be asked, and, based on the knowledge and rules held, a conclusion will be given. The main function of a KBS system is to help the organisation to identify and analyse new ideas and information to enable the organisation to be more effective and profitable. KBS can also be used to ensure high-quality standards of services provided or goods produced. KBS tend to be used by the technical people involved in the organisation. The main role of technical staff is to identify and investigate technical information that can then be analysed, processed and integrated into the organisation's systems. Each KBS is specific to a particular area. For example, a KBS may be used in the translation of documents into a different language (i.e. German into English).

There are a number of ways in which KBS extract data to provide the information needed to carry out analysis or to identify implications, impacts or trends. Some methods are straightforward, involving the sorting or filtering of

information using application software. However, there are specific tools and techniques that can be used. These include the use of expert systems.

Expert systems

Expert systems support a decision-making process. They contain the experience and specialised knowledge of specialists and provide this information to non-specialists so that he or she can have access to the information. Expert systems are based on a reasoning process that resembles the human thought processes. The thought process is dependent upon rules and reasons that have been provided by specialists/experts in the field. The main function of an expert system is to provide a knowledge base that can be accessed to assist non-specialists in their own decision-making process. Many expert systems have the built-in ability to justify the reasoning on which any conclusion is reached. This enables the reasoning to be checked and either accepted or rejected.

For example, MYCIN was developed by Edward Shortcliffe in 1970 to assist doctors in the diagnosis and treatment of meningitis and bacterial septicaemia. The patient systems and any test results are input as data into MYCIN. The output from the system includes a diagnosis, and recommended treatment.

Key terms

Expert systems: systems in which human expertise is held in the form of rules which enable the system to diagnose situations without the human expert being present.

Management information systems (MIS): computer systems for an organisation which collect and analyse data from all departments, and are designed to provide an organisation's management with up-to-date information (such as financial reports, inventory, etc.) at any time.

Theory into practice

Investigate other KBS and expert systems that are used. Identify the specific area of use, and the purpose.

Profiling systems

Profiling systems allow data gathered about a group of people to be analysed to determine which one of them meets a given set of criteria. The profiling system sorts through information based on a given set of sensible and relevant criteria. These criteria are input into the system before the profiling and selection begins. The situation for which the profile is being created needs to be analysed carefully to select the appropriate skills, qualifications, interests and other requirements needed. Profiling systems are more frequently being used in large organisations when selecting interviewees based on the information given on their application forms. However, there has also been an increased use of profiling systems in criminal investigations.

Theory into practice

Investigate other uses of profiling systems.

Management information systems (MIS)

Management information systems (MIS) are sets of integrated software packages that can be used at tactical level in an organisation. They provide support for managers in forecasting, planning, organising, controlling and decision making in the organisation. Generally MIS bring together information from a variety of sources, both internal and external, sorting, collating, merging and analysing it as necessary to provide only the relevant and necessary information to the manager involved. MIS are usually specific to the person/persons they support, so they are usually bespoke systems.

The system provides managers with a variety of different types of information or support such as easy-to-understand tables, responses to direct queries, graphical output, output resulting from the input of a 'what if' scenario or even a warning signal as a result of data exceeding a set limit. There are many different types of MIS (an example is shown in Figure 5.11) but typical systems include:

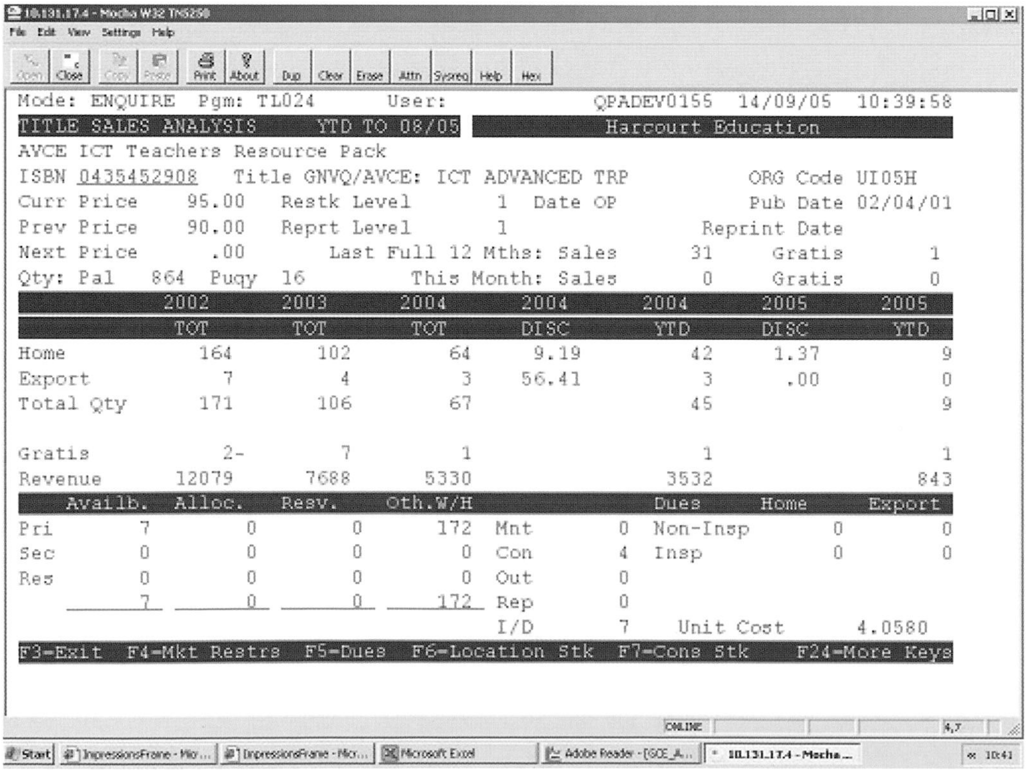

FIGURE 5.11 *A screen shot of an MIS report – projected sales of a suite of books, orders at any given time and number of copies printed*

* a comprehensive database holding all the different types of information processed by the organisation to regularly provide managers with ready-made reports

* the analysis and comparison of data in a database over a period of time to provide the information about items such as sales, purchases, wages or stock levels

* warning signals to indicate that decisions are required such as low stock levels, expenditure exceeding income, numbers of faulty goods exceeding expectations

* daily calculation methods of productivity levels by analysis of costs and outputs

* monthly graphs of price comparison with competitors' goods and services resulting from regular market research

* audio and visual warnings when incoming orders exceed production levels

* a model of the organisation that enables 'what if' queries to be input to forecast the effects of items such as policy decisions, market conditions, production rates, VAT or tax changes.

The main types of software that will be used at strategic level will be decision support systems (DSS) and executive information systems (EIS).

Theory into practice

Identify which aspects of an MIS system would be used in an estate agents. Explain your choices.

Decision support systems

Decision support systems (DSS) enable decision making to take place in situations that cannot be defined in advance. This type of system takes information, internal and external, and combines this information with a variety of appropriate models. These models can relate to financial, statistical marketing, human resource or production. This approach enables 'what if' questions to be asked. Decision support systems have three main components. They are:

* a database management system to provide access to all relevant information

* models of the different situations involved

* a user interface that can provide graphs and charts and reports.

The main feature of a DSS is that it is able to provide and perform a greater depth of analysis than software used at operational and tactical levels. A simple example of a DSS is the system that is used in many schools and colleges to produce the yearly staff and student timetables.

Executive information systems

Executive information systems (EIS) enable a manager at strategic level to see the results of an automatic analysis of large amounts of information. The information is presented in a clear and concise way to enable an informed decision to be made. An EIS is designed to be used by people who are not necessarily skilled in the use of ICT and do not make use of spreadsheets or databases. EIS provide a simple user interface, sometimes using touch screens or voice-activated commands, and enable the user to change the parameters easily and quickly. These systems include their own database and use data from outside and inside the organisation. The EIS must provide the required information quickly and within a given period to enable decisions to be made rapidly. As the data used by these systems is from both internal and external sources they must be able to interact easily and effectively with other systems to retrieve the data required. The EIS must be flexible and adaptable to continue to meet the changing needs and requirements of the organisation over time.

Theory into practice

Suggest how an estate agent could make use of a DSS and an EIS.

* REMEMBER!

Although it is possible to say in general terms the type of software that will be used at each level this is not always true. Different types of software can be used at other levels within the information structure of an organisation.

Quality procedures

When a solution to a problem is being developed it is important that the goals, aims and objectives of the solution are defined. This should be done at the beginning of the problem-solving process. The definition of the aims, goals and objectives enables the users of the solution to check that the solution will meet his or her needs and requirements. It will also ensure that the solution stays 'on track'.

There are many quality procedures that can be used during the development of a solution, and which procedure is used will depend upon the type of solution being developed. The most popular quality procedure used is that of total quality management (TQM). One of the aims of TQM is to keep the clients happy. If a client is happy and pleased with the solution that has been provided then he or she will return and may recommend the firm to other organisations.

You will have found many graphical tools that can be used during TQM, including histograms. Histograms can be used to show the results of the occurrences of an event over a given period or periods. For example, a histogram can be developed to show the number of people who call into an estate agents during a Saturday (see Table 5.2).

TIME	NUMBER OF PEOPLE
9am–10am	3
10am–11am	7
11am–12 noon	12
12 noon–1pm	15
1pm–2pm	22
2pm–3pm	14
3pm–4pm	9

TABLE 5.2

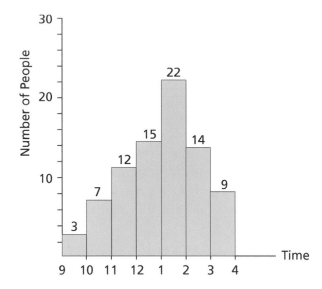

FIGURE 5.12 *Histogram of results*

By putting these figures into a histogram (see Figure 5.12), the developer producing the solution will be aware that there is a busy time slot on a Saturday and that any solution must be able to cope with this. It would also be possible to compare the number of people over a longer period, i.e. a week, month or year. This would clearly show when the peak times in the demand for the solution might be.

One of the tools and techniques that can be used to gather information from the users of the solution is a check sheet (also known as a questionnaire). A check sheet is a data-gathering and interpretation tool.

A check sheet is used for:

1 distinguishing between fact and opinion (for example: how do the customers of the estate agents perceive the usefulness of the information held on the information sheets about each property?)

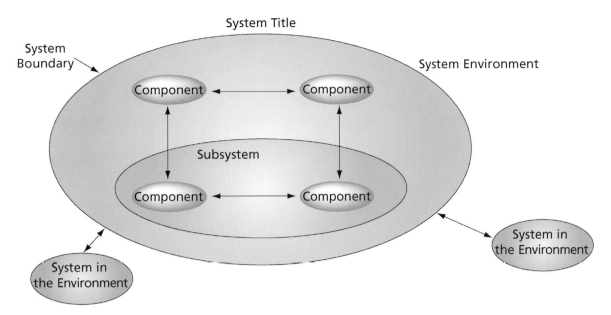

FIGURE 5.13 *A system diagram*

2 gathering data about how often a problem is occurring (for example: how often are errors found in the information held on each property?)

3 gathering data about the type of problem occurring (for example: what is the most common type of error found on the information sheet – wrong room sizes, incorrect asking price, grammar/punctuation?).

Other tools and techniques you may have found may include flowcharts, audit trails and statistical analysis. It is important that the TQM tools you use relate to the aims, goals and objectives of the solution.

One part of TQM is directly concerned with the development of solutions. This is known as software quality assurance (SQA). SQA is applied to the whole development of a solution to a problem. The basic aim of SQA is that the final solution meets the needs of the users and provides satisfaction with the solution and can be achieved through the development of aims, goals and objectives.

The aims, goals and objectives of any solution are interlinked. The aims of a solution are the broad, long-term goals. The goals are the required end results, with the objectives being specific and measurable means for accomplishing goals.

Your aim for taking this course might be to have a career where you travel; your goal might

be to become an IT consultant; and your objectives to achieve good grades in your exams and successfully study for a degree in IT.

Systems

A system is a set of connected 'things' or items. A single item is not a system, but when separate things interact together they form a system. System components are the things or parts that make up a system. These can be materials, machines, money, people, activities or ideas. They form the components of a system. On a system diagram (see Figure 5.13), they are shown as ellipses. Components may also be sub-systems (components of a given system but ones that are themselves systems comprising components). Thus there usually exists a nested set of systems at different levels. The choice and level of detail of components needed depends on the purpose of analysis.

The components of the system will be connected through their interactions and relationships. They are shown on a system diagram as arrows. They may be physical, material, energy, money or information flows. The total relationship between a pair of components may include several of these different types of connection. Relationships are not just the flows between components. Some relationships exist wholly within the system but others will relate to other, external systems.

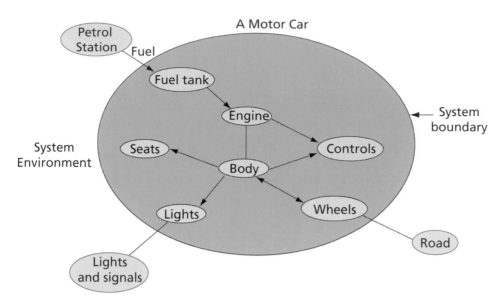

FIGURE 5.14 *A system diagram of a car*

A **system boundary** is a dividing line separating the things in a system from the things that are not in the system. It is shown on a system diagram as a large circle around the components of the system. Defining the boundary of a system defines the system (its components and its objectives). A boundary should be clearly defined to help to determine the functional area in which the solution will fully solve the problem.

The **environment** of a system is the set of other systems outside the defined system. A thing is inside a system if it influences the behaviour of the system and is controlled by it. Something in the environment is outside the system and influences it but is not controlled by it. A system influences things both inside and outside the system boundary. It may be that a system has no relationship with anything outside itself. This is known as a 'closed' system. Most systems, however, do interact with their environment and these are called 'open' systems. Open systems operate within and interact with their environment.

The inputs and outputs of a system are the relationships between the things inside and outside a system. They are relationships that cross the system boundary. The behaviour of a system is the outputs of a system in response to its inputs. The system diagram shows how the components interact together.

A **system diagram** is an attempt to show the system on paper. It is a useful way of trying to understand a system. What is drawn will depend on the purpose of analysis and the perception of the person drawing the diagram. In a complex system several diagrams may be needed to show the different levels of system with different boundaries.

Figure 5.14 shows how a car would be represented. A car is a simple system. It comprises a few thousand components – all physical, inanimate things – mainly made of metal and plastic.

Clearly, to be of any use, cars are driven by people. The driver sets the objectives, uses skills and perception to control the car in order to achieve the desired outputs, adapting to a changing environment. The car is a component (and a sub-system) of this system. The system diagram is shown in Figure 5.15.

The system diagram does not pretend to be a complete graphical representation of a car. There is a limit to how much can be shown on a diagram. It shows the major components of the system. The lines between components are an attempt to show a relationship, but clearly some labels and verbal description are necessary.

Evaluation of the solution

The final part of this unit is to produce a final conclusion and evaluation of your proposed solution to the problem. When the proposed

FIGURE 5.15 *A system diagram of a person driving a car*

solution is being evaluated the original problem of the organisation should be considered. The proposed solution must fully solve this problem. It is possible that some parts of the problem have not been solved. If this is the case then an explanation of why this has happened must be included in the evaluation. When a proposed solution has been produced, part of the evaluation is to compare the solution to the aims, goals and objectives that were defined at the beginning of the problem-solving process.

The impact of the proposed solution must be explained to the end-users. The benefits and disadvantages of the proposed solution to the problem also need to be explained to the users. Most computerised solutions to problems have disadvantages – these may include training for users and money required for new hardware and software. But there should be a greater number of benefits than disadvantages brought to the organisation.

Assessment evidence

Task 1

When you are attempting to solve a problem using ICT it is important that you clearly identify the problem to be solved. This is to ensure that the solution you develop fully solves the problem.

CASE STUDY

Peters Perfect Cars

Peters Perfect Cars has recently expanded the number of car showrooms it operates. As a result of this, a head office has been opened. The owner and the directors of the company are based in this head office along with the administration staff for the group.

In each office in the group, details of each car for sale by that showroom are kept on a database. Staff in the office are responsible for maintaining and updating this database.

Within each office there is a showroom manager, an office manager and a number of salespersons. There are differing levels of access to the database for the different members of staff:

* **the salespersons are able to access only details of the cars for sale and to print reports based on a client's requirements. For example, they can produce a report of all cars within a price range or of a particular make (e.g. Land Rover, BMW, Ford) that a client requires**

* **the showroom manager within each office can amend the car details held on the database**

* **the office manager can access any details held on the database and print reports relating to the sales of cars, the sales completed by each salesperson and the financial results of the office.**

Each office has access to email both within the Peters Perfect Cars group and externally.

Following the expansion, the directors of the group need to have access to all details from every office. They want to ensure that a new system would also be able to cope with any future expansion. They would also like to carry out investigations such as to find out the most popular car buying periods in the year, the most popular make of car sold, or the best performing office in the group.

Currently there is no software used within the group that will enable the directors to fulfil these requirements.

You must:

∗ identify the problem to be solved for Peters Perfect Cars.

To achieve mark band 2, you will identify the problem and produce a simple explanation of the problem, with some of the benefits to the organisation explained. To achieve the highest mark band you should identify the problem, providing a detailed explanation of the problem to be solved and the benefits that the solution will bring to Peters Perfect Cars.

Task 2

Once you have identified the problem, you must develop a solution using ICT that solves the problem you identified.

You must:

∗ produce a solution to the problem you identified in Task 1, including the goals, aims and objectives of your solution.

To achieve mark band 2, the solution you propose will be appropriate to the organisation. To achieve the highest mark band you should produce a detailed solution that fully solves the problem you identified in Task 1 and is appropriate to the organisation.

Task 3

When you are developing a solution to a problem it is important that you describe the information that will be used. In many cases the information either used or produced by the solution will be employed at different levels within the organisation. The use of the information will change depending on the level at which it is being used. The format of the information will also change depending on the level at which it is being used.

You must:

∗ describe the information that will be used by your proposed solution.

To achieve mark band 2, you should describe the information that is used by your proposed solution and identify the organisational levels at which it is used. To achieve the highest mark band you should

describe the information that will be used by your proposed solution and explain how this information will be used at each organisational level.

Task 4

Different levels within an organisation may use different types of software. Each level within an organisation will process information using different types of software. When you are developing a solution to a problem you must identify the level at which the solution will be used and the software that is currently being used at that level.

You must:

∗ identify the different types of software that are used at different levels within Peters Perfect Cars.

To achieve mark band 2, you should also give examples of the different types of software that are used at different organisational levels. To achieve the highest mark band you will provide a range of examples of the differing types of software that are used at different organisational levels.

Task 5

When you are developing a solution to a problem it is essential that you use quality procedures to ensure that your proposed solution will actually solve the problem. You should already have identified, in Task 2, the goals, aims and objectives of your proposed solution.

You must:

∗ identify the quality procedures that could be used when developing your proposed solution.

To achieve mark band 2, you should provide an explanation of the quality procedures that could be used when developing the proposed system. To achieve the highest mark band the explanation you produce will be detailed.

Task 6

The problem you are solving may be affected by other systems or sub-systems that are currently being used in Peters Perfect Cars. System boundary diagrams can be drawn to demonstrate the boundaries of a system that is solving a problem, and how it interacts with the other systems within the organisation.

When you are developing a solution it is important that you think about the environment in which the new system will fit. It is also important that you investigate the current environments and properties to ensure that the new system is appropriate and will interact within the current systems.

You must:

* produce a system boundary diagram for the system you are developing

* identify the system boundaries and environment that will be affected by your proposed solution.

To achieve mark band 2, your system boundary diagram will show either the inputs or the outputs of the proposed solution and you should produce an explanation of the system boundaries and environment that are affected by the proposed system. To achieve the highest mark band the system diagram you produce will be detailed, showing the inputs and outputs of the system. The explanation of the system boundaries and environment that are affected by the proposed system will be detailed.

Task 7

It is important that all proposed solutions to a problem are evaluated to ensure that the solution fully meets the needs and requirements of the end-user and the organisation.

You must:

* produce an evaluation of your proposed solution

* comment on your actions and role in producing this solution.

To achieve mark band 2, the evaluation you produce will consider the aims, objectives or goals and the benefits or disadvantages of the proposed system. The impact of the new system should also be considered. You should evaluate your own performance when completing this work, and consider the good and poor features of the way in which you tackled and solved the problem. You should also suggest ways in which your performance could be improved. To achieve the highest mark band the evaluation you produce will be detailed and will consider the aims, objectives and goals along with the benefits and disadvantages of the proposed system. You will also need to analyse your own experiences and suggest how you could improve your own performance when solving a similar problem in the future.

 ## Signposting for portfolio evidence

Currently, all of your evidence must be produced on paper. You need to organise your work carefully. Make sure each piece of work is clearly labelled to show what it is and that your name is on each page. For each task, put the work for each task in a logical order. When you have put all your work in a sensible order, number all the pages and create a contents page to show where each piece of work is located.

Software development – design

Introduction

Before a software system is installed it must be designed, created and tested. Before the software is designed a study must be undertaken to ensure that it is possible and feasible to design the software based on the end-users' needs and requirements. It is also important, before beginning to design the software, to understand why, how and where the software will be used and by whom. In order for a computerised software system to fully meet the needs and requirements of the end-users it is important to follow a plan and to investigate the current system fully. Once the existing system has been fully investigated, it is possible for the new software system to be designed.

In this unit you will learn about four stages that must be completed. These stages are the:

* feasibility stage
* investigation stage
* analysis stage
* design stage.

Each stage has a range of tools and techniques that can be used within it. You will learn about the tools and techniques which are used during each stage, understand why they are used and the benefits of each one.

The assessment for this unit will require you to produce a design for a solution to a given problem.

By studying this unit you will:

* be able to understand the tasks which must be completed in the four stages of feasibility, investigation, analysis and design. You will be able to complete the tasks within each stage based on the given problem

* be able to identify and explain the tools and techniques that are used in the analysis and design stages. You will need to select and use the most appropriate tools and techniques for the given problem

* identify and explain the investigation methods that are used when designing solutions to problems. You will need to be able to select the most appropriate investigation method for the given problem and explain why the method you have selected is the most appropriate

* be able to produce a solution to the given problem

* learn about data flow modelling and entity relationship diagrams and the documentation that is associated with these tools. You will produce data-flow models and documentation for your proposed solution to the given problem.

You will also produce an entity relationship diagram for your proposed solution with the associated documentation.

* be able to produce a conclusion and an evaluation of your proposed solution to the given problem. You will need to be able to discuss the advantages and disadvantages of your proposed solution to the end-users of your solution.

What you need to learn

You need to learn about:

* feasibility studies

* the investigation stage

* structured analysis

* design of forms and layouts

* producing a conclusion.

The systems life cycle

All projects, resulting in a solution to a problem, go through a number of stages before they are complete – the systems life cycle (see Figure 6.1). As the term 'cycle' suggests there is no clear start or finish point but it may be useful to think that the start is when a new software system is being considered. It may be that the existing system is unable to cope with the demands of the end-users, or the volume of work has increased, leading to a reduction in the efficiency of the current system.

The life cycle is a continuous loop with each stage leading into the next.

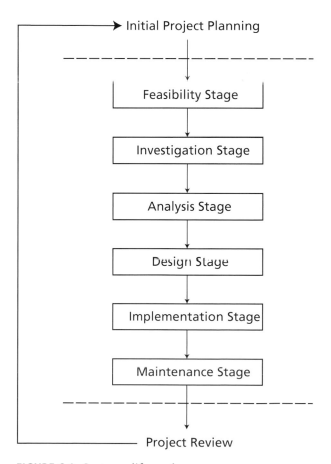

FIGURE 6.1 *Systems life cycle*

Each stage has a dependency on the stages that occur immediately before and after it. If you look at the diagram of the systems life cycle you can see that the analysis stage will depend upon the feasibility stage (the stage before) and the design stage (the stage after). In this unit we are just concerned with the stages of feasibility, investigation, analysis and design. These stages are collectively known as *SSADM*. There are many other methodologies that are available and can be used when designing software systems. SSADM is the basic methodology on which all others are built. If you continue your study of this area of ICT, it is important that you learn about this basic methodology before you learn about any others.

The investigation stage is sometimes combined with the analysis stage. But, the methods used for investigation are very important as is the understanding of what is to be achieved by the investigations. The tasks completed within the analysis stage will be based on the findings from the investigation stage.

Key terms

SSADM: structured systems and design methodology.

Systems analyst: the person who is responsible for the analysis of a system to assess its suitability for the proposed changes.

In Figure 6.1 you will see two stages that are outside the systems life cycle. These are initial project planning and project review. Usually the initial project planning stage is considered to be part of the feasibility stage. But, the **systems analyst** will have to be prepared for the main investigation as to the feasibility of the proposed changes to the system. This preparation may include investigations into the organisation/business and the current system in place.

Today most systems analysts are known as systems analysts/designers where they are responsible for both the analysis and for the new system design. This change has occurred over time as the boundaries between the stages of feasibility, investigation, analysis and design have become blurred.

To help you understand the processes involved in software development this unit will be applying each of the stages to a case study.

Feasibility studies

The *feasibility study* is the initial look at the existing system to see how it can be improved or if it is possible to meet the needs and requirements of the end-users. The end result of this stage is a *feasibility report*.

Key terms

Feasibility study: an initial look at an existing system to see how it can be improved.

Feasibility report: the final product from the feasibility stage.

CASE STUDY

SAMS Theatre Company, based in Cumbria, provides a range of theatrical experiences. The company works with youth groups and schools, putting on workshops to help young people gain acting and singing experience. The theatre company also puts on larger theatrical productions that tour the country.

The theatre company now needs some way of managing the touring productions. The system should be user-friendly, with the user being able to manage bookings, invoices, contracts and other data related to a touring theatre company.

The feasibility study answers a very important question – can the need for a new software system be justified? Is it technically feasible and economically desirable for the end-users?

During this stage a number of important questions may be asked. These include:

* can the solution be designed and implemented within the given constraints of time-scale allocated and budget?
* will the solution have a positive impact on the end-users; will the new system bring benefits?
* will the solution fulfil all the needs and requirements of the end-users?

For the project to continue the answer to all these questions must be yes, there is the time, money and resources, and the impact of the proposed solution will be positive.

The benefits a new system may bring include:

* greater efficiency
* reduced costs and overheads
* standardised way of working and sharing of information across the organisation
* increased end-user satisfaction.

The feasibility study begins with an initial investigation that involves the systems analyst obtaining some general information:

* the system currently being used, its benefits and limitations
* the additional requirements the end-users require from a new software system.

Once these investigations have been completed, a feasibility report is produced. From these investigations and findings a report can be produced clearly detailing the feasibility of the project – a feasibility report.

The main sources of information for the feasibility report are the end-users of the current system. However, the management of the organisation will also need to be consulted. The requirements of both these groups may be quite different – the analyst must ensure, as far as is feasible, that the needs and requirements of both groups are incorporated into the new software system.

One of the main questions which need to be covered in the feasibility report is 'Why is a new software system required?' The analyst needs to identify why the current system is not meeting the needs of the organisation. There are many reasons a new system may be required:

* the organisation wants to computerise a part of its operations that is currently done manually
* the capacity of the existing software system is too small to carry out the work now demanded of it
* the existing system is now outdated and no longer suits the needs of the organisation
* the existing system has come to the end of its life and needs to be replaced.

During the feasibility stage the analyst must determine which one, or more, of these reasons is why a new software system is required.

CASE STUDY

Currently SAMS Theatre Company keeps all records manually. This is causing problems, e.g. searching for available production dates can be very lengthy, if any details change they have to be rewritten by hand, records can easily get misplaced or damaged. There are many other problems with the current manual system.

A new system is needed to replace the current manual system and to remove the difficulties that this system is causing. There are currently no computers used during the administrative procedures in SAMS. The budget for the new system is £20,000 with a time-scale of 16 weeks.

Once the reason(s) for a new software system has been identified, the analyst must describe the role of the current system. Based on these findings the analyst, in consultation with the end-users and management of the organisation, must state what the new system needs to do. This is called a 'statement of purpose'.

The analyst must draw up a list of what is wrong or the problems with the current system. This list will be based upon investigations already

Theory into practice

Based on the information given write a statement of purpose for SAMS.

completed. It is also important that the analyst makes a note of those parts of the current system that are working well so that they can be kept in the new software system.

CASE STUDY

The current system used by SAMS Theatre Company is:

A theatre makes a booking for one performance of a production on a given day. Details of all productions (e.g. plays) that are available are kept in a production file. Each production is available for a set start date to a set finish date. The file holds details about the current production, including the actors and production staff involved and the scenery and costumes needed. If the booking from the theatre is possible then the booking is made.

Blank forms are currently used to monitor bookings of productions. When a theatre makes a booking this form is completed with all the relevant details. When a booking is made a contract is sent from SAMS to the theatre making the booking.

The contract is several pages long but only the first page changes based on the theatre making the booking, the production and the terms of the booking. The standard contract and a signed copy of the first page of each individual contract are returned by the theatre and kept in a contracts file. SAMS keeps all contact details for each theatre, such as name, address and box office telephone number.

SAMS tours with scenery only, so they need the theatre management to be available when they arrive at the theatre, at a time agreed in advance. These details are recorded on the booking form and confirmed by the theatre when the signed contract is returned.

The theatre pays SAMS a guaranteed fee for each performance (typically £1000) that will be paid irrespective of the money taken at the box office. SAMS then gets an agreed percentage of the box office takings if these takings exceed the guaranteed fee. The percentage is based on the number of seats in the theatre: over 200 seats the percentage of takings is 50 per cent, theatres with 200 seats or less agree to 40 per cent of the takings.

SAMS can provide programmes for each performance, at £2 each, on a sale or return basis. If programmes are provided, the theatre will keep 10 per cent of the takings (20p per programme) with SAMS getting the remaining 90 per cent (£1.80 per programme).

On the day after the performance the theatre must inform SAMS of the number of seats sold, the box office takings and the number of programmes sold. These details are recorded on the booking form. The income owed to SAMS from the sale of programmes and the total box office takings are calculated, based on the details recorded on the booking form. SAMS will then send an invoice for the total due from the theatre. Details of the income made from each production are kept in an accounts file. This file is updated each time an invoice is sent to a theatre. A copy of the invoice sent to the theatre is kept in an invoice file.

CASE STUDY

The **problems** with the current system used by SAMS are:

* searching for available dates can be time-consuming
* as the production bookings are written by hand, if changes are needed then they have to be rewritten
* searches are difficult to perform on the manual system, e.g. it is not easy to see all bookings for a particular production
* manual calculation of income from each performance can lead to user error
* sorting manual records is difficult, e.g. for sending a mailshot letter.

CASE STUDY

Some of the **needs and requirements** of the new system for SAMS are:

* enter and edit dates of booking for performances from theatres
* print details of each booking made for a performance
* enter details about a particular booking, including guaranteed fees, time of arrival, percentage of takings agreed, and number of programmes required
* print a report showing the income received from each performance.

A statement of user requirements should also be produced at this time. This will be developed in very close consultation with the end-users of the current system and the management of the organisation. The needs and requirements of the new software system should be prioritised as not all those needs and requirements may be possible, or feasible, given the time and money which has been allocated to the project.

Theory into practice

Some of the needs and requirements of the system for SAMS have been given to you. Using the information about the current system used in SAMS, identify the remaining needs and requirements.

Every project has a limit on the money that is available. This budget is set by the management of the organisation who requires the new software system. During the feasibility stage the analyst may not be aware of the budget. The feasibility study will need to estimate the cost of completing the project, including the cost of any new hardware which may be required, the cost of developing and implementing the software required and any training costs for the end-users of the new software.

Other questions which should be considered at the feasibility stage may include:

* what hardware and software does the current system use (if any)?
* how is the data needed by the current system collected?
* how is this data entered onto the system?
* where is this data stored?
* how is the data processed?
* what types and format of output are used?
* who uses the output and is it helpful?

These questions will be fully answered during the analysis stage but it is important, during the feasibility stage, that the analyst has as complete a picture of the current system as possible so that the right conclusions can be made and included in the feasibility report.

Once all the information has been collected, the analyst will be able to draw conclusions and make recommendations. The recommendations will have to be achievable within the given time-scale and budget (if known). If a sensible solution cannot be achieved within the constraints of time and money then the analyst must explain why. If a solution is possible, based on the given constraints, then the analyst must recommend solutions to the problem.

> ## ✱ REMEMBER!
>
> As the feasibility report is written by an analyst for the management of the organisation needing the solution it is very important that it is written in non-technical language so that the contents of the report can be clearly understood. The report should also describe the project from the end-users' perspective.

> ## Knowledge check
>
> 1 What is the purpose of the feasibility study?
>
> 2 Why is the feasibility stage so important?

Types of solution

In the recommendation in the feasibility report the analyst has to make suggestions for a proposed solution. Usually, analysts will provide more than one solution to the problem, all of which will meet the needs and requirements but may have different budget implications.

There are three main software approaches that the analyst can use to provide the solutions. These are to use *bespoke* (or *custom written software*), *off-the-shelf software* or a *customised off-the-shelf (COTS) approach*.

Bespoke or custom written software

Bespoke or custom written software is developed to meet the needs of a single organisation. It is specially written to fully meet their needs and requirements. It is very expensive and time-consuming to produce a bespoke system yet this system will totally meet the needs of the end-users and the organisation. For example, the software written to handle customer transactions using ATMs (automated teller machines – cash machines)

> ## Key terms
>
> *Bespoke* or *custom written software*: software which is designed and created to meet the needs of a specific organisation or a specific role.
>
> *Off-the-shelf software*: software which has already been developed and is ready to buy, install and use on a computer system.
>
> *Customised off-the-shelf (COTS) approach*: software that is purchased off-the-shelf as a package and then modified to meet the needs of a particular organisation.

is bespoke software. It has been specially written for an organisation – a bank – to meet a specific requirement. It is not only large organisations that will use bespoke software. Smaller organisations may also require bespoke software to be written as their needs and requirements of the software will be very specific to the nature of their business.

Off-the-shelf software

Off-the-shelf software has already been developed and tested. This software is already written and can be installed and used immediately. It is available from high street stores, through e-commerce or a mail-order software supplier. These software solutions are normally sold as whole packages. They are supplied on a CD-ROM or DVD-ROM with any updates to the software being supplied on storage media or through downloads from the Internet. Off-the-shelf software can be used in many different types of organisations. They are generally cheaper to buy than bespoke or COTS and have the advantage of having been fully tested. As this software can be installed and used very quickly this approach has the time advantage over the other two approaches. The main disadvantage with this approach is that the software may not fully meet the needs and requirements of the organisation and end-users.

Customised off-the-shelf software

Customised off-the-shelf software has the advantages of both bespoke and off-the-shelf software and is often sold to specific organisations that perform the same activities. For example, all DVD/video rental shops will need software which handles customer records, keep records of loans and returns, stock lists and borrower requests. But, each shop will also have specific needs that will not be shared with other shops: some may stock games or sweets and drinks. An off-the-shelf solution is not appropriate as it will not be flexible enough to meet all the needs of the shops whilst a bespoke system will probably be too expensive for a single shop. A customised solution can be bought from a software house that will be able to modify the software, selecting from a range of pre-written functions, to fully meet the needs of an individual shop. The user interface will then be tailored to suit the end-users of the software and to give the impression of a bespoke software package.

Theory into practice

Investigate the software that is used at your centre. Try to find out which approach was taken when the software was being developed. Consider why the software was developed using that approach.

In this unit we will be concentrating on the processes, tasks, tools and techniques that are used when developing bespoke software systems.

Following the production of the feasibility report and the authority given for the project to continue, the analyst must begin the investigations into the current system.

Theory into practice

Using the following headings, develop a feasibility report for SAMS Theatre Company.

* Purpose of the system

* Problems with the current system

* User needs and requirements

* Conclusions and proposed solution.

Investigation stage

During the investigation stage the analyst must discover how the current system is used, the processes which are carried out using the current system, and the needs and requirements for the new software system. The analyst may find out that the end-users are already carrying out the processes using software but the effectiveness of the current system is no longer viable. The proposed software solution will simply replace the current system. However, it may be that the current system is a manual one or the proposed software solution will add additional functions to an existing software system.

The analyst needs to investigate how data is put into the current system (input) how the data flows around the system, how it is processed and what types of output are produced.

The main topics that need to be considered during investigation are:

* the people involved

* the data capture methods

* data types, sources and flows

* decisions taken and types of processing

* storage methods

* documents used

* types of output

* manual and any automatic processes currently carried out.

There are different methods of investigation that can be used to gather the information on these topics. The main methods are interviews, questionnaires, document analysis, observation.

Interviews/meetings

Through interviewing users the analyst can clarify that the information already gathered is correct (see Figure 6.2). Interviews, if the questions are planned in advance, can reveal new information and give the analyst the opportunity to understand the system through the end-user perspective. The analyst should always plan an interview in advance. When planning the questions to be asked at the interview it is important to keep referring to the objectives of the interview.

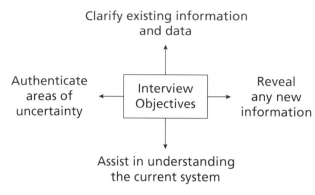

Clarify existing information and data

Authenticate areas of uncertainty → **Interview Objectives** → Reveal any new information

Assist in understanding the current system

FIGURE 6.2 *Interview objectives*

It is very important when interviewing that the analyst ensures they can talk to all different types of end-users, from management to staff at all levels, and that the interviewee feels comfortable and at ease with the questioning. There are four factors which should be considered when arranging interviews. They are who to interview, where and when to conduct the interview, what questions are to be asked and how the answers to the questions are to be recorded. If all these points are carefully considered then the interview will go well and all the information required by the analyst will be gathered.

Think it over...

Working in pairs, draw up some questions that could be asked of all the end-users of the current system used in SAMS.

Questionnaires

Questionnaires are an excellent way of gathering information. However, the questionnaire must be structured clearly and correctly, the return of the questionnaires must be strictly controlled and the correct end-users should have been sent the questionnaire. The questionnaire should provide opportunities for short answers based on facts and figures and descriptive answers. The balance of types of questions will ensure that all the information required by the analyst will be gathered. The return of a questionnaire may cause a problem to the analyst. One idea

may be to put a time constraint on the return of the questionnaire (e.g. please return within four working days). Another idea may be to distribute the questionnaire at a meeting and collect them in at the end of the meeting – this is not always feasible and this approach should be carefully considered. When designing a questionnaire it is important to consider who the questionnaire is aimed at. End-users of a system can interpret questions differently given their job role within the organisation. (More information about the types of questions and use of questionnaires can be found in Unit 1: Using ICT to Communicate.)

Theory into practice

Collect some questionnaires. Look at the different types of questions that are asked. Identify the open and closed questions. Using this information, design a questionnaire to find out what administrative procedures are carried out in SAMS Theatre Company. Your questionnaire should try to find out what improvements the administrative staff feel could be made to the system currently used in SAMS.

Document analysis

The analysis of documentation used in the current system is a good way of identifying the format of the input, processing and outputs that occur in a system. The drawback is that this method of investigation can be used only when the information flow is document based. This method can be used to clarify the information given by the end-users and can also trace the source and recipients of a particular piece of information used by the current system. The analyst should collect copies of all documents used by the current system. The common documents analysed include invoices, purchase orders, goods received notes, receipts, stock records and customer records.

Observations

If lots of activities are taking place in the system being investigated then observation may be the best method for collecting the information. For example, on a factory production line there will not be much documentation that can be analysed and, because of the nature of the activity, interviewing or questionnaires will not be appropriate. When the analyst observes the current system he or she will be able to identify all the processes that occur in the current system, how long it takes to perform a specific task and what hardware, software (if any) and people are involved. One thing the analyst must be aware of, although he or she is simply interested in the current system, is that people will be involved. The analyst must always ask the permission of the people involved before beginning his or her observation. To ensure that observation gathers the information required by the analyst the following factors should be carefully considered: how the observation findings are to be recorded, where and when the observation is to take place, and what part of the current system is to be observed.

Table 6.1 shows the advantages and disadvantages of each method of investigation we have looked at.

METHOD	ADVANTAGES	DISADVANTAGES
Interviews/meetings	• A rapport can be developed with the people who will use the system • Questions can be adjusted as the interviews proceed • Additional questions can be added to gather more information	• Can be time-consuming and costly • Poor interviewing can lead to misleading or insufficient information being gathered • In a large group it is not possible to interview everyone
Questionnaires	• Large numbers of people can be asked the same questions, therefore comparisons are easy to formulate (e.g. 72% of people said they were unhappy with the current system) • Cheaper than interviews for large numbers of people • Anonymity may provide more honest answers	• Must be designed very carefully. Questions need to be simple and easy to answer • Questions cannot be ambiguous • Cannot guarantee 100% return rate: may be lower with some groups
Observation	• The effects of office layouts and conditions on the system can be assessed • Work loads, methods of working, delays and 'bottlenecks' can be identified	• Can be time-consuming and costly • Problems may not occur during observation • Users may put on a performance when being observed
Document investigation	• Good for obtaining factual information, e.g. volume of sales over a period of time, inputs and outputs of the system	• Cannot be used when input, output and information is not document based

TABLE 6.1

It may be that, based on the information required about the current system, the analyst will use a combination of investigation methods.

Structured analysis

When the feasibility report has been developed and approved by the organisation, the next stage is to analyse the current system and to suggest a number of options for the solutions.

There are a number of tools and techniques that can be used when analysing a system. These include data flow modelling and entity relationship diagrams (ERDs). All the tools and techniques used in the analysis stage have documentation associated with them.

Data flow modelling

The two main techniques used to model data flows are:

* data flow diagrams (DFDs) – these are formal methods of modelling data flows

* rich picture diagrams (RPDs) – these are informal methods of modelling data flows.

Data flow diagrams

DFDs focus on the processes that transform incoming data flows (inputs) into outgoing data flows (outputs). The processes that perform this transformation create and use data (held in data stores). The DFD will also show who the system interacts with: *external entities*.

There are many different sets of symbols that can be used when constructing DFDs (see Figure 6.3). It does not matter which set of symbols you decide to use to construct your DFD but what is important is that once the set of symbols has been selected they are used consistently and are not changed part-way through the analysis stage.

In this unit the symbols we are going to use to construct DFDs are shown in Figure 6.3.

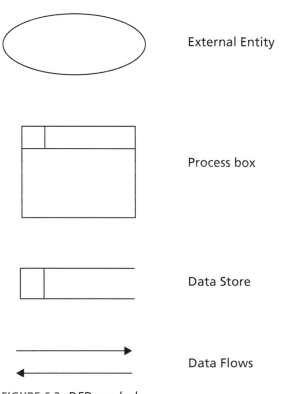

FIGURE 6.3 *DFD symbols*

A DFD does not show the hardware or software required to operate the system. The analyst will use the DFD to show the:

* external entities that the system interacts with
* processes that happen
* data stores that are used
* flow of the data and information.

External entities are used to represent people, organisations or other systems that have a role in the system under development but are not necessarily part of it. The external entities either put data into the system or receive data from it.

A **process** represents activities that take place within and are linked to the system. All activities within a system have a process attached to them. A process models what happens to the data. It transforms incoming data flows into outgoing data flows. Usually a process will have one or more data inputs and produce one or more data outputs.

Data stores show where data is stored. Examples of data stores include a database file, a paper form or a folder in a filing cabinet. A data store should be given a meaningful descriptive name, e.g. a customer file.

The **data flows** indicate the direction or flow of information within the system. Data flows provide a link to other symbols within the DFD. Each flow should be given a simple meaningful descriptive name. There are certain rules about which symbols can be linked. These are shown in Table 6.2.

So, looking at the table, you can see that in a DFD it is not possible to link an external entity with a data store.

Three of the symbols used must also be identified in some way. The **process** box is labelled with a number (see Figure 6.4). Each number given to the processes should follow on with the numbers representing when in the system the process is taking place. For example, process 1 would come before process 7. The process box should also state what the process is. This example shows the process of producing an invoice.

Sample process Box

FIGURE 6.4 *Sample process box*

The **data stores** are labelled dependent upon the type of data store they are (see Figure 6.5). The two main types are:

D: a computerised data store, i.e. files on a database

M: a manual data store such as a filing cabinet or paper form.

Sample manual data store

FIGURE 6.5 *Sample manual data store*

DATA FLOW LINKS	DATA STORE	EXTERNAL ENTITY	PROCESS
Data store	✗	✗	✓
External entity	✗	✗	✓
Process	✓	✓	✓

TABLE 6.2

It is possible to have a data store used more than once in a system. These are called repeating data stores (see Figure 6.6). If a data store is repeated then the same numbering and description is used but a second line is inserted.

| | D1 | Invoice database |

Sample computerised data store

FIGURE 6.6 *A repeating data store*

The **external entities** are labelled with the name of the person, organisation or system they represent. The external entity depicted in the following diagram shows the theatre as an external entity (see Figure 6.7a). It is possible to have repeating external entities (see Figure 6.7b). As with the data stores, the original name is kept and a line is used to show that it is repeated.

(a) A sample external entity   (b) A repeating external entity

FIGURE 6.7 *(a) A sample external entity (b) A repeating external entity*

Knowledge check

1 Name the four symbols used to create a DFD and describe the purpose of each.

2 Which two symbols can be repeated?

3 What does it mean when a data store is labelled with M and D?

In this unit we are looking at two levels of DFD – the Level 0 or context diagram (a diagram which shows how the system interacts with the outside world) and the Level 1.

Level 0 DFD/Context diagram

The Level 0 or context diagram gives a summary of the system. It shows the main external entities and the information that flows into and out of the system. A Level 0 DFD does not show the processes that occur or the data stores that are used within the system – it simply provides an overview of the system under investigation.

The first thing that should be done is to identify the external entities. In SAMS Theatre Company there is only one external entity used in the system under investigation – the theatre who are going to stage the performance by SAMS. Some systems will have more than one external entity; the process of constructing the Level 0 DFD will be the same despite the number of external entities and flows involved.

The next thing to be done is to identify the flows of data that occur between the system and the external entity – the theatre.

Theory into practice

Using the information given in the case study, identify the flows of data which occur between the SAMS system and the theatre.

The main flows you should have identified are:

* theatre places booking
* a contract is sent
* an agreed contract is returned
* details about the performance are given
* an invoice is sent.

When the flows of data have been identified it is important to identify which way the flow of information goes, i.e. from the theatre to the SAMS system or from SAMS to the theatre. This is known as defining the *source* or the *recipient*.

In Table 6.3 the flows of data, the source and the recipient have been defined. By putting this information in a table it becomes clear to the analyst and this table can then be used to draw the Level 0 DFD.

Once all this information has been gathered the analyst can draw the L0 DFD. This diagram for the SAMS Theatre Company is shown in Figure 6.8.

FIGURE 6.8 *L0 DFD/Context diagram*

It is convention that the flows that happen first in the system are at the top whilst the flows that happen last are at the bottom. It is very clear from the diagram that the start of the system is the theatre placing a booking and the final flow of the system is the invoice being sent by SAMS.

Once the L0 DFD diagram has been completed it is then time to begin developing the L1 DFD.

Level 1 DFD

The L1 DFD provides an overview of what is happening within the system. The system is represented in the L0 DFD by a process box. The overview includes types of data being passed within the system, documents and stores of data used (**data stores**), the activities (**processes**) and the people or organisations that the system interacts with (**external entities**).

The method you are going to use is only one of a wide range of methods that can be used to construct a L1 DFD.

Ten-step plan for constructing a L1 DFD

1 Read through the information collected during the feasibility and investigation stages.

2 Sort the information into clear sections, identifying the people or organisations external to the system under investigation but who interact with it, the documents used in the system under investigation, the activities that take place within the system under investigation.

3 Produce a data flow table.

4 Convert external users to external entities.

5 Convert documentation to data stores.

6 Convert activities to processes identifying when in the system the activity takes place, who is involved, and any data stores used.

DATA FLOW	EXTERNAL ENTITY	SOURCE/RECIPIENT
Theatre places booking	Theatre	Source
A contract is sent	Theatre	Recipient
An agreed contract is returned	Theatre	Source
Details about the performance are given	Theatre	Source
An invoice is sent	Theatre	Recipient

TABLE 6.3

ACTIVITY	ACTIVITY OVERVIEW	ACTIVITIES	DOCUMENTS USED
1	Check booking	Check requested booking against production file and start booking form	Production file Booking form
2	Contract issued	First page of standard contract amended for specific theatres booking	Contracts file
3	Update files	Signed copy of contract put in contracts file, booking form updated with confirmed details	Contract file Booking form
4	Check performance details	When performance details are received from the theatre the details of box office takings and programme sales are recorded on the booking form	Booking form
5	Invoice created	Money owed to SAMS from box office takings and sales of programmes is calculated based on details recorded on booking form. An invoice is created and sent to the theatre, a copy invoice is put in the Invoice file and the Accounts file is updated	Booking form Invoice file Accounts file

TABLE 6.4

7 Look at the inputs and outputs for each process with the data stores that are used and use data flows to 'link' these.

8 Link each data store and external entity with the associated process.

9 Link the processes (remember the rules about the labelling of processes!).

10 Check for consistency (check the initial findings to ensure all documentation has been included, check that the flows between external entities given on the context diagram are included, check with the end-users of the current system to ensure nothing has been forgotten).

We are now going to construct a L1 DFD for SAMS Theatre Company using the 10-step plan.

Step 1: The information given in the case study, the findings from the feasibility and investigation stages have been read. The system under investigation and development is the touring production system.

Steps 2 & 3: The information is sorted and a data flow table is developed. It is useful to include the activities in the order in which they occur in the system. This will help you when you begin to develop your L1 DFD. The data flow table for the SAMS Theatre Company system is shown in Table 6.4.

Steps 4, 5 & 6: Using the information from the data flow table and the L0 DFD the activities are converted to processes, documents used converted to data stores and the external entities are confirmed. It is also useful at this stage to give the identifiers to the processes and data stores that will be used in the L1 DFD. The external entities, data stores and processes, with the associated identifiers, used in SAMS system are shown in Table 6.5.

EXTERNAL ENTITIES	DATA STORES	PROCESSES
The theatre	Production File (M1)	Check booking (1)
	Booking Form (M2)	Contract issued (2)
	Contract File (M3)	Update files (3)
	Invoice File (M4)	Check performance details (4)
	Accounts File (M5)	Invoice created (5)

TABLE 6.5

Steps 7 & 8: Each process now needs to be drawn as a single process DFD (see Figure 6.9). This is done using the DFD symbols linking the external entities, data stores and the process together using data flows. The following diagram shows the first process DFD that occurs in the SAMS system.

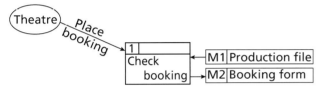

FIGURE 6.9 *First process DFD*

Theory into practice

Using the single process DFD for process 1 as an example, develop the single process DFD for the remaining 4 processes (processes 2–5).

Step 9: Link the processes together. You can have more than one process using a data store but remember the data flow lines must not cross. You can use repeating data stores to stop the data flow lines crossing. Each person will develop a DFD in a different way. This is because we all look at things in a different way. What is important to remember is that all the processes, external entities and data stores used within the system under investigation must be included, with each process linked to the associated data stores. An example L1 DFD for SAMS Theatre Company is shown in Figure 6.10.

Theory into practice

Link the five single process DFDs you have created together to produce a complete L1 DFD for the SAMS Theatre Company System.

You will notice on the L1 DFD that there is a repeating data store (M2: Booking Form) and the external entity (Theatre) is also repeated. This is to ensure that no data flow lines cross in the final DFD. Do not worry if your L1 DFD does not look identical to the example given. What is important is that the data stores, processes and external entities are linked correctly.

Before the DFD is shown to the organisation the analyst should perform some final checks. These are detailed in the following final checks list.

Step 10 L1 DFD final checks!

✱ Does each process receive all the data it needs?

✱ Does any data store have only data flows out and not in?

✱ Does any data store appear to have data in that is never used?

✱ Are all data flows consistent across the L0 and the L1 DFD?

✱ Are all external entities shown on the L1 DFD also shown in the L0 diagram? Are all flows labelled? Are they documented in the data dictionary?

✱ Are there any data flows between two external entities, external entities to data stores and two data stores?

✱ Do any data flows cross other data flows on the diagram? If they do, use repeating external entities or data stores.

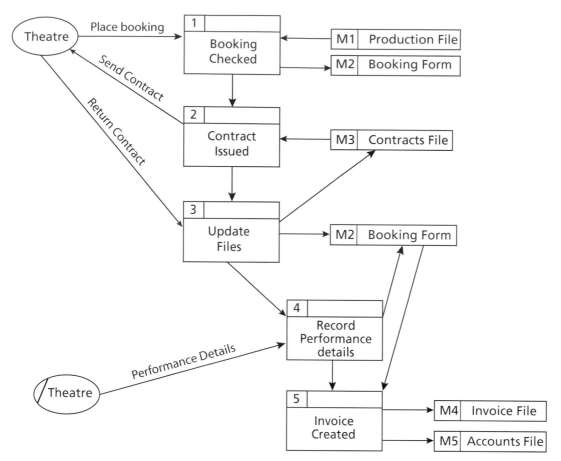

FIGURE 6.10 *L1 DFD for SAMS Theatre Company System*

Rich picture diagrams

Rich picture diagrams (RPDs) are an informal method of modelling data flows. A RPD shows what the system is about and is developed using simple 'pictorial' representations of the system under investigation. It is sometimes easier for end-users to visualise a system in RPD format rather than as a formal DFD. The RPD is sometimes developed prior to the formal DFD being developed. An RPD can be used by the analyst to check that all the activities within the system under investigation are included and are being considered during the analysis stage.

Rich picture diagrams (see Figure 6.11) are self-explanatory as they are designed and developed to help during the analysis stage as well as to help the analyst visualise the system. The RPD has three elements:

1 The structure of the system under investigation

2 What takes place in the system, the activities and processes

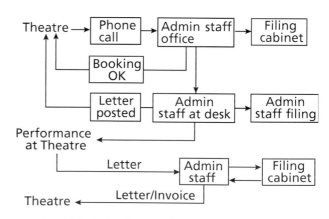

FIGURE 6.11 *Rich picture diagram*

3 The relationships between different parts of the system being investigated.

Data flow modelling documentation

Both formal and informal data flow modelling need to be accompanied by some documentation. The documentation accompanies the diagrams and is used to support and clarify the information contained within the diagram. The documentation you will need to produce for your DFD or RPD includes external entity descriptions, input/output descriptions and process descriptions.

External entity descriptions identify the role and responsibilities they have as part of the system. There is only one external entity involved in the SAMS system – the theatre.

One possible description of the theatre is:

> A venue that places a booking for SAMS to perform their current production and agrees to a contract for this booking. The theatre provides the information, box office takings and programme sales, which allows the SAMS admin staff to produce a correct invoice.

Input/output descriptions provide written descriptions of the data flows that exist between the system under investigation and the external entities. These flows will have been detailed in the context diagram and integrated into the Level 1 DFD.

You should have identified five inputs/outputs between the theatre (external entity) and the SAMS system. These are the:

* booking (input into the system)
* unsigned contract (output from the system)
* signed contract (input into the system)
* performance details (input into the system)
* invoice (output from the system).

It is important that the analyst defines the inputs/outputs between the system and the external entities. It is useful for the end-users of the system to check, at this stage, that the analyst has missed no important inputs or outputs.

The final piece of documentation that needs to be produced is a description of the activities or operations that occur within each process. This was completed during steps 2 & 3, the data flow table, of the plan you followed to develop the L1 DFD.

Entity relationship diagrams

Entity relationship diagrams (*ERDs*) are one of the tools and techniques that can be used to produce the logical data model. This tool provides a detailed graphical representation of the information that is used within a system and identifies the relationships which exist between the items of data. As with data flow modelling a set of tools and documentation is used. In this unit we are concerned with three elements of ERDs. These are entities, relationships and the degree of the relationships. The set of symbols we are going to use is shown in Figure 6.12.

⬜	Entity
——	Relationships
	Different degrees of Relationships
——	One to One Relationship (1:1)
——←	One to Many Relationship (1:M)
→——←	Many to Many Relationship (M:M)

FIGURE 6.12 *ERD symbols*

When the analyst is completing the analysis stage they will have sufficient knowledge and understanding of software development to be able to identify the entities, attributes and primary and foreign keys that will need to be used in the proposed system. In this unit the entities and attributes will be given to you. You will develop the ERD based on the information given to you.

Key terms

ERDs: techniques for representing the structure of data in a software system using entities and the relationships between those entities.

Attributes: elements that define an entity.

Entities are usually real-world things, i.e. books, students, products that need to be represented in the software system. For example, in the SAMS system one of the entities might be theatre; this is because information is held about theatres in the current system. This would be represented by:

```
┌─────────────────┐
│                 │
│     Theatre     │
│                 │
└─────────────────┘
```

Each entity has *attributes*. Attributes make up the information that is held on a system about the entity, as shown in the table below.

ENTITY	BOOK
Attributes	ISBN Number
	Title
	Author
	Publisher
	Publication Date

You may have defined the following attributes:

STUDENT(Student number, Surname, First name, Tutor group, Course, Contact number) COMPUTER_GAME(Name, Platform, Price)

The entities and attributes are given in a specific format. There are many different formats that can be used. As with DFDs it is important that once a format has been selected it is used consistently throughout the ERD development. In this unit we are going to use the following format. The entity name is shown in capitals with the attributes contained within brackets ( ). But, when the ERD is developed the entity name is shown with an initial capital letter, i.e. 'Student'.

Each set of attributes for an entity should have a unique field that identifies each *occurrence* of an entity. This unique field is called the *primary key*. In our example of STUDENT the primary key would be Student_ID as no two students will have the same student ID number. It is the primary key that provides the links between the entities.

In the SAMS system the entities are defined as: PRODUCTION, PERFORMANCE and THEATRE. In an ERD these would be represented as:

```
┌────────────┐  ┌─────────────┐  ┌───────────┐
│ Production │  │ Performance │  │  Theatre  │
└────────────┘  └─────────────┘  └───────────┘
```

Relationships are used to show how entities are linked together. Each relationship is given a degree. The degrees of relationships that may be used are:

1 One to One (1:1) – shows that only one occurrence of each entity is used by the linked entity (see Figure 6.13).

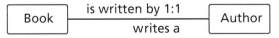

A single author writes a single book.

FIGURE 6.13 *One to One relationships*

2 Many to One (M:1) or One to Many (1:M) – shows that a single occurrence of one entity is linked to more than one occurrence of the linked entity (see Figure 6.14).

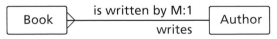

A single author writes many books

A single book is written by many authors

FIGURE 6.14 *One to Many/Many to One relationships*

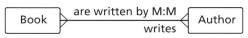

An author can write a
number of books and books can
have more than one author.

One book can relate to many contracts
and many contracts can be awarded to
one author.

FIGURE 6.15 *Many to Many relationships*

3 Many to Many (M:M) – shows that many
occurrences of one entity are linked to more
than one occurrence of the linked entity.
Although many to many occurrences are
common, a linked entity must be used to break
down or decompose the many to many
relationship (see Figure 6.15).

To define the relationships the attributes of each
entity must be listed. In the SAMS software
system the entities and attributes are:

PRODUCTION(ProductionName, StartDate,
EndDate)

PERFORMANCE(InvoiceNumber,
PerformanceDate, *ProductionName, TheatreID*,
ContractSent, ContractReturned,
GuaranteedFee, AgreedPercentage)

THEATRE(TheatreID, VenueName, Address1,
Address2, Town, County, Postcode,
BoxOfficeNumber)

If a database were being built for SAMS the
analyst would use the entities and their attributes
as tables (entities) with each attribute being a field
within that table.

In the format we are using in this unit the
primary keys are underlined and are shown as the
first attribute in the list. The primary keys for the
SAMS software system are:

PRODUCTION – ProductionName

PERFORMANCE – InvoiceNumber

THEATRE – TheatreID

In the SAMS software system each of the
primary keys is a number; remember a
primary key uniquely defines each occurrence
of the entity.

You will notice that some of the attributes are
in *italics*. These are known as foreign keys.
A foreign key is simply the primary key from
another entity used as an attribute in an entity.
For example, in the SAMS system the foreign key
ProductionName is an attribute in the entity
PERFORMANCE but is also the primary key of
the entity PRODUCTION.

Once the entities, attributes and primary and
foreign keys have been identified the ERD can
start to be developed. The method you are
going to use to develop the ERD is only one of
a wide range of methods that can be used to
construct an ERD.

The entities and attributes need to be shown in
boxes. In this diagram the primary keys are
shown in **bold** with the foreign keys shown in
italics. For the SAMS system this is shown in
Figure 6.16.

Theatre	Performance	Production
Theatre ID Venue Name Address 1 Address 2 Town County Post Code Box Office Number	*Invoice Number* Performance Date *Production Name* *Theatre ID* Contract Sent Contract Returned Guaranteed Fee Agreed Percentage	*Production Name* Start Date End Date

FIGURE 6.16 *Entities and attributes for the SAMS system*

We can now begin to think about the relationships that will link the entities together to form an ERD. There are many ways of thinking about the relationships but it is best to concentrate on one relationship at a time.

There is a link between the THEATRE and PERFORMANCE entities – we know this, as the primary key of THEATRE is a foreign key of PERFORMANCE. It is not possible that one theatre holds one performance. Theatres have many performances that are held over the course of time. So the relationship would be:

One THEATRE holds Many PERFORMANCES

We also know there is a relationship between PERFORMANCE and PRODUCTION.

Theory into practice

Define the relationship between PERFORMANCE and PRODUCTION. Explain your choice.

The relationship between PERFORMANCE and PRODUCTION is a M:1. This is because

Many performances can be done of **One** production.

Now the relationships have been defined it is possible to complete the ERD. Go back and look at the notation that is used to represent the relationships.

The notation we use to represent a M:1 relationship is:

To represent the 1:M relationship we use:

We now need to show the relationships on the ERD we have partially completed. The final ERD is shown in Figure 6.17.

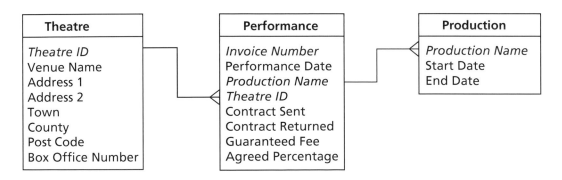

FIGURE 6.17 *ERD for the SAMS system*

ENTITY NAME: PRODUCTION			
Relationships:			
Related to:	**Type**	**Which end?**	
Performance	1:Many	Many	
Attributes:			
Name	**Key type**	**Format**	**Length**
Production name	Primary	Text	30
Start date		Date	
End date		Date	

TABLE 6.6

As with the DFDs, documentation needs to be developed to clarify and support the ERD. The documentation includes **Entity Descriptions** and **Attribute Lists**.

Each entity in the ERD should have an associated entity description that details the entity name and description, the entity attributes and any relationships/links associated with it. The method we used to develop our ERD has already detailed the information that is needed in the documentation. It is simply a matter of putting the information into a format that can be easily understood.

One format that could be used to show this information is a table. The documentation for the entity PRODUCTION has been completed as shown in Table 6.6.

Flowcharts

There are three other tools and techniques that the analyst can use at this stage. These are:

* flowcharts
* decision tables
* structured English.

Flowcharts are good for providing a general outline of the processing that is involved in the system under investigation but, generally, do not relate very well to the actual software system which is eventually developed.

Flowcharts, as with DFDs and ERDs use sets of symbols. There are many different formats that can be used. As with DFDs and ERDs it is important that once a format has been selected it is used consistently throughout the flowchart development. In this unit we are going to use the symbols shown in Figure 6.18.

Flowcharts can be used to model all kinds of systems, not just computer systems. They can be used to break a process into small steps or to give an overview of a complete system. People who are not involved in the IT industry can easily understand them. However, flowcharts do not translate easily into code and they can sometimes become so complex they can be hard to follow.

For these reasons flowcharts are used by the analyst to give a generalised overview of a system or the functions which make up a specific process. Decision tables or structured English can then be used to provide more detailed information. One of the processes that happens in the SAMS system that could be shown in a

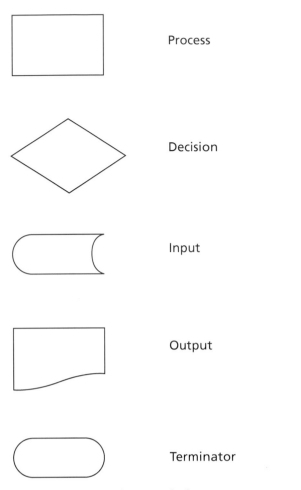

Process

Decision

Input

Output

Terminator

FIGURE 6.18 *Flowchart symbols*

flowchart is the development of the invoice. During this process decisions have to be made. The decisions are:

❋ guaranteed income (£1000) exceeded?

❋ number of seats in the theatre?

❋ programmes supplied?

The flowchart in Figure 6.19 shows the steps that are taken in the SAMS system when an invoice for a theatre is produced.

Theory into practice

Draw a flowchart to show the processes that occur in the SAMS system before the development of the invoice. (Hint: refer back to the L1 DFD.)

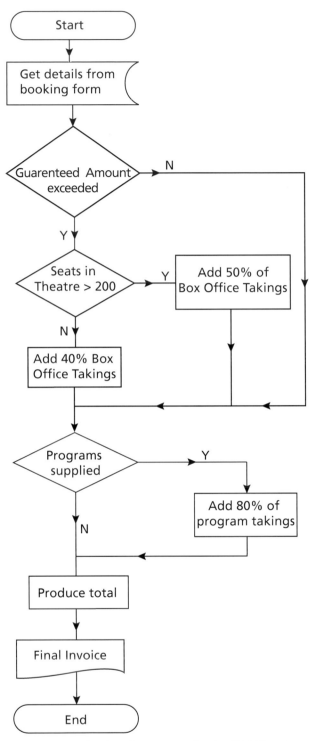

FIGURE 6.19 *The invoice process in the SAMS system*

Decision tables

Decision tables are useful where there are options (the conditions) which need to be chosen and the analyst needs to identify what happens in each circumstance (the actions).

RULES	1	2	3	4
Conditions				
	Y	Y	N	N
	Y	N	Y	N
Actions				

TABLE 6.7

They are used when the processing that occurs includes a range of true or false conditions. Depending on the combination of conditions different actions need to be taken. The advantage of a decision table is that all the combinations of the rules have to be considered and it is very easy to check that all the rules have been included. Decision tables are best used for processes involving complex combinations of up to six decisions. More than six decisions can make the decision tables very large and difficult to read. There is a standard layout for decision tables that means that all the information included in the table can be understood by the end-users of the system under investigation.

A decision table is made up of two parts (see Table 6.7):

* the conditions are listed at the top of the table – all combinations of conditions must be listed

* the actions (what to do in each condition) are listed in the bottom part of the table.

In this decision table there are two conditions with four rules. Each condition is shown to be either yes/no or true/false. The actions are based upon the rules.

In the SAMS systems there are several decisions that have to be made when the invoice is being developed. These have been used to draw the flowchart of this process. To remind you the decisions are:

* guaranteed income (£1000) exceeded?

* number of seats in the theatre?

* programmes supplied?

The condition part of the decision table would be as shown in Table 6.8.

So if we look at the decision table shown, we can quickly tell that if the guaranteed income has been exceeded, the theatre has more than 200 seats and SAMS has provided the programmes (Rule 1), then to calculate the invoice the processing needed to develop the invoice is:

£1000 + 50% of takings + 80% of programme sales.

RULES	1	2	3	4	5	6	7	8
Conditions								
Guaranteed income exceeded?	Y	Y	Y	Y	N	N	N	N
Seats in theatre > 200	Y	Y	N	N	Y	Y	N	N
Programmes supplied?	Y	N	Y	N	Y	N	Y	N
Actions								
Only charge £1000					X	X	X	X
Takings % = 50%	X	X						
Takings % = 40%			X	X				
Add 80% of programme sales	X		X		X		X	

TABLE 6.8

Structured English

Structured English is very detailed; it is a 'half-way' house between actual programming code and normal spoken English. It is used to describe the steps in a process without being concerned about the programming syntax. Structured English is also known as **pseudo-code**. Structured English is best used whenever a process combines sequences of actions with decisions and loops. There are no exact rules on how to use Structured English but it is important that the Structured English written should avoid ambiguity. There are many constructs which can be used in structured English and which ones you use will depend upon your programming knowledge. The most common constructs are:

If...Then...Else – used when a choice needs to be made based on a condition. This construct takes the format:

If (condition) Then (action)
Else (alternate action)

While Do or **Do While** – used when a loop is used, the loop continues until a condition disagrees with the condition given. The construct takes the form:

While (condition) Do (action) or
Do (action) While (condition)

Repeat...Until – this loop is used when a set of commands must be carried out an unknown number of times until a condition becomes true. The construct takes the format:

REPEAT
any number of instructions put here
UNTIL a condition is true

CASE – this is very closely linked with a decision table. The decision table identifies the actions to take in all the different combinations of actions. The CASE construct follows each rule identified in the decision table. The CASE Structured English for the Invoice process, rule 1, in the SAMS system is shown as follows.

Select CASE Invoice Process

CASE (GIE = Y) and (seats > 200) and (programmes supplied = Y)

Invoice total = £1000 + 50% of takings + 80% of programme sales.

Design of forms and layouts

When the analysis stage has been completed, and the analyst has checked with the end-users of the system that nothing has been missed, the next stage is the design stage.

In this unit you will need to produce proposed designs for:

* data input forms
* screen layouts
* screen report layouts
* printed report layouts.

At this stage hand-drawn designs need to be developed. These will then be shown to the end-users of the proposed software system and any feedback given will be used to refine the designs until they fully meet their needs and requirements. When the end-users are happy with the designs then final designs are produced. What is important to remember is that the designs must be hand-drawn. It is only later in the systems life cycle that these hand-drawn designs will be computerised.

When designing the forms and screen layouts the analyst will refer to any documents used in the current system. These documents will have been collected and analysed during the investigation stage.

For each type of document designed the following questions will have to be answered, and with the answers accompanying the hand-drawn designs.

* Type – Is the format paper-based or displayed on a screen?

* Purpose – Who will use the form or screen? What is the purpose of the form or screen? Who will the output go to? Is a corporate style needed?

* Data required – What is required for input, are any calculations required, does any data need to be grouped or sorted?

Other considerations include:

* if the design is screen-based then it is important that the screens follow a consistent layout so that end-users will become familiar and confident with the screens. Data should be input onto the screen in a logical order

* the colour of the screens is important; bright or clashing colours should not be used. It may be that the company has a corporate colour scheme that can be used. The style and size of the font should also be carefully considered. If the font is too small, end-users may have to strain their eyes to see the text; conversely, if the font is too large, then all the information may not be seen on a screen

* if the output is to be printed should it be in colour or black and white?

An initial design of an invoice for SAMS is shown in Figure 6.20.

Production of a conclusion

The final part of this unit is to produce a final conclusion and evaluation of your proposed system. When the analyst has produced a proposed solution he or she must justify it to the end-users. The benefits of the proposed software system must be explained to the end-users along with any potential problems or disadvantages.

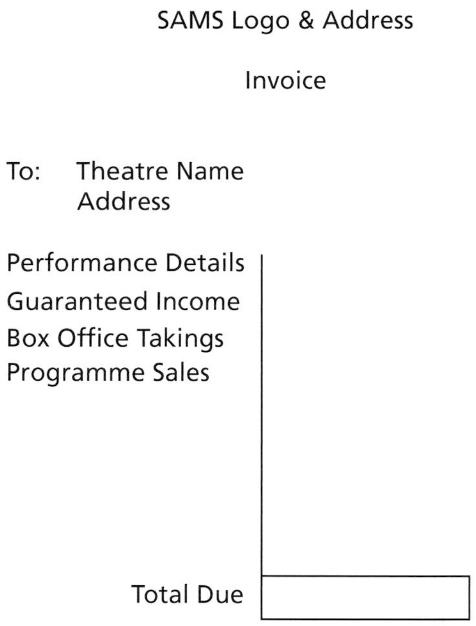

SAMS Logo & Address

Invoice

To: Theatre Name
     Address

Performance Details
Guaranteed Income
Box Office Takings
Programme Sales

Total Due

FIGURE 6.20 *Initial design of invoice*

Although a proposed solution has been identified and designed it is good practice to identify alternative solutions that would solve the problems with the current system. It may be that, as in this unit, the analyst has designed a bespoke system, and an alternative solution may be to suggest using an off-the-shelf piece of software which can be tailored to meet the needs of the end-users.

Alternative proposals should also be suggested in terms of hardware. The analyst may have suggested a colour laser printer as the output device to produce the printed reports. An alternative would be a black and white printer or an inkjet printer.

Theory into practice

Produce a conclusion for the SAMS system. You should consider the benefits and disadvantages of the proposed system and any alternative solutions that are available.

Assessment evidence

Task 1

There are a range of tools and techniques that can be used by the analyst during the analysis stage of the system life cycle. The tools and techniques selected by the analyst willdepend on the nature of the system being analysed.

To be able to select the most appropriate tools and techniques to be used at the analysis stage you must be aware of the range of tools and techniques that are available.

You must:

* identify the tools and techniques that can be used during the analysis stage of the system life cycle.

To achieve the mark band 2 or higher marks; you should identify and give a simple explanation of a range of tools and techniques that may be used during the analysis stage of the systems life cycle. You should include the advantages or limitations of each tool and technique you have identified. To achieve the highest mark band you should provide a detailed explanation of the tools and techniques, including advantages and limitations, and give an example of a situation where each tool and technique could be used.

Task 2

There are also many tools and techniques that can be utilised during the design stage of the system life cycle. The nature of the system being designed may define the tools and techniques being used by the analyst at this stage of the systems life cycle. To be able to select the most appropriate design tools and techniques you must be aware of the range of tools and techniques that are available.

You must:

* identify the tools and techniques that can be used during the design stage of the systems life cycle.

To achieve the mark band 2, you should identify and give a simple explanation of a range of tools and techniques that may be used during the design stage of the systems life cycle.

You should include the advantages or limitations of each tool and technique you have identified. To achieve the highest mark band you should provide a detailed explanation of the tools and techniques, including advantages and limitations, and give an example of a situation where each tool and technique could be used.

Task 3

When the analyst is developing the system some investigation of the current system must be undertaken. There are many different investigation methods that can be used by the analyst. To be able to select the most appropriate investigation method you must be aware of the different investigation methods that are available.

You must:

* identify the different investigation methods that are available.

To achieve the mark band 2, you should identify and give a simple explanation of a range of investigation methods that may be used. You should include the advantages or limitations of each investigation method you have identified. To achieve the highest mark band you should provide a detailed explanation of the investigation methods, including advantages and limitations, and with an example of a situation where each investigation method could be used.

Task 4

The purpose of undertaking the initial stages of the systems life cycle is to provide a report to the client that details the feasibility of the proposed system, and proposed solutions to solve the problems of the current system and meet the needs of the end-users. The report will also include initial designs of the proposed input/output requirements.

You must:

* read the attached scenario and provide a report that includes:

    – the feasibility of the proposed system

    – a proposed solution to the problem

    – the design of the input/output requirements.

To achieve mark band 2, your report should be detailed and include alternative solutions to the problem. The solutions and designs you propose should meet the needs and requirements of the end-user. To achieve the highest mark band you should recommend your preferred solution to the client with justification of your selection of this solution. The solution you propose and the designs of the input/output requirements must fully meet the needs of the end-user.

Task 5

It is important to analyse the flow of data within the current system. This will enable the analyst to get an overview of the processes and associated data stores that are currently used. By doing this, it will also help to ensure that no processes are ignored when developing the new system.

You must:

* produce a data flow model of the current system used, with the associated documentation. This documentation should include:
  – external-entity descriptions
  – input/output descriptions.

To achieve mark bands 1 and 2, a simple graphical representation of the data flow may be used. To achieve mark band 2, the documentation you produce should be complete, appropriate and relate to the data flow model you have produced. To achieve the highest mark band you will need to use one of the formal graphical representations that can be used to develop a data flow model and provide detailed, complete documentation that relates to the data flow model.

Task 6

One of the tools and techniques that can be used in the designing of the new system is the ERD. An ERD provides a detailed graphical representation of the information used within the new system and identifies the relationships that exist within it.

You must:

* produce an ERD for the proposed system, with associated documentation. This should include:
  – entity descriptions including
    * the name of the entity
    * a description of the entity
  – the entity attributes
  – the relationships and links.

To achieve mark band 2, you should produce an ERD with complete documentation that is appropriate and relates to the ERD you have produced. To achieve the highest mark band the ERD you produce should be fully complete, with the associated documentation being complete to an appropriate level of detail.

Task 7

It is important that all proposed solutions to a problem are evaluated to ensure that the solution fully meets the needs and requirements of the end-user.

You must:

* produce an evaluation of your proposed system and comment on your actions and role in producing this solution.

To achieve mark band 2, you must produce a conclusion about your proposed system considering the benefits or the disadvantages. You should also identify an alternative proposed solution to the problem. You should evaluate your own performance when completing this work, considering the good and poor features of the way in which you tackled and solved the problem. You should also suggest ways in which your performance could be improved. To achieve the highest mark band you should justify your conclusion, discussing the benefits and disadvantages of the proposed solution. You should identify the strengths and weaknesses in the strategies you used to solve the problem, explaining how these were refined to meet the purpose more closely. You should also include a consideration of how a more efficient approach could be used when solving a similar problem in the future.

Signposting for portfolio evidence

Currently, all of your evidence must be produced on paper. You need to organise your work carefully. Make sure each piece of work is clearly labelled to show what it is and that your name is on each page. For each task, put the work for each task in a logical order. When you have put all your work in a sensible order, number all the pages and create a contents page to show where each piece of work is located.

CASE STUDY: SAMPLE SCENARIO

The Organic Box

The Organic Box is a small business in Bath. The main function of the business is to deliver organic produce boxes to customers to their workplace or home address. The boxes available contain organic vegetables, meat, fish or fruit that can also be delivered. All boxes can be ordered to be delivered weekly or fortnightly.

The boxes are available in small, medium or large sizes. A small box costs £7.50; a medium box costs £10.00 with the cost of a large box at £12.50.

Delivery is extra, with a small box having a delivery charge of £1.50, a medium box £2.00 and a large box £2.50. If a customer orders two or more boxes, the delivery charge is reduced. This is shown in the table below:

Number of boxes	Reduction
1	0
2	50p
3	£1.00
4	£1.50

If customers have their boxes delivered fortnightly, a surcharge of 50p is added once any reduction in delivery charge has been applied. For example, a customer ordering two large boxes on a weekly delivery would pay a delivery charge of (£2.50 + £2.50) − 50p = £4.50, whilst a customer ordering three small boxes delivered fortnightly would pay a delivery charge of (3 × £1.00) − £1.00 + 50p = £2.50.

Most of the customers of The Organic Box place regular orders but deliveries can also be made as a one-off order.

The main office of The Organic Box is situated in the farmhouse of the farm where most of the vegetables are grown. Regular customers can arrange any change to their order, and businesses can place one-off orders, by calling into, faxing or phoning this office. The owner and the administration staff are based at this office.

The boxes are made up in a barn on the farm about four miles away from the main office. This is also where the delivery vans are kept and where the boxes are put on the correct van each morning.

At the moment all communication between the two sites is by phone or fax, or by the owner walking between the two sites to deliver the information by hand. This information may be on paper or on a floppy disk.

There are two desktop computers at the main office. One computer (the delivery system) is used by the administration staff to:

* keep records of all the orders made by customers

* print out the invoices that are given to customers

* record any payments that are received.

The other computer is in the owner's office. This computer is used for keeping staff personnel records and recording the company accounts.

There is one desktop computer at the barn. This computer is situated in the office and is

(continued)

supposed to be used to keep records about the customer orders and deliveries. However, there is no formal method for keeping these records, and the computer is very rarely used. Most of the information is stored on paper and pinned to the notice board on the wall in this office. This method of storing the information is very disorganised and information is often lost or misplaced.

There have been instances in the past when orders have been delivered incorrectly, leading to customer dissatisfaction. There are also other problems that need to be solved.
The main ones are:

* orders still being delivered when regular customers have cancelled their order because they are away

* invoices not being given to customers, resulting in loss of revenue for The Organic Box

* changes to regular customer orders not being actioned.

It is hoped that a new computer system will solve these problems.

The owner of The Organic Box would also like to be able to produce reports including:

* the sales for each type of box (meat, fish, vegetable, fruit)
* the amount of profit that each type of box brings to the business.

The owner wants three computers in the main office and two computers at the kitchen site. These should be interconnected within each site and also linked between the two sites.

The new system must be implemented within 20 weeks. The budget is £20,000.

Appendix one – procedures

When a customer wants to **start** a regular order the following procedure takes place within The Organic Box.

* The customer advises a member of the administration staff of the start date, frequency of delivery and boxes required.

* The member of the administration staff enters these delivery details onto the delivery system.

* The information about the delivery is sent to the barn.

* In the barn, a record of the delivery start date is made – this is done by hand.

When a customer wants to **cancel** a regular order the following procedure takes place within The Organic Box.

* The customer advises a member of the administration staff of the final delivery date.

* The member of administration staff enters the final delivery date onto the delivery system.

* The cost of the products not yet paid for, up to and including the final order, is calculated and totalled, and an invoice produced.

* The information about the final delivery date and the invoice are sent to the kitchen.

* In the barn, a record of the final delivery date is made – this is done by hand.

* On the final delivery date the invoice is left with the delivery.

* The customer calls into the main office to pay the outstanding invoice.

When a customer wants to **change** a delivery the following procedure takes place within The Organic Box.

* The customer advises a member of the administration staff of the changes he or she wishes to make to the order. This may be, for example, a change of size of box, type of box, or frequency of delivery.

* The member of administration staff enters the changed order onto the delivery system.

* The information about the changed delivery is sent to the barn.

* In the barn, a record of the changed delivery is made – this is done by hand.

Following all the procedures just detailed the appropriate member of the delivery staff is notified and the delivery changes are actioned.

Customers can also request an invoice at any time to bring their account up to date.

Appendix two – entities

The following **entities** could be used when developing the new system. You will need to amend and add to the entities given to design a working system to incorporate these assumptions.

DELIVERY (**Del_Number**, *Cust_ID*, *Round_Number*, start_date, end_date, frequency, *Box_Number*)

CUSTOMER (**Cust_ID**, address, contact_number)

BOX (**Box_Number**, type, size, cost)

DELIVERY ROUND (**Round_Number**, *Del_Number*, *Staff_Number*)

STAFF (**Staff_Number**, staff name)

Key

Primary Keys are in **bold**
Foreign Keys are in *italics*
Assume the following:

* one member of the delivery staff may do one or more delivery rounds

* one customer may have one or more boxes delivered.

UNIT 7

Communicating using computers

Introduction

The use of intranets and the Internet has expanded rapidly over the last few years. Many organisations use computers to communicate and make use of the Internet to share information amongst themselves, and intranets to share information with other people and organisations and to find out information about other people. Websites are no longer static, looking like representations of pieces of paper, they are dynamic and interactive – a communication medium in their own right.

Being able to understand how the Internet and intranets are used by organisations and to define a specification and set up and manage websites are valuable commodities to today's companies. You will learn about the different components that make up a website and how to develop a specification to implement it.

ICT moves very rapidly, particularly networking, intranets and the Internet. It is important that you do your own research and include the latest developments in the reports that you produce. No company would want a specification that uses outdated technology.

Learning outcomes

By studying this unit you will:

* develop an understanding of how the Internet and intranets are used by organisations. You will need to investigate an organisation and document its current provision and use

* know how the Internet is organised and services that can be provided by the Internet. You will need to understand protocols and standards relating to the Internet and what services can be provided and how they can be used. Different Internet service providers (ISPs) provide different services. You will need to be able to compare different ISPs for a given task

* develop an understanding of the costs associated with connecting to and accessing the Internet. This includes an understanding of the different bandwidths and connection methods and of the hardware and software required

* be able to select the appropriate software and tool for a given task. This involves configuring software, such as email clients, data compression and communication logs for use on a network

* understand the technical terms relating to the Internet and communication services and know about data compression and communication logs

* be able to follow standard ways of working, including managing your work effectively, keeping information up to date, such as records of faults found and repaired, and working safely.

What you need to learn

You need to learn about:

* acronyms and technical terms used in communicating using computers
* the Internet and intranets
* the Internet and communication systems
* web server requirements
* Internet tools
* Internet websites
* setting up a computer system for use on the Internet.

Acronyms and technical terms used in communicating using computers

The ICT industry is very fond of its acronyms and makes use of many of them. There are lots of terms specific to communications technology that you need to know. The main ones are flagged up as you go through this unit. Over time, new technical terms and acronyms will be introduced. You must keep up to date with the terminology used.

The Internet and intranets

The Internet is often thought of as just being the *World Wide Web* (WWW). It is not. The Internet is a vast collection of interconnected computers that run the same protocol (TCP/IP). The computers are used for communication purposes. This may include:

* web pages/sites
* newsgroups
* email
* video conferencing
* telephone calls.

Key term

World Wide Web: it is a system of Internet servers that uses HTTP to transfer specially formatted documents. The documents are formatted in a language called HTML (hypertext mark-up language). This language supports links to other documents, as well as graphics, audio and video files.

A *website* can have many different purposes depending on the nature of the company. Advertising is one of the main purposes of the majority of websites. To sell a product or service is becoming very common. In 1998, 9 per cent of UK homes had Internet access. In 2004 that had risen to 53 per cent – 12.3 million homes. Since 2000, sales of goods on the Internet has doubled every year. In 2004, over 40 billion pounds was spent on-line. The top most visited on-line retail websites included Tesco (see Figure 7.1), Argos and Next. Organisations need to advertise their product. With more and more money being spent on-line, unless a company has a web presence it is going to lose out on a potential market. The number of homes with Internet access is increasing and the use of the Internet to

FIGURE 7.1 *Tesco on-line*

shop is increasing. No retailer can ignore it if they want to survive.

Once a product has been sold, it needs to be supported. This is particularly common with computer items and software where support forums exist as well as troubleshooting guides and patches and upgrades.

Other purposes can include giving out information – such as news sites, surveys, lecture notes and articles. Some of these may be subscription based.

Theory into practice

Investigate four different Internet sites and list all the services that they offer. What are the similarities between these services? How do the Internet sites make money from the services they offer?

An *intranet* is a private network inside a company or organisation, which uses software similar to that used on the *Internet*, but is for internal use only and is not accessible to the public. An intranet allows computers to communicate but only with other computers within the organisation.

The purpose of the intranet is to disseminate information to the employees within the organisation. There may be diaries and calendars with events and meetings, on-line email for employees, and policies, procedures and forms to fill in, available on-line. The intranet is a method of organising information that the employees will require in a co-ordinated and intuitive manner.

Extranets are intranets that can be accessed by computers that are not part of the company. They have security features set up within them to allow other computers and users to access the information stored on the intranet. It is not open access, but controlled, usually by passwords and available only to a select few.

The extranet is used to allow selected individuals access to restricted areas. This might be a customer support area which allows access only to individuals who have purchased the product. Extranets could be used to assist team working from different parts of the country – a shared repository of documents available to all involved. If a sales team needed product information whilst at exhibitions and shows, they could log on to the extranet to retrieve the required information.

Key terms

Intranet: private network accessible only by those machines internal to the organisation.

Internet: collection of computers accessible from any other Internet connected computer.

Extranets: intranets with specific external access allowed.

Many intranets and extranets are set up without having an aim in mind. There is acknowledgement from senior management that one is required and the task is then usually delegated without a purpose or vision being given. It is left to those with knowledge and experience of setting up websites to determine the content and purpose.

Evaluating what is currently present requires the same approach as when setting up the services from scratch. You need to address the following issues:

* what is the purpose?
* who is the audience?
* what service is to be provided?

Once each issue is addressed, further questions will arise that need answering.

What is the purpose?

It is important to know the purpose of the website. This will enable you to create specific targets which will allow the success or failure of the project to be gauged. Examples of purpose can include:

* to reduce the number of telephone calls to a product support line
* to increase sales of a product
* to use an on-line survey to collect opinions of customers
* to support suppliers by giving them on-line access to their account.

It is likely that there will be more than a single purpose. The Internet, for example, involves more than the WWW: it includes other elements which can also be used:

* to reduce the costs of telephone calls overseas by the use of *VOIP* (voice over Internet protocol) or email
* to reduce travel costs when holding discussions with sales managers from across the UK.

The purpose will determine the audience and web server requirements.

Key term

VOIP: this is a method of using networks and the Internet to make telephone calls.

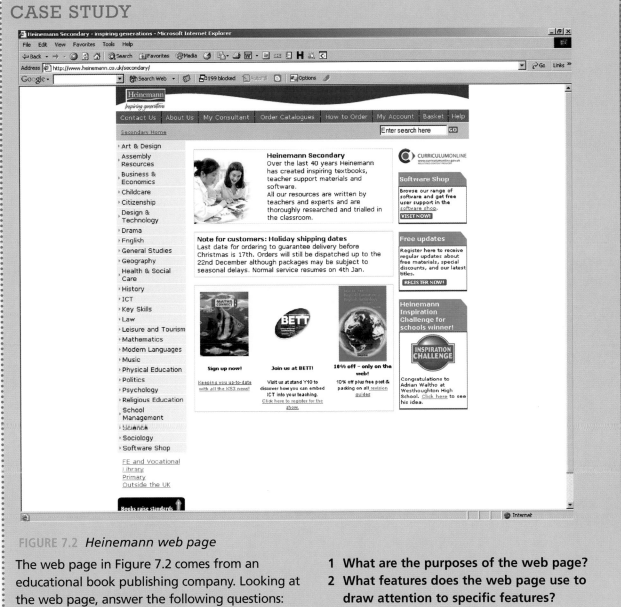

FIGURE 7.2 *Heinemann web page*

The web page in Figure 7.2 comes from an educational book publishing company. Looking at the web page, answer the following questions:

1 What are the purposes of the web page?
2 What features does the web page use to draw attention to specific features?

Who is the audience?

Identification of the *audience* is important as it will enable the correct technologies to be selected and the ideal interface. There are three main groups who could be the audience:

1 employees accessing information from within the organisation

2 individuals accessing internal information from external to the organisation

3 individuals accessing external information.

> **Key term**
>
> *Audience*: the audience is the person or persons who is going to see the end result. It is who the website has been created for. There is no point in creating something that you like if it will not appeal to the audience.

Employees accessing information from within the organisation

These people will be utilising an intranet, shared diary and internal email. They will require an easy to use interface but can be trained directly, as they are known to the organisation. The organisation can keep accurate logs on what information is required and being used. The technical ability of the audience is known and the interface can be specially adapted to suit different employees; for example, sales could have a different homepage from customer support. Since all of the audience is internal the technologies and software being used is known and can be utilised.

Individuals accessing internal information from external to the organisation

This group of individuals may be known to the organisation – sales staff, those involved in shared activities, for example. Equally, they may be unknown. If the extranet is used to support customers and suppliers then the individuals will not be known. This will affect the interface and technologies used as not everyone who accesses the extranet will have the same platform or software.

Individuals accessing external information

It is necessary to view two different types of audience when looking at external information. External information that is placed onto the Internet is available to anyone who can access the Internet. These individuals may be customers, prospective customers, business rivals observing the competition, suppliers or casual browsers. There are also the individuals whom the external information is targeting – customers, individuals with support requests or suppliers.It is essential to consider them first but always to look with a critical eye at other people who can access the information. With any external audience, the platform, software and level of technical expertise are unknown and can range greatly.

Knowledge check

Look at the BBC website. Who is the audience for the BBC website? How does the website target the different audiences?

Services provided

The Internet is more than the WWW. The services available on the Internet and intranet are more than the use of a web browser to access information. In many cases the WWW can be used as the portal to access the other services. For example, we have web-based email, web browsers can be used to access FTP sites, and media files can be played from within the browser.

Email

You use *email* to send text messages to individuals or groups of individuals. An individual or a group address book can be kept. In an organisation, emails which have been sent internally can be retrieved (provided they have not been opened by the recipient). Email can be used to send text files and pictures as attachments. Email allows for discussions to be recorded and kept and email can send a message to the sender when it is opened. Using an extranet or Internet it is possible to send and receive emails from any Internet connected computer anywhere in the world.

In an organisation, individuals change. They move position, get new jobs and retire. If, as an organisation you are giving out an email address you do not want it to be continually changing – for example admissions at a college or sales at a firm. In order to keep the email address the same, even if the individual changes, email redirection is used. This is when one email address is mapped onto another. For example, an organisation may have an email address called Sales@organisation.co.uk. The person responsible for sales may be J Bloggs with an email address of Bloggs@organisation.co.uk. Any emails sent to Sales@organisation.co.uk are diverted to J Bloggs. When J Bloggs leaves, the emails are diverted to the new person responsible for sales and there is no need for the public who use the email address to know that anything has changed.

Key term

Email: email is a method of sending messages from one computer to another. It is an abbreviation of electronic mail.

WWW

The World Wide Web – websites – is a particularly important method of communicating. Websites can be used as the host for a number of services. They can be used for bulletin boards, file transfer, email and text conferencing. Websites can be used on intranets, extranets or the Internet. They are, if written correctly, hardware and browser independent and intuitive to use. They can reinforce the organisation's corporate image with

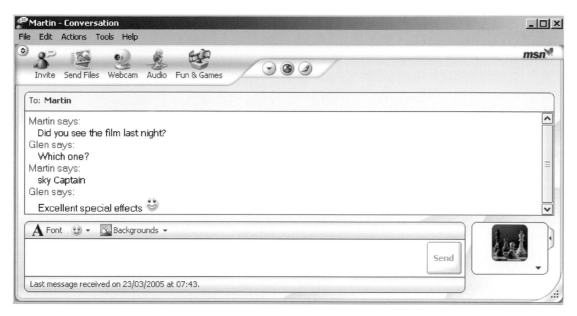

FIGURE 7.3 *Webmail*

the use of colour schemes and can control the resources and information available.

The WWW has only been around since the early 1990s. It was invented as a means to locate and access scientific documents. *HTML* (hypertext mark-up language) was created as the means to write the pages and in 1990 the first browser was demonstrated. The WWW as we know it today was released to the world in 1993.

Many of the most popular sites on the Internet are search sites. These sites allow users to enter searches and return web pages that match the criteria. There are many different search engines available and they provide different results.

Theory into practice

Investigate four different search engines. Compare the features that they offer. Search for the same criteria on all four and see how the sites they return are similar or vary. Investigate the advanced search options within each site.

IRC, conferencing

The ability to talk to other individuals over a network is a great benefit. *IRC* (Internet relay chat) allows for text conferencing, video conferencing is voice and images whilst VOIP is voice. A comparison of the features available can be seen in Table 7.1. All three of these technologies make

	TEXT	VIDEO	VOIP
Recorded discussions	Yes	Yes	No
Bandwidth implications	No	Yes	Yes
Specialist software/hardware required on all machines	Yes	Yes	Yes
Training required	No	Yes	No
Most useful in an intranet, extranet or Internet	Internet	Internet Extranet	Intranet

TABLE 7.1 *A summary of the services offered by text, video and VOIP*

FIGURE 7.4 *MSN homepage*

use of the existing network with the requirement for additional communications media. Video conferencing and VOIP do, however, take up a large amount of bandwidth and this is a consideration when looking at using them.

Text based conferencing is a useful way to hold discussions with multiple individuals anywhere in the world. One of the most common forms of text conferencing is MSN (see Figure 7.4), which allows multiple individuals to communicate and share files.

> ### Key term
>
> *IRC*: this is a chat system that allows two or more Internet users to communicate by text in real time.

Newsgroups, Newsnet and bulletin boards

Newsgroups, Newsnet and bulletin boards (see Figure 7.5) are particularly good for customer support. They allow products to be discussed within a controlled environment. The organisation can react to complaints and promote products. Bulletin boards can contain links to files, websites and allow both text and pictures to be represented. They can be internal or external. For the user, bulletin boards can offer private messaging (like email but restricted to the discussion board), notification of posts, searches, new posts, and different ways of viewing posts.

File transfer

File transfer is a valuable tool. It allows documents, images, sound files and movie files to be transferred between users. There are a variety of ways that file transfer can be done. It can be done by using a web page with hyperlinks to the files to be transferred. It is also possible to use specialist software FTP programs that are specifically designed to allow for files to be transferred. FTP programs are covered later on in the unit on page 228. It is also possible to open up part of the computer you are working on – to make a shared area. This shared area is accessible by other users, and documents that need to be shared can be placed there. On a network there is usually an area on a shared drive that can be used to upload and download shared files.

Telnet

Telnet is a *protocol* for remote computing on the Internet. Telnet is broken into two parts, the remote terminal and the telnet server. You need the protocol installed on both machines – server and remote terminal. A machine is running as a telnet server. You connect to it using your machine – the telnet remote client and it allows the server to accept input from your machine – as if you were sitting there using the server instead of being half way across the world. The output from any commands you run on the server is directed back

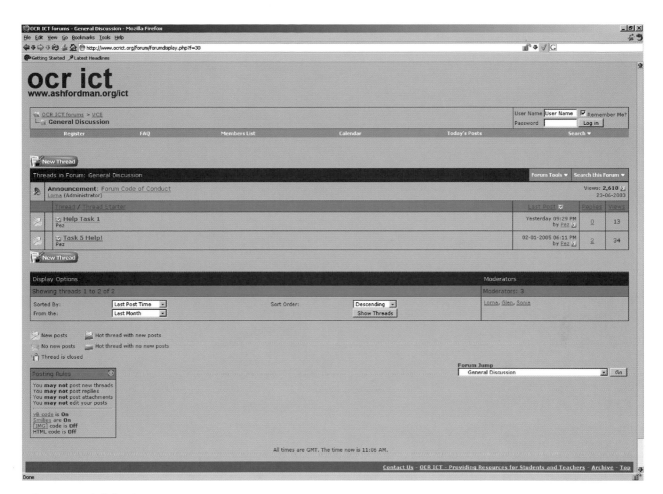

FIGURE 7.5 *Ashfordman*

to your machine. Library and information sources use telnet.

 ## Signposting for portfolio evidence

Within an organisation you will need to conduct an investigation. The focus of the investigation is on the use that the organisation makes of the Internet, intranet, and, if they use one, extranet. Begin by looking at the objectives that the organisation has for the Internet, etc., and compare how it is used, to the objectives. It is unlikely that any organisation is using the Internet/intranet to its full potential. To progress up the mark range, you must look at the advantages and disadvantages of the current use and suggest improvements. It may be that the layout and configuration is not effective, or parts of the Internet are not being used (remember that the Internet is not just the WWW).

Organisation of the Internet

Domains and DNS

Every text based Internet address ends with a specific code – .COM, .MIL, .ORG or a country code – .UK, .FR, .AU. These are known as domains. The domain name is the text based name for a given website:

www.bbc.co.uk

www.google.com

www.nasa.gov

Domain names are broken into top level, second level and third level. Domain names are read from the right to the left with the top-level domain being on the furthest right (see Table 7.2).

Not all domain names have three levels and some might have more than three levels.

Top-level domains are single words, such as com, info, org or they can be the country codes, uk, au, etc. Top-level domains are shared. For

example, there can be lots of domain names that end in .COM or .UK.

Second-level domain names in the UK identify the type of organisation, for example a company has co, a school has sch, not for profit organisations have org.

The third-level domain names are registered to individuals or organisations. They contain the memorable word or identifiable part of the domain name.

The example shown in Figure 7.6 is from Nominet, the body in the UK responsible for maintaining a database of all domain names with a top level domain of UK. It shows how a domain name is broken down.

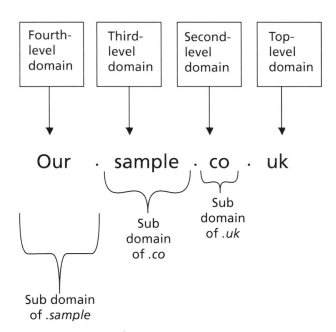

FIGURE 7.6 *Domain names*

Sub domains are websites that have fourth level domains. A *sub domain* is an additional name inserted after the third level. The sub domain

THIRD LEVEL	SECOND LEVEL	FIRST LEVEL
bbc	co	uk
	google	com
	nasa	gov

TABLE 7.2 *Domain levels*

could be used to separate different parts of the website – for example members.sample.co.uk or finance.sample.co.uk. Sub domains can be named anything you like. Because the domain is unique, the sub domain must also be unique.

In the UK, when you want to register a domain, you use a registration agent. There are organisations who specialise in registering domain names – they are registered with various bodies that control the issue of domain names around the world. The name you have chosen, along with the top level and second level domain names is checked against the database held at Nominet. If it is available, you are given ownership of the domain. It is necessary to renew the domain every year otherwise other individuals or companies could register it.

UK domain names have to be registered with Nominet – they control all the UK domain names available. Domain names that end with com, org or other country domain names are registered with different registration authorities, for example Canadian domain names (ending .ca) are registered with CIRA.

Selecting the right domain name to use is important. It must be intuitive. If the domain name is not known then it should be able to be guessed. The name should reflect the name of the organisation.

Theory into practice

Choose five worldwide organisations. Write down what you think their web address should be and then try it and see if you are correct. Once you have found out an organisation's web address, try slightly different versions, maybe changing a .co.uk to a .com. What have you found out? Why do some organisations have multiple web addresses?

Computers do not use text names to identify computers on the Internet. They use IP addresses. IP addresses are unique identifiers that every computer on the Internet has. However, because numbers are difficult to remember, those computers that host websites used by individuals tend to have an equivalent text name that is known as a domain name. For example, www.example.com is the domain name that might have the IP address of 198.105.232.3. Every domain name has an IP address linked to it, but not every IP address has a domain name.

DNS (domain name servers) are servers that translate domain names into IP addresses and vice versa. Domain name servers are the backbone of the Internet. They handle name queries for all hosts within a particular domain. Every domain needs a domain name server. The DNS is the authoritative source for addressing information about host names within its domain. In practice this means that when a computer needs to know the IP address of a host within that particular domain, it sends a message to the domain name server that controls that domain and asks that the host name be turned into an IP address and returned to the machine sending the query.

Domain name servers are required because the Internet runs on IP addresses, not domain names, but humans find numbers difficult to remember and so we work on domain names. The domain name server performs the translation between them.

There are many utilities that will translate domain names into IP addresses and vice versa. One is NSLOOKUP, an MS-DOS program, shown in Figure 7.7.

This shows that the IP address for www.bbc.co.uk is 212.58.224.82

Theory into practice

There are many websites that will perform translations from IP to domain name and vice versa. Find a site and try out some conversions of your own.

FIGURE 7.7 *NSLOOKUP.bmp*

Mode of access to the Internet, IAP, ISP, POP and Internet services

Connecting to the Internet has two aspects – connecting a machine to the Internet to get access to other websites or creating and setting up a website so that others on the Internet can access it.

There are three elements that are required before you can connect a computer to the Internet:

* Internet access provider (IAP)/Internet service provider (ISP)

* connection medium

* appropriate hardware and software.

The terms IAP and *ISP* are used interchangeably; however, there is a difference between them. Traditionally, an IAP provides access only to the Internet. It provides the portal through which the connection is made. An ISP can provide additional services and the line itself. For simplicity both IAPs and ISPs will be referred to as service providers.

Before any connection to the Internet can be made it is necessary to procure the services of a service provider. They will provide an account and access point to connect to the Internet. The access point is known as a *point of presence.*

Key terms

ISP: Internet service provider – the company that provides the connection to the Internet.

Point of presence: a point of presence (POP) is the physical location where the service provider's equipment is held. This will include computers and telecommunications lines. The POP is the access point to the service provider's network.

There are many different service providers, each offering a different service. The main differences include:

* cost of the service – the fee charged, either a flat monthly fee, a fee per M/byte of material downloaded or a dial-up fee

* limits on the service – some providers will limit the amount that can be downloaded and uploaded. Downloaded is material that comes from the Internet to you – the web pages and files. Uploaded is material you send to the Internet – for example emails or requests for web pages

* technologies offered – some service providers will offer only a limited range. Technologies include CGI, PHP, ASP etc. (languages that can be used to write interactive web pages)

* services offered – such as FTP (covered in detail on page 228), number of email accounts, web-based email, front page extensions, newsgroups, etc.

* technical support – how many support staff are there, is there web support and telephone support, is there a user group?

* provision for backup and running specialised programs needs to be examined.

* history of the service provider – how long have they been in business, records of their downtime over the last year, and customer recommendations need to be examined.

International standards and protocols

The Internet is machine independent. This means that different types of computer running different operating systems can connect and use it. In order for the computers to communicate they must be talking the same 'language'. This language is known as a protocol. A protocol is a standardised means of communication among machines connected to the network – in this case the network is the Internet. This means that all machines that are connected to the Internet need to run the same protocol. The protocols used with the Internet are TCP/IP (transmission control protocol/Internet protocol) and HTTP (hypertext transfer protocol). TCP/IP allows all Internet users and service providers to communicate with each other regardless of what equipment they are using. The HTTP protocol is used when requesting and transferring web pages.

Connection medium

How the data from the Internet gets to the computer is an important consideration. The *medium* used will determine how much data can be transferred and in which direction (upstream or downstream) and the cost to the organisation of the medium. Not all types of medium are available to all organisations – geographical restrictions apply. When talking about bandwidth and communication medium it is worth bearing in mind that various factors affect the bandwidth – the quality of the line, the standard being used (V.90 or V.92, for example) and the compression used will affect how much data can be downloaded/uploaded per second.

The connection can either be analogue or digital (see Figure 7.8). Computers work using digital signals. Analogue signals are continuous

signals and require an analogue connection. Digital signals can only take on one of two discrete levels – 0 or 1. Digital communication using a digital connection is quicker than analogue as conversion does not need to take place and there is less chance of errors creeping in.

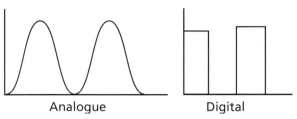

FIGURE 7.8 *Analogue and digital waves*

If you are using a computer with an analogue connection, a modem is required. The modem converts the digital signal from the computer to an analogue one and sends it along the analogue medium. The modem at the receiving end converts the analogue signal to a digital one that the computer can understand (see Figure 7.9).

FIGURE 7.9 *Connecting two computers together via a phone line*

When using a digital medium a modem is not required.

When talking about methods of connection and medium the term 'bandwidth' often crops up.

Bandwidth is defined as the range of frequencies, usually expressed in kilobits per second, that can be sent/received over a given data transmission medium within a certain time. The greater the bandwidth, the more information that can be sent in a given amount of time. Bandwidth is officially concerned with the volume of information in a given amount of time, not the speed.

Analogue telephone

Known as POTS (plain old telephone system), this uses an analogue phone line. A modem is required at each end. The bandwidth will vary but, typically, speeds of 56Kbps (kilobits per second) are possible. Sharing an analogue phone connection is possible but drastically reduces the bandwidth to each individual computer. When the telephone line is in use by the modem it cannot be used for voice calls.

Digital telephone – ISDN, xDSL

ISDN is a dialup connection. It typically involves two channels of 64 Kbit/s giving 128 Kbit/s bandwidth. ISDN 30 is 30 channels bonded together to give 1.92 Mbit/s bandwidth. Each channel is charged as a separate telephone line and there is the cost of the phone call on top.

xDSL is a catch-all name for all DSL (digital subscriber line) technologies. These include *ADSL*, SDSL and HDSL. These can offer download speed of up to 52 Mbit/s and upload speed of 64 Kbit/s to 2 Mbit/s. A subscription is paid for the line and there are no call charges. The more bandwidth required, the higher the subscription. These lines are typically used in small businesses and can be easily networked. There are also distance implications with xDSL.

Cable modems are provided by companies that supply television, telephone and the Internet connection. Speeds are equivalent to xDSL.

Leased lines are direct connections between two locations. No other users have access to the line: it is dedicated. Leased lines have a monthly subscription and are permanently connected. If you are hosting your own website then a leased line is recommended. There are two main types of leased line, T1 and T3, T3 being the faster line.

> **Key terms**
>
> *ISDN*: a digital phone service that allows a computer to be connected to the Internet and transmit/receive data at a higher speed than with a modem. It requires a separate line and is a dial-up connection.
>
> *ADSL*: a high-speed digital connection that is always on and allows for voice and data to be transmitted at the same time.

Satellite is useful where the telephone exchange is too far away for digital lines to be used. Satellite dishes are used to transmit and receive the signal from satellites (see Figure 7.10). Some systems use the satellite for two-way communication, others use the satellite for downloading but a normal ISDN or dial-up for uploading. In some systems there is a time lag, called latency. This is a delay caused by the distances involved.

As can be seen from Table 7.4, there is a considerable transmission time difference between the various connection media.

TYPE	UPSTREAM	DOWNSTREAM	DISTANCE (FEET)
ADSL	128 Kbit/s–1 Mbit/s	600 Kbit/s–7 Mbit/s	18000–25000
HDSL	2.048 Mbit/s	2.048 Mbit/s	12000
SDSL	1.544–2.048 Mbit/s	1.544–2.048 Mbit/s	10000
VDSL	1.6–2.3 Mbit/s	12.96 Mbit/s	4500
		25.82 Mbit/s	3000
		51.84 Mbit/s	1000

TABLE 7.3

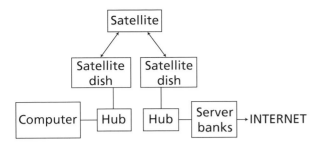

FIGURE 7.10 *Connecting digital telephones via satellite*

The speeds are the average speeds on a reasonable line. Different companies will provide different speeds on the same type of line, for example it is possible to get a faster ADSL or satellite connection. The technical term used to determine the speed of a modem is *baud rate*.

When considering the bandwidth requirements, what it is being used for must be looked at. A single user can use a T3 bandwidth if moving animation or movies, whilst an entire office of thirty people can use an ISDN line if using it just for occasional web searching and email. Contention must also be considered.

Hardware and software

On the software side it is necessary to set up the appropriate protocols on the computer (TCP/IP) and the necessary applications software – browser, FTP, newsreader, email, video conferencing, IRC, etc. The service provider will supply usernames and passwords and set up the domain name (if required).

TYPE OF CONNECTION AND SPEED	TIME TO TRANSMIT 250 KBYTE FILE (MIN:SEC)	TIME TO TRANSMIT 3 MBYTE FILE (MIN:SEC)
Modem – 28.8 Kbps	1:28	18:00
ISDN (1 B–channel) – 64 Kbps	0:39	8:00
ISDN (2 B–channels) – 128 Kbps	0:20	4:00
ADSL – 512 Kbps	0:05	1:00
Satellite – 512 Kbps	0:05	1:00
Leased Line (T1) – 1.544 Mbps	0:02	0:22
Leased Line (T3) – 45 Mbps	0:00.1	0:00.7

TABLE 7.4

The methods of connection to the Internet will depend partly on the connection medium and the number of computers that are to be connected.

The equipment used in networking includes modems, hubs/switches, routers/gateways and network interface cards (NICs). A modem links a computer to the analogue phone line. A hub and a switch allow multiple machines to be connected to a single point and for that point to be connected to the telephone line by a gateway/router. The gateway/router allows the signal from the Internet to be split between several machines. Computers are connected to hubs/switches by network cables. NICs are hardware devices in computers that allow the network cable to be plugged in.

Dial-up requires a modem and is useful only for a single machine. A gateway/router can be connected to a hub/switch and used to share the connection to all network enabled computers (see Figure 7.11). With a wireless gateway, computers do not have to be physically connected to the network to use the Internet connection. PDAs (personal digital assistants), mobile phones and laptops with wireless capability can be configured to use the connection.

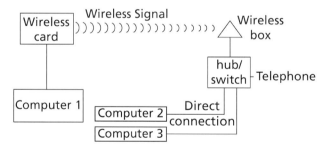

FIGURE 7.11 *A home wireless computer network*

The Internet and communications systems

The Internet is not free. Using the Internet and setting up a domain on the Internet both cost money. The costs of connecting can be a pay-as-you-go fee with only the costs of the telephone calls being paid or the costs of the telephone calls and a subscription to the company providing the connection. It may seem silly to pay for a connection if you can get it free, but there are some advantages. The contention ratio is likely to be lower, the technical support will be cheaper (not a peak rate telephone number) and the service more stable over the long term. There will also be less risk of the company going out of business and having to change email addresses.

If you are looking for a web host – someone to host your website then there will be additional costs. With your service provider you may get some free web space with which to create a website. However, if you are looking to create a professional, high-demand website then this will not be suitable. You will require a company that specialises in providing a web hosting service. This will cost a monthly fee. On top of this there is the domain name registration fee. It is important to make sure that you are on time renewing the domain name. If you are late, it is possible for someone else to renew it and have all your traffic redirected to their site.

 ## Signposting for portfolio evidence

You need to create a report looking at hosting a website and connecting to the Internet. Your report needs to identify the costs of the ISP and the connection method. To get higher marks, you must describe the costs and connection method and you must actually find a suitable ISP and host. For full marks, you must evaluate the ISP and host against a set of technical requirements from the organisation.

Web server requirements

When hosting an intranet or extranet the website is hosted internally, not by an external organisation. It is therefore necessary to have a web server that is capable of running the required services.

The web server requires a basic set of computer components. The following list makes up a basic computer, each component is listed by its generic name:

* motherboard
* processor
* fan
* random access memory (RAM)
* graphics card
* hard disk drive (HDD)
* CD/DVD drive
* floppy disk drive
* monitor
* mouse/keyboard.

When building a web server it is not possible to pick a list of components and expect them to work. One wrong component will slow the speed of the machine down drastically. It is essential to ensure that all components are compatible. There are choices that need to be made:

* type, speed and number of processors
* type and amount of RAM
* number, type and capacity of hard disk drive.

Floppy disk drives, CD and DVD drives are relatively standard components. Since a web server is unlikely to run any other processes within the organisation, the graphics card and monitor do not need to be of the highest quality.

You cannot select a computer just by naming the components. An analogy would be to try to buy a holiday by giving just a place and a date. You need to select other options – place of departure, type of accommodation, number of people, etc. The same applies to computers. For example, a processor for a computer might be AMD or Intel; it may be Itanium, Xeon, Athlon or Opteron to name a few. Processors come in different speeds and have different advantages and disadvantages.

The component market changes rapidly, with new items of hardware appearing daily. Any specification of server listed here would be out of date within a few months. To be up to date you need to do your own research on all of the components just listed to find the best mix and match. A good starting point is www.dell.co.uk where you can look at servers in detail and customise components to see the effect on price.

There are specific items which are required for a computer that is to host a website:

* network interface card (NIC)
* backup device.

These two devices are vital – the network card is going to be the route by which the web server communicates with the rest of the network. The type and speed of network card need to be carefully considered. A backup device is important – it may be integral to the web server (a tape device for example) or it may make use of a RAID (redundant array inexpensive/independent disks – a way of storing the same data on different disks) or a separate duplicate server.

Additional hardware within the network will include routers to connect to the Internet and hubs/switches to connect other machines to the intranet. These are likely to already be in place within the organisation.

Operating system

The web server will require an operating system. There are many different operating systems available, the main ones being Microsoft®, Novell and Linux. All are capable of supporting a web server and have their own advantages and disadvantages. The operating system that is going to be used needs to be chosen in conjunction with the web technologies that are to be run on the server – ASP, for example, is Microsoft® based. PHP integrates very well with Linux.

IP address

Other considerations include the IP address – if the web server is just on an intranet then it can be given an internal IP address. If the web server was to be used on an extranet or the Internet then it needs a publicly assigned IP address so that it can be accessed from anywhere in the world.

Organisations with many computers use NAT (network address translation) to allow their computers to access the Internet. Not every computer has a unique IP address. You need to differentiate between internal and external IP addresses. An internal IP address is one that is given to a computer that is not directly facing the Internet. There are internal IP address ranges that are used by different organisations – for example, 192.168.1.101 might be used by many different computers internally. Because the same IP address cannot appear on more than one computer on the Internet, when the computer connects to the Internet its IP address is translated by a router using NAT.

Network address translation (NAT)

NAT is the translation of an Internet protocol address (IP address) used within one network (internally) to a different IP address known within another network (externally). Usually, an organisation would map its local internal network addresses to one or more global outside IP addresses and unmap the global IP addresses on incoming packets back into local IP addresses.

The advantages of NAT are that it helps ensure security, as each outgoing or incoming request must go through a translation process. When it goes through this translation process the request can be qualified or authenticated (see Figure 7.12), or matched to a previous request. NAT also conserves on the number of global (external) IP addresses that an organisation needs and it lets the company use a single IP address in its communication with the world.

A NAT table is created that does the global-to-local and local-to-global IP address mapping. Cisco's version of NAT lets an administrator create tables that map:

* a local IP address to one global IP address statically
* a local IP address to any of a rotating pool of global IP addresses that a company may have
* a local IP address plus a particular TCP port to a global IP address or one in a pool of them
* a global IP address to any of a pool of local IP addresses on a round-robin basis.

The main advantage of NAT is that it reduces the need for a large amount of publicly known IP addresses by creating a separation between publicly known and privately known IP addresses. This means that fewer publicly known IP addresses are required and the depleting IP address pool will last a little longer.

An organisation will also have firewalls to stop access to the web server, and proxy servers to store commonly used web pages and filter requests may also be required.

Firewalls are a combination of hardware and software that sits between the network and the Internet. They examine both incoming and outgoing traffic and can filter unwanted material and users. Firewalls are used to protect the resources of an organisation from outside intrusion.

Proxy servers sit between the network and the Internet. They hold commonly used web pages. When a computer sends a request for a web page, the proxy will see if it has a copy of the file. If it does, the computer is sent that copy. If it does not have a copy, it will retrieve it from

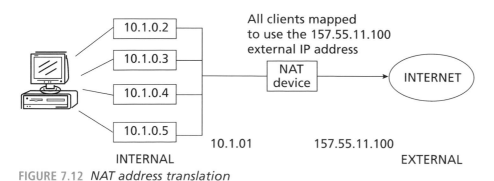

FIGURE 7.12 *NAT address translation*

the Internet and send that copy to the computer. The proxy will also make a copy of the file for future requests. The proxy server enables faster delivery of web content to the computer – it is quicker to get it from the proxy server than the Internet and whilst doing this for some of the traffic, it means that more bandwidth is available for other traffic, thus speeding up the Internet connection. Proxy servers can also be used to filter requests and add another layer of protection.

Internet tools

Web browser

Having set up the web server, content needs to be placed on the web server and made accessible by all users. The tool used to access the content is the web browser. The web browser takes the programming code used to write the web page and converts it into text and images for the user. There are many different types of web browser – Internet Explorer, Netscape, Mozilla and Firefox to name a few. There are also different versions of the web browser. When creating a website it is important to make the website compatible with as many browsers as possible. This means that you need to have as many browsers as possible installed on a computer.

The browser allows you to access search pages, create favourites/bookmarks and control how pictures and pages are displayed. The browser can also be used to set the proxy address. The proxy is a server which is used as the primary point of connection. It can filter requests, websites and users and hold a cache of common files, which allows displaying files to be speeded up.

The image (Figure 7.13) shows the proxy settings that can be set with Firefox.

FTP tools

FTP tools allow files to be transferred from one computer to another. FTP was in use prior to the WWW. FTP allows anonymous accounts to be created so anyone can log in or for security to be applied so that a username and password must be given before access is granted (see Figure 7.14). FTP tools are used to upload websites created locally to the web server.

FIGURE 7.14 *Settings for FTP*

When setting up an FTP session, the IP address of the site to connect to and a username and password are required. Once a connection has been made files can be downloaded and, if the user has permission, files can be uploaded.

FIGURE 7.13 *Proxy settings in Firefox*

Web editing software

There are many different web editors available. Web editing software is used to write the codes used to display web pages. Fundamentally, web pages are text pages. This means that the simplest web editor is a basic text editor, such as notepad. More complex web editing software gives the user the ability to view the code as the end-user would (WYSIWYG), add complex reusable code and view a site map of the entire site. Advanced software can check links to see that they exist and automatically upload the website to the Internet.

In Dreamweaver (see Figure 7.15), for example, you can edit a web page either by HTML code or by a preview window. Both are linked and update automatically. Specialised web editing packages have many tools and wizards built into them to assist in the process of creating web pages.

 Signposting for portfolio evidence

You need to create a report looking at the hardware and software required to create and host a website. Your report needs to identify hardware and software required. To get higher marks, you must describe the hardware and software.

The software that is required can be of different types. It can be purchased from a shop/on-line – the user owns a licence to run the software. The software could be public domain software. This is software that is not copyrighted and can be used without any restrictions – you do not need to pay for public domain software. Shareware software is also available. This is copyright software that the user is allowed to run and use for a limited period of time. If, at the end of that period they decide to keep the software they must pay for a licence.

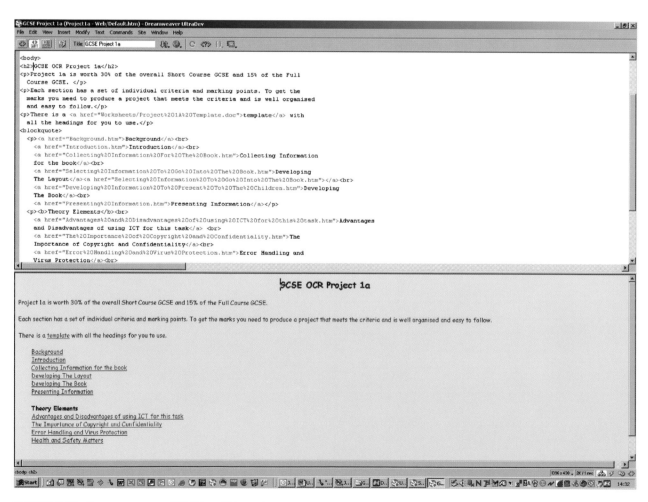

FIGURE 7.15 *Dreamweaver HTML editing view*

Internet websites

Web pages can be static or dynamic depending on the code used to write them. Initially, web pages

were static. This means that the only way to change the content was to upload new pages.

Static web pages are written in HTML. The following example shows HTML code for a simple page with a title, heading, some centred text and a bulleted list.

```
<html>
<head>
<title>www.ashfordman.org</title>
</head>
<body>
<h1 style="text-align: center;">OCR
ICT</h1> <p>
<strong style="font-weight: normal;">
A web site to support OCR ICT
qualifications:</strong></p>
<ul>
<li><strong style="font-weight:
normal;">
GCSE Syllabus A</strong></li>
<li>AGCE AS/A2 ICT</li>
<li>VGCSE ICT<br> </li>
</ul>
</body>
</html>
```

All the code that performs an action is included within '<' and '>'. A style is a set of formats applied to the text. A / closes a set of instructions. So, for example, <center>**This is Centered**</center>**This is not** will appear on the page as:

> **This is Centered**
>
> **This is not**

There are many programs available that allow you to create web pages in a word processing type application and then save the content to HTML code.

OCR ICT

A web site to support OCR ICT qualifications:

- GESE Syllabus A
- AGCE AS/A2 ICT
- VGCSE ICT

FIGURE 7.16 *Output of code sample*

The code sample gives the output shown in Figure 7.16.
If the content of the page needed to be changed, because it is static, the HTML code would need to be altered.

Dynamic web pages allow the content to change without uploading any new pages. A simple example is the time and date. A static web page cannot change the time and date but a dynamic one can display the correct time and date. Dynamic websites are written using a different code from static pages – PHP, ASP and CGI are the most common languages.

PHP is an open source language that is a server side embedded scripting language. To take each of these phrases in turn – open source means that the actual language used to write the code is free. You do not have to buy a copy of the program. Server side means that all code is executed by the server not by the client. (The client is the machine that the browser is operating on, the server is the machine where the website resides.) This means that the code is not viewable by the client, which makes it more secure and reduces the use of client side resources and increases compatibility, as no specific software is required. Embedded scripting language means that the code is combined with HTML and embedded between tags, which reduces the amount of code and makes it easier to write.

ASP and PHP can connect to many different databases, making them extremely useful for different applications such as shopping carts and discussion boards.

The following code examples are from ASP and PHP. They create a database connection to the Northwind database. As you can see, both types of code are embedded within HTML tags. Both are run at the server – the code itself runs on the server and presents the output to the user as HTML. There is no way that the end-user can see the code below.

ASP Code Example

```
<HTML>
<HEAD><TITLE>ASP Database
Connection</TITLE></HEAD>
<BODY BGCOLOR=white>
<H1>Northwind Database Contacts</H1>
<% Dim Connect, selectSQL, RecSet
Set Connect = CreateObject
("ADODB.Connection")
Connect.Open "DSN=Northwind"
selectSQL = "SELECT * FROM Customers"
Set RecSet = Connect. Execute
(selectSQL)
If NOT RecSet. EOF
THEN
DO UNTIL RecSet. EOF
Response. Write RecSet("Companyname")
& ", " & RecSet("Contactname") &
"<BR><BR>"
RecSet. MoveNext
Loop
End If
RecSet. Close
Connect. Close
Set RecSet = Nothing Set
Connect = Nothing %>
</BODY>
</HTML>
```

PHP Code Example

```
<html>
<body>
<?php
$conn=odbc_connect
('northwind','','');
if (!$conn)
{
exit ("Connection Failed: " . $conn);
}
$sql="SELECT * FROM customers";
$rs=odbc_exec($conn,$sql);
if (!$rs)
{
exit("Error in SQL");
}
echo "<table><tr>";
echo "<th>Companyname</th>";
echo "<th>Contactname</th></tr>";
while (odbc_fetch_row($rs))
{
$compname=odbc_result($rs,"CompanyName");
$conname=odbc_result($rs,"ContactName");
echo "<tr><td>$compname</td>";
echo "<td>$conname</td></tr>";
}
odbc_close($conn);
echo "</table>";
?>
</body>
</html>
```

As you can see from the code, there is a lot of similarity between the two languages. If the data in the underlying table was to change then the results would change. The same code can produce dynamic pages.

Knowledge check

Copy out the HTML, ASP and PHP code and go through it indicating what each line of the code is doing.

CGI is a set of standards by which web pages can communicate and run programs on the server. Instead of running the code to access a database, as PHP and ASP do, a CGI script would run an external program that accessed the database and passed the results, via the CGI gateway, back to the web page. CGI can be written in any programming language; Perl is one of the most popular.

Other technologies include Java and Flash which are applet based. This means that a small application – applet, is downloaded and run on the computer. These technologies require software installed on the client machine in order to work.

In the applet from Sun Java (see Figure 7.17), the aim is to adjust the angle and velocity to hit the target. Actions made by the user directly impinge upon the applet. Although the applet is run in a web browser, it requires Java to be installed on the computer for it to work. Unlike PHP, CGI and ASP it is not server side technology.

Dynamic HTML (DHTML) is an HTML extension that allows web pages to react to the end-user's input, such as displaying a web page based on the type of browser or changing text or colour based on the mouse position. It uses HTML, JavaScript, CSS – Cascading Style Sheets, and the DOM – Document Object Model, to produce dynamic content.

Signposting for portfolio evidence

For a nominated website you need to define its purpose and look at two of the services that it offers, for example ordering, product support, patches and upgrades, etc. The selection of the website is important as it must not be a plain HTML site but contain, for full marks, two Internet technologies – PHP, Java, JavaScript, etc. For full marks, you need to describe all of the services offered by the website and look at two technologies offered.

Signposting for portfolio evidence

You need to create a web page for a planned website. For higher marks you will need to identify an Internet technology that you have used in the web page. For full marks the web page must be hosted on-line. The whole site does not need to be created but there must be a purpose and a plan and one page. Consideration should be given to the Internet technology that is going to be used. It could be something as simple as a JavaScript menu or a full-blown logon system written in PHP or ASP.

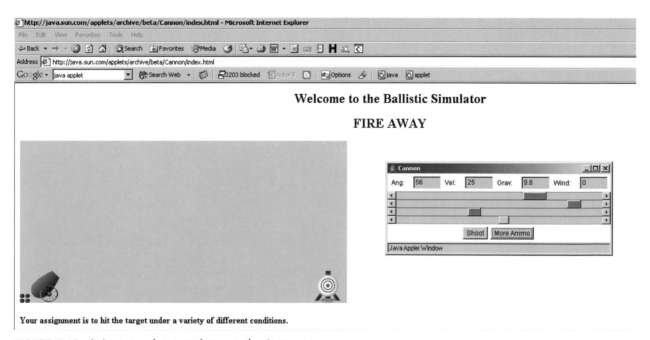

FIGURE 7.17 *A Java applet running on the Internet*

Signposting for portfolio evidence

You need to evaluate and comment on your actions and role in creating and getting the page hosted on-line. For higher marks your evaluation needs to include an analysis of your performance, and for full marks must include reflection on how your experiences would help you if you attempted the task in the future.

The website that is presented to the user is navigated by using hyperlinks. Clicking a hyperlink will load up a new page. This may be a completely new page or a page within a frame. The website and links that are presented to the user need to have a detailed plan behind them – what pages and links go where. This is done by producing a *diagrammatic structure* of the website.

This example is a very simple site but it demonstrates how to lay out a sitemap. When designing a web page the structure is very easy to map out, as you are starting from

Key term

Diagrammatic structure: this is a computer generated or hand-drawn layout of how the pages link to each other within a website.

scratch. When trying to map the structure of an exiting website there are two ways of doing it. The first is to use a web editor that can create site maps. By pointing it to the start page, usually index, it will automatically follow links and create a site map. The second method is to click links manually and write down the results using a pen and paper. Once all the links have been exhausted and documented a map can be drawn.

Theory into practice

Start with a simple website, maybe your college intranet or Internet site and draw a diagrammatic structure of it.

A diagrammatic representation of the website is required if you are to make any changes or have any problems with the website. It helps to know what pages link to what, and the effects of changing a page name or adding a new page.

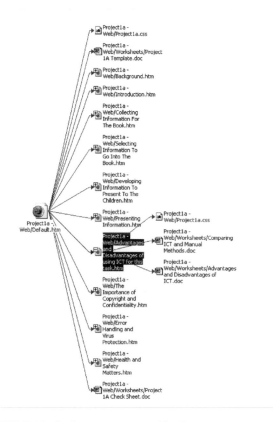

FIGURE 7.18 *A sitemap created in Frontpage*

Signposting for portfolio evidence

You need to select a website and take it apart, producing a diagrammatic structure. The structure needs to show hyperlinks and the titles of the pages. To get more marks you need to print off the code from at least three of the pages and annotate what it is doing. For full marks, you not only need to annotate the code but give an explanation of why it has been used.

Setting up a computer system for use on the Internet

Having an Internet, extranet or intranet that meets its designated purpose is useful only as long as users can access it. Organisations are not static; they are constantly changing – individuals moving offices, employees leaving and new employees arriving. Within today's modern organisation all will require a computer.

When setting up a computer, the first step is to determine the purpose. This will lead to the requirements and to the settings and software that are required. It needs to be done before the computer is even taken out of its box. A specific form may be used to determine what needs to be done (see Figure 7.19).

Installation Form

Computer Name _____	Location _____
Date _____	Installer _____
IP Address _____	DNS Settings _____

Software To Install

Email Server Settings   POP _____
SMTP _____

Additional Settings

Comments

Customer Signature _____   Installer Signature _____

FIGURE 7.19 *Example of an installation form*

Once all the relevant information has been assembled the computer can be set up. It is important that all the health and safety regulations are followed when dealing with any electrical device.

You need to identify all the information required to set up a computer for email and Internet access.

The two methods of connection are modem or network. The network connection may be cable or wireless. In a modem connection the settings required include username, password, DNS settings and IP settings. (DNS and IP may be obtained automatically.) A phone number to dial up is also required. In a network connection all of the settings required for a modem, except telephone number, are required. In addition, the workgroup/server name is required.

The software that needs to be installed onto the computer will include web browser (see Figure 7.20), FTP, virus checker, compression software and email. The web browser will need to be set up with the correct favourites for the organisation and a homepages set.

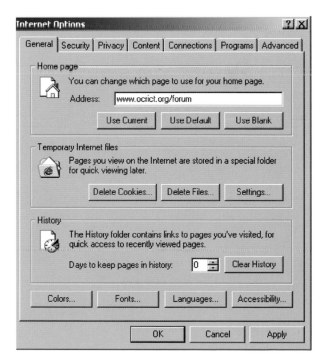

FIGURE 7.20 *Internet options*

Communication software allows a computer to communicate with another computer. This can include FTP, IRC, email, browser and Telnet.

A configuration change is a setting within the software that alters how it appears, starts up or deals with events. It could be changing the homepage, history or cache or altering security levels.

In Internet Explorer, as with other web browsers, it is possible to set the homepage – the first page that appears when you open the browser, as well as history and caching options. Other tabs give access to other options that can be set. If relevant, a proxy server and exceptions can be added.

 Signposting for portfolio evidence

You need to make two configuration changes to a browser. You need to provide evidence of the changes, and for full marks you need to describe what you have done.

FTP software needs to know the site address, username and connection method. The virus checker needs to know the method of connection and how to automatically update itself to ensure continued protection. In order to check emails the virus checker will need to know which email client is being used, and in some circumstances, the path to the client exe file. Compression software does not require any additional network settings to run.

Email

There are two types of email software – client and server. Email server software contains all email addresses within the organisation and acts as a postmaster – sorting and putting the mail in the appropriate box (see Figure 7.21). The email client software is used by individual users to access their own mailboxes to look

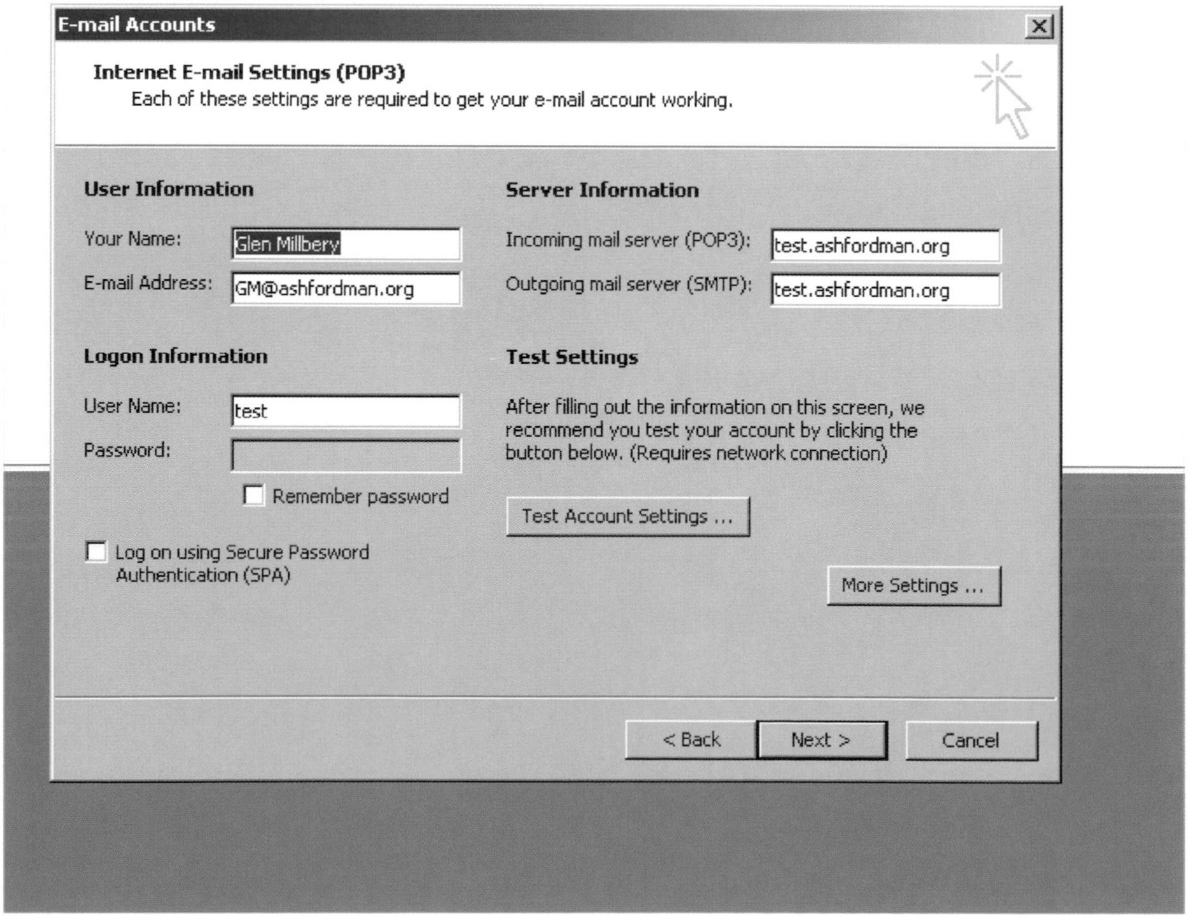

FIGURE 7.21 *Email.bmp*

at received mail and send mail to the email server for delivery.

To set up an email client you need to know the SMTP server (name of the email server used to send the messages), the name of the POP server (the mailbox where messages sent to you are received) and a username and password.

Signposting for portfolio evidence

To get marks in the higher mark bands you need to install at least one, and for full marks, three, pieces of communication software.

You need to produce a technical guide. This will detail the installation process. For full marks it will be a complete installation guide with all settings and stages involved in setting up a computer from scratch with all the required communication software.

There comes a time when you need to find an email that has been sent to you. You know it is somewhere but cannot find it. A sensible filing system eliminates these problems. There is no correct solution to a filing system; however, it must be intuitive – this means that it is easy to use and it is immediately obvious where every message needs to go. If your filing system is intuitive then you will be able to be given any topic or subject and know where it has been filed. A filing system usually involves the use of directories and sub-directories allowing messages to be categorised according to the topic.

A fundamental part of email is the ability to send and receive messages. You need to provide evidence that you can send and receive an email, both with and without attachments, and deal appropriately with any attachments. Attachments in emails could be viruses so it is important that they are dealt with responsibly. Knowing who has sent you the message is not enough to guarantee that it is virus free. Having a virus check program that checks attachments is an absolute requirement.

Signposting for portfolio evidence

You need to produce a suitable filing structure for emails. For higher level marks, you need to

provide additional evidence proving that you can send and receive email.

Assessment evidence

Record keeping and reports

When there are many individuals working for an organisation and there is a large turnover of those individuals, it is important that any work that is done is presented in such a way that it can be understood, and, if necessary, repeated by other individuals. This requires good record keeping.

You are installing up to three pieces of communications software and showing how changes have been made to a browser. Good technical documentation will give another individual all the required information that he or she needs to repeat the task. He or she will need to know:

* what was the software and where it is located
* are there any licensing keys/disks required? If so, where are they located?
* what directories were used to install the software to
* what choices were made during the installation process
* what shortcuts/menu options were set up
* what settings were changed in the software
* what tests were done to make sure it works.

This information needs to be presented neatly and spellchecked. It should have a cover detailing what the contents are about and, as necessary, headers/footers with page numbers and a table of contents.

The other audience for reports, apart from technical staff, is decision makers within the organisation. You will be required to produce reports for management as part of the evidence for this unit. These should be presented with a title page, table of contents, numbered pages and appropriate use of font, styles and images.

UNIT 8

Introduction to programming

Introduction

A computer system is a collection of pieces of equipment that we use to do a variety of tasks. In order for the computer to be able to carry out the tasks we require of it, we need to be able to give it a set of instructions. If we buy software such as Microsoft Office® then someone has already compiled a long list of instructions to tell the computer how to process documents, how to print documents, how to save documents, and many other things. The list of instructions used by the software is stored in computer language (a series of 1s and 0s put together to form many sequences, each of which constitutes an instruction – see Figure 8.1).

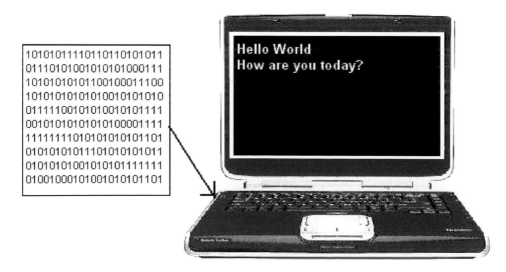

FIGURE 8.1 *Computer language*

New software is being programmed all the time but we humans are ill-equipped to write instructions in computer language. To write new software we need to be able to write instructions for the computer in a language that means something to us and then to translate those instructions into machine language.

To help with the translation there is a variety of software available that will take instructions written by you, the programmer, and translate them into machine language. In order for the software to be effective, it needs you to write the instructions in a particular format. If you use the correct format, the software can easily interpret what you have written and will produce the correct machine instructions to carry out your instructions (see Figure 8.2).

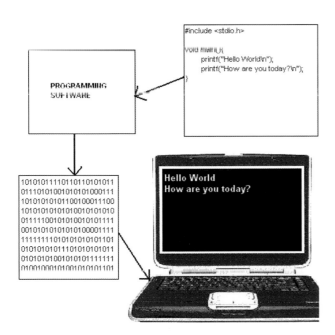

FIGURE 8.2 *Translating instructions into machine language*

A programming language is the format used by a software package that does the translation. There are many programming languages available, including Visual Basic, C, C++, Java and Pascal. This unit will introduce you to a variety of programming languages and will guide you through the first stages of learning Visual Basic.

What you need to learn

You need to learn about:

* programming languages
* program structure.

Think it over...

There are a number of different programming languages to choose from. How many can you name? Why have different languages?

Programming languages

All software is written to carry out specific tasks. Games software will produce graphical images and allow users to move characters around the screen. Web pages contain software that allows interactivity between users on different computers. Complex machines such as underground trains are controlled by software that monitors and adjusts.

Each of these types of software performs a very different task and will use very different sets of instructions. Rather than have one programming language that contains a vast amount of different instructions, there are a number of programming languages each with a different defined set of instructions.

Low-level languages

Languages are chosen because they have the best set of instructions for a particular purpose.

Software that controls parts of the computer system or hardware connected to it must be very specialised, so specialised that it is often best to write the programs directly in the processor's own language. Each processor has its own set of *machine code/machine language* instructions and so there is a different language for each. These languages are known as low-level languages.

Assembly language is an example of a low-level language. Each processor will have its own assembly language that is very close in format to that processor's particular *instruction set* but that uses letter codes in place of 1s and 0s. These letter codes are then translated into the collections of 1s and 0s understood by the processor.

MOVE #9, D0   store 9 in a data register

MOVE #5, D1   store 5 in a data register

ADD D0, D1   add contents of two data registers

Example of assembly language instructions

Intermediate-level languages

Assembly languages are well suited for writing programs that directly control parts of the computer system such as hardware drivers. They are ideal languages for writing operating systems such as Windows® or network operating systems such as Windows NT®. However, operating systems are huge programs and to write in assembly language would be a difficult and lengthy task. Languages such as C have such a versatile set of instructions that they can be almost as good as assembly language in writing programs for specific systems. C, however, has the advantage of being able to be translated into a variety of different machine languages. This means that one C program could be translated to work on a number of different processors. C is known as an intermediate-level language, specialised enough to contain low-level instructions but versatile enough to be used for different processors and simple enough to enable large complex programs to be quite easily written.

```
int  *p  &names[1];
add = p & F000;      /* determine the first
                        four bits of a
                        memory address */
```

Example of low-level C instructions

High-level languages

Most of the software you use will deal more with what the user wants to do than with the hardware. For instance, when you use a word processor you are using a program whose main aim is to allow the user to create and format documents to suit his or her needs. When the user needs to print, the word processor will generally use the operating system to do this. This type of program needs to be written in a language that can be translated for use on any type of processor and the language will be chosen more for its instructions that are suited to text processing. High-level languages provide instructions suited to particular types of software.

Different language, different purpose

Many *web applications* are written in Java. Java has instructions for creating *graphical user interfaces* that look the same no matter which machine or operating system the program is running on. It has instructions for operating over networks, including the Internet. Java might be chosen as a language because it contains the right sort of instructions for programs that will be accessed by web pages. Java is object-oriented, which means that it is very well suited to applications with graphical user interfaces. An object-oriented language treats windows, menus and other controls as individual objects with sets of properties and sets of actions they can carry out.

Other object-oriented languages, such as C++, Visual C++, Smalltalk and Visual Basic. NET are organised in a similar way and so are well suited to graphical applications on individual machines.

Other languages suited to graphical user interfaces are:

* Visual Basic

* Delphi.

These languages are not strictly object-oriented but have similar features in that they deal with properties and actions. Most of the software you are likely to use will have a graphical user interface, and so any of the languages mentioned might be considered suitable for writing this software. A graphical user interface is generally event-driven, that is it responds to events that the user requests in the order in which they occur. When you are using a word processor you might click on various parts of the page, select from menus, click on icons in toolbars or use shortcut keys. Each of these things is an event and the word processing software must respond to the events when they happen. It can't be programmed to do things in a particular order, as it doesn't know what the user will want to do.

More specialist software is often written in languages specially designed for that type of software. Knowledge based systems such as medical expert systems and neural networks are based on sets of facts and rules. For example, a fact might be that Bob is Dave's father and that Alan is Bob's father. This might be written:

    father (Bob, Dave) :- true

    father (Alan, Bob) :- true

A rule might be that X is the grandfather of Y if X is Z's father and Z is Y's father. This might be written:

    grandfather (X,Y) :-

        father(X,Z)

        father(Z,Y)

From the facts and rules you can determine that Alan is Dave's grandfather.

    ?- grandfather(Alan,Dave)

    yes

This sort of program will be written using many conditions. Languages such as Prolog and Lisp contain instructions that allow facts and rules to be stated and linked together to manipulate data. Prolog, in particular, is an example of a declarative language. It contains the facility to state facts and rules but does not have the right instructions to allow complex mathematical calculations or to carry out repetitive processes such as counting or producing animated graphics on a screen.

Table 8.1 shows a variety of different types of software and the programming languages that contain the features that each particular type of software requires.

While there are a variety of different types of programming language there are some similarities between them. Most are able to define data to be processed by the program. All programming languages can be used to create lists of instructions of some sort. Some instructions will describe the data that a program will be able to process, other instructions will state what will be done (change data, repeat a set of instructions, select a particular set of instructions, etc.). Most languages allow instructions to be organised into sections so that they are easier to follow. When learning a language you will need to become familiar with how it:

* describes (or declares) data of different types;

* manipulates (or changes) data;

* repeats instructions;

* selects particular instructions to carry out in certain cases;

* groups instructions into sections (subroutines);

* organises all these things into a complete program.

Think it over...

The language you choose to learn is likely to be determined by what is available to you. Which of the languages just listed are you likely to be able to use? What sort of programs are you likely to be able to produce with these languages?

TYPE OF SOFTWARE	FEATURES REQUIRED	SUITABLE PROGRAMMING LANGUAGES
Hardware drivers	Specialised instructions to control hardware for a particular processor	Assembly language for particular processor
Operating systems	Specialised instructions to control the running of hardware and software within a computer system	Assembly language for the particular processor, C
Network operating systems	Specialised instructions to control the running of hardware and software on different computer systems within a network	Assembly language for each particular processor, C for all processors (translated into correct machine language for each processor)
General user applications such as word processors, spreadsheets, email, etc.	Instructions to deal with a graphical user interface, ability to deal with events	C++, Smalltalk, Java, Visual Basic.Net, Visual Basic, Delphi, Visual C++
Web applications and web pages	Instructions to deal with web page format, ability to work across different types of system, instructions for moving data across the Internet	Java (for applications) JavaScript (for interactive web pages) HTML (for general web pages)
Database manipulation software	Instructions to search a database and display the results in a specified format	SQL
Application customisation (e.g. macros in spreadsheets and databases)	Instructions especially suited to the application that is being customised by adding macros to manipulate its documents	Visual Basic for Applications (VBA)
Specialist mathematical or scientific software	Complex mathematical formula processing instructions	FORTRAN
Artificial intelligence software (e.g. expert systems)	Ability to state and process facts and rules	Prolog, Lisp
Embedded systems (such as flight control systems or machine control systems that exist within a bigger system such as an aeroplane or a washing machine)	Specialist processing instructions suitable for the individual systems (e.g. parallel processing for real-time systems)	Ada (used in a number of defence systems where real-time processing is essential) C (used for more general-purpose systems)
Computer animation and games software	Instructions for producing graphics and animation on a screen in real time	C, C++, Java
Software produced by programmers while learning	Easy-to-learn instructions, easy-to-follow structure	Pascal (designed as a teaching language for simple general-purpose programming) BASIC (very easy to learn for simple general-purpose programming)

TABLE 8.1

A language tutorial for Visual Basic

In order to supplement the content of this unit, a tutorial will run all the way through giving you a step-by-step guide to writing programs in Visual Basic (version 6.0).

This tutorial will guide you through the process of writing one program step by step. You will see how to create a new program project, how to structure a simple program, how to declare variables, manipulate data, use instructions to repeat and select and how to write subroutines.

Tutorial 1 – Creating a Visual Basic project

To write a very basic Visual Basic program you will:

* create an application (Standard .exe) project

* set the properties of the main program form

* add controls such as labels, text boxes and buttons

* run an application.

First run the Visual Basic 6.0 application. You will see this screen.

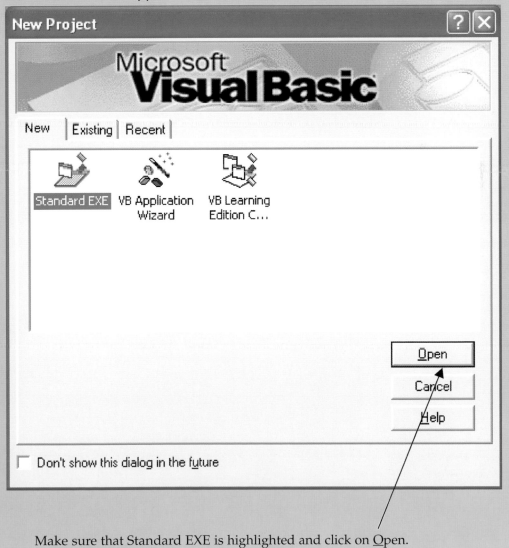

Make sure that Standard EXE is highlighted and click on Open.

The main project window will open with an empty form.

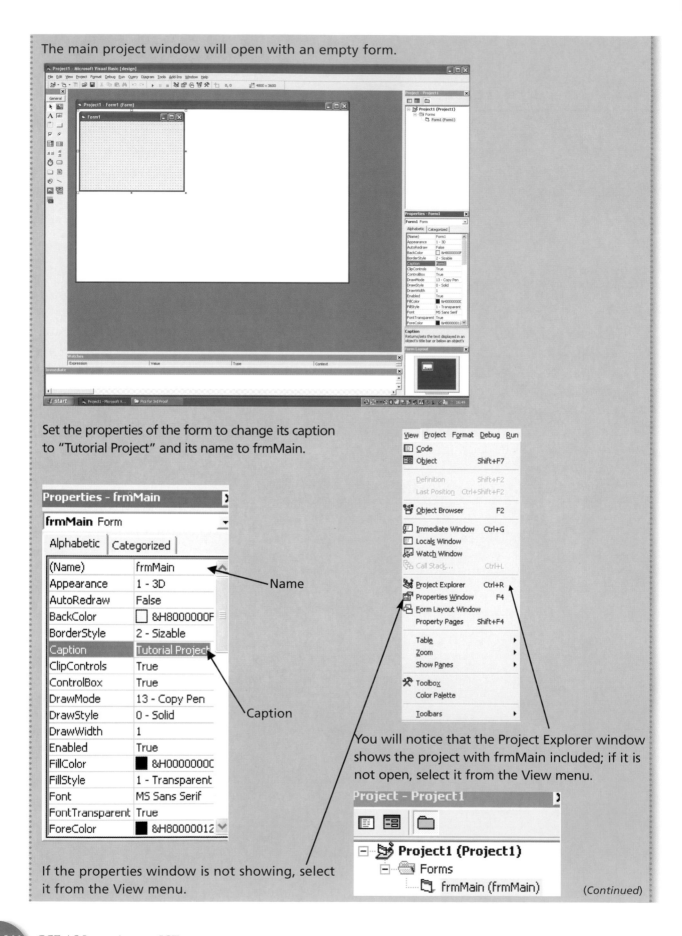

Set the properties of the form to change its caption to "Tutorial Project" and its name to frmMain.

Name → (Name) frmMain

Caption → Caption Tutorial Project

If the properties window is not showing, select it from the View menu.

You will notice that the Project Explorer window shows the project with frmMain included; if it is not open, select it from the View menu.

(Continued)

Now to add some controls. We will add a label, a text box and a button.

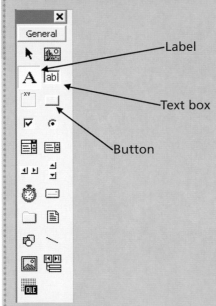

Label

Text box

Button

Use the controls to create one Label. Set its **Name** property to "lblTitle" and its **Caption** property to "Title".

Use the controls to create one Button. Set its **Name** property to "cmdExit" and its **Caption** property to "Exit".

Use the controls to create one Text Box. Set its **Name** property to "txtHello" and look at its Text property – we will leave it as Text1 for now.

Here's what it should look like.

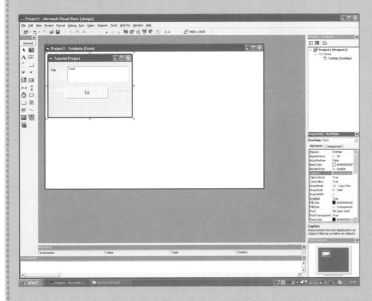

We now have a program that we can run. Do this by clicking on the Run icon on the toolbar.

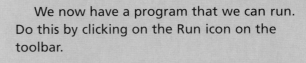

You won't be able to close the application using the Exit button as it hasn't been programmed yet. To close the application, click on the close box in the top right-hand corner.

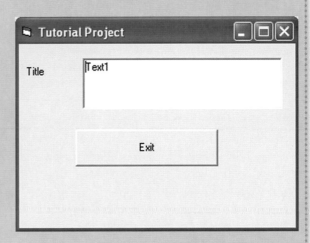

You have made your first Visual Basic 6.0 application! Make sure you save it (call it "Hello World") and remember what you have called it.

Program structure

Each programming language uses a different structure. When learning a language, you will need to become familiar with the way that particular language requires you to set out your programs. There will be set places for declaring variables, adding subroutines and writing instructions.

Visual Basic

When you use Visual Basic, you will design forms and then you will enter program instructions for each control on the form. Program instructions are typed into a text document linked to a form. Visual Basic itself will set out the program code so that you know where to type individual instructions. For example, if you are entering the instructions for what to do if the user clicks on a button, Visual Basic will create an area for the click event of that button and you will type the instructions in there. All instructions that need to be carried out when a form first loads are placed in a particular area for the load event of the form. Visual Basic has one instruction per line and an instruction ends at the end of that line. 'End' instructions allow you to mark the end of a group of instructions that are together for a particular reason (e.g. they must all be repeated together).

A typical structure of a Visual Basic program is as follows:

```
<<general section – all data is
  described here>>
<<event subroutines – one for each
  control that does something>>
e.g.
Private Sub cmdOK_Click()
  Instructions for OK button
End Sub
e.g.
Private Sub frmMyform_Load()
  Instructions to be carried when
    form is first loaded
End Sub
```

C

Program instructions for a C program are typed into a text file. C programs have a set structure that dictates where everything must be placed in the file that contains the program code. C programs have a set structure that dictates where everything must be placed in the file that contains the program code. There are sections for naming library files you will use, for declaring data requirements, for adding your own subroutines of program instructions, for writing the main program instructions. In a C program, the include instructions must be at the top and the main() function must be at the bottom. All instructions in a C program are terminated with a semi-colon (;). Any instructions that need to be grouped together so that they are treated in the same way (e.g. they are repeated a number of times, they are selected to run in certain conditions or they all belong to a subroutine) are grouped by enclosing them in curly brackets { }.

A typical structure of a C program is as follows:

```
List of library files to be included
  (e.g. #include stdio.h)
Data declarations e.g. int Num;
void main() {
  program instructions;
  program instructions;
  ...
}
```

> **Key term**
>
> *Library files*: these are files containing sets of instructions for particular tasks, written by someone else and put in a file so that you don't have to write them.

Pascal

Program instructions for a Pascal program are typed into a text file. Pascal programs have a set structure that dictates where everything must be placed in the file that contains the program code.

There are sections for:

* naming the program
* naming *library files* you will use
* declaring data requirements
* adding your own subroutines of program instructions
* writing the main program instructions.

In a Pascal program, the name of the program must be on the first line and this will be followed by any libraries the program needs. Data requirements are entered below this, followed by any subroutines you write.

The main program instructions must be at the bottom. All instructions in a Pascal program are separated with a semi-colon (;). If instructions need to be grouped together so that they are treated in the same way (e.g. they are repeated a number of times or they are selected to run in certain conditions) they are surrounded by the words BEGIN and END.

The final END, at the bottom of the program has a full stop to indicate that the program code is complete.

A typical structure of a Pascal program is as follows:

```
PROGRAM program_name;
USES library files to be included
  (e.g. WinCrt);
CONST
  Data declarations for data that will
    not change (e.g. Pi = 3.14159;)
VAR
  Data declarations for variable data
    (e.g. Num:INTEGER;)
BEGIN
  program instructions;
  program instructions;ß
  ...
END.
```

JavaScript

Program instructions for a JavaScript program are typed into an HTML file. The HTML file will already have some instructions written in HTML and the JavaScript will be inserted as appropriate. Because JavaScript is entered into the HTML file you will need to know just enough HTML to make a working document. JavaScript is inserted in the file and surrounded by HTML tags indicating that there is JavaScript code there. HTML tags are identified by angle brackets < >.

Within the JavaScript section of the HTML document, there are no particular rules for layout. A typical structure of JavaScript within an HTML document is as follows:

```
<html>
<title>" Page Title here"</title>
<head>
<script language = "JavaScript"
  type = "text/javascript">
  data declarations might go here
  program instructions
  program instructions
  ...
</script>
</head>
</html>
```

Theory into practice

Find a book that gives instruction in one particular programming language. Find two programs and highlight where the structure of the two programs is similar – i.e. show what goes where in a typical program. (Show data declarations, library files, groups of instructions if and where they appear.)

Tutorial 2 – Adding some Visual Basic code

To add code to a Visual Basic application you have created you will:

* open the code window for a form
* select the form load event and add some code
* select the exit button click event and add some code
* run the application.

Open the application you created in the last tutorial. To open an existing application from Windows Explorer, double click on the Visual Basic Project.

The main form should automatically open (if not, find it in the Project Explorer window and double click on it).

We want to add some code so we will need to open the code window. Click on the icon for the code window in the Project Explorer window.

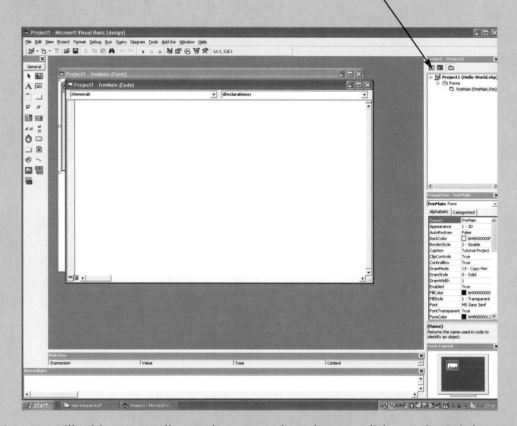

First, we will add some outline code to run when the user clicks on the Exit button.

Select cmdExit from the controls drop down menu. The events drop down menu will automatically change to "Click".

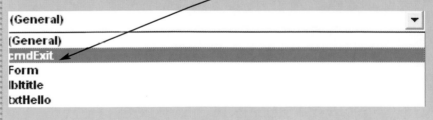

(Continued)

Next, we will add some outline code to run when the program first loads up. Select Form from the (General) controls drop down menu. The events drop down menu will automatically change to Load.

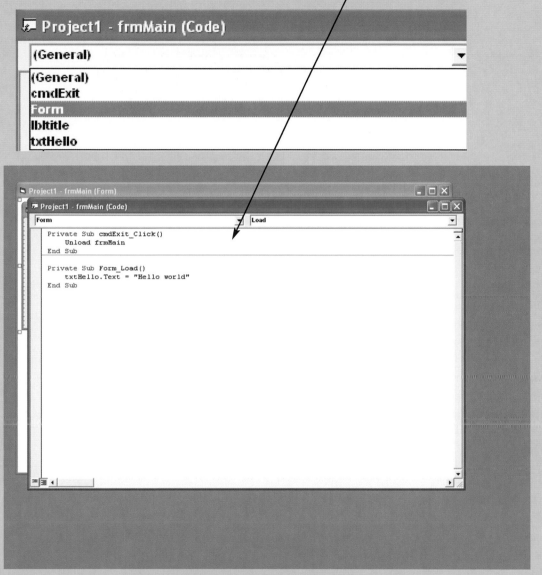

Type the code displayed in the window just shown. The Exit button will now close the program when it is clicked and the text in the Text Box will automatically be changed to "Hello World" when the program runs.

Run the program (by clicking on the Run icon in the toolbar). It will look like this and you will be able to click on the Exit button to exit the program.

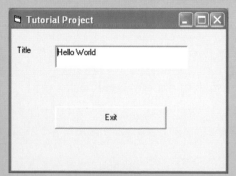

Save your project again.

Data types

All computer programs will carry out a series of instructions on various items of *data*. This data can be one of a number of types and must be stored while the *program* needs to use it.

All programming languages will include the facility to allocate areas of memory in which to store data. The amount of memory allocated will depend on the type of data. Data can be any of:

* whole numbers (integer)
* decimal numbers (floating point or real)
* characters
* a simple True or False (Boolean).

For example, a program might read two whole numbers and add them together. The program will need to allocate three areas of memory, one for holding each of the two whole numbers and one for holding the sum, which will also be a whole number.

Variable data

Data can be variable, constant or can appear literally within a program. The allocation of memory for storage of data that will be changed while the program is running is called **declaration of variables**. Programming languages vary in the way they declare variables but, in general, variables must be declared before any set of instructions that use those variables.

1. Integer variables

These hold whole numbers only and are allocated at least 4 bytes of memory.

> **Example**
> Declare a variable to hold the number of people in a department.
> → Declare a variable named NumPeople of type Integer (see Table 8.2).

2. Floating point/real variables

These hold any numbers and store them in such a way that very small and very large numbers can be stored in a small space.

> **Example**
> Declare a variable to hold the exact length of a building in metres.
> → Declare a variable named Length of type floating point/real (see Table 8.3).

3. Character variables

These hold any one ASCII character and typically use only one byte of storage.

> **Example**
> Declare a variable to hold a letter typed by a user.
> → Declare a variable named Letter of type character (see Table 8.4).

4. Boolean variables (true or false)

These can hold values representing true and false only and typically use only one byte of storage.

IN VISUAL BASIC THIS IS WRITTEN:	IN C THIS IS WRITTEN:	IN PASCAL THIS IS WRITTEN:	IN JAVASCRIPT THIS IS WRITTEN:
Dim NumPeople As Integer	int NumPeople;	VAR NumPeople: INTEGER;	var NumPeople = 0 Note: the type is implied

TABLE 8.2

IN VISUAL BASIC THIS IS WRITTEN:	IN C THIS IS WRITTEN:	IN PASCAL THIS IS WRITTEN:	IN JAVASCRIPT THIS IS WRITTEN:
Dim Length As Double	float Length;	VAR NumPeople: REAL;	var NumPeople = 0.00 Note: the type is implied

TABLE 8.3

IN VISUAL BASIC THIS IS WRITTEN:	IN C THIS IS WRITTEN:	IN PASCAL THIS IS WRITTEN:	IN JAVASCRIPT THIS IS WRITTEN:
Dim Length As String	char Letter;	VAR NumPeople:CHAR;	var NumPeople = "c" Note: the type is implied

TABLE 8.4

IN VISUAL BASIC THIS IS WRITTEN:	IN C THIS IS WRITTEN:	IN PASCAL THIS IS WRITTEN:	IN JAVASCRIPT THIS IS WRITTEN:
Dim SwitchOn As Boolean	bool SwitchOn;	VAR SwitchOn: BOOLEAN;	var SwitchOn = new Boolean() Note: this creates a Boolean object

TABLE 8.5

> **Example**
> Declare a variable to hold whether or not a switch is on.
> → Declare a variable named SwitchOn of type Boolean.

Constant data

Sometimes, a particular value must be used over and over again but will always remain the same. For example, there may always be 10 items in a list and so the end of the list is always the tenth item. You might want to use a data name such as EndOfList to indicate where the end of the list is and to set its value permanently to 10. EndOfList is declared as constant data.

> **Example**
> Declare a constant to hold the value of Pi (3.14159).
> → Declare a constant named Pi with the value 3.14159 (see Table 8.6).

Literal data

When you write programs you will want to use instructions to give specific values to variables. For example, the number of people at a party might be 20.

You can name literal data and store it in a variable.

> **Example**
> Set the number of people at a party to 20 (see Table 8.7).

The literal value must have the same data type as the variable in which it will be stored.

The following gives examples of literal values of the main data types: integer, real, character and Boolean:

integer:	10, − 32000, 3000
real:	0.1, 1, − 567.4567
character:	'c', 't', 'T'
Boolean:	true, false

IN VISUAL BASIC THIS IS WRITTEN:	IN C THIS IS WRITTEN:	IN PASCAL THIS IS WRITTEN:	IN JAVASCRIPT THIS IS WRITTEN:
n/a (no constant declaration method available – literal values will be used instead)	const float Pi = 3.14159;	CONST Pi = 3.14159;	n/a (no constant declaration method available – literal values will be used instead)

TABLE 8.6

IN VISUAL BASIC THIS IS WRITTEN:	IN C IN PASCAL THIS IS WRITTEN:	IN JAVASCRIPT THIS IS WRITTEN:	THIS IS WRITTEN:
NumPeople = 20	NumPeople = 20;	NumPeople = 20;	NumPeople = 20

TABLE 8.7

Knowledge check

Write a definition of each of the following and give an example of its uses in the language you are studying:

integer

real/floating point

character

Boolean

Theory into practice

Write data declarations for the following variables and give an example of a literal value for each and declare a constant using the literal value:

1 the number of sweets in a jar

2 the price of a new dress

3 a letter typed to choose from a menu

4 whether or not a bin is full.

Tutorial 3 – Declaring and using variables and literals

To write Visual Basic programs that use variables and literal values you will:

* Create a new application (Standard EXE) project

* Set the properties of the main program form

* Add controls such as labels, text boxes and buttons

* Declare variables of type string, integer, double and Boolean

* Add code to the form load event, text box change events and a button click event. Disable and enable a button within the program code.

* Run the application.

First run the Visual Basic 6.0 application and start a new project. The main project window will open with an empty form. Change the form's name to "frmMain" and the Caption to "Tutorial Project"

(Continued)

Add the labels Name, Age and Height *naming* them "**lblName**", "**lblAge**" and "**lblHeight**" respectively and set the *Captions* to "**Name**", "**Age**" and "**Height**" respectively.

Add two command buttons *named* "**cmdExit**" and "**cmdShow**" with *Captions* "**Exit**" and "**Show**".

The result should look like this.

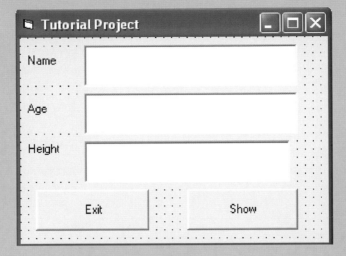

We are going to add some code, so open the code window.

Your program will need somewhere to store the name, age and height entered by the user. You will enter variable declarations in the code window as shown below (just type them in at the top).

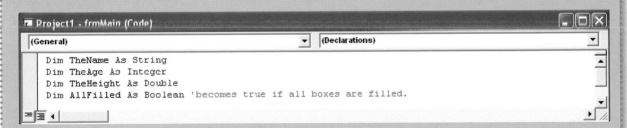

Now we will add some code for the form load event. Select form from the controls drop down list and make sure that Load is selected in the events drop down list. The code will set the variables to empty values and will disable the cmdShow button because all variables are not yet set.

Add the code as follows:

```
Project1 - frmMain (Code)
txtName                                    Change

    Dim TheName As String
    Dim TheAge As Integer
    Dim TheHeight As Double
    Dim AllFilled As Boolean 'becomes true if all boxes are filled.

    Private Sub Form_Load()
        TheName = ""
        TheAge = 0
        TheHeight = 0
        AllFilled = False
        cmdShow.Enabled = AllFilled
    End Sub
```

Now add the code to change TheName to what the user entered in the text box txtName. Select txtName from the controls drop down list and change from the events drop down list. The code will set up TheName and check to see if all three boxes are full. It will then enable or disable the cmdShow button appropriately.

Add the code as follows:

```
Project1 - frmMain (Code)                                              [_][□][X]

txtName                              ▼    Change                        ▼

   Dim TheName As String
   Dim TheAge As Integer
   Dim TheHeight As Double
   Dim AllFilled As Boolean 'becomes true if all boxes are filled.

   Private Sub Form_Load()
       TheName = ""
       TheAge = 0
       TheHeight = 0
       AllFilled = False
       cmdShow.Enabled = AllFilled
   End Sub

   Private Sub txtName_Change()
       TheName = txtName.Text
       AllFilled = (TheName <> "" And TheAge <> 0 And TheHeight <> 0)
       cmdShow.Enabled = AllFilled
   End Sub
```

Add the code for changing TheAge to what the user typed in (it will need to be changed to an integer using int(val()).

```
Project1 - frmMain (Code)                                              [_][□][X]

txtName                              ▼    Change                        ▼

   Dim TheName As String
   Dim TheAge As Integer
   Dim TheHeight As Double
   Dim AllFilled As Boolean 'becomes true if all boxes are filled.

   Private Sub Form_Load()
       TheName = ""
       TheAge = 0
       TheHeight = 0
       AllFilled = False
       cmdShow.Enabled = AllFilled
   End Sub

   Private Sub txtName_Change()
       TheName = txtName.Text
       AllFilled = (TheName <> "" And TheAge <> 0 And TheHeight <> 0)
       cmdShow.Enabled = AllFilled
   End Sub

   Private Sub txtAge_Change()
       TheAge = Int(Val(txtAge.Text))|
       AllFilled = (TheName <> "" And TheAge <> 0 And TheHeight <> 0)
       cmdShow.Enabled = AllFilled
   End Sub
```

(Continued)

Finally, add the code for changing TheHeight, similar to TheName and TheAge.

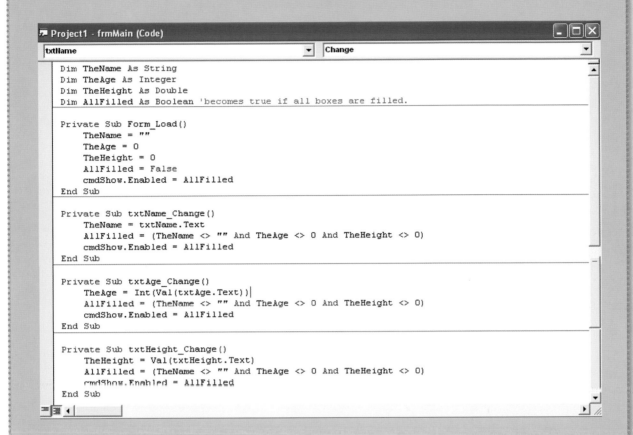

```
Project1 - frmMain (Code)

txtName                                          ▼   Change                                ▼

    Dim TheName As String
    Dim TheAge As Integer
    Dim TheHeight As Double
    Dim AllFilled As Boolean 'becomes true if all boxes are filled.

    Private Sub Form_Load()
        TheName = ""
        TheAge = 0
        TheHeight = 0
        AllFilled = False
        cmdShow.Enabled = AllFilled
    End Sub

    Private Sub txtName_Change()
        TheName = txtName.Text
        AllFilled = (TheName <> "" And TheAge <> 0 And TheHeight <> 0)
        cmdShow.Enabled = AllFilled
    End Sub

    Private Sub txtAge_Change()
        TheAge = Int(Val(txtAge.Text))|
        AllFilled = (TheName <> "" And TheAge <> 0 And TheHeight <> 0)
        cmdShow.Enabled = AllFilled
    End Sub

    Private Sub txtHeight_Change()
        TheHeight = Val(txtHeight.Text)
        AllFilled = (TheName <> "" And TheAge <> 0 And TheHeight <> 0)
        cmdShow.Enabled = AllFilled
    End Sub
```

These snippets of code give examples of declaring variables, assigning literal values, assigning entered values, changing text to integer and to double values and assigning a value to a Boolean variable. Make sure that you are happy with what you have done here before moving on.

The last bit of code for now is the code to exit the program using the Exit button.

Add the following code to the click event of the cmdExit button:

```
Project1 - frmMain (Code)

Form                                             ▼   Load                                  ▼

    Private Sub cmdExit_Click()
        Unload frmMain
    End Sub
```

Now the program is ready to try. Run the program by clicking on the Run icon in the toolbar. You should see the following (notice that the Show button is disabled)

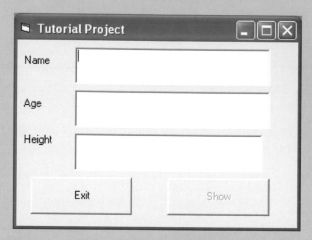

Enter a name into the Name text box and an age into the Age text box (the Show button is still enabled):

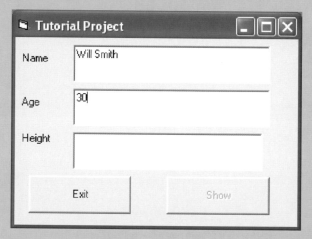

Enter a height into the Height text box. The Show button will become enabled. If you delete any of the text in any of the boxes the Show button will become disabled again.

The Show button will not do anything if you click on it because we haven't added any code to get it to do anything yet.

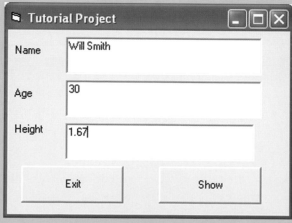

Save your project in the same way as you did before, this time naming it "NameAgeHeight".

Input and output (data manipulation)

All programming languages provide methods for getting *input* from a keyboard or other input device and for sending *output* to a screen, printer or other output device. Programs with a graphical user interface will use controls such as *drop-down lists, text boxes, form fields* and *option buttons* to get input from the user.

The language you are using will have either built-in functions for input and output or will have library files that contain pre-written input and output functions.

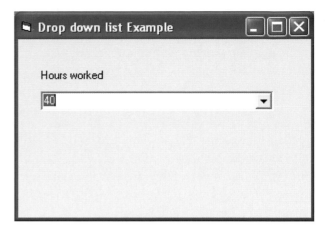

FIGURE 8.3 *Example of drop-down list*

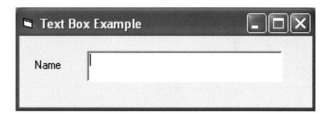

FIGURE 8.4 *Example of text box or form field*

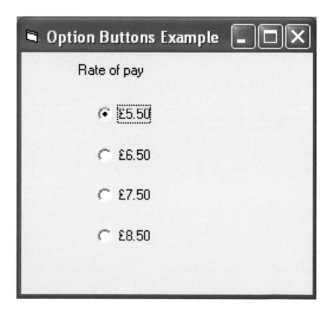

FIGURE 8.5 *Example of option buttons*

Examples of input are:

Visual Basic: all input comes through controls on forms. These controls might be input boxes or text boxes but might also be control buttons or drop-down lists (see Table 8.8).

C: there are a number of pre-written functions available for input. These include 'cin' and 'scanf()', both of which are designed to input a variety of different types of data. There are also functions for reading strings and characters such as 'gets() and 'getch'() (see Tables 8.9 and 8.10) .

Pascal: the standard functions for input are 'Read()' and 'ReadLn()'. These both read data of any type from the keyboard (see Table 8.11) .

JavaScript: for simplicity, examples will show Script prompt boxes being used to get text input (see Table 8.12).

Examples of output are:

Visual Basic: output will often be made through text boxes, labels or message boxes (see Table 8.13).

C: there are a number of pre-written functions available for output. These include 'cout ()' and 'printf'(), both of which are designed to output a variety of different types of data. There are also functions such as 'puts()' specifically for writing strings (see Tables 8.14 and 8.15).

Pascal: the standard functions for output are 'Write()' and 'WriteLn()'. These both write data of any type and WriteLn will end on a new line (see Table 8.16).

JavaScript: output is made either using an alert box or by writing directly to the current window (see Table 8.17).

EmpName = Text1.Text	'string input from text box called Text1
Hours = Text2.Text	'integer input through text box called Text2
HoursList.Index	'Index has the value of the item selected and this will be used to set the value of Hours.
PayRateButtons(Index).Checked	'The value of Index indicates which button is selected and the value of 'PayRate' is set from this

TABLE 8.8 *Examples of Visual Basic input*

cin>>PayRate;	/*reads data from the keyboard for PayRate */
cin>>Hours;	/*reads data from the keyboard for Hours */
scanf ("%f",&PayRate);	/* does the same as cin but only allows float */
scanf ("%d",&Hours);	/* does the same as cin but only allows integer */

TABLE 8.9 *Examples of C input of a floating point value 'Payrate' and an integer 'Hours'*

cin>>EmpName;	/*reads a string from the keyboard for EmpName*/
scanf ("%s",&EmpName);	/*does the same as cin*/
gets(EmpName);	/*reads EmpName from the keyboard as a string*/
Initial = getch();	/*reads a single character from the keyboard buffer*/

TABLE 8.10 *Examples of C input of a string value 'EmpName' and a character value 'Initial'*

```
ReadLn(PayRate, Hours, EmpName);        {Note: the return key indicates that all have been
                                         entered, even if only one has been}

Read(PayRate, Hours, EmpName);          {Note: the return key is ignored by Read, all will be read,
                                         even if return is pressed in between}
```

TABLE 8.11 *Examples of Pascal input of a real value 'PayRate', an integer value 'Hours' and a string value 'EmpName'*

```
EmpName = prompt ("Enter employee name","") //read a string

PayRate = parseFloat(prompt ("Enter pay rate","")) //read a decimal number

Hours = parseInt(prompt ("Enter hours worked","")) //read an integer
```

TABLE 8.12 *Examples of JavaScript input of string, float and integer values*

```
Label1.Caption = EmpName
Label2.Caption = PayRate
Label3.Caption = Hours

Text1.Text = EmpName
Text2.Text = PayRate
Text3.Text = Hours

MsgBox (EmpName,0,"Name") 'box titled "Name" with OK button only
MsgBox(PayRate,1,"Pay Rate") 'titled "Pay Rate" with OK & cancel buttons
MsgBox(Hours,0,"Hours Output") 'box titled "Hours" with OK button only
```

TABLE 8.13 *Examples of Visual Basic output*

```
cout<<"The rate of pay is: " << PayRate;

cout<<"Number of hours worked: " << Hours << "\n"; /* \n = new line */

printf ("The rate of pay is: %f", PayRate);

printf ("Number of hours worked: %d \n", Hours);
```

TABLE 8.14 *Examples of C output of a floating point value 'Payrate' and an integer 'Hours'*

```
cout<<"Employee Name: " << EmpName << " \n"; /* \n makes a new line */

printf ("Employee Name: %s \n",EmpName);

puts(EmpName); /*no message, to add, use strcat()*/
```

TABLE 8.15 *Examples of C output of a string value 'EmpName'*

```
Write('Employee Name: ', EmpName);

WriteLn('The rate of pay is', PayRate, ' Number of hours worked: ', Hours);
```

TABLE 8.16 *Examples of Pascal output of a string value 'EmpName' immediately followed by a real value 'PayRate' and an integer value 'Hours' and all written on the same line. After writing the cursor will move to the next line.*

```
alert ("Employee Name" + EmpName + ".\")

document.writeln ("The rate of pay is: " + PayRate +" Number of hours worked: " + Hours)
```

TABLE 8.17 *Examples of JavaScript output*

Theory into practice

Try writing a simple program to read a name and then to display the same name back on the screen as a message ("The name you entered was <name>").

Tutorial 4 – Displaying output

The last program got input from the user through text boxes. This one will produce some output as well. To do this you will:

✳ open an existing project

✳ add some code to the Show button to display name, age and height in a Message Box

✳ run the application.

Open the project you saved in the last tutorial – NameAgeHeight – remember to open the Project file and not the form.

Open the code window.

We are going to program the Show button to display a message box containing all the information collected from the text boxes. The information will be collected together into one single message.

Add the following code:

```
Private Sub cmdShow_Click()
    MsgBox "Your name is " + TheName + ".  Your age is " + Str(TheAge) + ".  You are " + Str(TheHeight) + "m tall"
End Sub
```

Now try running the program. Enter all the information as before and click on the Show button.

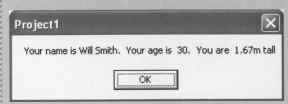

Save your project.

Data structures

All programs you write will need to store and read data. The four simple *data types (integer, real, character, Boolean)* can hold single items of data. But data often comes in groups.

Programs often need to store names. Names consist of characters but the characters must be held together in the correct order. Data structures allow you to group data so that it is organised in a useful way. The data structures you will need to be able to use are:

* string – a set of characters stored together

* array – a set of variables of one data type stored together

* record – a collection of variables of different types held together

* file – a collection of variables of different types held together on some form of storage media (disk, CD, tape).

1. Strings

These hold whole sets of characters and must be declared to have a length (although some languages will have a default/built in length for strings). This length is the maximum number of characters that can be stored in the string. One of the characters, however, will often be a length character (stored at the beginning of the string) or a terminating character (stored at the end). These extra characters allow the program to detect exactly how long the stored string is so that it processes only the required number of characters.

> **Example**
> Declare a variable to hold the name of an employee.
> → Declare a variable named EmpName of type string (see Table 8.18).

2. Arrays

These hold sets of variables of one type. You might use an array to hold a list of numbers, a list of prices, a list of names or values for a set of switches. To declare an array you must state the type of the variables in it and the number of items in the array. To refer to an item in an array, you will use the array name and the position of the item in the array.

> **Example**
> Declare an array to hold the prices of a set of five items. Assign the prices 1.50, 2.45, 3.65, 2.86, 9.10 to the items in the array.
> → Declare a variable named Prices of type array and size 5 (see Table 8.19).

3. Records

These hold sets of variables of different types. You might use a record to hold a set of data about an employee, as you would when using a database. Records have names and fields. To refer to data in a record you will use the record name and the field name.

IN VISUAL BASIC THIS IS WRITTEN:	IN C THIS IS WRITTEN:	IN PASCAL THIS IS WRITTEN:	IN JAVASCRIPT THIS IS WRITTEN:
Dim EmpName As String	char EmpName[30];	VAR EmpName: STRING[30];	var EmpName ="Will Smith Note: the type is implied

TABLE 8.18

IN VISUAL BASIC THIS IS WRITTEN:	IN C THIS IS WRITTEN:	IN PASCAL THIS IS WRITTEN:	IN JAVASCRIPT THIS IS WRITTEN:
Dim Prices(5) As Double	float Prices[5];	VAR Prices : Array [1..5] OF REAL;	var Prices = new array(5)
			Note: the type is implied when data is stored in the array.
Prices(0) = 1.50;	Prices[0] = 1.50;	Prices[1] := 1.50	Prices[0] = 1.50
Prices(1) = 2.45	Prices[1] = 2.45;	Prices[2] := 2.45	Prices[1] = 2.45
Prices(2) = 3.65	Prices[2] = 3.65;	Prices[3] := 3.65	Prices[2] = 3.65
Prices(3) = 2.86	Prices[3] = 2.86;	Prices[4] := 2.86	Prices[3] = 2.86
Prices(4) = 9.10	Prices[4] = 9.10;	Prices[5] := 9.10	Prices[4] = 9.10

TABLE 8.19

Example
Declare a variable to hold a set of details about an employee.
→ Declare a variable named Employee of type record with fields to hold name (string), number of years of service (integer), salary (real) and whether or not they are in the pension scheme (Boolean) (see Table 8.20). Assign the data:

> name → Will Smith
>
> number of years of service → 5
>
> salary → 21,682.85
>
> in pension scheme → yes

Example
A file (filename) holds a list of names and money owed. It is organised as follows:

> Name
>
> Money owed
>
> Name
>
> Money owed
>
> Name
>
> Money owed
>
> …
>
> …

Write instructions to open the file, read the first two items of data (one name and one money owed) and close the file.
→ Open the file for reading, read the first two items of data, close the file (see Table 8.21).

4. Files

A file holds data in a particular order on some form of storage media (e.g. hard disk, floppy disk, CD-RW). You will write programs that will read data from and write data to a file on a disk. In order to do so, you must know how the file is organised (i.e. what data is where) and your program must read and write the data in this way. Before files can be read from or written to, they must be opened for the required purpose (e.g. open for reading, open for writing a new file, open for adding data to the end of a file).

Programming languages will include instructions for opening, closing, reading from and writing to files.

Example
A file (filename) will hold a list of house numbers and roads. Write instructions to open a new file, add one house number and one road to it, and close the file. The resulting file will look like this:

> House number
> Road

→ Open the file for writing, write the house number and road, close the file (see Table 8.22).

IN VISUAL BASIC THIS IS WRITTEN:	IN C THIS IS WRITTEN:	IN PASCAL THIS IS WRITTEN:	IN JAVASCRIPT THIS IS WRITTEN:

Public Type Employee
  Name As String * 30
  YearsService As Integer
  Salary As Double
  InPension As Boolean
EndType
 	
Dim Emp As Employee
Emp.Name = "Will Smith"
Emp.YearsService = 5
Emp.Salary = 21682.85
Emp InPension = True
	struct Employee{
	  char Name[30];
	  int YearsService;
	  float Salary;
	  bool InPension;
	}
	
	Employee Emp;
	
	strcpy(Emp.Name, "Will Smith");
	Emp.YearsService = 5;
	Emp.Salary = 21682.85;
	Emp InPension = True;
		TYPE Employee = RECORD
		  Name : String[30];
		  YearsService: INTEGER;
		  Salary : REAL;
		  InPension: BOOLEAN;
		END;
		
		VAR
		  Emp : Employee;
		
		  Emp.Name : = Will Smith);
		  Emp.YearsService := 5;
		  Emp.Salary := 21682,85;
		  Emp.InPension := TRUE;
			n/a (JavaScript variables are part of the object to which they relate and so records are generally not required).

TABLE 8.20

IN VISUAL BASIC THIS IS WRITTEN:	IN C THIS IS WRITTEN:	IN PASCAL THIS IS WRITTEN:	IN JAVASCRIPT THIS IS WRITTEN:

Open filename For Input As #1
 	
Input #1, name
Input #1, owed
Close #1
	FILE myfile;
	
	myfile = fopen(filename,"r");
	if (myfile != 0){
	  fscanf(myfile, "%s", &name);
	  fscanf(myfile, "%f", &owed);
	  fclose(myfile);
	}
		VAR
		myfile: TEXT;
		BEGIN
		ASSIGN(myfile,filename);
		RESET(myfile);
		ReadLn(myfile, name);
		ReadLn(myfile,owed);
		RESET(myfile);
			n/a (JavaScript programs cannot read or write files on client machines and so there is no version of file handling)

TABLE 8.21

Knowledge check

Can you write a definition and give an example of your own, in the language you are studying, for each of the following?

String

Array

Record

File

Theory into practice

Write data declarations for the following data structures and show how values are assigned for each:

1 the name of a sweet

2 a list of the weights of sweets in a jar

3 data about an item of clothing, including item code, description and price

4 a list of variables each holding whether or not a switch is on

5 a file of data in list form of book title, author and price (in this case, show how one set of data might be read and how one set of data might be written to the file).

IN VISUAL BASIC THIS IS WRITTEN:	IN C THIS IS WRITTEN:	IN PASCAL THIS IS WRITTEN:	IN JAVASCRIPT THIS IS WRITTEN:

Open filename For Output As #1
 	
Print #1, house_no
Print #1, road
Close #1
	FILE myfile;
	myfile = fopen(filename,"w");
	
	if (myfile != 0){
	  fprintf(myfile, "%d\n", house_no);
	  fprintf(myfile, "%s\n", road);
	  fclose(myfile);
	}
		VAR
		  myfile : TEXT;
		'BEGIN'
		ASSIGN(myfile,filename);
		REWRITE(myfile);
		WriteLn(myfile, house_no);
		WriteLn(myfile,road);
		RESET(myfile);
			n/a

TABLE 8.22

Tutorial 5 – Using data structures – records

The last program got name, age and height details and treated them as three separate items. This program will use a record structure to group the details together into a "Person" record. To do this we will:

* open an existing project – NameAgeHeight

* change the data declarations to use a record instead of individual variables

* change the code to use the record variables instead of individual variables

* run the application.

Open the project you saved in the last tutorial – NameAgeHeight – remember to open the Project file and not the form.

Open the code window.

We are going to change the data declarations so that a record is used instead of individual variables for TheName, TheAge and TheHeight.

Change the code at the top of the window as shown below.

Now we have a record "TheMan" which contains name, age and height information. When we want to use the name we must now refer to it as belonging to the record: TheMan. TheName; similarly, TheAge now becomes TheMan.TheAge, and TheHeight becomes TheMan.TheHeight.

We will need to change the code so that every time TheName appears it is changed to TheMan.TheName, TheAge is changed to TheMan.TheAge everywhere and TheHeight is changed to TheMan.TheHeight.

```
Project1 - frmMain (Code)
mdShow                                  Click

    Public Type Person
        TheName As String
        TheAge As Integer
        TheHeight As Double
    End Type

    Dim TheMan As Person
    Dim AllFilled As Boolean
```

(Continued)

Make sure your code looks like the following:

```
Project1 - frmMain (Code)

cmdShow                                              ▼  Click                                              ▼

Public Type Person
    TheName As String
    TheAge As Integer
    TheHeight As Double
End Type

Dim TheMan As Person
Dim AllFilled As Boolean

Private Sub Form_Load()
    TheMan.TheName = ""
    TheMan.TheAge = 0
    TheMan.TheHeight = 0
    AllFilled = False
    cmdShow.Enabled = AllFilled
End Sub

Private Sub txtName_Change()
    TheMan.TheName = txtName.Text
    AllFilled = (TheName <> "" And TheAge <> 0 And TheHeight <> 0)
    cmdShow.Enabled = AllFilled
End Sub

Private Sub txtAge_Change()
    TheMan.TheAge = Int(Val(txtAge.Text))
    AllFilled = (TheName <> "" And TheAge <> 0 And TheHeight <> 0)
    cmdShow.Enabled = AllFilled
End Sub

Private Sub txtHeight_Change()
    TheMan.TheHeight = Val(txtHeight.Text)
    AllFilled = (TheName <> "" And TheAge <> 0 And TheHeight <> 0)
    cmdShow.Enabled = AllFilled
End Sub

Private Sub cmdExit_Click()
    Unload frmMain
End Sub

Private Sub cmdShow_Click()
    MsgBox "Your name is " + TheMan.TheName + ".  Your age is " + Str(TheMan.TheAge) + ".  You are " + Str(TheMan.Th
End Sub
```

Now try running the program. Enter all the information as before and click on the Show button. You should find that everything is exactly the same. It is only the way the data is stored that is different.

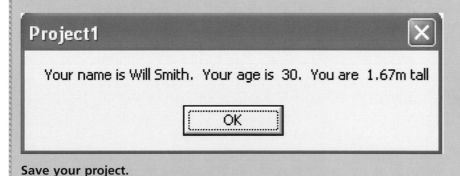

Project1

Your name is Will Smith. Your age is 30. You are 1.67m tall

OK

Save your project.

Tutorial 5a – Using data structures – arrays

This program will use an array structure to group the details together into a set of names and a set of ages. To do this we will:

* create a new project
* declare two arrays – names and ages
* copy and paste text boxes to create control arrays on the main form
* create an output form with a control array of labels
* run the application.

Run Visual Basic 6.0 and create a new Standard EXE application. Name the form frmMain and give it the Caption "Tutorial Project".

Create a label called "lblNames", with Caption "Names".

Then create a text box called "txtNames". Delete the text in the Text property so that the box is empty.

Copy and paste the text box. You will see an alert box that says "A control called txtNames already exists. Do you want to create a control array?" Click Yes.

The two text boxes are now called txtNames(0) and txtNames(1). Make three further copies of the text box.

Now add a label "lblAges" with Caption "Ages".

Add a text box "txtAges" with blank text. Copy the text box to create an array of five text boxes (txtAges(0) to txtAges(4)).

Add two command buttons: "cmdShow" with Caption "Show List" and "cmdExit" with Caption "Exit".

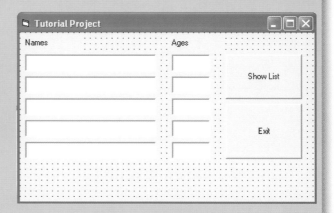

The form now contains TWO control arrays – txtNames and txtAges. Each has five items in the array. We now need to declare some variables in which to store the names and arrays. Open the code window.

Type in the following to declare two arrays "TheNames" and "TheAges". Each array will hold five items, either Strings or Integers. Also add an "AllFilled" variable to store whether all boxes are filled or not.

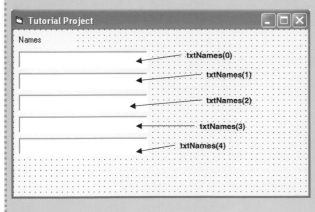

Now add code to run when the main form loads. This sets all the names and ages in the array to blank values and sets the AllFilled variable to false and the Show List button to disabled because the variables have no values.

(Continued)

```
Private Sub Form_Load()
    TheNames(0) = ""
    TheNames(1) = ""
    TheNames(2) = ""
    TheNames(3) = ""
    TheNames(4) = ""
    TheAges(0) = 0
    TheAges(1) = 0
    TheAges(2) = 0
    TheAges(3) = 0
    TheAges(4) = 0
    AllFilled = TheNames(0) <> "" And TheNames(1) <> "" And TheNames(2) <> "" And TheNames(3) <> "" And TheNames(4) <> ""
    AllFilled = AllFilled And TheAges(0) <> 0 And TheAges(1) <> 0 And TheAges(2) <> 0 And TheAges(3) <> 0 And TheAges(4) <> 0
    cmdShow.Enabled = AllFilled
End Sub
```

Select txtNames from the control drop-down list. Because the names are an array, you can write code to do the same whichever text box is selected. The actual text box selected is identified by **Index**.

```
Private Sub txtNames_Change(Index As Integer)
    TheNames(Index) = txtNames(Index).Text
    AllFilled = TheNames(0) <> "" And TheNames(1) <> "" And TheNames(2) <> "" And TheNames(3) <> "" And TheNames(4) <> ""
    AllFilled = AllFilled And TheAges(0) <> 0 And TheAges(1) <> 0 And TheAges(2) <> 0 And TheAges(3) <> 0 And TheAges(4) <> 0
    cmdShow.Enabled = AllFilled
End Sub
```

Now add the code to run when the text in one of the txtAges text boxes changes.

```
Private Sub txtAges_Change(Index As Integer)
    TheAges(Index) = Int(Val(txtAges(Index).Text))
    AllFilled = TheNames(0) <> "" And TheNames(1) <> "" And TheNames(2) <> "" And TheNames(3) <> "" And TheNames(4) <> ""
    AllFilled = AllFilled And TheAges(0) <> 0 And TheAges(1) <> 0 And TheAges(2) <> 0 And TheAges(3) <> 0 And TheAges(4) <> 0
    cmdShow.Enabled = AllFilled

End Sub
```

Add the code for the cmdExit button.

Run the program.

You should get the following with the Show List button disabled.

The Show List button will remain disabled until all boxes are filled.

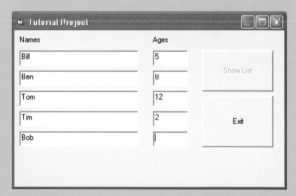

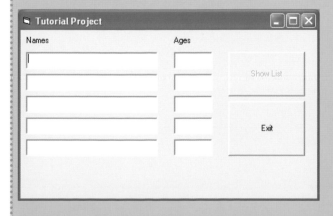

When all boxes are filled the Show List button will become enabled.

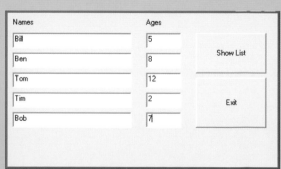

This program is going to display a list of all names and ages on an output form.

To create a new form, use the Project menu and select Add Form. Select Form and click on Open.

Create a label called "lblNameAge" with a blank Caption. Copy and paste this label so that you have an array of five labels called "lblNameAge(0)" to "lblNameAge(4)".

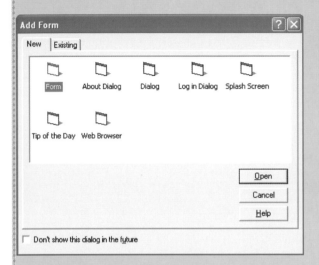

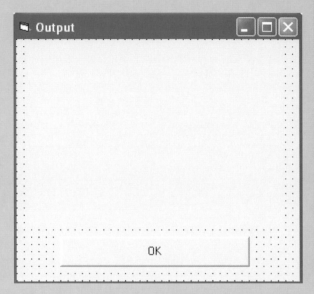

You will have a new form added to the project. Change the name of this form to "frmOutput" and the Caption to "Output". Look in the Project Explorer window. You should see the form added to the Project.

Open the code window for frmOutput and add the following code. The code in the Form_Load event will copy the names and ages from the variables in frmMain and will join them together to make a Caption for the labels on frmOutput.

We will need to add the following two sections of code:

Firstly, add some code to the click event of the Show List button on frmMain to get it to put the correct text in the labels of frmOutput before it shows it.

```
Private Sub cmdShow_Click()
    frmOutput.lblNameAge(0).Caption = TheNames(0) + " " + Str(TheAges(0))
    frmOutput.lblNameAge(1).Caption = TheNames(1) + " " + Str(TheAges(1))
    frmOutput.lblNameAge(2).Caption = TheNames(2) + " " + Str(TheAges(2))
    frmOutput.lblNameAge(3).Caption = TheNames(3) + " " + Str(TheAges(3))
    frmOutput.lblNameAge(4).Caption = TheNames(4) + " " + Str(TheAges(4))
    Load frmOutput
    frmOutput.Show
End Sub
```

(Continued)

Next, we will add some code to frmOutput so that the OK button closes the form.

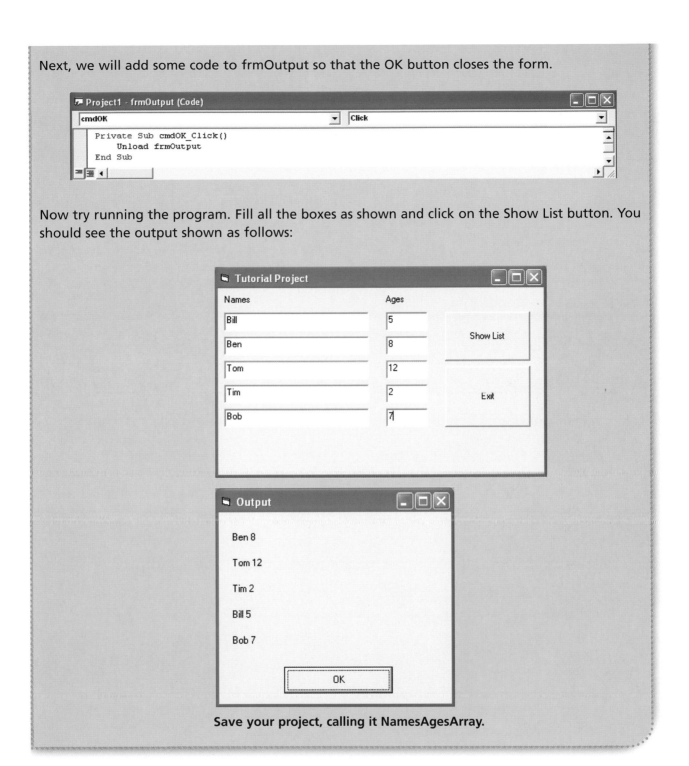

```
Project1 - frmOutput (Code)
cmdOK                                    Click

    Private Sub cmdOK_Click()
        Unload frmOutput
    End Sub
```

Now try running the program. Fill all the boxes as shown and click on the Show List button. You should see the output shown as follows:

Tutorial Project

Names | Ages
Bill | 5
Ben | 8
Tom | 12
Tim | 2
Bob | 7

Show List

Exit

Output

Ben 8

Tom 12

Tim 2

Bill 5

Bob 7

OK

Save your project, calling it NamesAgesArray.

Operators

Data is stored in variables of different types. Once it has been stored you will want to write program instructions to use the data. Various operators can be used to manipulate data and these operators can be used with *variable*, *constant* and *literal data*. Operators can be used to manipulate data of all types.

Arithmetic operators

Your program might read two numbers and find their sum. It might find the difference between two prices. It might calculate VAT on a price or it might find the average of three ages. For these operations, you will need to be able to use *arithmetic operators* (see Tables 8.23 and 8.24).

Variable data: data that can change while a program is running. It is stored in the computer's memory and accessed by the program using an identifier (variable name). Example – an age might be stored as a variable called 'Age'.

Constant data: data that is given a value at the beginning of the program and remains the same while the program runs. The data is stored in the computer's memory, given a name to identify it, and marked as constant so that it can't be changed by accident. Example – the size of an array of items might be set as Arraysize = 8.

Literal data: data that is explicitly identified in the program. Literal data can be numeric or textual. Example – to set the initial value of a variable 'Total' to zero, the variable is assigned the literal value 0, e.g. Total = 0.

addition	+
subtraction	–
multiplication	*
division	/
assignment	= or :=

TABLE 8.23

below 10°C, find out if a count has reached 5, or check if menu option 4 has not been chosen. For these operations you will need to be able to use *relational operators* (see Tables 8.25 and 8.26).

Logical operators

Your program might need to use a combination of relational operators to check, for instance, if someone's height is greater than 1.75m and their age is less than 18. Your program might need to check if the result of a division is an error and the divisor was not 0. For these operations you will need to be able to use *logical operators* (see Table 8.27 and 8.28)

Relational operators

Your program might find the highest of two temperatures, check if a temperature has fallen

find the sum of two numbers (Num1 and Num2) and assign the answer to Sum	Sum = Num1 + Num2 Sum = Num1 + Num2; Sum:= Num1 + Num2; Sum = Num1 + Num2
find the difference between two prices (Price1 and Price2) and assign the answer to Diff	Diff = Price2 - Price1 Diff = Price2 - Price1; Diff:= Price2 - Price1; Diff = Price2 - Price1
calculate the VAT on a price	Vat = Price * 0.175 Vat = Price * 0.175; Vat := Price * 0.175; Vat = Price * 0.175
find the average of three prices (already added and called Total) and assign the answer to Average (a real variable)	Average = Total / 3 Average = (float)Total / 3; Average := Total / 3; Average = Total / 3
assign the value 0 to a variable Count	Count = 0 Count = 0; Count := 0; Count = 0

TABLE 8.24 *Examples of arithmetic operators (all given in the order Visual Basic, C, Pascal, JavaScript)*

less than	<
greater than	>
less than or equal to	<=
greater than or equal to	>=
equal to	= or ==
not equal to	<> or !=

TABLE 8.25

Logical operators are used in conjunction with relational operators and/or Boolean variables. Brackets are often required to ensure that comparisons and operations are done in the correct order.

Find the largest of two numbers (Num1 and Num2) and assign the largest number to the variable 'Largest'	If Num1>Num2 Then
	   Largest = Num1
	Else
	   Largest = Num2
	Endif
	
	if(Num1>Num2)
	   Largest = Num1;
	else
	   Largest = Num2;
	
	IF Num1>Num2 THEN
	   Largest := Num1
	ELSE
	   Largest := Num2;
	
	if(Num1>Num2){
	   Largest = Num1
	}
	else{
	   Largest = Num2
	}

Set a Boolean variable 'Negative' to true if Num1 is less than or equal to 0	If Num1 <= 0 Then
	   Negative = TRUE
	Else
	   Negative = FALSE
	Endif
	
	Negative = (Num1 <=0);
	
	Negative:= (Num1 <= 0);
	
	Negative = (Num1 <= 0)

Display a greeting on the screen if a menu choice of 3 is chosen	If MenuChoice = 3 Then
	   Text1.Text = "Hello"
	Endif

(Continued)

	if(MenuChoice == 3)
	   puts ("Hello")
	
	IF MenuChoice = 3 THEN
	   Writeln ("Hello");
	
	if(MenuChoice == 3){
	   document.write("Hello")
	   }

Set a Boolean variable 'Value' to true if Num1 is not 0	If Num1 <> 0 Then
	   Value = TRUE
	Else
	   Value = FALSE
	Endif
	
	Value = (Num1 != 0);
	Value:= (Num1 <> 0);
	Value = (Num1 !=0)

TABLE 8.26 *Examples of relational operators (all given in the order Visual Basic, C, Pascal, JavaScript. The use of 'IF' is explained in the next section)*

NOT	NOT or !
AND	AND or &&
OR	OR or ||

TABLE 8.27

Set a Boolean variable éTalí to true if a personís age is less than 18 and their height is greater than 1.75m	If (Age < 18) And (Height > 1.75) Then
	   Tall = TRUE
	     Else
	   Tall = FALSE
	Endif
	
	Tall = (Age < 18) && (Height > 1.75);
	Tall := (Age < 18) AND (Height > 1.75);
	Tall = (Age < 18) && (Height > 1.75)

Read names from a file while the end has not been reached	While Not EOF(1)
	     Input #1, Name
	Wend
	
	while(!eof(file1))
	  fscanf(file1, ì%sî, &name);
	
	WHILE NOT EOF(File1) DO
	  Readln(File1, name);
	
	n/a
	                                    (Continued)

Add one to a counter variable if Num1 is not between 1 and 5 (ie it is less than 1 or greater than 5)	If (Num1 < 1) Or (Num1 > 5) Then
	  Counter = Counter + 1
	Endif
	
	if((Num1 < 1) || (Num1 > 5))
	  Counter++;
	
	IF (Num1 < 1) OR (Num1 > 5) THEN
	  Counter := Counter + 1;
	
	if((Num1 < 1 || (Num1 > 5)){
	  Counter++
	
	}

TABLE 8.28 *Examples of logical operators (all given in the order Visual Basic, C, Pascal, JavaScript)*

Knowledge check

Can you write a definition, and give an example of your own, in the language you are studying, for each of the following?

- Arithmetic operator
- Relational operator
- Logical operator

Theory into practice

1 Write a program that reads two numbers and displays their sum.

2 Write a program that reads two prices and outputs their difference.

3 Write a program that reads two words and joins them together with the second word appearing before the first.

4 Write a program that reads a price and calculates 17.5% of the price for VAT.

5 Write a program that reads a person's age and height and determines whether they are a small adult (at least 18 years of ages and under 1.75m tall).

6 Write a program that reads two numbers and displays a message if they are the same.

7 Create a text file containing the following text:

Anderson
Brown
Chang

Write a program that reads the file and displays the names on the screen (see Figure 8.6). The following example shows the output for this program using a visual programming language. If you are programming in a non-visual language, you should create something equivalent.

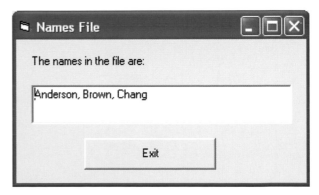

FIGURE 8.6 *File displaying names*

Tutorial 6 – Using operators

We will use the previous program but change the output form to display the result of some operations on the data. To do this we will:

✱ change the output form "frmOutput"

✱ change the Show List button to say "Show" and to output the total and average ages

✱ run the application.

Open the project you created in the last activity "NamesAgesArray".

Open the output form by double clicking on it in the Project Explorer window. Delete the labels "lblNameAge(0)" to lblNameAge(4)" and create two new labels called "lblAverage" and "lblTotal".

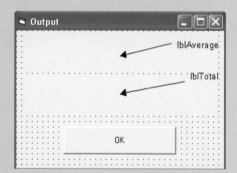

We will now need to change the code in frmMain for the click event of the Show List button so that it now creates a total and an average rather than a set of names and ages.

Save the project by selecting File, Save.

Open frmMain by double clicking on it in the Project Explorer window.

First, change the Caption on the button cmdShow to "Show".

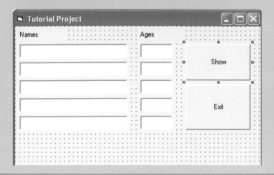

Open the code window. We will need two new variables: one to store the total age and one to store the average age. Add the following variable declarations:

```
Dim TheNames(5) As String
Dim TheAges(5) As Integer
Dim AllFilled As Boolean
Dim Total As Integer
Dim Average As Double
```

We will also need to change the cmdShow event code to calculate and display the total age and the average age. Change it so that it looks like this:

```
Private Sub cmdShow_Click()
    Total = TheAges(0) + TheAges(1) + TheAges(2) + TheAges(3) + TheAges(4)
    frmOutput.lblTotal.Caption = "The total age is: " + Str(Total)
    Average = Total / 5
    frmOutput.lblAverage.Caption = "The average age is: " + Str(Average)
    Load frmOutput
    frmOutput.Show
End Sub
```

Now try running the program.

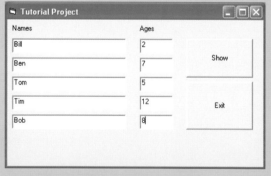

Save your project.

Sequence and selection

As we have seen in previous sections, programs consist of instructions to manipulate data. Those instructions might set up variables or constants to hold data:

```
int EmpNum;          /* C */
const int ArraySize = 10;
```

Think it over...

Can you remember what the four simple data types are?

The instructions might declare data structures to hold data in a particular way:

```
Dim EmpName As String     'Visual Basic
```

Think it over...

Can you remember the four main data structures?

The instructions might, alternatively, manipulate data using operators:

```
Total := Num1 + Num2;     { Pascal }
```

Think it over...

Can you list all the arithmetic, relational and logical operators?

Any computer program you write will consist of SEQUENCES of these instructions. If the instructions are in the correct order the program will do what is required.

Selection

Sometimes, you will want your program to make a choice and to carry out one set of instructions in one situation and a different set of instructions in another situation. All programming languages will have special control structures to allow selection of the required set of instructions.

1. Simple selection

Selection can take place in a number of ways. You might want your program to add a number on to a running total <u>only</u> if it is a positive number. In this case you want it to select to carry out an instruction or ignore it. This type of selection is performed using the IF...THEN instruction.

Example

Add a number to a running total only if it is a positive number.

```
IF Num > 0 THEN
      ADD number to Total
ENDIF
```
(See Table 8.29a and 8.29b.)

Theory into practice

Write a program that reads a number and displays the square of the number (the number multiplied by itself) if the number is not 0.

2. Two-way selection

You might want your program to read a salary and display a message stating that the salary is at least average or below average salary. In this case there are two possible outcomes: a message stating that the salary is at least average or a message stating that the salary is below average. This type of selection is performed using the IF...THEN...ELSE instruction.

Example

Read a salary and if the salary is at least average salary (£17,000), add it onto a total and display a message stating that it is at least average salary. Otherwise, display a message stating that it is below average.

```
READ Salary
IF Salary >= AverageSalary THEN
      ADD Total to TotalSalaries
      DISPLAY "Salary is at least average"
ELSE
      DISPLAY "Salary is below average"
ENDIF
```
(See Table 8.30a and 8.30b.)

IN VISUAL BASIC THIS IS WRITTEN:	IN C THIS IS WRITTEN:

If Num > 0 Then
    Total = Total + Num
Endif
	if (Num > 0);
	   Total += Num
	/* same as Total = Total + Num; */

TABLE 8.29a

IN PASCAL THIS IS WRITTEN:	IN JAVASCRIPT THIS IS WRITTEN

IF Num > 0 THEN
    Total := Total + Num;
	if (Num > 0) {
	   Total += Num
	}

TABLE 8.29b

IN VISUAL BASIC THIS IS WRITTEN:	IN C THIS IS WRITTEN:

If Salary >= Average-Salary Then
   TotalSalaries = TotalSalaries + Salary
   MsgBox "Salary is at least average"
Else
   MsgBox "Salary is below average
Endif
	if (Salary >= AverageSalary){
	  TotalSalaries + = Salary;
	  puts("Salary is at least average");
	}
	else
	   puts("Salary is below average");

TABLE 8.30a

IN PASCAL THIS IS WRITTEN:	IN JAVASCRIPT THIS IS WRITTEN

IF Salary >= Average Salary THEN
  BEGIN
  TotalSalaries := TotalSalaries + Salary;
  WriteLn ('Salary is at least average');
  END
ELSE
  WriteLn ('Salary is below average');
	if (Salary >=AverageSalary) {
	  TotalSalaries += Salary
	  alert("Salary is at least average")
	else{
	  alert("Salary is below average")
	}

TABLE 8.30b

Write a program that reads a number and displays a message stating either that the number is between 1 and 10 or that the number is out of range.

Write a program that reads a number and if that number is at least 50, displays a message stating that it is at least 50. Otherwise the program will add the number onto a total, display a message stating that it has added the number onto the total and display the new total (for this exercise, set the initial total to 10).

3. Multi-way selection

You may want to write programs where there are a number of choices of action depending on the value of one variable. For example, if your program uses a menu it will want to do something different for each menu option. A special instruction is used for this called a SELECT CASE instruction.

Example

Read a menu choice and display which option has been chosen. If option 1, 2 or 3 has been chosen display the option number; if option 4 is chosen display exit messages and if any other option is chosen, display an error message (See Table 8.31a and 8.31b).

```
READ MenuChoice
SELECT CASE MenuChoice
  1: DISPLAY "Option 1 chosen"
  2: DISPLAY "Option 2 chosen"
  3: DISPLAY "Option 3 chosen"
  4: DISPLAY "You have chosen to exit"
     DISPLAY "Goodbye!"
  OTHERWISE: DISPLAY "Invalid choice made"
END SELECT
```

Write a program that will display the following menu and carry out the appropriate instructions:

1 Add two numbers

2 Find the difference of two numbers

3 Multiply two numbers

4 Exit.

Give an example of each of the following in the language you are studying:

IF...THEN

IF...THEN...ELSE

SELECT CASE

There are some occasions when you might want to give three possible outcomes but you can't use a SELECT CASE (for example, if you want your program to state that a number is in one of three given ranges such as 1 to 10, 11 to 20 or above 20). Could you use IF...THEN...ELSE to cope with this?

Write a program that reads two numbers and displays the largest of the two numbers.

Write a program that will read two numbers and display their average on the screen only if both numbers are between 1 and 10.

IN VISUAL BASIC THIS IS WRITTEN:	IN C THIS IS WRITTEN:
| ```
MenuChoice = Text1.text
Select Case MenuChoice
   Case 1
      MsgBox "Option 1 chosen"
   Case 2
      MsgBox "Option 2 chosen"
   Case 3
      MsgBox "Option 3 chosen"
   Case 4
      MsgBox "You have chosen to exit"
      MsgBox "Goodbye!"
   Case Else
      MsgBox "Invalid choice made"
End Select
``` | ```
scanf("%d", &MenuChoice);
switch(MenuChoice){
   case 1:
      printf ("Option 1 chosen");
      break;
   case 2:
      printf ("Option 2 chosen");
      break;
   case 3:
      printf ("Option 3 chosen");
      break;
   case 4:
      printf ("You have chosen to exit");
      printf ("Goodbye!");
      break;
   default:
      printf ("Invalid choice made");
}
``` |

TABLE 8.31a

IN PASCAL THIS IS WRITTEN:	IN JAVASCRIPT THIS IS WRITTEN:
| ```
ReadLn (MenuChoice);
CASE MenuChoice OF
1: WriteLn ('Option 1 chosen');
2: WriteLn ('Option 2 chosen');
3: WriteLn ('Option 3 chosen');
4: BEGIN
  WriteLn ('You have chosen to exit');
  WriteLn ('Goodbye!');
  END;
ELSE
  WriteLn ('Invalid choice made');
END;
``` | ```
n/a
JavaScript does not
support a multiway selection statement
and you will need to use a series of 'if'
statements instead
e.g.
MenuChoice = prompt ("Enter choice")
if(MenuChoice==1){
   alert("Option 1 chosen")
}
if(MenuChoice==2){
   alert("Option 2 chosen"
}
if(MenuChoice==3){
   alert("Option 3 chosen"
}
if(MenuChoice==4){
   alert("You have chosen to exit,
goodbye")
}
``` |

TABLE 8.31b

Tutorial 7 – Selection

This version of the program will add some selection. We will add a drop-down list (or combo box) to select the output we want and we will use selection code to choose the correct output and to select the oldest or the youngest person. To do this we will:

* open an existing project – NameAgeHeight

* add a combo box with the choices – Find Oldest, Find Youngest and Find Average

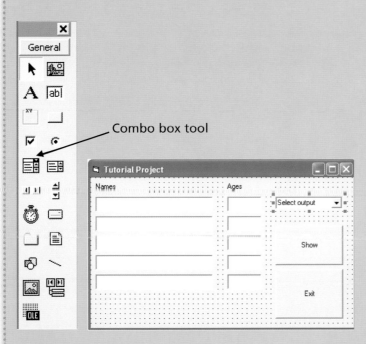

Combo box tool

* change the code for the Show button click event to select the correct type of output

* run the application.

Open the project you saved in the last tutorial – NameAgeHeight – remember to open the Project file and not the form.

First we will add a drop-down list or combo box. Move the Show and Exit buttons down to make room for a combo box. Use the control bar to select combo box and draw the box. Set the Name property to "cmbOutput" and the Text property to "Select output".

We now need to add the items to the list. The items go in the List property. Click on the List property and a list will open. Type the items into the list. Once you have entered an item you can press the return key and the next time you open the List you can add the next item.

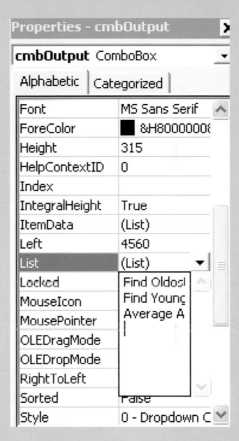

The input form is now ready. We will need to change the output form because now there will be only one output which will be either the oldest person, the youngest person or the average age.

Open the output form by double clicking on it in the Project Explorer window. Remove lblTotal and rename lblAverage to lblResult.

We will use a Select Case statement to select the correct output. We can identify which item was chosen in the combo box as its number will be stored in the property ListIndex.

Open frmMain and open the code window. First, add variable declarations for the oldest age, youngest age, position of the oldest and position of the youngest.

```
Dim TheNames(5) As String
Dim TheAges(5) As Integer
Dim AllFilled As Boolean
Dim Total As Integer
Dim Average As Double
Dim Oldest As Integer
Dim OldIndex As Integer
Dim Youngest As Integer
Dim YoungIndex As Integer
```

Change the code in the cmdShow click event as follows:

Try running the program to see that it does what it should.

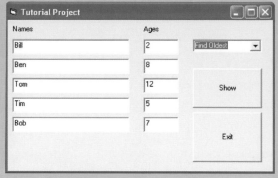

```
Private Sub cmdShow_Click()
    Select Case cmbOutput.ListIndex
        Case 0
            Oldest = 0
            If TheAges(0) > Oldest Then
                Oldest = TheAges(0)
                OldIndex = 0
            End If
            If TheAges(1) > Oldest Then
                Oldest = TheAges(1)
                OldIndex = 1
            End If
            If TheAges(2) > Oldest Then
                Oldest = TheAges(2)
                OldIndex = 2
            End If
            If TheAges(3) > Oldest Then
                Oldest = TheAges(3)
                OldIndex = 3
            End If
            If TheAges(4) > Oldest Then
                Oldest = TheAges(4)
                OldIndex = 4
            End If
            frmOutput.lblResult.Caption = "The oldest person is: " + TheNames(OldIndex) + " at " + Str(TheAges(OldIndex)) + " years."
        Case 1
            Youngest = 32767
            If TheAges(0) < Youngest Then
                Youngest = TheAges(0)
                YoungIndex = 0
            End If
            If TheAges(1) < Youngest Then
                Youngest = TheAges(1)
                YoungIndex = 1
            End If
            If TheAges(2) < Youngest Then
                Youngest = TheAges(2)
                YoungIndex = 2
            End If
            If TheAges(3) < Youngest Then
                Youngest = TheAges(3)
                YoungIndex = 3
            End If
            If TheAges(4) < Youngest Then
                Youngest = TheAges(4)
                YoungIndex = 4
            End If
            frmOutput.lblResult.Caption = "The youngest person is: " + TheNames(YoungIndex) + " at " + Str(TheAges(YoungIndex)) + " years."
        Case 2
            Total = TheAges(0) + TheAges(1) + TheAges(2) + TheAges(3) + TheAges(4)
            Average = Total / 5
            frmOutput.lblResult.Caption = "The average age is: " + Str(Average)
        Case Else
            MsgBox "Invalid choice made"
    End Select
    Load frmOutput
    frmOutput.Show
```

(Continued)

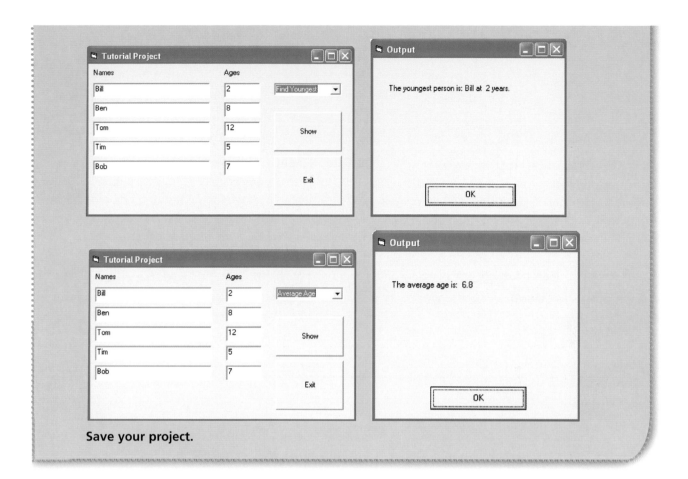

Save your project.

Repetition (iteration)

> ✳ **REMEMBER!**
>
> One of the main advantages of using computers is their ability to repeat a set of tasks over and over again until it is necessary or desirable to stop.

All programming languages will include special instructions, which cause a group of individual instructions to be repeated until a given condition arises.

For example, a program might read an input over and over again until the input is within a given range.

There are three distinct ways of repeating instructions.

1. Count-controlled repetition

The program repeats a set of instructions a given number of times. For example, a program might read a number ten times and each time add it on to a running total. A variable for holding a count is needed. This variable is often called i.

The instruction for count-controlled repetition is generally:

FOR...NEXT

Example
Read 10 numbers and add them to a running total.

    SET Total to 0
    FOR i = 1 to 10
        PROMPT for number
        READ number
        ADD number to Total
    NEXT
(See Table 8.32)

---

2. Repetition with test on entry

The program repeats a set of instructions a number of times. Each time it performs the instructions, it first checks to see if they should be performed. The set of instructions will never be performed if the check indicates that it shouldn't on its first go.

The instruction for test-on-entry repetition is generally:

WHILE...DO

Example

Read and add together numbers while the total of the numbers is less than 10.

```
SET Total to 0
WHILE Total < 10 DO
    PROMPT for number
    READ number
    ADD number to Total
ENDWHILE
(See Table 8.33)
```

3. Repetition with test on exit

The program repeats a set of instructions a number of times. After each time it will check whether it should perform them again. The set of instructions will always be performed once. This type of loop is used extensively in validation of input.

The instruction for test-on-exit repetition is generally:

DO...WHILE or REPEAT...UNTIL

Example

Read a number between 1 and 10.

```
DO
    PROMPT for number
    READ number
    IF number < 1 OR number > 10 THEN
        DISPLAY "Number out of range"
    ENDIF
WHILE number < 1 OR number > 10
(See Table 8.34a and 8.34b)
```

IN VISUAL BASIC THIS IS WRITTEN:	IN C THIS IS WRITTEN:	IN PASCAL THIS IS WRITTEN:	IN JAVASCRIPT THIS IS WRITTEN

Total = 0
For i = 1 To 10
   number = Int (Text1.Text)
Total = Total + number
Next
	Total = 0;
	for(i=0; i<10; i++){
	   scanf("%d", &number);
	   Total = Total + number;
	}
		Total := 0;
		FOR i := 1 TO 10 DO
		  BEGIN
		  ReadLn(number);
		  Total := Total + number;
		  END;
			Total = 0
			for (i=0; i<10; i++){
			   number = parseInt (prompt(""))
			   Total = Total + number
			}

TABLE 8.32

IN VISUAL BASIC THIS IS WRITTEN:	IN C THIS IS WRITTEN:	IN PASCAL THIS IS WRITTEN:	IN JAVASCRIPT THIS IS WRITTEN

Total = 0
While Total < 10
   Number = Int(Text1.Text)
   Total = Total + number
Wend
	Total = 0;
	while(Total<10){
	   scanf("%d",&number);
	   Total = Total + number;
	}
		Total := 0;
		WHILE Total < 10 DO
		  BEGIN
		  ReadLn (number);
		  Total := Total + Number;
		  END;
			Total = 0;
			while(Total<10){
			   number = parseInt (prompt(""))
			   Total = Total + number
			  }

TABLE 8.33

IN VISUAL BASIC THIS IS WRITTEN:	IN C THIS IS WRITTEN:
```Repeat Number = Int(Text1.Text) If number < 1 Or number > 10 Then MsgBox "Number out of range" End If Until number >= 1 AND number < = 10```	```do{ scanf("%d", &number); if(number<1 ||number > 10) printf("Number out of range"); }while(number<1 || number > 10);```

TABLE 8.34a

IN PASCAL THIS IS WRITTEN:	IN JAVASCRIPT THIS IS WRITTEN
```Total := 0; REPEAT ReadLn (number); If number <1 OR number>10 THEN Write Ln ('Number out of range'); UNTIL (number > = 1) AND (number < = 10);```	```Total = 0; do{ number = parseInt(prompt("")) if (number <1 || number >10) { alert ("Number out of range") }while(number<1 || number > 10)```

TABLE 8.34b

Theory into practice

Write a program that will read a number between 10 and 100 and display the number on the screen.

Knowledge check

Write a definition of each of the following and give an example of each in the language you are studying:

count-controlled repetition

test on exit

test on entry

There are some occasions when repetition is required indefinitely. Find out how to write an infinite loop (one that never ends) in the language you are studying.

Theory into practice

Write a program that reads 8 numbers and finds the largest and smallest of those 8 numbers.

Write a program that reads 8 numbers while the largest of the 8 numbers is less than 10.

Write a program that will read two numbers between 1 and 10 and display their average on the screen.

Tutorial 8 – Repetition

This version of the program will add some repetition. We will add a new item to the drop-down list (or combo box). This item will select the output to produce a string of names. Also, we will add some code to check that each age entered is between 5 and 50. The program will now check an age once it has been entered, then if it is out of range it will use an input box

to get a new age. It will do this repeatedly until the age is within range. To do this we will:

* open an existing project – NameAgeHeight

* add an extra item to the combo box choices – List all names

* change the code for the Show button click event to deal with the extra output using a FOR...NEXT loop

* use the LostFocus event of the Age text boxes to add validation code

* run the application.

Open the project you saved in the last tutorial – NameAgeHeight – remember to open the Project file and not the form.

First we will add an item "List all names" to the drop-down list or combo box.

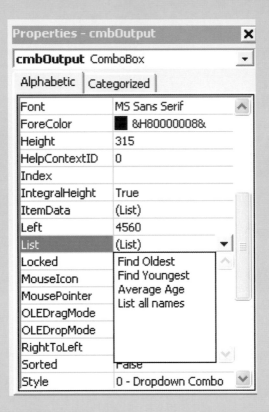

Open the code window and add some extra code into the Select Case statement in the click event of the Show button to deal with the new output using a FOR...NEXT loop. The output will be put in the same label on the output form as the other choices. We will also need to add "Dim NameStr As String" and "Dim i as Integer" to the variable list (i will hold the current position in the arrays while working through the names).

```
    Case 2
        Total = TheAges(0) + TheAges(1) + TheAges(2) + TheAges(3) + TheAges(4)
        Average = Total / 5
        frmOutput.lblResult.Caption = "The average age is: " + Str(Average)
    Case 3
        NameStr = ""
        For i = 0 To 4
            NameStr = NameStr + TheNames(i) + " "
        Next
        frmOutput.lblResult.Caption = NameStr
    Case Else
        MsgBox "Invalid choice made"
End Select
```

New code

(Continued)

Now we will add some code to validate the Age input. The Change event happens as soon as anything is typed into the text box. We want to check the code when the typing in that text box is finished so we will use the LostFocus event which happens when you move to the next control.

Remove the Change event code and add the LostFocus event code (select txtAges from the controls drop down list and then LostFocus from the event drop down list).

```
Private Sub txtAges_LostFocus(Index As Integer)
    TheAges(Index) = Int(Val(txtAges(Index).Text))
    While TheAges(Index) < 5 Or TheAges(Index) > 50
        txtAges(Index).Text = InputBox("You must enter a number between 5 and 50", "Age Error", "")
        TheAges(Index) = Int(Val(txtAges(Index).Text))
    Wend
    AllFilled = TheNames(0) <> "" And TheNames(1) <> "" And TheNames(2) <> "" And TheNames(3) <> "" And TheNames(4) <> ""
    AllFilled = AllFilled And TheAges(0) <> 0 And TheAges(1) <> 0 And TheAges(2) <> 0 And TheAges(3) <> 0 And TheAges(4) <> 0
    cmdShow.Enabled = AllFilled
End Sub
```

Now run the program. Enter some names and then try entering an age below 5. You will see the input box.

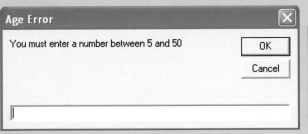

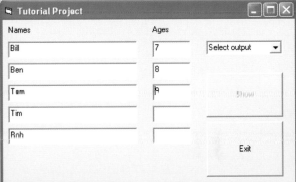

You can type in any invalid age and the box will keep reappearing until you type an age that is between 5 and 50.

Now, type in a valid age, such as 9 and click OK.

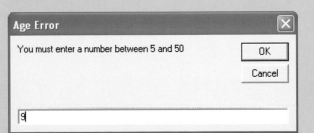

We will now look at the new output. Fill in all the boxes so that the Show button is enabled. Select "List all names" from the combo box then click on the Show button.

This time it will be accepted.

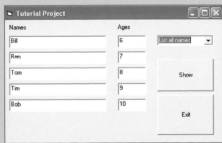

Save your project.

Data manipulation

Data comes in a number of different forms. For instance, it might be numeric, alphabetic, stored individually or stored together. Data is processed according to its type and structure. Single data types can be processed using standard operators. Data structures must be dealt with differently. This section explains how to deal with data structures such as strings, arrays and records.

Data, in whatever form, will be read into a program and will be written by the program. Data can be read from a keyboard, from a file or from some other input device. Data can be written to a screen, a printer, a file, or to some other output device. This section will cover input from keyboard and file and output to screen and file. You can write a wide variety of simple programs using these types of input and output. You may want to do some research of your own to find out how the programming language you are using deals with other sorts of input and output.

Dealing with strings

Some languages use the standard operators for dealing with strings. To assign a string to a variable the assignment operator (= or :=) is used. To join two strings together the addition operator is used (+) and to remove part of a string the subtraction operator is used (–). Languages such as C use special instructions for strings.

Examples of string operations

Assign an employee's surname to a string variable 'EmpSur' and an employee's first name to a string variable 'EmpFirst' (see Table 8.35).

Join the two strings together, with a space in between, to form the new string 'EmpName'.

Other functions and methods are available in each programming language for dealing with strings (see Table 8.36).

IN VISUAL BASIC THIS IS WRITTEN:	IN C THIS IS WRITTEN:	IN PASCAL THIS IS WRITTEN:	IN JAVASCRIPT THIS IS WRITTEN

Dim EmpSur As String
Dim EmpFirst As String
 	
EmpSur = "Smith";
EmpFirst = "Will"
	#include <string.h>
	char EmpSur [30];
	char EmpFirst [30];
	
	strcpy(EmpSur ,"Smith");
	strcpy(EmpFirst, "Will");
		VAR
		EmpSur : STRING[30];
		EmpFirst: STRING[30];
		
		EmpSur := 'Smith';
		EmpFirst := 'Will';
			var EmpSur = "Smith"
			var EmpFirst = "Will"

TABLE 8.35

IN VISUAL BASIC THIS IS WRITTEN:	IN C THIS IS WRITTEN:

Dim EmpSur As String
Dim EmpFirst As String
Dim EmpName As String
 	
EmpSur = "Smith"
EmpFirst = "Will"
EmpName = EmpFirst + " " + EmpSur
	#include <string.h>
	char EmpSur [30];
	char EmpFirst [30];
	char EmpName [60] = "";
	
	strcpy(EmpSur ,"Smith");
	strcpy(EmpFirst, "Will");
	strcat(EmpName, EmpFirst);
	strcat(EmpName, " ");
	strcat(EmpName, EmpSur);

TABLE 8.36a

IN PASCAL THIS IS WRITTEN:	IN JAVASCRIPT THIS IS WRITTEN

VAR EmpSur : STRING[30];
  EmpFirst: STRING[30];
  EmpName:STRING[60];
 	
EmpSur := 'Smith';
EmpFirst := 'Will';
EmpName := CONCAT (EmpFirst,' ', EmpSur);
	var EmpSur = "Smith"
	var EmpFirst = "Will"
	var EmpName = ""
	EmpName = EmpFirst + " "+Empsur

TABLE 8.36b

Theory into practice

Can you find out how to do the following in the programming language you are studying?

get the length of a string

remove part of a string

get the first three characters of a string

Arrays and records

Arrays and records are dealt with by accessing each element or field separately. Each element or field is a simple data type and can be processed using the standard operators.

Key terms

Arrays: collection of data of the same type, stored together. Example – a set of ages might be stored together so that they can be sorted into order and used for calculating statistics such as averages. Each item in an array is called an element and is referred to by its position in the array.

Records: collection of data of different types stored together because all data refers to the same thing. Example – a set of data might be stored about an address. This address might include a house number (integer), a road name (string), a town name (string) and a postcode (string). Each item of data is called a field and is referred to using the record name and the field name.

File handling

Key terms

A file: a collection of data stored on disk, CD, tape or other storage media. Data is organised in a set order and the program must read and write the data in that order. You will need to know the instructions available for opening, closing, reading from and writing to files in the language you are studying.

A file's location: where the file exists on the storage media. For instance, if a file is stored on the main hard disk of a system running the Windows® operating system, its location will include 'C:\' to indicate that it is stored on the hard disk and the full directory path of the file, e.g. 'C:\My Documents\Data Files\Myfile.txt'

You are expected to write simple programs and these will read and write data from simple *file* organisations. In most cases, the data in the file will be organised as it would if it were read from the keyboard, that is, each line contains a separate data item. The examples used here will assume this to be the case and will show files created as text files with the suffix '.txt'.

Before a file can be manipulated it must be opened. To open a file you must know the exact *location* and name of the file, as it would be recognised by the operating system. You will use this name and the 'open' instruction to ensure that the file is opened, ready to be either read from or written to.

Find out how to do the following in the language you are studying:

Open a file for reading

Open a file for overwriting (either creating a new file or overwriting what was there)

Open a file for appending data (adding data to the end of the file)

Check to see if the end of a file has been eached

Read data from a file

Write data to the current end of the file

Close a file

Tutorial 9 – File handling

This time we will get input from a file instead of through a form. We will create a new project to read five names and ages from a file and create the same outputs as before (oldest, youngest, total age and all names). To do this we will:

* create a new project

* create a text file using Notepad and containing five names and ages

* add code to read the file and store the names and ages in two arrays

* add all other code as in the last project

* run the application.

Create a new Project. Name the main form frmMain and add three buttons and a combo box as shown.

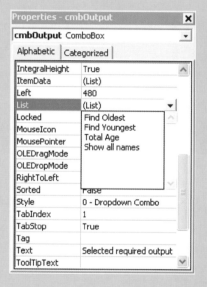

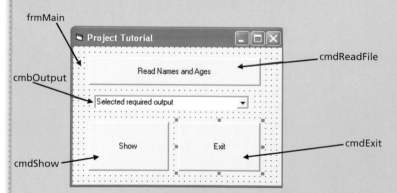

Add items to the combo box List. After you have typed each item, hold down the Control key and press Enter: this will give you a new line.

Now we will create an output form. Name it frmOutput and change its Caption to "Output". Add controls as shown.

(Continued)

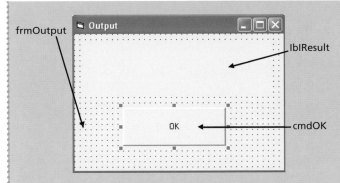

frmOutput

lblResult

OK — cmdOK

Data will now be read from a file – so we had better create one!

Open Notepad and create a new text file as shown. Save it as a text file with the name "DataFile" and keep note of the full path name to where it is saved. (The full path to this file is "C:\Documents and Settings\Brian\My Documents\DataFile.txt").

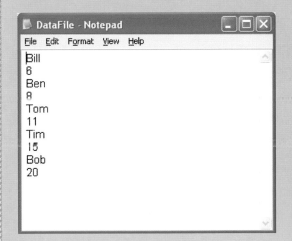

We now need to add some code. Open frmMain and open its code window.

First we will add some variables to hold the names, ages, Oldest, Youngest, Total, string of names and other data.

```
Dim TheNames(5) As String
Dim TheAges(5) As Integer
Dim AgeStr As String
Dim Total As Integer
Dim NameStr As String
Dim Oldest As Integer
Dim OldestIndex As Integer
Dim Youngest As Integer
Dim YoungestIndex As Integer
Dim i As Integer
```

Next add the code for the cmdExit button, the frmMain load event and the cmdReadFile button.

```
Private Sub cmdExit_Click()
    Unload frmMain
End Sub

Private Sub cmdReadFile_Click()
    Open "C:\Documents and Settings\Brian\My Documents\DataFile.txt" For Input As #1
    For i = 0 To 4
        Input #1, TheNames(i)
        Input #1, AgeStr
        TheAges(i) = Int(Val(AgeStr))
    Next
    Close #1
    cmdShow.Enabled = True
End Sub

Private Sub Form_Load()
    cmdShow.Enabled = False
End Sub
```

Now let's add the code to produce the output. Add the click event for the cmdShow button. It is almost identical to the code in the last project.

```
Private Sub cmdShow_Click()
    Select Case cmbOutput.ListIndex
        Case 0
            Oldest = 0
            For i = 0 To 4
                If TheAges(i) > Oldest Then
                    OldestIndex = i
                    Oldest = TheAges(i)
                End If
            Next
            frmOutput.lblResult.Caption = "The oldest person is " + TheNames(OldestIndex) + " at " + Str(TheAges(OldestIndex))
        Case 1
            Youngest = 32767
            For i = 0 To 4
                If TheAges(i) < Youngest Then
                    YoungestIndex = i
                    Youngest = TheAges(i)
                End If
            Next
            frmOutput.lblResult.Caption = "The youngest person is " + TheNames(YoungestIndex) + " at " + Str(TheAges(YoungestIndex))
        Case 2
            Total = 0
            For i = 0 To 4
                Total = Total + TheAges(i)
            Next
            frmOutput.lblResult.Caption = "The total of the ages is " + Str(Total)
        Case 3
            NameStr = ""
            For i = 0 To 4
                NameStr = NameStr + TheNames(i) + " "
            Next
            frmOutput.lblResult.Caption = NameStr
        Case Else
            MsgBox "You have selected an invalid option"
    End Select
    If cmbOutput.ListIndex >= 0 And cmbOutput.ListIndex <= 3 Then
        Load frmOutput
        frmOutput.Show
    End If
End Sub
```

Try running the program.

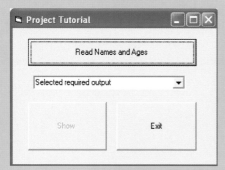

Click on the Read Names and Ages to read the file and enable the Show button.

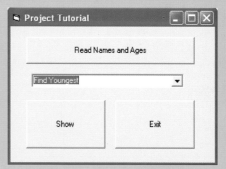

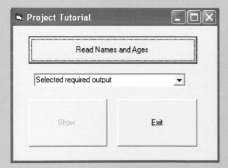

Select Find Youngest from the combo box and click on Show.

Save your project – naming it "FileHandling".

By now you will be able to write a program in the language you are studying, using the correct structure for a program. You will be able to:

* declare variables and constants;
* use operators to manipulate and create new data;
* write program instructions to carry out the required processing;
* use selection and repetition as required;
* declare data structures;
* use appropriate instructions to manipulate data structures;
* handle data that comes from files.

When you are confident that you can do these, you will be able to complete the following case study.

Subroutines

As programs get larger and larger they become much more difficult to read and to follow. As your programs get larger you will find it more difficult to keep track of what you have done and more difficult to find and correct errors.

Your programs will be much easier to follow and to maintain if they are organised into sections. Subroutines are small sections of

CASE STUDY

A company needs a new program that will read a file of employee details and produce a report. The file format is shown in Table 8.37.

FIELD NAME	FIELD TYPE
Surname	Text/String
First Name	Text/String
Years Service	Integer
Salary	Real/Floating point

TABLE 8.37

The data in the file will look like the following:

```
...
Smith
Will
5
21832
Patel
Raj
10
28840
...
```

The program must read all the records in the file and print the details out on the screen in the form of a report similar to that shown below:

EMPLOYEE NAME	YEARS SERVICE	SALARY
...	...	...
Will Smith	5	21832
Raj Patel	10	28840
...	...	...
	TOTAL SALARIES	...

program (almost mini programs) that carry out one particular task. When you create subroutines you are creating your own new instructions and defining how those instructions will work.

If you are using a language such as Visual Basic you will be forced to write your programs in separate sections. Visual Basic itself makes sure that the individual sections happen at the correct time.

If you are using C, Pascal or JavaScript you could well have written all your programs so far without writing any subroutines. You will need to learn how to separate your program instructions into subroutines and to write your programs so that those subroutines run in the correct order.

Defining subroutines

Visual Basic – many subroutines are defined for you. Visual Basic uses Sub to refer to subroutines. When you write the code for the click event of a command button you will be given an outline subroutine:

```
Private Sub cmdOK_Click()

End Sub
```

All the instructions to be carried out when the OK button is clicked are entered into this subroutine and Visual Basic deals with making sure it runs at the correct time.

However, there might be a lot of instructions to be carried out when the OK button is clicked and so it might still be good to divide the code up. There might be a lot of instructions used to collect data from text boxes. You could define your own instruction "GetData" which will collect all the data from the text boxes.

To do this you would add the instruction "GetData" to the cmdOK_Click() subroutine:

```
Private Sub cmdOK_Click()

  GetData

End Sub
```

Then, somewhere **above** this, you would define what "GetData" does by writing the instructions for getting data from individual text boxes.

```
Private Sub GetData()

  Num1 = int(Text1.text)

  Num2 = int(Text2.text)

  Num3 = int(Text3.text)

  Num4 = int(Text4.text)

End Sub
```

Now, whenever the instruction "GetData" appears, the processor will know to collect four numbers from the four text boxes.

C – subroutines in C are called functions. Many functions are already written and you will already be using them (e.g. printf(), scanf(), gets()). You will already be familiar with writing the int main() function or the void main() function. All program instructions will so far have been entered into the main() function.

The following code gets four separate numbers from the user and will then go on to do something with those numbers.

```
void main() {
    printf ("Enter 1st number: ");
    scanf ("%d", &Num1 );
    printf ("Enter 2nd number: ");
    scanf ("%d", &Num2 );
    printf ("Enter 3rd number: ");
    scanf ("%d", &Num3 );
    printf ("Enter 4th number: ");
    scanf ("%d", &Num4 );
    ...
    ...
}
```

You could define your own instruction GetData() which will collect all the data from the user.

To do this you would replace the printf() and scanf() instructions in the main() function with the instruction GetData():

```
void main() {
    GetData();
    ...
    ...
}
```

Then, somewhere **above** this, you would define what GetData() does by writing the instructions for getting data from the user.

```
void GetData() {
    printf ("Enter 1st number: ");
    scanf ("%d", &Num1 );
    printf ("Enter 2nd number: ");
    scanf ("%d", &Num2 );
    printf ("Enter 3rd number: ");
    scanf ("%d", &Num3 );
    printf ("Enter 4th number: ");
    scanf ("%d", &Num4 );
}
```

Now, whenever the instruction 'GetData()' appears, the processor will know to collect four numbers from the user.

Key term

Void: all C functions have a type (e.g. int main()) and they produce one item of data of this type that must be stored or used each time the function is used. However, if the function's type is void, no data is produced. To keep things simple, you will use functions of type void only and so won't have to worry about what to do with the function's resulting data.

Pascal – subroutines in Pascal are called either procedures or functions. A procedure carries out a set of instructions and a function does the same but also produces an item of data to be stored in memory. You will need to be able to use only procedures for this unit. Some procedures are already written and you will already be using them (e.g. Write(), WriteLn(), ReadLn()). All program instructions will so far have been entered into the program between the BEGIN and END keywords.

The following code gets four separate numbers from the user and will then go on to do something with those numbers.

```
BEGIN
    Write ("Enter 1st number: ");
    ReadLn (Num1 );
    Write ("Enter 2nd number: ");
    ReadLn (Num2 );
    Write ("Enter 3rd number: ");
    ReadLn (Num3 );
    Write ("Enter 4th number: ");
    ReadLn (Num4 );
    ...
    ...
END.
```

You could define your own instruction GetData() that will collect all the data from the user.

To do this you would replace the Write() and ReadLn() instructions in the main part of the program with the instruction GetData:

```
BEGIN
    GetData;
    ...
END.
```

Then, somewhere **above** this, you would define what GetData does by writing the instructions for getting data from the user.

```
PROCEDURE GetData;
BEGIN
    Write ("Enter 1st number: ");
    ReadLn (Num1 );
    Write ("Enter 2nd number: ");
    ReadLn (Num2 );
    Write ("Enter 3rd number: ");
    ReadLn (Num3 );
    Write ("Enter 4th number: ");
    ReadLn (Num4 );
END;
```

Now, whenever the instruction 'GetData' appears, the processor will know to collect four numbers from the user.

JavaScript – subroutines in JavaScript are called functions. Many functions are already written and you will already be using them (e.g. alert(), prompt()). All program instructions will so far have been entered into the main body of code.

The following code gets four separate numbers from the user, using prompt(), and will then go on to do something with those numbers.

```
<script language = "Javascript"
type = "text/javascript">
    Num1 = prompt("Enter 1st number: ","")
    Num2 = prompt("Enter 2nd number: ","")
    Num3 = prompt("Enter 3rd number: ","")
    Num4 = prompt("Enter 4th number: ","")
    ...
    ...
</script>
```

You could define your own instruction GetData() which will collect all the data from the user.

To do this you would replace the prompt() instructions in the main script with the instruction GetData():

```
<script language = "Javascript
type = "text/javascript">
    GetData()
    ...
    ...
</script>
```

Then, somewhere **above** this, you would define what GetData() does by writing the instructions for getting data from the user.

```
function GetData() {
    Num1 = prompt("Enter 1st number: ","")
    Num2 = prompt("Enter 2nd number: ","")
    Num3 = prompt("Enter 3rd number: ","")
    Num4 = prompt("Enter 4th number: ","")
}
```

Now, whenever the instruction 'GetData()' appears, the processor will know to collect four numbers from the user.

Theory into practice

Write a program that reads three numbers, finds the average of those three numbers and displays the average and the total of those three numbers. Your program should consist of three subroutines (GetNumbers, FindAverage, DisplayAnswers).

Knowledge check

Subroutine – a set of instructions which, together, carry out one particular task. A subroutine is defined and, once defined, its name becomes a new instruction that can be used by a program.

Function – another name for a subroutine used by C, Pascal and JavaScript. All functions produce one single piece of data as a result.

Procedure – another name for a subroutine used by Pascal. A procedure is a simple function.

Defining a subroutine – this is done in a different way by each language.

    Private Sub GetData()

    void GetData()

    PROCEDURE GetData

    function GetData()

Calling a subroutine – once a subroutine has been defined it can be called from any point in the program as long as it is below where the subroutine is defined. A subroutine is called simply by using its name as given in its definition (GetData() or GetData).

Tutorial 10 – Subroutines

The last project used a case statement to select the required output. The case statement had all the code for finding the oldest, youngest, total and list of names. The code would look much neater if we could separate out the bits that do the actual output from the bits which select the type of output. We will create subroutines to produce the same outputs as before (oldest, youngest, total age and all names). We will replace the code in the case statement with the names of the subroutines.

To do this we will:

* open the project "FileHandling"

* open the code window for frmMain and add four subroutines

* change the code in the case statement to use the subroutines

* run the application.

Open the project "FileHandling". Make sure that frmMain is open and open the code window.

Type in the subroutines "Find_Oldest", "Find_Youngest", "Find_Total" and "Show_Names". They must be added **above** the click event for the Show button – "CmdShow_Click".

```
Private Sub Find_Oldest()
    Oldest = 0
    For i = 0 To 4
        If TheAges(i) > Oldest Then
            OldestIndex = i
            Oldest = TheAges(i)
        End If
    Next
    frmOutput.lblResult.Caption = "The oldest person is " + TheNames(OldestIndex) + " at " + Str(TheAges(OldestIndex))
End Sub

Private Sub Find_Youngest()
    Youngest = 32767
    For i = 0 To 4
        If TheAges(i) < Youngest Then
            YoungestIndex = i
            Youngest = TheAges(i)
        End If
    Next
    frmOutput.lblResult.Caption = "The youngest person is " + TheNames(YoungestIndex) + " at " + Str(TheAges(YoungestIndex))
End Sub

Private Sub Find_Total()
    Total = 0
    For i = 0 To 4
        Total = Total + TheAges(i)
    Next
    frmOutput.lblResult.Caption = "The total of the ages is " + Str(Total)
End Sub

Private Sub Show_Names()
    NameStr = ""
    For i = 0 To 4
        NameStr = NameStr + TheNames(i) + " "
    Next
    frmOutput.lblResult.Caption = NameStr
End Sub
```

Now change the code in the Show button click event to use the subroutines.

```
Private Sub cmdShow_Click()
    Select Case cmbOutput.ListIndex
        Case 0
            Find_Oldest
        Case 1
            Find_Youngest
        Case 2
            Find_Total
        Case 3
            Show_Names
        Case Else
            MsgBox "You have selected an invalid option"
    End Select
    If cmbOutput.ListIndex >= 0 And cmbOutput.ListIndex <= 3 Then
        Load frmOutput
        frmOutput.Show
    End If
End Sub
```

Run the program. Make sure you try all the different types of output.

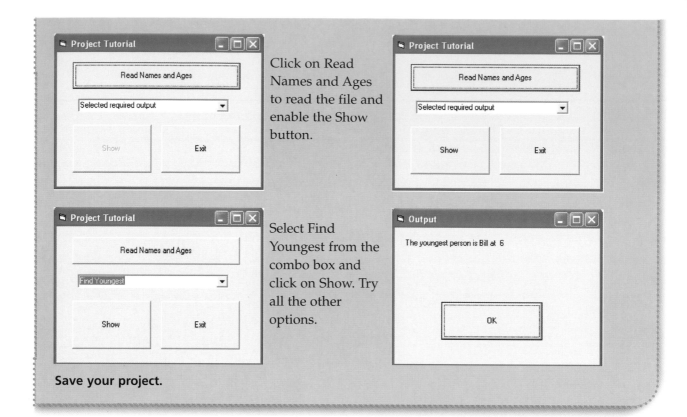

Click on Read Names and Ages to read the file and enable the Show button.

Select Find Youngest from the combo box and click on Show. Try all the other options.

Save your project.

Local and global variables

You will already have learnt how to declare variables of different *data types* and of different *data structures*.

So far, you have learnt to declare variables at the top of each program you write. This is because you want to be able to use these variables anywhere within the program.

In the last section you learned to break your program into smaller sections called *subroutines*.

When you declare variables, the computer will allocate memory for data of the given type and will store its name so that it can remember where the data is.

Example
Dim Num As Integer

The computer will allocate a piece of memory just the right size for an integer (often 4 bytes) and will store the name of the variable (Num) in a table alongside the address of the allocated memory (see Table 8.38).

VARIABLE NAME	MEMORY ADDRESS
Num	00000FFF

TABLE 8.38

All variables declared at the top of your program are allocated a memory address. This memory remains allocated until the program ends. All parts of the program can access this memory using the name of the variable. Because these variables are available for the duration of the program and can be used by any part of the program they are known as *global* variables.

When a program has been written to use subroutines, there might be variables that are only used by one subroutine. If these variables are declared at the top of the program, they take up memory for the entire time the program runs, when they are used only while a particular subroutine is running. This is not an economic use of memory and makes your program larger than it needs to be.

When you write subroutines, you can declare variables inside those subroutines. The variables will then be allocated when the subroutine starts and will be deleted when it ends. If the subroutine is used again, new memory is allocated and then deleted when the subroutine ends the second time. This is good housekeeping. Memory is being used only when needed and is free for use at other times.

You declare local variables in exactly the same way as global variables but you do so inside the subroutine code. Local variables can be used only by the subroutine in which they are declared and it is important to remember that they are destroyed as soon as the subroutine ends (i.e. as soon as the new instruction defined by the subroutine has been carried out).

Example
A subroutine named FindAverage will calculate the average of three numbers. The average is needed elsewhere in the program, where it will be written on the screen. However, in calculating the average the subroutine will find a total. This total is needed only to calculate the average and will not be used anywhere else.

The 'Total' variable can be a local variable, used only in the FindAverage subroutine.

The 'Average' variable must be a global variable as it is used in the FindAverage subroutine AND in the main program or other subroutines.

→ Declare a global variable 'Average' of type real and a local variable 'Total' of type integer (see Table 8.39).

IN VISUAL BASIC THIS IS WRITTEN:	IN C THIS IS WRITTEN:	IN PASCAL THIS IS WRITTEN:	IN JAVASCRIPT THIS IS WRITTEN

Dim Average As Double
 	
Private Sub FindAverage()
  Dim Total As Integer
  Total = Num1 + Num2
    + Num3
  Average = Total / 3
End Sub
	float Average;
	
	void FindAverage() {
	  int Total;
	  Total = Num1 + Num2
	    + Num3;
	  Average = Total / 3;
	}
		VAR Average: REAL;
		
		PROCEDURE FindAverage;
		VAR Total: INTEGER;
		BEGIN
		  Total := Num1 + Num2
		    + Num3;
		  Average := Total / 3;
		END;
			var Average = 0.00
			
			function FindAverage(){
			  var Total = 0
			
			  Total = Num1 + Num2
			    + Num3
			  Average = Total / 3
			}

TABLE 8.39

Tutorial 11 – Using local variables

Now that we have a selection of subroutines, we will have some variables that are used only in one subroutine. If this is the case then it is more efficient to declare the variables in the subroutine that are at the top of the code. We will move some variables from the top of the code to within the subroutines where they are used. To do this we will:

* open the "FileHandling" project

* cut and paste various local variables to the subroutines where they are used

* copy and paste the counting variable i to all the subroutines it is used in

* run the application.

Open the project "FileHandling" and open frmMain. Open the code window.

First we will move the variables used in the Find_Oldest function. These are not used anywhere else so we will cut and paste them.

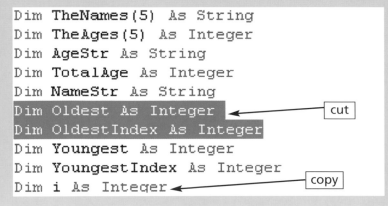

```
Dim TheNames(5) As String
Dim TheAges(5) As Integer
Dim AgeStr As String
Dim TotalAge As Integer
Dim NameStr As String
Dim Oldest As Integer            ← cut
Dim OldestIndex As Integer
Dim Youngest As Integer
Dim YoungestIndex As Integer
Dim i As Integer                 ← copy
```

```
Private Sub Find_Oldest()
Dim Oldest As Integer                    ←————— [paste]
Dim OldestIndex As Integer
Dim i As Integer
    Oldest = 0
    For i = 0 To 4
        If TheAges(i) > Oldest Then
            OldestIndex = i
            Oldest = TheAges(i)
        End If
    Next
    frmOutput.lblResult.Caption = "The oldest person is " + TheNames(OldestIndex) + " at " + Str(TheAges(OldestIndex))
End Sub
```

Now move the variables for the Find_Youngest subroutine.

```
Dim TheNames(5) As String
Dim TheAges(5) As Integer
Dim AgeStr As String
Dim TotalAge As Integer
Dim NameStr As String
Dim Youngest As Integer              ←————— [cut]
Dim YoungestIndex As Integer
Dim i As Integer                     ←————— [copy]
```

```
Private Sub Find_Youngest()
Dim Youngest As Integer              ←————— [paste]
Dim YoungestIndex As Integer
Dim i As Integer
    Youngest = 32767
    For i = 0 To 4
        If TheAges(i) < Youngest Then
            YoungestIndex = i
            Youngest = TheAges(i)
        End If
    Next
    frmOutput.lblResult.Caption = "The youngest person is " + TheNames(YoungestIndex) + " at " + Str(TheAges(YoungestIndex))
End Sub
```

And finally, the Show_Names subroutine.

```
Dim TheNames(5) As String
Dim TheAges(5) As Integer
Dim AgeStr As String
Dim NameStr As String                ←————— [cut]
Dim i As Integer                     ←————— [copy]
```

```
Private Sub Show_Names()
Dim NameStr As String                ←————— [paste]
Dim i As Integer
    NameStr = ""
    For i = 0 To 4
        NameStr = NameStr + TheNames(i) + " "
    Next
    frmOutput.lblResult.Caption = NameStr
End Sub
```

(*Continued*)

Try running the program, using all the output options, to ensure that all is working.

Click on the Read Names and Ages to read the file and enable the Show button.

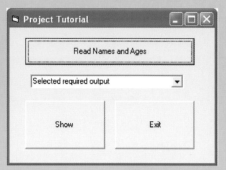

Select Find Youngest from the combo box and click on Show. Try all the other options.

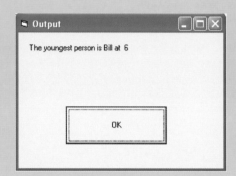

The variable AgeStr is only used in the cmdReadFile_click event and so it can be moved into the subroutine. Also, this is the last time we will need to move the counting variable i, so this time we will cut it.

```
Dim TheNames(5) As String
Dim TheAges(5) As Integer
Dim AgeStr As String              ⟵  cut
Dim i As Integer
```

```
Private Sub cmdReadFile_Click()              paste
Dim AgeStr As String
Dim i As Integer
    Open "C:\Documents and Settings\Brian\My Documents\DataFile.txt" For Input As #1
    For i = 0 To 4
        Input #1, TheNames(i)
        Input #1, AgeStr
        TheAges(i) = Int(Val(AgeStr))
    Next
    Close #1
    cmdShow.Enabled = True
End Sub
```

Save your project.

Comments and good practice

Now that you can write simple programs in the language you are studying you will have a collection of program listings, either stored in source code files or printed.

Meaningful names

You might identify what a program does by its name. A program that adds two numbers together might be called 'AddTwoNums' so it is fairly obvious what it does. A program called 'FindDifference' might be expected to find the difference of two numbers. Using meaningful names for all your program files will allow you to identify them more easily later on.

The name of a program, however, can only give a general identification of the program's purpose. Within a single program there will be many instructions. There may be a number of subroutines and there will be a number of variables. Each of these has a particular role to play in the program and, again, its name can be an indicator of its role. A variable that will hold a total should be called 'Total'. A variable to hold the price of an item might be called 'ItemPrice'. If variables are named meaningfully it makes it much easier to find all the parts of a program where the variable is used.

Subroutines, similarly, have a particular purpose and should be named according to that purpose. A subroutine that gets two numbers from the user might be called 'GetTwoNums'. A subroutine that finds the average of a set of numbers might be called 'FindAverage'. Again, it is much easier to find a particular subroutine if its name means something.

Comments

When correcting programs or updating them, you will want to go back and look at particular pieces of program code. For example, the part of a program that works out the final price for an item might calculate the VAT using a wrong value. You will have found this error when you were testing the program and you will want to find the part of your program listing that calculates the VAT. You might find the subroutine that works out the final price because its name is 'CalcFinalPrice', but within that subroutine you will need to find the part that calculates the VAT. There may be many numbers used in the calculations and you need to know which one is the VAT number. It will be easier to find this particular part of the program if it is labelled as the part that calculates the VAT. You can do this by adding a comment to your program code.

Comments are notes added to a program, written in plain English and marked in a way that the computer knows they are not part of the program, so doesn't try to treat them as program instructions. Most programming languages have their own methods for identifying a comment. The following are some examples of code with comments using Visual Basic, C, Pascal and JavaScript.

Visual Basic – a program that reads an item number and a price and calculates a 10% discount, adds 17.5% VAT and displays the final price.

Comments in Visual Basic are identified by an apostrophe (') at the start of the comment. The ' indicates that all text between ' and the end of the line are to be treated as comments.

```
'global variables
Dim ItemCode As String          'holds alphanumeric code
Dim ItemPrice As Double         'holds price entered by the user
Dim FinalPrice As Double        'holds final price, reduced and VAT added
```

```
Private Sub GetData()
'gets item code and price from the user
    ItemCode = InputBox("Enter item code: ", "Get Data") 'get item code from user
    ItemPrice = InputBox("Enter item price: ", "Get Data") 'get item price from user
End Sub

Private Sub CalcFinalPrice()
'calculates reduction and adds VAT
    Dim ReducedPrice As Double 'local variable for holding reduced price before VAT

    ReducedPrice = ItemPrice * 0.9        'reduce item price by 10%
    FinalPrice = ReducedPrice * 1.175    'add 17.5% VAT onto final price
End Sub

Private Sub DisplayFinalPrice()
'displays the final price, reduced and VAT added
    MsgBox ("The final price including VAT is: " + Str(FinalPrice))
End Sub
Private Sub frmCalcPrice_Load()
    GetData
    CalcPrice
    DisplayPrice
    Unload Me
End Sub
```

TABLE 8.40

C – a program that reads an item number and a price and calculates a 10% discount, adds 17.5% VAT and displays the final price.

Comments in C are identified by /* at the start of the comment and */ at the end. All text between /* and */ is treated as comments.

```
#include <stdio.h>

/* global variables */
    char ItemCode[8];            /* holds alphanumeric code */
    float ItemPrice;             /* holds price entered by the user */
    float FinalPrice;            /* holds final price, reduced and VAT added */

void GetData(){
/* gets item code and price from the user */
printf ( "Enter item code: " );
scanf ( "%s", &ItemCode );       /* get item code from user */
printf ( "Enter price: " );
scanf ( "%f", &ItemPrice);       /* get item price from user */
}

void CalcFinalPrice() {
/* calculates reduction and adds VAT */
    float ReducedPrice;          /* local variable for holding reduced price before VAT */
```

```
    ReducedPrice = ItemPrice * 0.9;      /* reduce item price by 10% */
    FinalPrice = ReducedPrice * 1.175;   /* add 17.5% VAT onto final price */
}

void DisplayFinalPrice() {
/* displays the final price, reduced and VAT added */
printf( "The price of item %s, including VAT is: %0.2f \n", ItemCode, FinalPrice);
}

void main() {
    GetData();
    CalcFinalPrice();
    DisplayFinalPrice();
}
```

TABLE 8.41

Pascal – a program that reads an item number and a price and calculates a 10% discount, adds 17.5% VAT and displays the final price.

Comments in Pascal are identified by { at the start of the comment and } at the end. All text between { and } is treated as comments.

```
PROGRAM CalcFinalPrice;

USES Wincrt;

VAR { global variables }
    ItemCode: STRING[8];              { holds alphanumeric code }
    ItemPrice: REAL;                  { holds price entered by the user }
    FinalPrice: REAL;                 { holds final price, reduced and VAT added }

PROCEDURE GetData;
{ gets item code and price from the user }

BEGIN
    Write ( 'Enter item code: ' );
    ReadLn ( ItemCode );              { get item code from user }
    Write ( 'Enter price: ' );
    ReadLn ( ItemPrice);              { get item price from user }
END;

PROCEDURE CalcFinalPrice;
{ calculates reduction and adds VAT }

VAR
    ReducedPrice: REAL;               { local variable for holding reduced price before VAT }

BEGIN
    ReducedPrice := ItemPrice * 0.9;        { reduce item price by 10% }
    FinalPrice := ReducedPrice * 1.175;  { add 17.5% VAT onto final price }
END;
```

(*Continued*)

```
PROCEDURE DisplayFinalPrice;

{ displays the final price, reduced and VAT added }

BEGIN
   WriteLn ( 'The price of item', ItemCode, 'including VAT is:', FinalPrice);
END;

BEGIN
   GetData;
   CalcFinalPrice;
   DisplayFinalPrice;
END.
```

TABLE 8.42

JavaScript – a program that reads an item number and a price and calculates a 10% discount, adds 17.5% VAT and displays the final price.

Comments in JavaScript are identified by two forward slashes '//' at the start of the comment, indicating that all text between // and the end of the line is to be treated as a comment.

```
<script language = "JavaScript" type = "text/javascript">
// global variables
var ItemCode = ""                    // holds alphanumeric code
var ItemPrice = 0.0                  // holds price entered by the user
var FinalPrice = 0.0                 // holds final price, reduced and VAT added

function GetData(){

// gets item code and price from the user
   Itemcode = prompt ( "Enter item code: " , "" ) // get item code from  user
   ItemPrice = prompt ( "Enter price: " , "" )        //get item code from  user
}

function CalcFinalPrice() {
// calculates reduction and adds VAT
var ReducedPrice = 0.0               // local variable for holding reduced price before VAT
ReducedPrice = ItemPrice * 0.9       // reduce item price by 10%
FinalPrice = Reduced * 1.175         // add 17.5% VAT onto final price
}

function DisplayFinalPrice() {
// displays the final price, reduced and VAT added
alert ( "The price of item " + ItemCode + " including VAT is: " + FinalPrice )
}
   GetData()
   CalcFinalPrice()
   DisplayFinalPrice()
</script>
```

TABLE 8.43

Indentation

Where comments help us to understand what the program is doing, they add to the text of the program and don't necessarily make it easier to read. We often want to look only at a subroutine or only at a FOR NEXT loop to find out how it works or if there are any errors in it. Indentation can be used to show where the beginning and end of subroutines, control structures and variable declarations are.

Look again at the program listings just shown. Each subroutine has a heading followed by some program code. The program code is indented further in than the heading. The end of the subroutine (indicated by End Sub, }, END; or }) is indented to the same level as the heading. This means that it is easy to spot where the subroutine starts and ends.

The same technique can be used with control structures such as loops and selection statements.

> **Example**
> Suppose a program included a *count-controlled loop* and part of that loop used a *two-way selection*.
>
> The code in Table 8.44 is part of a program that reads eight numbers and counts and reports even and odd numbers. It is intended to show examples of good practice: meaningful variable names, meaningful subroutine names, comments and indentation. Notice how the indentation allows easier identification of parts of the loop and the two selection possibilities. The first indentation is for instructions inside the for loop. The second indentation is for instructions inside each part of the if statement.

Visual Basic	

	``
	EvenCount = 0
	OddCount = 0
	
	For i = 1 to 8
	    Num = InputBox("Enter a number")
	    If Num Mod 2 = 0 Then
	        EvenCount = EvenCount + 1
	        MsgBox ("Even numbers counted so far: " + EvenCount)
	    Else
	        OddCount = OddCount + 1
	        MsgBox ("Odd numbers counted so far" + OddCount)
	    End If
	Next
	``

C	```
	EvenCount = 0;
	OddCount = 0;
	
	for(i=0; i<8; i++) {
	    printf ("Enter a number: ");
	    scanf ("%d", &Num);
	    if (Num%2 == 0){
	        EvenCount++;
	        printf("Even numbers counted so far: %d\n" , EvenCount);
	    }
	    else{
	        OddCount++;
	        printf("Odd numbers counted so far: %d \n" , OddCount);
	    }
	}
	``

| Pascal | ```
EvenCount := 0;
OddCount := 0;

FOR i:= 1 TO 8 DO
  BEGIN
  Write ('Enter a number: ');
  ReadLn (Num);
  IF Num MOD 2 = 0 THEN
    BEGIN
    EvenCount := EvenCount + 1;
    WriteLn ( 'Even numbers counted so far: ', EvenCount );
    END
  ELSE
    BEGIN
    OddCount := OddCount + 1;
    WriteLn ( 'Odd numbers counted so far: ', OddCount );
    END;
  END;
``` |
|---|---|
| JavaScript | ```
EvenCount = 0
OddCount = 0

for ( i=0; i<8; i++) {
  Num = prompt ( "Enter a number: ")
  if ( Num%2 == 0 ) {
    EvenCount++
    alert ("Even numbers counted so far" + EvenCount )
  }
  else {
    OddCount++
    alert ("Odd numbers counted so far" + OddCount )
  }
}
``` |

TABLE 8.44

Key terms

Count-controlled loop: a loop that executes a set number of times. Examples are FOR...NEXT, for(), FOR...DO, for().

Two-way selection: an IF statement with an ELSE part. There are two possible sets of instructions that might be carried out and one set will always be chosen depending on a given condition.

Theory into practice

Look at three programs you have written so far. Amend these programs so that they are indented appropriately and add comments.

For each program, check variable names and change them if you can think of a more suitable name. You will need to be careful to change the name through the program, not just where the variable is declared. If you have used subroutines, check and amend the names of these, remembering again to change all occurrences in the program.

Meaningful variable name – a name that indicates the purpose of the data that will be stored in that variable. Variable names can be made up of more than one word but must have no spaces so must be joined using underscore or by removing the spaces (e.g. Running_Total, RunningTotal are both valid names, but Running Total is not).

Meaningful subroutine name – a name that indicates what the subroutine does. Again, subroutine names must not contain spaces.

Comments – annotations added to a program listing to explain what each part of the program does. Comments are identified by special marks that the language understands and all text marked as a comment is ignored by the program when it gets ready to run.

Indentation – using TAB or spaces to start particular instructions further across the page. All program instructions that are grouped together for a reason (i.e. because they are all included in a particular loop, all included in part of a selection or all included in a subroutine) are indented to the samelevel.

Good practice – this includes using meaningful variable names, meaningful subroutine names, comments and indentation to make program listings more readable and more understandable. It also includes dividing your program up into subroutines to, again, make it more readable and understandable. If a program has been well designed it will be easy for anyone who understands the language to find any particular part of the program.

Tutorial 12 – Adding comments

This activity is designed to show you how to add comments and to give an idea of the amount and quality of comments to add for assessment of Unit 8: Introduction to Programming:

* open the project "FileHandling"

* open the code window for frmMain

* add comments to subroutines to explain what the code does

* print the code and screen print the form while running.

Open the project "FileHandling". Open frmMain and open the code window. Type comments into the code as shown below. These comments will not change the way the program runs in any way.

```
Dim TheNames(5) As String        'Global variables
Dim TheAges(5) As Integer


Private Sub cmdExit_Click()       'Exit button to close program
    Unload frmMain
End Sub

Private Sub cmdReadFile_Click()  'Open the file, read the names and ages.  Must be exactly 5 of each
Dim AgeStr As String
Dim i As Integer
    Open "C:\Documents and Settings\Brian\My Documents\DataFile.txt" For Input As #1
    For i = 0 To 4                'read 5 names and 5 ages from file
        Input #1, TheNames(i)
        Input #1, AgeStr
        TheAges(i) = Int(Val(AgeStr))    'store in array
    Next
    Close #1
    cmdShow.Enabled = True        'enable Show button when file read
End Sub
```

(Continued)

```
Private Sub Find_Oldest()     'find position of highest age
Dim Oldest As Integer
Dim OldestIndex As Integer
Dim i As Integer
    Oldest = 0                 'start low and look for higher ages
    For i = 0 To 4             'read through all 5 ages and look for highest
        If TheAges(i) > Oldest Then
            OldestIndex = i
            Oldest = TheAges(i)        'keep highest so far
        End If
    Next
    frmOutput.lblResult.Caption = "The oldest person is " + TheNames(OldestIndex) + " at " + Str(TheAges(OldestIndex))
End Sub


Private Sub Find_Youngest()  'find position of lowest age
Dim Youngest As Integer
Dim YoungestIndex As Integer
Dim i As Integer
    Youngest = 32767           'start high and look for lower ages
    For i = 0 To 4             'read through all 5 ages and find lowest
        If TheAges(i) < Youngest Then
            YoungestIndex = i
            Youngest = TheAges(i)   'keep lowest so far
        End If
    Next
    frmOutput.lblResult.Caption = "The youngest person is " + TheNames(YoungestIndex) + " at " + Str(TheAges(YoungestIndex))
End Sub

Private Sub Find_Total()       'add up all ages
Dim TotalAge As Integer
Dim i As Integer
    TotalAge = 0
    For i = 0 To 4             'read through all 5 ages and add to total
        TotalAge = TotalAge + TheAges(i)
    Next
    frmOutput.lblResult.Caption = "The total of the ages is " + Str(TotalAge)
End Sub

Private Sub Show_Names()       'make list of names separated by spaces
Dim NameStr As String
Dim i As Integer
    NameStr = ""
    For i = 0 To 4             'read through all 5 names and add each to string
        NameStr = NameStr + TheNames(i) + " "
    Next
    frmOutput.lblResult.Caption = NameStr
End Sub

Private Sub cmdShow_Click()
    Select Case cmbOutput.ListIndex  'select required output
        Case 0
            Find_Oldest
        Case 1
            Find_Youngest
        Case 2
            Find_Total
        Case 3
            Show_Names
        Case Else
            MsgBox "You have selected an invalid option"     'if user hasn't selected anything
    End Select
    If cmbOutput.ListIndex >= 0 And cmbOutput.ListIndex <= 3 Then   'display output if valid option chosen
        Load frmOutput
        frmOutput.Show
    End If
End Sub

Private Sub Form_Load()        'disable Show button until file has been read.
    cmdShow.Enabled = False
End Sub
```

Notice that the comments turn green as you add them. This makes them easy to spot.

To print the code, select print from the file menu while the code window is open. If you have a black and white printer you might find it better to select all the code and paste it into a word processor. You can then embolden all comments so that they are more obvious when they are printed out.

To get a screen shot, run the program until it is in the state you want to show and then use the print screen function to get a shot of the screen. You might need to open an application such as Paint or Notepad to paste the screen shot in or you might be able to save it to a file (this depends on the system you are using).

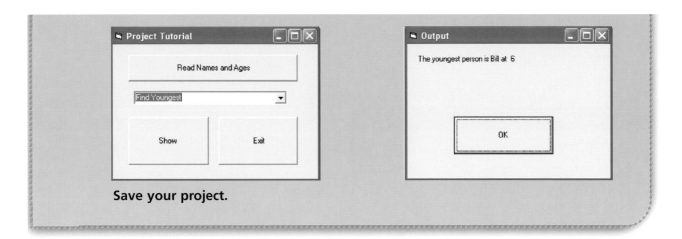

Save your project.

Assessment evidence

Programming is about being able to break a problem down into small logical steps and then about knowing how to write instructions to carry out those steps in a particular language. This unit has guided you through the various features of a programming language and you will have had a chance to practise writing programs in one particular language.

To pass Unit 8: Introduction to Programming you will need to demonstrate that you can

identify and use the features of two different programming languages. You will write simple programs using a language with which you are very familiar and you will be given a program in a different language with which you are less familiar. You will be expected to add comments to the written program to show that you can identify features of the language such as loops, selection statements, subroutines or variable declarations.

Your program will need to read the file until it reaches the end and produce a price list with individual product details, the total price of all products and the average product price.

The price list will look as follows:

Item Code	Description	Price
123456	Hand Cream	£2.99
274736	Face Cream	£4.99
568374	Body Lotion	£3.49
968475	Hair Conditioner	£1.99
837564	Nail Nourishing Oil	£2.49
	Total of products on file	£15.95
	Average product price	£3.19

Write the program and produce a program listing with comments and screen dumps showing the program working.

The second program will display information about five products on the screen and ask the user to enter how many of each product they would like to buy (up to five of each). The program will calculate how much is owed for each product, how much overall, how much VAT

(17.5%) to be added, and how much the overall price including VAT is. Figure 8.7 is an example of an input screen and Figure 8.8 shows output screen.

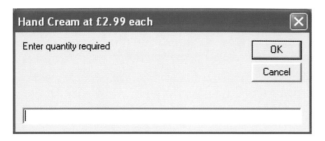

FIGURE 8.7 *Input screen*

FIGURE 8.8 *Invoice screen*

Now try this

The code in Figure 8.9 is a program written in JavaScript. You will need to try it out to see what it does and then add comments to the code to explain each part of the program (in case you are unable to run this code some screen prints are included to illustrate the program working). To create the program, make a new file using Notepad. Type the JavaScript code into the file and save it as a text file named assessJava.html, exit Notepad. You can now double-click on your file and it should automatically run in Internet Explorer. If it doesn't run you might have to enable pages containing script and ActiveX® controls or you may have typed some of the code incorrectly.

And this!

Write an evaluation of the programs you have written and the one you have annotated. Answer the following questions:

1 Was the language you used to write the two programs the most suited to the task? If not, which features of the language were suited and which were not?

2 Was JavaScript the best language to use for the program you have annotated? If not, which features of the language were suited and which were not?

3 Explain the stages you went through in producing the two new programs. Did you create forms first and then think about what each control would do? Did you have to change the form layout or the way the program worked at all while you were writing the program; why did you have to change it? How might you prevent this happening in the future?

4 Now that you have written, tested and used the new programs, how easy were they to use? Suggest something that might be changed to make them easier or more efficient to use.

```
assessJava - Notepad
File  Edit  Format  View  Help

<HTML>
<title>"Numbers Program"</title>
<head>
<script language = "JavaScript" type = "text/javascript">
var number=0
var firstnum=0
var secondnum=0
var total=0

function get_valid_num(){
        do{
                number = Math.round(prompt("Please enter a number: ",""))
                if(number<1||number>10){
                        document.write("Invalid: try again" + "<br \/>")
                }
        }while((number<1||number>10))
}

function find_total(){
        total=firstnum+secondnum
}

get_valid_num()
firstnum=number
document.write("The first number entered was: " + firstnum + "<br \/>")

get_valid_num()
secondnum=number
document.write("The second number entered was: " + secondnum + "<br \/>")

find_total()
document.write("The total of the two numbers was: " + total + "<br \/>")

</script>
</head>
</HTML>
```

FIGURE 8.9 *JavaScript example*

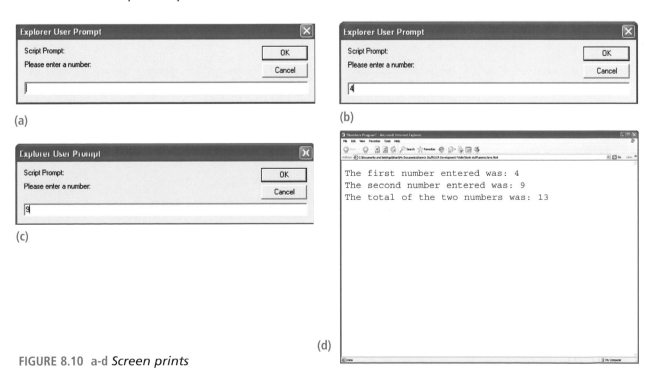

(a)

(b)

(c)

(d)

FIGURE 8.10 a-d *Screen prints*

5 Now that you have tried the pre-written program, how easy was it to use? Suggest something that might be changed to make it easier or more efficient to use.

6 Explain the stages you might go through in the future to produce new programs. Identify things that you would do the same way, explaining why you think they went well this time. Identify things that you would do differently, explaining why you think they might need changing.

GLOSSARY

Access time
The time taken to access data on a disk measured in milliseconds.

Address
A unique number identifying a memory location.

ADSL
A high-speed digital connection that is always on and allows for voice and data to be transmitted at the same time.

AGP (accelerated graphics port)
A direct high speed bus between the system memory and a graphics card.

Appendix
Numbered sections at the end of a document that contain relevant information referred to in the document but not part of it.

Array
A collection of data of the same type, stored together.

Assets
Anything of monetary value that is owned by an organisation.

Attributes
Elements that define an entity.

BACS (Banks Automated Clearing System)
A system that transfers money electronically from one bank account to another.

Balance sheet
A financial statement that lists the assets of an organisation.

Bandwidth
The number of bits per second that can be transmitted.

Batch processing
Processing where all the data is collected or input and then all the records are processed in a single operation.

Baud rate
In common usage, this is the amount of bits that can be sent and received per second – also known as bps. Technically, the baud rate is the amount of times the sound frequency on the line changes (the carrier signal shifts value – for example a 1200 bit-per-second modem actually runs at 300 baud, but it moves 4 bits per baud (4 × 300 = 1200 bits per second).

Bespoke or custom written software
Software which is designed and created to meet the needs of a specific organisation or a specific role.

Bespoke software
Software specially designed and written for an organisation.

Bitmap images
Images that are made up of a two-dimensional array of dots or pixels, each of which corresponds to one or more bits in the computer's memory.

Browser software
Software that allows you to access and view web pages.

Buffer
Memory in a peripheral device that acts as a buffer between faster bus speeds and slower peripherals.

Bus
The channels that carry data between devices such as the processor and memory and the address the data is to be sent to or fetched from.

Cache
Fast access memory on the CPU that stores the most recently accessed data and instructions to speed up subsequent retrieval.

Capacity
The amount of data that can be stored on a disk usually measured in MB or GB.

Cash flow
A measure of the money coming into and going out of the organisation, usually on a monthly basis.

CD-ROM
Pre-written optical disks with a capacity of 720 Mb that can only be read by a CD drive.

CD-RW
CDs that can be erased and rewritten many times using a CD rewriter.

Centronics
A type of parallel connector that usually plugs into the device, e.g. a printer.

Clock
A quartz crystal that oscillates at a known fixed rate and that is used to synchronise the actions of the processor.

Colour mode
The number of bits used to hold the colour information for each pixel and hence the number of possible colours.

Commercial organisation
An organisation that sells products or services in order to make a profit.

Computer viruses
Small computer programs that can copy themselves from one computer to another and that are almost always written to cause damage to the computers they infect.

Configure
Make changes to the way the software looks or performs.

Connectors
The plugs and sockets that allow devices to be connected to a computer.

Constant data
Data that is given a value at the beginning of the program and remains the same while the program runs. The data is stored in the computer's memory, given a name to identify it and marked as constant so that it can't be changed by accident.

Context
Taking the data and giving it an environment where our prior knowledge and understanding can make sense of it.

Co-processor
A second processor that carries out specific processing to reduce the burden on the main processor.

Count-controlled loop
A loop that executes a set number of times. Examples are FOR…NEXT, for(), FOR...DO, for().

Curriculum vitae (cv)
A document that includes your personal details and your education and employment history (called a resume in the US).

Customised off-the-shelf (COTS) software
Software that is purchased off-the-shelf as a package and then modified to meet the needs of a particular organisation.

Data compression
Reducing the size of a data file by removing unnecessary characters.

Data controller
The person(s) who determines the how and for what purpose personal data will be used.

Data structures
Sets of data of the simple data types, organised in such a way that they are stored together. Data structures include strings, arrays, records and files.

Data subjects
The individuals whose information is stored and processed.

Data types
Data used by a program can be integers (whole numbers), reals (any numbers), characters (all printable characters) and Boolean values (either true or false).

Data
Small pieces of information coded and structured for processing by a computer program. Data is meaningless until it is put into a context.

Database
An organised collection of data stored in a computer system.

DB series
A term used to describe any connector between a serial or parallel cable and a data bus.

Department
A group of people performing a particular job function under the direction of a department manager.

Design brief
A summary of the specification of a product or service.

DFDs
Diagrammatical ways of representing the flow of data and information in a system.

Diagrammatic structure
This is a computer generated or hand drawn layout of how the pages link to each other within a website.

Digital television broadcasting
Transmits multimedia data in streamed *bits* (binary digit, i.e. 0 or 1) of data.

DIL (dual in-line) switches/DIP (dual in-line package) switches
Small two way switches on a circuit board used to change its settings.

Direct marketing
Sending marketing information directly to a list of potential customers.

Drop-down lists
Pop-up menus or scrolling lists and are sometimes called combo-boxes. Drop-down lists are a control which displays a list of items and produces a number relating to the item that was selected by the user.

DVD-RAM
DVDs that can be written to (DVD-R) or erased and rewritten too many times (DVD-RW) using a DVD writer/rewriter.

DVD-ROM
Pre-written optical disks with a capacity of 4.7 Gb or more that can only be read by a DVD drive.

Electronic data interchange (EDI)
The exchange of standardised document forms between computer systems for business use.

Email
Written information that is communicated electronically.

Employees
The people who work for and are employed by an organisation.

Encryption key
Key needed to unscramble encrypted data so that it is meaningful.

Encryption
A security method that involves scrambling information transmitted so that it cannot be read if it is intercepted.

ERDs
Techniques for representing the structure of data in a software system using entities and the relationships between those entities.

Expansion cards
Circuit boards that plug into or connect to the motherboard to provide sound, graphics or networking capabilities, for example.

Expansion slots
Spaces, usually on the back of the case, that allow expansion boards to be inserted. These too have easily removed blanking plates so that the connectors are accessible for connecting external devices.

Expert systems
Systems in which human expertise is held in the form of rules which enable the system to diagnose situations without the human expert being present.

External entities
Sources for data which is input into the system or destinations for data that leaves the system. Examples of external entities include people and other systems.

Extranets
Intranets with specific external access allowed.

Feasibility report
The final product from the feasibility stage.

Feasibility study
An initial look at an existing system to see how it can be improved.

File location
Where a file exists on the storage media.

File
A collection of data stored on disk, CD, tape or other storage media. Data is organised in a set order and the program must read and write the data in that order.

Firewire
A fast serial connection often used for fast transfer of audio and video. It allows peer-to-peer connection as well as connection to a computer.

Flatbed
A scanner where the image to be scanned is placed on a flat surface and the light source moves or a plotter where the paper is placed on a flat surface and the pens move to draw the image.

Flat-file database
A database consisting of a single table of data.

Floppy disk
A small portable magnetic disk that can store 1.44 Mb of data.

Font
Typeface.

Frequency
The particular waveband at which radio signals are broadcast or transmitted.

Graphical user interfaces (GUI)
Windows, icons, menus, drop-down lists, etc. All software that allows the user to use these controls rather than having to type all commands is said to have a graphical user interface.

Gutter
The blank area of margin on the inside edge of pages that are to be bound that will be within the binding.

Hard disk
A disk that is made up of one or more rigid platters, either within the main processing unit (internal) or in a separate case outside of it (external). Hard disks can store a minimum of 40 GB of data and programs.

Hardware
The parts of a computer system that you can physically touch.

HTML
The language that is used to create hypertext documents. It is code that is interpreted by the browser to display what you see in a web page.

Hyperlink
An area of an on-screen document or presentation that takes the user to another part of the presentation or to a different location, such as another file or a web page, when it is clicked on.

IDE
Integrated drive electronics – a method of connecting internal disk drives to the motherboard where the controller and disk drive are combined.

Inkjet
A printer that sprays dots of ink onto the paper to create the image.

Input
Data is entered into a computer system for a program to read. For example, the user might input their name by typing it on the keyboard or they might select a menu choice by clicking on it.

Instruction set
The set of machine code instructions understood by a processor.

Interlace
The blending of changes between repeated displays of images.

Internet
A world-wide network of computer networks.

Internet
Collection of computers accessible from any other Internet connected computer.

Intranet
Private network only accessible by those machines internal to the organisation.

Invoice
A document that lists the products or services purchased from an organisation together with the cost of each, any additional costs such as carriage, the VAT due and the total amount to be paid.

IRC
This is a chat system that allows two or more Internet users to communicate by text in real time.

ISA (integrated systems architecture)
An older type of bus that allowed only 16 bits (0s and 1s) to be transferred at a time.

ISDN
A digital phone service that allows a computer to be connected to the Internet and transmit/receive data at a higher speed than with a modem. It requires a separate line and is a dial-up connection.

ISP
Internet service provider – the company that provides the connection to the Internet.

Job functions
Staff who are responsible for carrying out specific tasks within an organisation, such as sales or finance.

Laser
A printer that uses heat to fuse dry ink powder onto electrically charged areas of the paper.

Library files
Files containing sets of instructions for particular tasks, written by some else and put in a file so that you don't have to write them.

Literal data
Data that is explicitly identified in the program. Literal data can be numeric or textual. Example – to set the initial value of a variable 'Total' to zero, the variable is assigned the literal value 0, e.g. Total = 0.

Machine code

The language of the computer, it is made up of 0s and 1s. All programs written for a computer must be translated into machine code before they can run.

Machine language

Another name for machine code.

Management information systems (MIS)

Computer systems for an organisation which collect and analyse data from all departments, and are designed to provide an organisation's management with up-to-date information (such as financial reports, inventory, etc.) at any time.

Meaning

Putting data into the correct structure and putting it into a context.

Media

Medium used to express or communicate information.

Medium

The means that signals use to transfer from one device to another. The medium can be telephone, cables or through the air in the case of wireless.

Motherboard

The main circuit board in a computer that holds the processor, memory and other components and connects them together.

Multimedia

Using more than one medium to express or communicate information.

Occurrence

A specific example of an entity.

Off-the-shelf software

Software which has already been developed and is ready to buy, install and use on a computer system.

Optical disk

A disk that uses changes in the optical properties of a surface, rather than magnetism to store and retrieve data.

Optical storage medium

A disk that stores data by altering the optical characteristics of the surface material, e.g. the way light is reflected off it.

Orphan

Where the last line of a paragraph ends up on its own at the top of a new page.

Output

Data is displayed in a form in which it can be read or interpreted by a user. Output data is often displayed on a screen or on a printer but can take other forms such as sound or movement.

Parallel port

A port on the computer that transmits 8 bits of data down 8 separate wires simultaneously.

PCI (peripheral component interconnect)

Originally a 32-bit bus that provided a bridge between the much faster internal processor bus and the slower peripheral devices.

PDA (personal digital assistant)

A handheld computer that provides facilities for maintaining a diary, address book, notebook etc.

Permanent contracts

Employment contracts that have no end date.

Personal data

Data that relates to a living individual who can be identified from the data on its own or from the data along with other information held.

Point of presence

A point of presence (POP) is the physical location where the service provider's equipment is held. This will include computers and ecommunications lines. The POP is the access point to the service provider's network.

Ports

More correctly called I/O (input/output), ports are the means of connecting peripheral devices such as keyboards and printers to the computer for the input and output of data.

Premium
The amount of money you pay to an insurance company to provide insurance cover.

Primary key
An attribute which has a unique value for each occurrence of the entity.

Processor (CPU)
The main integrated circuit (chip) that carries out the processing of data.

Profit and loss statements
List the income and expenditure of an organisation.

Program
A series of instructions to a computer's processor to manipulate and create data and information.

Protocol
A protocol is a formal set of rules for transmitting data. It tells the devices being used to communicate how to send and receive the data. There are many different protocols.

Purchase ledger
The section of the accounts system that keeps records of all the purchases made by the organisation and the money paid out for these purchases.

Purchase orders
Documents that list the goods or services that an organisation wants to purchase from a supplier.

Questionnaire
A document designed to gather information and opinions from large numbers of individuals, often as part of a survey or to gain feedback on services provided

Quotation
Details of what a product or service will cost.

RAM (random access memory)
Volatile memory that can be written to and read from. Used for the temporary storage of data and programs.

Range of cells
A block of cells that is defined by the addresses of the top-left and bottom-right cells.

Recipient
Where the data goes to.

Records
Collection of data of different types stored together because all data refers to the same thing. Example – a set of data might be stored about an address. This address might include a house number (integer), a road name (string), a town name (string) and a postcode (string). Each item of data is called a field and is referred to using the record name and the field name.

Refresh rate
The number of frames that can be displayed on a CRT monitor per second.

Report
A long document that presents the results of some research or the activities an organisation has undertaken during the previous year and its financial position.

Resolution
A measure of the number of pixels on a VDU or the dots per inch in a printed or scanned image.

RJ (registered jack) series
A series of small square connectors used to connect devices to the telephone line or a network.

Robotics
Computer controlled devices that are able to carry out tasks that would have previously been done by people.

ROM (read only memory)
Non-volatile memory that can only be read from. Used for storing system start-up files, including BIOS.

Rotation speed
The speed at which the platters of a hard disk rotate measured in rpm.

Sales ledger
The section of the accounts system that keeps records of the sales made by the organisation and the money paid in for the goods or services sold.

SATA
Serial advanced technology attachment – similar to IDE but using serial rather than parallel connection.

Scan frequency
In a CRT monitor, number of rows of pixels that can be displayed in a second.

SCSI
A small computer system interface – a fast parallel connection used to connect devices such as hard disks. Devices can be daisy-chained.

Search engines
Computer programs that search a database to find the information required, either within a website or on the WWW.

Semantic
The meaning of the sentence.

Serial port
A port on the computer that transmits data in a single stream down a single wire.

Set-top box
A box about the size of a DVD player that is connected between the satellite dish, aerial or cable input and the television set.

Short-term fixed contracts
Employment contracts that last for a specified time, for example one year.

SMS (short message service)
Telephone text messaging.

Software
The programs needed to make the hardware perform useful tasks.

Source
Where the data comes from.

Specify
Select and produce a detailed list of all the components and features of those components required to make up a computer system.

Spreadsheet
A tool for analysing and manipulating numerical data.

SSADM
Structured systems and design methodology.

Staff development plan
A document that identifies the existing knowledge and skills of employees and how these can be extended and updated to improve performance.

Subdomain
A subsection of a domain. It does not have its own IP address but uses folder redirection to find the right pages.

Subroutines
Sets of instructions that will carry out one particular task. The set of instructions is given a name and this name becomes a new instruction that the main program can use.

Syntax
The rules of a sentence.

Systems analyst
The person who is responsible for the analysis of a system to assess its suitability for the proposed changes.

Tax code
A code issued by the Inland Revenue and based on each individual's personal circumstances that is used to calculate how much income tax should be deducted from their wages or salary.

Telesales
Selling goods or services by taking orders over the telephone.

Template
A template allows you to set the style and size of fonts and the position of items so that these are the same in every document.

Textual hotspots
Words within a web page that, when clicked on, take you to another part of the site, or even to an external site.

Touch screen
Screens that allow people to interact with a computer without the need for a keyboard, mouse or other input device.

Two-way selection
An IF statement with an ELSE part. There are two possible sets of instructions that might be carried out and one set will always be chosen depending on a given condition.

URL
Uniform Resource Locator – the unique address of the page on the Internet.

USB (universal serial bus)
A standard serial connection for a wide range of devices.

Utility companies
Companies that provide utilities such as water, electricity, gas and telephone services.

Validation
Computerised checking to detect any data that is unreasonable or incorrect.

Variable data
Data that can change while a program is running. It is stored in the computer's memory and accessed by the program using an identifier (variable name). Example – an age might be stored as a variable called 'Age'.

Vector graphic
Images that are made up of simple geometric shapes. Geometric information is stored, such as the co-ordinates of the start and end point of a straight line.

Verification
The process of ensuring that data entered into the computer matches the original.

Void
All C functions have a type (e.g. int main() and they produce one item of data of this type that must be stored or used each time the function is used. However, if the function's type is void, no data is produced. To keep things simple, you will use functions of type void only and so won't have to worry about what to do with the function's resulting data.

VOIP
A method of using networks and the Internet to make telephone calls.

Volatile
Memory is volatile if the content is lost when power is removed.

WAP
Wireless application protocol.

Web applications
Programs that run on a web server and are accessed from a web page. The database software used by a search engine is an example of a web application.

Web browser
Software that allows you to view web pages. The most common is Internet Explorer.

Website
A virtual location on the WWW. It is a group of pages that, when taken together, represent a company, organisation or an individual on the WWW.

Widow
Where the first line of a paragraph is left on its own at the bottom of a page.

Working practices

The way that work is organised and carried out.

World Wide Web

A system of Internet servers that uses HTTP to transfer specially formatted documents. The documents are formatted in a language called HTML (hypertext mark-up language). This language supports links to other documents, as well as graphics, audio and video files.

Write protect

The ability to prevent data being written to a floppy disk or flash memory.

INDEX

BBC website   91, 92, 101
bespoke software   70, 188
bibliography, creation of   25
BIOS software   140, 156
bit   10
bitmap graphics software   151
    images   27
bold   20
borders   24, 28, 111
boxes, text and picture   26
branding   30
briefs   63
broadcasting websites   97–8
brochures   30, 36, 76
browsers   4, 8, 94, 150, 230, 236
buffer   131, 138
bullet points   24
bulletin boards   219
bus
    address   127
    control   127
    data   127
    external   127
    internal   127
business letters   27, 30, 33–4
business reports   13, 14, 15, 36–7

C programming language   242, 244
    code with comments   300–301
    declaration of variables   252, 253, 254, 295
    functions (subroutines)   290
    good practice example   304
    input and output   256, 257, 258
    operators   268, 270
    program structure   248
    repetition   280–81
    selection   273, 275–6
    strings   257, 258, 259, 284
cable modems   225
cache   131
CAD (computer aided design)   67, 137, 138, 151
capacitive touch screen   9
cash flow spreadsheet   70
CDs   133, 134
cell formats   109–10, 117
cell referencing   112–14
centronics connector   129, 130
CGI 232,   234

character variables   252, 253
charts 26,   117–18
check sheet, quality   174
clipart images   27, 117
clock   127
Closed Circuit Television (CCTV)   4, 7
closed questions   14
CMOS   130–1
co-processor   127
colour   24, 28, 110–11
command line interface (CLI)   140–1
commercial companies   47
communicating using computers   212–37
    assessment evidence   237
    see also Internet
communication   1, 8, 12–17
    creation of   28–30
    of facts   13
    impact of WWW   99–100
    methods of   5–8
    paper-based   5, 12
    screen-based   5–6, 12
    summarising information   13–14
    technologies supporting   8–12
    writing to impress   13
compression software   132, 133, 236, 237
computer aided design (CAD)   67, 137, 138, 151
computer aided manufacturing (CAM)   67
Computer Misuse Act (1990)   86–7
computers   8–9, 12, 76
    setting up for Internet   235–7
        installation form   235
        required software   235, 238–9
concept keyboard   134–5
conferencing
    text based   219
    video   218, 219
confidential information   39, 40, 67, 85, 139, 159, 160
configuration of OS and GUI   141–6
    application software icons   147
    checking and setting system properties   147
    desktop and display set-up   146–7, 148
    device drivers   142
    directory structure and settings   143–5
    multimedia   145
    passwords   142, 143
    scheduled tasks   142
    time and date   142

power supply   126
Management of Health and Safety at
   Work Regulations (1999)   87–8
management information systems (MIS)   172–3
management and security procedures   159–60
managers, information about   63
manufacturers   62–3
margins   17–18
market research analysis   69
marketing function   53–4
master page layout   29
memory   130–3
   cache   131
   flash memory   132–3
   RAM   130–1
   ROM   131
meta-search engines   102
microphone   136
Microsoft Access   107–8
Microsoft Windows   140, 141, 228
mobile phones   4, 6, 11, 12, 78
   WAP enabled   4, 78
   and working location   78
modem   224, 225, 236
   baud rate   226
motherboard   125, 126
mouse   135
   configuration   145–6
   ergonomics   158
MS-DOS   140, 141
multi-level numbering   22
multimedia   3, 12, 38
   configuration   145
   reference software   150
museum websites   94

naming cells   113
naming files   39–40
National Health Service website   95
National Rail website   96–7, 99
navigation bars   91, 92
network address translation (NAT)   228
network interface card (NIC)   227
networking hardware   227
news on-line   97
newsgroups   219
newsletters   34, 35
Newsnet   219

newspaper printing industry   82
NHS Direct   95
Nominet   221, 222
Novell OS   228
numbering paragraphs   22

observation   191
off-the-shelf software   188
Office of National Statistics   100, 116, 117, 119
office software   168–73
on-line
   banking   73, 99, 100
   directory services   95
   information   4–5, 12, 91–9
open punctuation   31
open questions   14
open source   140, 228, 232–3
operating systems   140–1, 156
   configuring   141–8
operational information   164
operators   267–72
   arithmetic   267, 268
   logical   268–70
   relational   268
optical character recognition software   135
optical disk   10, 132, 133
option buttons   255
order forms   60, 61
ordering goods   14–15
organisational structure   58–9
organisations   46–89
   collection of information   60
   corporate image   32
   functions within   49–58
   information types   59–64
   key information systems   64–73
   movement of information   73–6
   types of   47–8
   use of databases   105
   use of information   59–60
output devices   136–9

page layout   17–19, 28
page orientation   18–19
page setup   18
pagination   19
paper production   82–3
paper size   19